Collected essays

Collected essays

Volume I
The Englishness of the English novel

Q. D. LEAVIS

EDITED BY G. SINGH

CAMBRIDGE UNIVERSITY PRESS

CAMBRIDGE

LONDON   NEW YORK   NEW ROCHELLE
MELBOURNE   SYDNEY

Published by the Press Syndicate of the University of Cambridge
The Pitt Building, Trumpington Street, Cambridge CB2 1RP
32 East 57th Street, New York, NY 10022, USA
296 Beaconsfield Parade, Middle Park, Melbourne 3206, Australia

© Cambridge University Press 1983

First published 1983

Printed in Great Britain by the University Press, Cambridge

Library of Congress catalogue card number: 83–1978

British Library Cataloguing in Publication Data
Leavis, Q.D.
Collected essays.
Vol. 1: The Englishness of the English novel.
1. English literature—19th century
—History and criticism
I. Title   II. Singh, G.
820.9′008   PR461

ISBN 0 521 25417 5 hard covers
ISBN 0 521 27677 2 paperback

Contents

Plates

Sources and acknowledgments

'Jane Austen: novelist of a changing society' was delivered as a public lecture at Queen's University, Belfast, on 15 April 1980. In a shortened form the same lecture had been given at the University of Newcastle-upon-Tyne in 1974 and as Jane Austen Bicentenary Lecture in 1975. 'The Englishness of the English novel' was delivered as the Cheltenham Festival Annual Literature Lecture in 1980 and appeared first in *New Universities Quarterly* (Spring 1981) and subsequently in *English Studies*, 62, no. 2 (April 1981). The four parts of 'A critical theory of Jane Austen's writings' appeared in *Scrutiny* (vols. x and xii) and 'A fresh approach to *Wuthering Heights*' was published in *Lectures in America* by F. R. and Q. D. Leavis (Chatto, 1969). The introductions to *Sense and Sensibility*, *Mansfield Park*, *Jane Eyre*, *Villette* and *Silas Marner* appeared respectively as follows: Macdonald, London, 1958; Macdonald, London, 1957; Penguin Books, 1966; Harper Colophon Books, Harper and Row, New York, 1972; Penguin Books, 1967. 'Dating *Jane Eyre*' was first published in *The Times Literary Supplement*, 27 May 1965.

The editor and publishers are grateful to Chatto and Windus Ltd for permission to reprint 'A fresh approach to *Wuthering Heights*', to Penguin Books Ltd for permission to reprint the introductions to *Jane Eyre* and *Silas Marner* from the Penguin English Library editions of the novels, and to Harper and Row Publishers, Inc. for permission to reprint the introduction to *Villette*.

Editor's introduction

On the occasion of her death *The Times* obituary referred to the formidable critical partnership between Q. D. Leavis and her husband F. R. Leavis. The reference was apt and – as far as it went – illuminating. But it did not suggest the singularly independent character of Q. D. Leavis's pioneering and influential criticism of the novel, which, in its tone, ethos and direction, was as sharply distinguishable from her husband's as her husband's was from hers. Inevitably, in the course of a long collaborative life together, they influenced one another. But any influence or collaboration was not, by its nature, such as to turn their independence of judgment and enquiry into interdependence. That is why both could pursue their individual drift quite freely and single-mindedly, as indeed each did.

Q. D. Leavis's lifelong preoccupation was with fiction. The copious notes and jottings she made, or the quotations from or references to books she read or consulted, show the unusually varied scholarship – historical, biographical, sociological and anthropological – that she brought to bear on whatever she wrote or lectured on. Her trenchant lucidity of style, with its wealth of suggestively relevant and amply authenticated detail, and its fluent forthrightness, distinguish her temperament, attitude and procedure from those of her husband. Concerned with offering a critical account of what constitutes artistic maturity and originality, it was not of primary interest to Q. D. Leavis whether a writer was major or not, and she could write as cogently on Mrs Oliphant as on Dickens, on Charlotte Yonge as on George Eliot, on Edith Wharton as on Henry James. This does not mean that the critical perception of what constitutes major creativity was less present in Q. D. Leavis's criticism than in F. R. Leavis's; or that it did not affect her treatment of a minor writer, however interesting or relevant such a writer might have been to her particular line of enquiry. Hence, one might say that the contact between the critic and the writer in Q. D. Leavis's writing is made at more varied levels than in that of F. R. Leavis; and the form as well as the degree and proportion in which the social historian and the critic in her combine are also more varied and more manifest.

Fiction and the Reading Public came out in the year (1932) in which *Scrutiny* was launched; the ethos of *Scrutiny*, so far as the critical reviewing of the novel is concerned, was very much determined by what Q. D. Leavis had achieved in that book – a method of investigation which she preferred to describe as 'anthropological'. It consisted, to quote her own words, 'in examining all the material that seemed to bear on the question " what has happened to fiction and the reading-public since the eighteenth century?" in an unbiased but inquisitive frame of mind and concentrating on registering shifts of taste and changes in the cultural background, allowing such conclusions as I arrived at to emerge simply by comparison and contrast and analysis'. But even in *Fiction and the Reading Public*, in the course of such 'comparison and contrast and analysis', Q. D. Leavis offers critical considerations and perceptions of a more general kind concerning the nature of the novel and what the criticism of it ought to aim at. As, for instance, when she distinguishes between 'merely popular novels and stories', and the novel 'which has come to be literature' and points out how a popular bestseller provides 'wish-fulfilment in various forms' or 'compensation for life' in a way the latter does not. And this comes out through characterization as well as through other aspects. For instance, the highbrow novelist, if he 'creates' characters at all 'is apt to produce personalities that do not obey the literary agent's rule ("The principal characters must be likeable. They must be human"), and that do not lend themselves to fantasizing but cause disturbing repercussions in the reader's emotional make-up'. Such a 'confusion of fiction with life and the demand that fiction should compensate for *life*', according to Q. D. Leavis, prevents popular enjoyment of novelists like Charlotte Brontë, Jane Austen, Henry James and D. H. Lawrence – novelists who are artists and whose works 'are not much more numerous than those English dramatic works which are, strictly speaking, tragedies'.

It is such novelists that Q. D. Leavis writes about in this

volume, which may be regarded as an indispensable supplement to F. R. Leavis's *The Great Tradition*. The premises and principles formulated in *Fiction and the Reading Public*, and the methods of approach and analysis outlined there underlie both these books, which, together with the collaborative *Lectures in America* and *Dickens the Novelist*, attest to the concrete results of a lifelong collaboration which continued even through divergencies of method, analysis and scope, and of which the Leavises speak in dedicating their Dickens book to each other. The bulk of this volume consists of her essays on Jane Austen – from the earliest critiques published in *Scrutiny* ('A critical theory of Jane Austen's writings') to the subsequent introductions to *Sense and Sensibility* and *Mansfield Park*, and the Jane Austen Bicentenary Lecture which was later elaborated into a larger and more specific lecture 'Jane Austen: novelist of a changing society' delivered at Queen's University, Belfast, just a year before Q. D. Leavis died.

The other essays included in this volume are 'A fresh approach to *Wuthering Heights*', her well-known introductions to Charlotte Brontë's *Jane Eyre* and *Villette* and to George Eliot's *Silas Marner*, and her Cheltenham Festival Annual Literature Lecture 'The Englishness of the English novel' delivered in 1980.

This volume, therefore, contains all Q. D. Leavis's criticism of the major English novelists other than that which appeared in *Dickens the Novelist*. Volume II will collect the essays on the American novel, as well as notes on the European novel. Volume III will collect unpublished essays and extended comments on the women writers of the nineteenth century, 'The novel of religious controversy', 'The Anglo-Irish novel', 'Hans Christian Andersen', '*Miss Marjoribanks*' and Mrs Leavis's Introduction to the *Autobiography and Letters of Mrs Margaret Oliphant*, and a selection of reviews and essays from *Scrutiny*.

In essay after essay in the present volume, while evaluating a particular novel or novelist, Q. D. Leavis applies with critical and analytical rigour the principles and assumptions she had formulated in *Fiction and the Reading Public*, examining the 'environment of literature', 'the climate of opinion' and the various stages of social and intellectual development rather than discussing the subject in what she called 'an aesthetic vacuum'. It is through this process that, early in her career, Q. D. Leavis recognized the importance of the Puritan conscience in English literary history – a recognition that was to prove pivotal to her thinking on the novel and determine her view of the English novel as having 'from its start an essentially and profoundly moral (I do not mean moralistic) framework and intention'. This perception underlies the whole treatment of Jane Austen's novels, and the conviction that she is a great novelist. Mrs Leavis gives Jane Austen's culture its historical and social perspective and shows how it impinged upon her, providing her with 'objective forms to symbolize and incarnate convincingly her preoccupation with the psychological changes she observed, and indeed registers in part as her own'. Such an account is an integral part of the kind of criticism Q. D. Leavis pioneered – a criticism based on the dual but interrelated approach to the novel as a composite product of art, reflection and observation on the one hand, and of the social and cultural milieu on the other.

This approach gives her summing up of Jane Austen's genius the edge and authority as well as the wide exegetical framework within which she distinguishes the novelist from the Romantic poets and other novelists whose works 'she knew of but was unimpressed by'. She also links Jane Austen with the Augustans, since her mode of writing too was developed out of satire and irony, and shows how her attitudes, like those of any eighteenth-century novelist, 'are always critical, her characters held away from herself, and her vocabulary is that of a system of values which is not emotional, but moral, critical and rational'.

The later introductions to *Sense and Sensibility* and *Mansfield Park* synthesize the views on the two novels expressed in 'A critical theory of Jane Austen's writings', and at the same time elaborate them in a firmer and more balanced assessment of these novels and their relationship to Jane Austen's total *oeuvre*.

In her Introduction to *Jane Eyre* Q. D. Leavis's critical evaluation of the novel is placed within a comprehensive and detailed background of Charlotte Brontë's character and personality. She shows how Charlotte Brontë was 'precipitated into writing fiction' as a result of the impact that going to study in Brussels made on her and her sister Emily, resulting in the shock 'for these very Protestant and Yorkshire-bred sisters at encountering the unimaginable culture of a Catholic boarding school'. She goes on to analyse Charlotte Brontë's handling of her theme – 'an urgently felt personal one, an exploration of how a woman comes to maturity in the world of the writer's youth' – which dictated the form of the novel. Thus criticism of the novel goes hand in hand with insight into Charlotte Brontë's character and personality which, as much as her narrative art, determine the ethos of the novels. Mrs Leavis also analyses Charlotte Brontë's handling of religion, observing how 'all the representatives or mouthpieces of religion in *Jane Eyre* are either "placed", or destroyed by ironic analysis'. In distinguishing Charlotte Brontë from Jane Austen and George Eliot, Q. D. Leavis analyses her 'suggestive use of language and the magical quality of her writing'.

Like F. R. Leavis, Q. D. Leavis thought George Eliot a very great novelist, although the way she brings out George Eliot's greatness in her Introduction to *Silas Marner* is different from the way Dr Leavis does it in *The Great Tradition*. For her this novel more than any other by George Eliot offers a full portrait of the novelist as 'the editor of the Benthamite review, the admirer of Comte, the student of all the ancient and modern languages, the friend of Herbert Spencer and the consort of G. H. Lewes, that middleman of all the arts and sciences'. Moreover it embodies George Eliot's ideas about the novel at their maturest – ideas that George Eliot tried to incarnate in this novel, as she herself said, 'as if they had revealed themselves to me first in the flesh and not in the spirit'. Q. D. Leavis then goes on to discuss what George Eliot learnt from her vast reading and what bearing it had on the kind of novel she wanted to write. For instance what she learnt from reading Greek tragedy is closely linked with her own concept of what a novel should be, since 'they [the Greeks] had the same essential elements of life presented to them as we have, and their art symbolized these in grand schematic forms'. These schematic forms George Eliot herself achieves in her novels through what she calls 'symbolic situations' and 'the myth', and it is through these that she extends the scope and richness of the novel.

Silas Marner itself has an adequate framework within which to deal with the problems of life as George Eliot saw them. And compared with *Middlemarch* and *Felix Holt* it has a greater degree of concentration which puts it along with Shakespeare and Bunyan, rather than with other Victorian novels. As for the character of Silas Marner, Q. D. Leavis sums it up in terms of the ethos and social and historical background to which he belonged. We are told that he 'never does acquire the pieties inborn with the villagers. He gets along eventually by adopting all the village customs without questioning them, but never, of course, has the traditional associations which make people benefit by them.'

Together with the influence of Greek tragedy there is also a Wordsworthian element in *Silas Marner* – not only in its descriptive passages, but also in the application of the Wordsworthian doctrine of 'the ties and charities' that bind families together. To these influences are to be added cultural, social and religious factors and George Eliot's particular way of reacting to them. Q. D. Leavis also draws the distinction between George Eliot's attitude to ideas and morals in the impersonal sense and ideas and morals as they affected her own life. For instance while commenting on the situation in which George Eliot placed herself by living with G. H. Lewes with whom marriage was legally impossible, she observes: 'The effect was peculiar. While she shows in her novels complete emancipation from restrictive ideas of class, and while her criticisms of its causes, manifestations and effects are always penetrating, sensitive and unbiased, she is surprisingly conventional about *moral* conduct in the narrow Victorian sense.'

After 'A critical theory of Jane Austen's writings', the longest essay included in this book is 'A fresh approach to *Wuthering Heights*' – a lecture which Q. D. Leavis gave in America and which was published in *Lectures in America*. As she explains in the 'Prefatory note', it was based on material for two lectures – one given at Harvard and the other at Cornell – the 'inseparable Siamese twins', as she calls them, and what we have now is the merging of that material into one essay. Her aim in this essay – one of the best and most convincingly argued that she ever wrote – is to put 'into circulation grounds for a responsible and sensitive approach to *Wuthering Heights* in its context (both literary and historical) as well as to provide a fresh assessment, which should also be corrective of its merits absolutely as a literary creation'. In doing so, Q. D. Leavis faces – and admirably resolves – not merely the difficulty of establishing that *Wuthering Heights* is a classic, but also the much greater difficulty of establishing *what kind* of classic it is. And as she examines other critics' views on the novel – for instance those of Lord David Cecil, P. Coveney, C. P. Sanger and Justice Vaisey – she offers her own view backed by a penetrating reassessment of those elements and scenes which other critics have ignored and which impinge on her as of fundamental importance. Thus with her richly informed historical sense underlying such a reassessment, Q. D. Leavis brings to bear, as always, a sharp and original critical perception which almost always turns into a moral response as well. Hence, for instance, she argues how 'the author's impersonality (deliberately maintained by the device of a narrator who records other narrators and all of whom are much less like their creator than Conrad's Marlow is)' is not inconsistent with a moral intention, and how 'the reader is obliged to draw moral conclusions, from the very nature of the scenes and actors in whose lives he is involved by sympathy and compassion or horror and repulsion'. Both as critic and as reader Q. D. Leavis does not so much condition our response to those scenes and actors as help us form one in the light of the new critical and psychological insights she provides in this essay.

The last essay included in this volume – 'The Englishness of the English novel' – is also the last public lecture Q. D. Leavis gave in her lifetime. Surveying the whole range of the English novel from its beginnings till its modern contemporary phase and comparing it with the Continental and American traditions of the novel, she analyses the grounds of the distinctive supremacy and originality of the English novel, and then traces those grounds to their origins in the history and development of the English people. Indeed, paraphrasing Matthew Arnold, she might well have said that in nothing is England so glorious as in her poetry *and* her novels. 'We of course take the English novel for granted', she argues, 'as the inevitable product of some literary law of Nature. But if we look at the novel as it has been established in other countries, as well as look at other countries which have failed to produce a national tradition at all (even one which, like Italy, has an old civilization and early achievement in poetry) we must realize that our English novel is a unique product.' This uniqueness Q. D. Leavis saw in terms of the values, inextricably moral and artistic, which she considered indispensable to the realization of the mature novel form, and she set out to show how the English novel, in the rich diversity of its talent and individuality, had achieved such a form by embodying those virtues to a greater degree than the French, the American, the Russian or the Italian novel had done.

What Q. D. Leavis found to be the most central and crucial factor in the development of the English novel is its profoundly moral framework and intention, its super-realism, and its 'sensitive open-minded exploration' of reality. All this is part of the tradition of 'radical and responsible inquiry into the human condition', with its moral and psychological problems, which constitutes the backbone of the English novel and which owes 'more than anything else to the fact that it had traditionally been the product of an essentially Protestant culture'. But whereas the English novelist of the past – say George Eliot – had a more mature and civilized tradition to work in, today, along with the decay of the traditional culture, we witness 'the withdrawal from moral responsibility of novelists – we see a parody of it in the novels of Graham Greene or *Brideshead Revisited* – and a consequent lapse of the novel into trivality or, in the cases of novelists like Greene and Waugh, spiritual pedantry'. Q. D. Leavis's apprehension for the future of the English novel, therefore, has to do with her apprehension about modern civilization itself and she cannot help noting 'how diminished the tradition [of the novel] has become in the hands of the most well-known practitioners of this age, who have uncritically been accepted as classics – as well as how commercialized'.

Approximately half the material in this volume deals with Jane Austen, on whom Q. D. Leavis wrote over the last forty years of her writing career on different occasions and in different circumstances. Hence there are some repetitions, mostly in the form of quotations from Jane Austen, but also in the form of Mrs Leavis's own comments, which necessarily occur here and there. The editor thought it improper or inadvisable to eliminate these repetitions, both in the interest of preserving the integrity of what Mrs Leavis originally wrote and observed and in the interest of avoiding such lacunae and excisions as would have been entailed in the process of elimination. Moreover, it is the editor's belief that the repetitions do not seriously interfere with Mrs Leavis's argument concerning particular aspects of Jane Austen's novels.

G. SINGH

A glance backward, 1965

Mrs Leavis wrote this paper (never published in her lifetime) some time in 1965–66 in response to a request from a research student (probably an American) asking for an account of the work she had been doing at Cambridge. Some of the projects she refers to as being in progress were later completed and published by her; others, unpublished at her death, will appear in the subsequent two volumes of Mrs Leavis's writings.

It's a formidable undertaking to give some idea of the work I've done, not only because my post-graduate career covers thirty-six years but because, while remaining always myself, I hope, I have changed direction from time to time, as my interests shifted with age and as the demands of teaching for different papers and specialisms in University English studies at Cambridge accidentally deflected my thoughts into different channels. It's over thirty years since *Fiction and the Reading Public* (1932) appeared (this book was a version of my doctoral thesis adapted for non-specialist reading) and this went out of print at the beginning of the War, though it is going to be republished soon as a paper-back.[1] It had a great *succès d'estime* but after the War Raymond Williams and Richard Hoggart[2] each brought out books which owed something to my original work and each (unlike my book) became a bestseller. My later work has been printed in *Scrutiny* and as articles in other English and American periodicals, sometimes reprinted in anthologies of criticism on subjects such as Hawthorne and Edith Wharton and Jane Austen, where I made pioneer or original studies. I've done a lot of work behind the scenes by directing research students, whose theses when published carry on my own lines in what I may call the sociology of literature, a subject whose value and identity were not in my youth at all decided.

I started as a research student knowing exactly what I wanted
to work at. I wanted to find out what part the reading-public
has played in determining the form and quality of English
imaginative writing. For my purpose Literature (with a capital
L) was simply the part of the iceberg that showed above the
water, though this top section, and not the whole, was what was
then selected as proper to be studied by university students. In
fact, when my book appeared in 1932, a leading senior academic
of the Cambridge 'English' School, writing an article on
'English Studies at Cambridge', held it and me up to oppro-
brium, since, he said, to read 'bestsellers' (as popular fiction was
then contemptuously labelled) showed a depraved taste and was
quite outside the literary field. I felt that part – the major
part – of the iceberg had been submerged by the passage of time
but was still not negligible from my point of view, since having
been read with pleasure by so many it must tell us something
important about the formation and taste of the reading-public
at any given time, and the climate of literature is determined
by public taste to a great extent. Also, books widely read though
of no permanent literary merit provide evidence as to the
quality of living and enable us to ask pertinent questions about
the nature of a community or society.

I was so stimulated by the accident that I preceded my purely
literary work as an undergraduate by taking Anglo-Saxon and
associated studies under a great Cambridge teacher and scholar,
Professor H. M. Chadwick, on whose death I wrote an
anonymous tribute in *Scrutiny*[3] which will make clear to you the
nature of his work as an educational influence and as writer of
a pioneer book in several volumes on the origin and growth
of Literatures. Professor Chadwick invented for us students at
Cambridge a course of study, highly educational and rewarding,
on the early history and literature of England which was
comparable with what the Classical Tripos at Cambridge or
Greats at Oxford do for the early history and literatures of
Greece and Rome. He put Anglo-Saxon back into its whole
context, not only making us study Anglo-Saxon literature along
with Early English arts and social system and history, but
putting all *that* back where it belonged, into the early cultural
history of the whole of Northern Europe, along with the Norse
and early Welsh and Irish literatures and arts and social life too.
This made us see Literature as something inseparable from the

whole culture that produced it and also made comparisons between cultures and their literatures possible, indeed inevitable. His students acquired an anthropological attitude because they had to study archaeology, myth, folk-lore, religious rites, early architecture and other arts while centring on literature and on the associated arts and beliefs as the expression and highest products of those cultures. This inspiring teaching, which made us acquainted with the whole evolution of Northern Europe from the Bronze Age to the Middle Ages, made it inevitable that when in our later purely 'Eng. Lit.' work we read Chaucer, we at once saw him *correctly*, not as a crude and naïve poet at the beginning of English Literature, but as the sophisticated artist who brought a slowly-developed tradition of several strands to a climax of achievement by enriching it with grafts from European poetic traditions. I think it due to this branch of my education that when reading for example the early nineteenth-century American novelist Hawthorne I naturally asked myself what does he tell us about the nature of the society in which he wrote, and then went on to enquire why the Calvinistic rural society of seventeenth- and eighteenth-century Scotland produced so *different* a literature from the similar theocratic society set up in New England by the Pilgrim Fathers who emigrated from England and were Hawthorne's ancestors – both directly in fact and artistically by determining the theme and values of his writings.

The next influence on my choice of research was the Victorian literary critic and philosopher Leslie Stephen – father of Virginia Woolf and described in her best novel *To the Lighthouse* – and more particularly I was impressed by the original line he took in his lectures on eighteenth-century literature published as *English Literature and Society in the Eighteenth Century*, a book that cannot be overpraised and has never been superseded. Besides having an unusually sensitive and thoughtful make-up as a literary critic, Leslie Stephen had a special training in his work on the English philosophers of the eighteenth century – he wrote the standard work on this subject – and in accidents of his personal history, which I have documented in an article in *Scrutiny* called 'Leslie Stephen: Cambridge Critic'.[4] Leslie Stephen started in his lectures on the eighteenth-century English poets and prose-writers by arguing from what then (in 1903) were quite unusual premises. For instance, he began by arguing that criticism 'must start from experience...begin by asking impartially *what* pleased men, and then inquire why it pleased them'. This was highly unorthodox, since the academic assumption was that there is good and bad, and what is good is literature while what is *not* is outside the scope of literary criticism and invisible, so to speak. This assumption was current a long while after Leslie Stephen tried to destroy it; I remember a very distinguished colleague at Cambridge who before the War was writing a comparative history of all European literature in the last decades of the nineteenth century. He was confident that his business was to deal only with the *good* writers, and that this did not require any exercise of literary criticism or involve any question of value-judgments. My husband said, 'Well, are you going to include Marie Corelli (a bestseller of the period, admired at the time she wrote by some of the most eminent of her contemporaries)?' 'Of course not.' 'Why not?' He couldn't say why not, but he thought the question irrelevant and in bad taste.

Leslie Stephen was prepared to explain in regard to the eighteenth century, which was his concern, what was the reason why those whom we now agree to be bad poets, for instance, were then often highly thought of, and what was the function of kinds of novels that were then popular and have since become unreadable. He thought the reasons were very relevant to the discussion of literature in general. He dwelt on the need for literary criticism to investigate what he called 'the environment' of literature – what has since become familiar to scholars under the name 'the climate of opinion' – saying: 'Fully to appreciate any great writer, therefore, it is necessary to distinguish between the characteristics due to the individual with certain idiosyncrasies and the characteristics due to his special modification by the existing stage of social and intellectual development...Even the greatest man has to live in his own century. The deepest thinker is not really – though we often use the phrase – in advance of his day so much as in the line along which advance takes place.' These have since become commonplaces in respect to the method adopted by serious literary critics (as distinct from belletrists) and research students, but in my young days these were heresies. And in fact they still need insistence. By recognizing the need to pursue this kind of enquiry we make Jane Austen or Burns, for instance, much more interesting writers than if we had merely classified them as geniuses. We find that in fact they are one particular kind of artist; their genius is not that of the great original creative artists (like William Blake, or Emily Brontë even though Blake and Emily Brontë are visibly and inescapably products of their age too), but that Jane Austen and Burns are respectively a novelist and a poet who brought superior faculty and intelligence to using techniques, material, stylizations and inventions that they had inherited from a long line of – in Jane Austen's case – less distinguished or mediocre fiction-writers, or – in Burns's case – ballad and lyric poets. This does not make Jane Austen or Burns less interesting, it seems to me that it makes them more so; and it makes us able to avoid a common fault, of praising them for what was not a personal creation but was the work of a long tradition finally perfected by such rarely endowed artists in words. Again the studies that have shown how much Bunyan had in common with earlier and contemporary Puritan polemic writers do not make the achievement of *Pilgrim's Progress* any the less wonderful.

Leslie Stephen, in this book that should be a classic for the literary critic and a model for the research student, goes on to ask many even more suggestive questions. 'Why did the *Spectator* suit one generation and Dr Johnson's *Rambler* its successors? Are we incapable of giving any answer?' he asks, and proceeds to investigate with great sensitiveness and subtlety his 'contention that there is a close relation between the literature and the general social condition of a nation' though 'the relation is hardly of a simple kind', he takes care to point out. In fact, his account of that relation is unlikely to give comfort to the Marxizing literary critic. Leslie Stephen comes to the conclusion that directed my work as a post-graduate student in the early 1930s: 'Briefly, in talking of literary changes, considered as implied in the whole social development, I shall have, first, to take note of the main intellectual characteristics of the period; and secondly, what changes took place in the audience to which men of letters addressed themselves, and how the gradual extension of the reading class affected the development of the literature addressed to them.'

In fact, this concept of literature as *a product of the interplay* between writer and reader, a collaboration between them (since no writer works except in the expectation of some kind of audience), which is governed by what the writer inherits from the tradition in which he works – *this* is the concept of literature that I have always had in mind when writing literary criticism myself and when teaching English literature. And Leslie Stephen in making this discovery found an approach which makes the study of the dullest and deadest works of past reputation have a relevance and significance. For instance, he says of *Ossian* that 'its popularity is a curious phenomenon': it is pseudo-poetry that appealed to Goethe and Napoleon, among others, and was admired by Blake to the last – its influence is visible in much of Blake's poetry. Leslie Stephen characteristically says finally of the taste for *Ossian* 'it was an indication of the state of mind which led to a new departure'.

I need not describe all the steps by which, fertilized by Leslie Stephen and by Dr I. A. Richards, a distinguished young Cambridge don who, psychologically trained, took this bent into literary criticism, and had recently published his famous book *Principles of Literary Criticism*, I decided to make my Ph.D. project an examination of popular fiction and the reading-public in England. Briefly, it had come to seem to me wasteful and dangerous to discuss a novel in an aesthetic vacuum, as if novels were written in a timeless contemporary void that E. M. Forster describes in his little book on the novel. 'A novel pulled up as a unit for inspection clings with its tentacles round so many non-technical matters that it cannot always be safely severed from them', I wrote in the Introduction to the part of my thesis which I published under the title *Fiction and the Reading Public*, and continued: 'I became interested in the general question: What has happened to fiction and the reading-public since the eighteenth century?' I found encouragement to pursue this kind of interest in hints thrown out by I. A. Richards in his book *Principles of Literary Criticism*, where he said that there is evidence perhaps that such things as bestsellers, mantel-piece pottery, popular songs, etc. have decreased in merit and added 'Bestsellers in all the arts, exemplifying as they do the most general levels of attitude development, are worthy of very close study. No theory of criticism is satisfactory which is not able to explain their wide appeal and to give clear reasons why those who disdain them are not necessarily snobs.' No one had then studied the subject.

Louis B. Wright was just beginning to investigate the Elizabethan reading-public. I asked Dr Richards (long since a professor at Harvard) to direct my research thesis and thus found myself committed to studying the history of English popular fiction, of magazines and other periodicals, including the history of the Press from Addison to Lord Northcliffe, and I made some discoveries which, though resisted with indignation at the time, have since become commonplaces of English literary criticism. The chief of these was the importance of the Puritan conscience in English literary history. I discovered in the publications of the English eighteenth and nineteenth centuries large numbers of artless and touching autobiographies and biographies of the humble, the poor who struggled to educate themselves and managed to do so wholly or partially even when illiterate until they were adult. They were impelled to this immense effort of self-education in the earlier period by the religious conscience and in later ages by the strong Radical trend among the English working class that first anticipated and then was generally the consequence of the French Revolution. This Radical complexion in England coloured (and largely in fact produced) the major literary creation of our English nineteenth century, the Victorian novel – novels of Emily Brontë, Mrs Gaskell, Kingsley, Dickens, Disraeli, George Eliot, which in spite of the widely different political and intellectual positions of these authors, were all instinctively Radical in sympathy. I found that such was the literary climate of England before the advent of Lord Northcliffe and the systematic exploitation of the Press which degraded popular taste (it was followed by allied phenomena such as the exploitations of amusements and general degradation of taste). I found evidence that the literary climate until then was such that the illiterate who had managed to learn to read could pull himself up to the best standard of taste of his age, the level of reading capacity of the educated public, with no difficulty. Even if his driving impulse was religious or atheistic, Radical in politics, or otherwise *un*aesthetically directed, the self-educated man had access to a good prose style, acquired standards of taste and discrimination and could read the fiction and the poetry that were read by even the best-educated men of his time. Thus when a novelist like Dickens appeared, who needed success – money *or* fame – and could like Shakespeare provide interest of all kinds, he made a great appeal. Being a novelist in spite of himself, he moved in stages from being an entertainer in a crude sense to writing to please himself, educating the lower levels of his public in the process. The integration of the reading-public effected in Dickens's time largely by Dickens, was what made George Eliot reap so rich a reward financially for her novels, novels in which she made no concessions of any kind but wrote to satisfy herself – and she was the most highly educated woman of her age, with the most sensitive taste, the highest literary standards and an uncompromisingly highbrow mode of expressing her insights and judgments. I also had to document the saddening disintegration of this public and the loss to the individual and the community alike, which followed on the Compulsory Education Act of 1870, which opened the eyes of journalists and popular entertainment to the new and innocent public which was then just literate enough to be exploited for gain.

But this line made me highly objectionable to the fashionable Marxism of the 1930s, which ruled in the high places of the literary world such as our left-wing intellectual weekly *The New Statesman* (the great law-giver of that time) and in corresponding academic quarters. Professor Harold Laski, the Marxist historian, then the dominating spirit of the London School of Economics and chairman of the British Labour Party, was furious, I was told, if he saw a student of his reading my book. My offence was to have challenged the automatic optimism on which the attitudes of the fashionable left-wing intellectuals were based. I had quoted at the beginning of my book John Stuart Mill's summary of his father's position: 'So complete was my father's reliance on the influence of reason over the mind of mankind, whenever it is allowed to reach them, that he felt as if *all* would be gained if the whole population were taught to read, if all sorts of opinions were allowed to be addressed to them by word and in writing, and if, by means of the suffrage, they could nominate a legislature to give effect to the opinions they adopted.' I also cited the enthusiastic salute to the future by the Victorian novelist Wilkie Collins, Dickens's friend and protégé, that 'A great, an unparalleled prospect awaits, perhaps, the coming generation of English novelists. The largest audience for periodical literature, in this age of periodicals, must obey the universal law of progress, and *must*, sooner or later, learn to

discriminate. When that period comes, the readers who rank by
millions will be the readers who give the widest reputations, who
return the richest rewards, and will therefore command the
services of the best writers of their time.' So it seemed to Wilkie
Collins, not unreasonably; but what happened later on that cut
off Henry James and Conrad, for instance, from the rich
rewards, I had demonstrated, and it ought to have been
recognized by the Laskis. But they could not afford to give up
their illusions. However, the advent of Fascism closed that era
in England. In Wilkie Collins's time, I pointed out, Dickens and
George Eliot were near neighbours, they had the same readers;
but 'there is an unbridged and impassable gulf between Marie
Corelli and Henry James', the situation we found at the
beginning of the twentieth century when the reading-public had
disintegrated.

I spent the next twenty years in writing for and helping to
edit *Scrutiny*, which my husband and I established to advance
our position in the field of literary criticism and criticism of the
other arts, for which, particularly music, we supplied a
comparable background, and we found – often by training them
ourselves – academics in other subjects, such as education,
philosophy, psychology, history, anthropology, and French,
German and Italian literatures, specialists who brought the
Scrutiny approach and adopted the *Scrutiny* platform. We provided
in this way a complete revaluation of Middle English poetry. We
were able at Cambridge University, behind the backs of a
largely hostile academic world, to smuggle in *Scrutiny*-type
research. For instance, a New Zealand research student who
was very miserable with an arid academic research-theme was
revived and made enthusiastic by taking on instead a subject he
had really at heart and was uniquely qualified to work on – an
enquiry into why New Zealand had not, like New England in
the early nineteenth century, evolved a literature of its own and
produced a school of novelists and poets characteristic of their
unique way of living. A very useful and thoroughly documented
examination of the equivalent theme in relation to Scotland and
Scottish literary history has been done more recently with my
stimulus and encouragement by Dr David Craig; it was
published in 1961 as *Scottish Literature and the Scottish People*,
1680–1830. *Scrutiny* had long before published a pioneer, completely original, examination of Scottish literary traditions and

achievement in a series of articles by my husband's pupil John Speirs, published in book form as *The Scottish Literary Tradition*. Another Cambridge associate, Martin Turnell, did something similar for the principal French writers, later published as well-known books. One of our young men, Wilfred Mellers, applied the *Scrutiny* line to music, and another, Denys Enright, contributed German poets and novelists for us; while L. C. Knights' work in *Scrutiny* on the Elizabethan literary world is well known. I must not give the impression that we were or ever have been under the delusion that there can be any substitute, whether in philosophy or sociology or psychology, for literary criticism, or that what we call for convenience *practical criticism* is not the absolutely indispensable basis for any discussion of literary questions. I may quote here from my own formulation, perhaps. As I wrote at the end of an article in *Scrutiny* in which I was investigating the work of a Victorian bestselling novelist Charlotte Yonge, who was then in danger of being thrust on us as a classic by the Anglo-Catholic enclave on grounds of belief: 'We are not concerned with her qualifications as a *Christian*, but as a *novelist*', and I ended after demonstrating that, before hailing a novelist on principle, it is necessary to discover (and this can only be done by the methods of practical criticism) *exactly what the writer is in fact doing*, which may be quite different from what the piece of writing alleges it is doing. The method of literary criticism practised by us in *Scrutiny* was 'to secure the maximum general agreement for evaluation by starting with something demonstrable – the surface of the work – and through practical criticism to proceed inwards to a deeper and wider kind of criticism commanding assent (or giving an opening for disagreement and discussion) at every step'.

In fact, particular investigations of the *complexity* and the *dangers* of easy generalization and naïve assumption in this field, were made in *Scrutiny* by my husband in a number of places, particularly in two articles; one was called 'Literature and Society', and was an address given very bravely to the London School of Economics which dealt with the Marxist assumptions about literature. The other, 'Sociology and Literature', started from a discussion of a German work by Schücking, called in English 'The Sociology of Literary Taste' (both these articles are reprinted in *The Common Pursuit*). The first of these essays ends with the conclusion proved by previous argument and demonstration: 'Without the sensitizing familiarity with the subtleties of language, and the insight into the relations between abstract or generalizing thought and the concrete of human experience, that the trained frequentation of literature alone can bring, without these the thinking that attends social and political studies will not have the edge and force it should.' In an exchange with Professor René Wellek, in the pages of *Scrutiny*, my husband clarified the objections that we had to the merely philosophic approach to literature – seen above all in the characteristic French method of extracting the philosophy of a poet or novelist and discussing this 'philosophy' as though that were the work of literature itself. Professor Wellek defended Shelley against the adverse findings of practical criticism of his poetry (made by my husband in *Revaluation*) on the grounds that 'Shelley's philosophy is astonishingly unified and perfectly coherent'. My husband's reaction to this position of Dr Wellek was to retort: 'If, in reply to my charge that Shelley's poetry is repetitive, vaporous, monotonously self-regarding and often emotionally cheap, and so, in no very long run, boring, Dr Wellek tells me that Shelley was an idealist, I can only wonder whether some unfavourable presumption has not been set up about idealism.'

Well, in the twenty years of *Scrutiny* we revalued the main English novelists, poets and dramatists and brought these creative writers into relation very fruitfully with the background of their times and traditions; and we did a good deal of the same kind for American literature, in particular bringing out its close interconnexion with English literature. I myself contributed pioneering essays of evaluation and elucidation on the American novelists Edith Wharton, Henry James, and (in *The Sewanee Review*) of Hawthorne, and I wrote similar studies on many English novelists, particularly Jane Austen, on whose writings I did some research resulting in a completely new account of the nature and value of her work. In consequence Jane Austen is no longer considered a light-weight comic artist but is accepted as being a major and deeply serious novelist concerned with the complexities of living, with its pressures and menaces, in a period of social and moral change. I have also (in teaching though not yet in published form) been concerned to relate Jane Austen to the tradition of novelists, principally women, that links her right back to the novels of the mid-eighteenth century, particularly Richardson's. What my particular interest in the nineteenth-century English novelists (in which I include Henry James) has given rise to is the desire to write a book that will consist of essays on the line of novelists from Jane Austen to Henry James, bringing Mrs Gaskell, Disraeli, Dickens, the Brontës and George Eliot into the line; my unifying theme would be to discuss their attitude to 'Art', which I find used in the nineteenth-century novel as a symbol (it includes architecture and sculpture too) for an achievement or ideal of living. Dickens uses the idea of art in order to explore the problem of what is wanting in the industrial society which has resulted in an England of Hard Times, a Bleak House, whose Great Expectations have turned out to be a bitter irony and cheat. As we must all have noticed, he uses throughout his novels the idea of the theatre, the racecourse, the circus, the waxworks – entertainment in which the individual escapes from his imprisoning identity as a member of a commercial society (Pancks). The Artist (Doyce) is the man who is master of his environment and free of it. Skimpole is the false artist and Gowan the anti-artist – and in his last whole novel, *Our Mutual Friend*, the gentleman whose sole justification is in the style and grace he brings to living, is the artist in living. These all are symbols of a kind of life, or possibilities in living, that have been fatally excluded from the prison-world of the Industrial Revolution. Dickens, I have found, is more systematic and comprehensive in this, but he is only carrying to fuller formulation ideas and techniques worked out by his predecessors from Jane Austen onwards, and in this George Eliot is wholeheartedly and more or less consciously the follower of Dickens at a higher level of aesthetic perception, and of course, being much more cultivated and intellectual, she brings more specialized knowledge to filling out such ideas. Henry James carries on from her, at the highest degree of conscious intellectual treatment of this question, which I imagine was the preoccupation of every major artist since the beginning of the Industrial Revolution, when Blake, perhaps our greatest creative artist since Shakespeare, undoubtedly gave his attention to the problem, as we can see from his prose epigrams as well as his poems. Matthew Arnold's preoccupation with it in *Culture and Anarchy* and many other related essays is better known than the novelists' handling of the same theme, but in spite of all his advantages such as a Classical education,

and a mind trained in polemic, and a nice line of irony, I don't
think his statement of the problems involved in making a society
which shall give a full life to all in an industrial and class-divided
country is as profound or helpful as what the novelists give us;
and it is certainly less convincing because Matthew Arnold's
argument is not expressed dramatically in terms of concrete
living as in those novels by his contemporaries.

Meanwhile I've written a long original introduction to *Jane
Eyre* for a new critical edition, and am doing another for *Silas
Marner*,[5] that short novel which is so fascinating an example of
George Eliot's impulse to give expression to the insights she
gained from her upbringing in the deep countryside of a
pre-industrial England as her parents remembered it and
transmitted it to her. *Silas Marner* contrasts very nicely with the
fully intellectualized and almost too schematic treatment of the
problem – how to live a full and satisfying life? – which we see
as the basis of *Middlemarch* in the history of Dorothea Brooke.
I could not study Dickens and his success in integrating a
reading-public, with his sympathetic feeling for the quality of
their lives and their deprivations, his urgent impulse to help
them by alerting them to their deficiencies and deprivations,
without examining the novels in all their aspects, which includes
the illustrations Dickens worked so hard at with successive
artists so that at best they are a collaborative achievement. I
cannot see how it is possible to separate Dickens's novels into text
and illustration: the whole, for their original readers and even
for us, consists of both together and intermingled. Thus I've
embarked on another side of that to me absorbing question,
what is the relation between writer and reading-public – in this
respect a seeing public too? The important part the illustrations
played in getting through to the readers what he intended to be
understood by the text, is best seen in *Dombey and Son*. I realized
how much better the aesthetic education of the masses was
visually through novels, since the art of Hogarth and his line
of successors in art was in common possession, a tradition well
understood and already drawn upon by the major English
novelists of the middle eighteenth century to help them in their
invention of a new fiction.

This has led me to examine (a neglected subject) the part
played by the illustrators of English nineteenth-century fiction,
and led me to reconsider the drawings in *Punch* and similar

Victorian comic papers, with which I had been delighted and
fascinated as a child and have gone back to with greater interest
and pleasure ever since. In fact, owing to a series of accidents
of a peculiarly English kind – the coincidence of the popularity
of Bunyan's *Pilgrim's Progress* with the occurrence later of
Hogarth, and then that Gillray the Regency political cartoonist
was Hogarth's pupil and George Cruikshank (Dickens's first
and best illustrator) was Gillray's pupil – owing to these
accidents the English *seeing* public was, it struck me, painlessly
and unconsciously educated into a reading-public skilled in
assimilating an ever-increasingly subtle and profound literary
art. It is a fact that illustrations of the Hogarth–Cruikshank
kind, along with the emblematic and pictorial moral scenes in
Pilgrim's Progress, were understood by everyone in England
however humble, since everyone read *Pilgrim's Progress* and
Hogarth's series of moralized pictures (the *Idle and Industrious
Apprentices* and *Marriage à la Mode*) hung in every alehouse and
farmhouse in old England. Then I saw the English moralistic
tradition in art and literature was not simply pious, but from
the beginning (as we can see in Bunyan) went along with quite
shrewd and sharp critical attitudes to people – to manifestations
of character and personality. This made it readily assimilate
with *political* caricature, such as Gillray's in the period of the
Napoleonic wars, and turned the current of popular interest into
criticism of the fashionable world; of political events, and of social
change, always with a moral intention and the implication of
a code of values that placed these events. We can see how the
folk-traditions drawn on by the poet Blake, taken over by him
from broadsheet ballads and folk-song, helped to feed this
culture of the people too. But the addition of the political
cartoon was what determined the trend of this popular art, and
Cruikshank, the pupil of Gillray and so indirectly of Hogarth,
fixed the style of the Dickens illustrations in the early novel
Oliver Twist, so that Phiz (the pen-name of Dickens's next artist
Hablôt Browne) reproduces the styles of all his predecessors to
suit the circumstances.

In *Punch*, one of the great formative influences of the
Victorian age from the beginning, the comic articles and the
illustrated jokes which started as quite sharply anti-aristocratic
and anti-royalist (*Punch* was at first Radical in politics) soon
narrowed down to humour about the family, the hunting-field,

the lower orders and children, with a corresponding mellowing of the engravings and drawings. The delightful drawings of Leech and Keene still have a generally satiric overtone, but it is not till the advent of George du Maurier that we again find an edge to the jokes, both in the text and the drawings. These acerbities are directed against the vulgar new rich and against the aristocracy that was insolent to intellectuals and did not know (unlike the aristocracy of our great age of the arts in the eighteenth century and the Regency period), how to treat artists and musicians with proper respect. They are also directed against the philistine, morally prudish and snobbish middle class. Du Maurier, in his famous drawings in *Punch*, also teased the aesthetic movement of Oscar Wilde and the Pre-Raphaelites, but only because of the affectations and insincerity the movement led to when taken up as a fashion at the drawing-room level. In Du Maurier I seem to see English satire cut free from its traditional base in politics and morals in order to serve as a weapon for the artist and intellectual against the enemies of his order. By this, pictorial satire separates itself from the people, always in England unsympathetic to these things: Du Maurier was, significantly, half French and shared none of the Victorian moral ethic; he always thought the English really rather tiresomely limited, and it is also significant that he was the friend and inspirer of Henry James, himself unEnglish since he was part New Yorker and part European. And again like his friend Du Maurier, James was consciously an artist without affiliations to any traditional system of morals or commitments to any social organization.

I think I can in this way make an investigation into the relations between literature and the arts of illustration in the nineteenth century, which will bring out and help to explain that divorce between people and the great novelists of the end of the century which is so much in contrast to the situation as Dickens and even George Eliot knew it. Of course I have had to realize that such an attempt needs great care in application, great delicacy. Much as one would like to be able to determine just how much Hogarth, or Bunyan, contributed to the formation of taste in the reading-public and to the equipment and aims of the English novelists, it will never be possible to do so with certainty. One can only conjecture; but one can certainly argue that without both Bunyan and Hogarth there would not have been a public for Dickens, or even Dickens's novels as we know them. We may contrast Jane Austen, in whose make-up neither Bunyan nor Hogarth counts specifically, though she shares the common English feeling for moralistic interpretation of the psychological and sociological observations she made of human nature. No one will ever be able to determine either just how much Dr Johnson's forbidding philosophic romance *Rasselas* contributed to the formation of taste, but we would be wrong to write off as negligible a work that was admired by Jane Austen, Charlotte Brontë and George Eliot – among other great novelists – and figures in both *Cranford* and *Jane Eyre* as a weighty symbol.

As an example of the care we must take, which extends to not believing what writers say themselves if their work tells us a different story, I can cite Henry James who in his (very interesting and valuable) book on Hawthorne expresses a dislike of, even contempt for, allegory in general and *Pilgrim's Progress* in particular. Yet Hawthorne himself was the un-doubted child of Bunyan and the English and New England Puritans (Bunyan's literary heirs); and Henry James started, and to a great extent always remained, Hawthorne's pupil, indebted to Hawthorne for the tools of his trade and even some of his subject-matter and attitudes.

I should, if challenged, sum up my work as literary criticism which is directed towards the sociology of literature and the arts in general. I have done a great deal of reviewing in *Scrutiny* and elsewhere – of novels, short stories, literary histories, biographies, literary criticism and essays – and written articles round such books or often round writers of no outstanding merit or less than no merit, because they have given the opportunity I wanted to make certain observations and deductions about literary questions. And also in order to arrive at a truer evaluation of interesting but till then neglected writers – such as Gissing the late Victorian novelist, Richard Jefferies the country writer from a Wiltshire farm, Charlotte Yonge the mid-Victorian bestseller whose novels were grounded in High Anglicanism and tell us some very interesting things about the quality of that creed in practice. These are a few of the writers on whom I did pioneer criticism, directed at placing them in a tradition and drawing conclusions about the taste of the reading-public. This kind of reviewing has become a matter of course since then and a pretence at it is part of the highbrow literary journalist's trade as regularly practised in the intellectual weeklies. But when I worked it out my writing (and the similar criticism by other members of the *Scrutiny* circle) was hotly resented by the old-style literary critics. They were belletrists, sometimes scholars too, but if so, outside their scholarly specialisms they were really quite frivolous, and freely stated that the high sense of responsibility for literature and its purpose that we showed in *Scrutiny* was priggish and objectionable. It is quite possible to combine an uncritical belief in the virtue of 'facts' or 'factual matter', or a professional interest in literary history with an irresponsible attitude to the contemporary situation in letters. Now *we* held that any genuine interest in the literature of the past must ask what the conditions were that made literature flourish and that will make it possible to keep literature going. Therefore we always pressed for value-judgments which the mere scholar *cannot* make and the belletristic critic does not *want* to have to make. Moved by these considerations I felt it essential to supplement my criticism of books and authors by substantial essays in *Scrutiny* on the achievements of the great Cambridge teachers in the humanities – such as Leslie Stephen and Professor Chadwick – along with other essays which analysed the dangerous influence of less admirable academic types at Cambridge and Oxford: this also didn't make me a very popular figure among those in power, though time has vindicated my judgments.

To sum up: what I have done was concentrated seminal work – throwing off fruitful ideas and suggestions that have been followed up by research students, doing exemplary pieces of criticism in new fields, opening up new lines of interest and finding fresh relations between writers and subjects, offering more helpful kinds of approach to the basic problems that arise for any serious and responsible literary critic or student. After all, a new method, a fresh kind of approach, brings more grist to the mill of the academic worker than anything else. Really I suppose what I have spent myself most on is showing other people where to dig, not having time to do intensive and exclusive digging myself. I am a dowser and not a navvy – and I must admit that whereas the higher navvying in the academic fields has always been considered respectable and praiseworthy, dowsing is a highly suspect activity.

Jane Austen: novelist of a changing society

Two hundred years is a long time for fame and affection to last, and we may well ask how it is that the fictions of a youngish spinster who was the daughter of a rather poor middle-class country parson, fictions apparently written originally to entertain her own family, should have spread over the whole world and now enjoy universal esteem, especially as it is only comparatively recently that her novels have been both highly esteemed and widely read. When her nephew wrote the memoir of his aunt to publish in 1869 he remarked that 'Seldom has any literary reputation been of such slow growth', and in fact, by 1870, only one complete edition of her novels had been published and bought, in spite of their having had a reputation in private circles in England of the highest social and intellectual rank, from the Prince Regent and Holland House to G. H. Lewes's household and Mrs Oliphant. But even enthusiasm is not necessarily judicious, and it is only in the last thirty years, I should say, that due appreciation of the nature of the Austen novels has come about. Even Henry James whose art (though presumably unconsciously) owes so much to hers, when writing about her in an essay, reprinted in *Partial Portraits*, takes the line that she was unconscious and naïve as an artist! In contrast, a more intelligent, and a woman novelist, Mrs Oliphant, argued in 1870 in *Blackwood's Magazine* that Miss Austen's 'is not the simple character it appears at first glance, but one full of subtle power, keenness, finesse and self-restraint – a type not at all unusual in women of high cultivation'.

Accepting this, which explains why the Austen novels could be so widely influential not only on such novelists as Trollope, Mrs Gaskell and Charlotte Yonge but on highly sophisticated novelists, even intellectual ones, such as Henry James, George Eliot, Mrs Oliphant herself and E. M. Forster, we still have to

ask why the Austen novels are read with deep interest by the
products not only of Anglo-Saxon cultures or even of European
cultures, but by peoples of cultures one would have thought
hopelessly alien to those. For instance, instructors in English
literature in African universities report that Miss Austen's
novels are often appreciated with little difficulty there, the secret
being that peoples with no written literature of their own but
possessing a strict code of manners and a social hierarchy
centring or having recently centred on a court, with a correspondingly developed linguistic system, have a good deal in
common with, and can therefore understand, the society that
forms the material of Jane Austen's novels. Her novels can
overcome the barriers of race, colour, time, religion, language
and education, not as *Macbeth* and *Hamlet* do (because they
have something universal and primitive in their actions and
theme), but for an opposite reason, that these novels deal with
the complexities of family life and the difficulties of personal life
in a society highly developed as regards *moeurs* but not yet
industrialized. The culture of the Austen novels was that of a
farming countryside with a traditional governing-class which was
still functioning as landowners, with an established religion, and
in which marriage was still primarily a matter of family
arrangements and interests, and in which property was settled
by law and custom. Life was a matter of obligations and duties
in all classes, and those classes were strictly defined as to their
rôles and in relation to each other, as were the sexes and the
different generations. Yet in her unduly short lifetime Miss
Austen saw some of these assumptions being questioned and
partly altered by a change of feeling in her own class. Her novels
are strictly and fundamentally the reflections of these changes –
social changes – and deal with the psychological and moral
problems to which the changes gave rise.

   This is only the groundwork of the novels, however. I started
by saying that Miss Austen is and has long been regarded with
affection as well as admiration and respect, and it is worth
asking why, since, if one thinks of it, it is *only* Jane Austen (no
longer Charles Lamb to the same extent or even Dickens, and
we don't *love* Dr Johnson though his life is incessantly being
investigated) – only Jane Austen who is loved and esteemed by
her readers as a *person*. Isn't it because, through her writings
alone, we acquire the impression of a delightful personality and

an admirable character, in spite of the impersonality of her novels? And this doesn't depend on Jane Austen's humour and wit – for we don't think fondly of Whistler or Oscar Wilde or W. S. Gilbert who were even wittier. And Jane Austen shows so uncompromising a critical mind that it would be natural for ordinary people to flinch from it; indeed, some academics and professional men of letters have gone on record as doing so, and one of her early admirers, Mrs Oliphant, thought that 'it is scarcely to be expected that books so calm and cold and keen would ever be popular'.

What sort of person is revealed by the Austen novels then? Underneath the changing themes and attitudes and characters of the novels there are many consistent expressions of values which are the skeletons of the structures and also give them an unequivocal flavour which we cannot but admire, respect and esteem if we are not frivolous or base. 'There is always something offensive in the details of cunning' is a characteristic remark and in her first novel the winding up, though clumsily expressed, enlarges on this:

The whole of Lucy's behaviour in the affair, and the prosperity which crowned it, therefore, may be held forth as a most encouraging instance of what an earnest, an unceasing attention to self-interest will do in securing every advantage of fortune, with no other sacrifices than that of time and conscience.

Elinor Dashwood perceives in Lucy Steele 'the thorough want of delicacy, of rectitude, and integrity of mind' while Henry Tilney approves of Catherine Morland for possessing an 'innate principle of general integrity'. And constantly and insistently the supreme value of sincerity, spontaneity and warmth of feeling is asserted. The novelist's evident detestation of Lady Middleton, the Ferrars clan and John Dashwood in her first novel, and similar characters in all her subsequent novels, endorses these expressions of values. Here we see the marks, over and over again, in the Austen novels, of a fastidious nature, a fine spirit and a keen sense of honour and of value for integrity, which seem to me to show Jane Austen to be closer to Conrad than any other novelist is. Both are natural aristocrats but both are concerned for human values. In spite of the impersonality sustained throughout her novels and which makes them so different from any Victorian novels, these values come through to the reader as personal. These qualities, as in Conrad, are somewhat daunting, but what makes them acceptable in her case is, surely, that they are combined in her with a degree of self-criticism that is disarming. Her heroines, especially the lively, witty, critical ones, ultimately criticize *themselves* for lacking 'humility, generosity, self-knowledge', qualities which always turn out finally to be what Jane Austen considers the most essential. Marianne Dashwood and Elizabeth Bennet express their admiration for their elder sisters for exemplifying 'candour', which meant the opposite of censoriousness. It is explained as the opposite of carping, the virtue of looking for the best in everyone and which corresponds in their form of society to the Christian concept of charity. This checks the tendency of a critical mind and a fastidious taste to foster prejudice and run to conceit, and we may deduce from the tendency to find people on the whole objectionable, that permeates the Austen letters, that Jane Austen recognized her own weakness to be a remorseless judgment of others. Essentially then, Jane Austen is a moralist, but one whose moral values are not theoretical or conventional but proceed from self-scrutiny. The novels really seem to be motivated by the need for investigating the author's own convictions, attitudes, assumptions and moral habits: they investigate through dramatic action and critical dialogue. 'Till now I never knew myself' is ultimately the cry of Marianne Dashwood, Elizabeth Bennet and Emma. Isn't it suggestive that Emma, the heroine who is most thoroughly chastened, is the Austen character who in physical appearance closely resembles her author – the hazel eyes, the brown complexion, the firm figure and look of abundant healthfulness, which Henry Austen described as his sister Jane's, is the description given to Emma too. In qualities not external the descriptions given by her relatives suggest that she was more like Anne Elliot than one might have supposed – sweet-voiced, sweet-natured, sympathetic and self-denying, though these accounts, perhaps significantly, are of her maturity only. Her brother wrote that she was 'formed for elegant and rational society' and that, as one might expect, 'she delivered herself with fluency and precision, excelling in conversation as much as in composition'. We see that she was essentially a social being.

The self-criticism, based on the conviction of the primary

importance of achieving self-knowledge, humility and generosity of mind, is what makes the Austen irony so different from, so totally other than, the contemptible – because always self-protective – irony of the Bloomsbury group, whether novelists, literary critics or historians, and what makes her satire so different from that of the literature and journalism of our own age, whose satire is characteristically an expression of animus against values superior in any respect to those of the common man – the commonest man. *Her* values are moral in the sense of being spiritual and this is what makes her novels more than the mere entertainment which they were often considered to be.

The society which is Jane Austen's subject-matter has been thought by some too civilized, narrow and restricted emotionally to allow the highest success in the creative form of literature that is the novel. Charlotte Brontë, though without prejudice, was bewildered by G. H. Lewes the critic and by her publisher, after she had examined *Pride and Prejudice* and *Emma*, for they had both advised her that Jane Austen was a great artist whom she might profitably study. She answered them separately in letters, saying among other things that Miss Austen deals not with men and women but with 'ladies and gentlemen in their elegant but confined houses', adding 'I should hardly like to live with them' and complaining that *Pride and Prejudice* is 'a carefully fenced, highly cultivated garden' but has 'no open country, no fresh air'.

What Charlotte Brontë did not realize, living a generation later and in a totally different world, is that Jane Austen was consistently a *critic* of the society she had to live in and that she was concerned in her novels to discover how it could be altered for the individual's greater happiness yet without sacrificing the benefits the individual received from being a member of a high culture.

There could be no greater contrast between the Austens' world – Southern England and Georgian – and the Brontës' in early Victorian Yorkshire, though both novelists lived in rural parsonages and only a generation apart. But *Wuthering Heights* and *Jane Eyre* and *Shirley*, in their complete absence of any conception of 'civility', may well make us realize the advantages of a code of conduct based on politeness and forbearance instead of brutal plain-speaking and aggressive individualism. Jane Austen could surely have retorted on Charlotte Brontë that *she* would not like to live with the *men* and *women* in the Brontë novels.

Though novels are generally a good, and sometimes the only, source of some aspects of social history, it is not always safe to base conclusions about social history on the work of any one novelist. However, the opposite – assembling facts as to social changes from non-fictional sources and seeing what use a novelist has made of them, and what that novelist's attitude to them is – can be a rewarding exercise. And particularly, I believe, in the case of Jane Austen. We can examine through her novels her changing attitude to the theory of society current in her youth and her response to the radical social changes she lived through; and indeed her novels are the result of the stimulus which these ideas, widely circulated and discussed, provided.

What determined her interests as a novelist was that after she had grown up, and was therefore fully formed by eighteenth-century attitudes and social conventions (having been born in 1775), she experienced the extensive changes in social life that marked the advent of the Regency period and the distinctive modes of thinking and life-style that age brought about. These changes were not merely of dress, furniture and architecture, the externals of social life; they were the result and the expression of changes in the very idea of a society and of the individual's relation to it; changes that at the time were so evident and so widely discussed that the novelist could assume a knowledge of them in her readers, though the average educated twentieth-century reader is hardly aware of these references and ideas. But that is disabling, for it prevents one seeing that each novel in the Austen *oeuvre* is a step forward in an argument or debate that the novelist has undertaken. In the end (in *Persuasion*) she is to be found occupying the opposite position from the one she had started with (in *Sense and Sensibility*).

We can see from her first novel, *Sense and Sensibility*, that though Jane Austen there shows a desire to find reasons for accepting the inherited social form, she was dissatisfied with it and is, through all her novels, a consistent critic of the society she had had to live in. She was concerned, as I said, to discover how it could be altered for the individual's greater happiness, yet without sacrificing the valuable benefits each received from being a member of a high or aristocratic culture. In the two first novels she shows the individual could cope with this dilemma by techniques known as 'address' and 'civility'. This social strategy she inherited, through the well-understood and widely implemented theory of Augustan society that Lord Chesterfield explained for us in the famous volume of letters to his son, and Jane Austen constantly uses his very phrases, as well as choosing to illustrate the theory on the same lines in dialogue in *Persuasion* and *Sense and Sensibility*. She also found La Rochefoucauld's insights and Molière's philosophy helpful – in her first novel Marianne Dashwood is an English Alceste, while her sister Elinor argues for the position of Molière's Philinte (in *Le Misanthrope*) – the object being how to retain one's integrity (which Jane Austen prized above all) without becoming objectionable to others. The Regency period was an age of optimism and social relaxation and this challenge to eighteenth-century values provided her with her theme and subject-matter. She welcomed these changes as on the whole beneficial, indeed she ended up by being in the forefront, as we see in *Persuasion* where a basically different revolutionary society is shown to be available and chosen, at some self-sacrifice, by a heroine who has been brought up in the stagnant air of an effete county family. 'Modern', a term to which the Regency gave a special meaning, to characterize itself approvingly – it's very unlike the use of 'modern' in Shakespeare and the Elizabethans – was adopted and is always used thus by Jane Austen and is associated by her with another characteristic Regency term, 'cheerful'.

She clearly felt that the Regency 'Improver' *was* improving on the past, for she shared the current reasons for dissatisfaction with the Georgian actuality of her youth. Yet, as we see in her novels, she was too intelligent to endorse unconditionally *all* departures from the old pattern of conduct, and she had misgivings about the new forms of Regency man and woman, who appear in *Mansfield Park* as the Crawford brother and sister and are played off against both the older generation, and two examples of the old-fashioned younger generation (Edmund Bertram and Fanny Price). It is this delicate and responsible work of scrutiny and dramatized discussion that puts Jane Austen into the same class of novelist as George Eliot, Dickens, Stendhal and Henry James, and answers the adverse case made out against her work by Charlotte Brontë and some more recent writers in the same sense.

Let me start by reminding you of the world Jane Austen was born and brought up in. Born in 1775 she was necessarily a thorough child of the eighteenth century; there is a silhouette picture of the Austen family which has picked out all the essential features of the eighteenth-century social mode [Plate 1]. Here we see the Rev. George Austen, Jane's father, introducing his second son Edward to his cousins the Knights, a wealthy childless couple who adopted Jane's brother Edward and left him their estates. The artist has stressed what struck him as the significant features of such a *milieu* – the bare floor and the meagre though elegant furnishings, the concentration on the card- or chess-table, the aloofness and elegancies and extreme formality of manners and the aristocratic dress and deportment which were even imposed on the clergy and also on childhood: the clergyman has no distinctive dress and the little boy is dressed and hair-styled as a miniature gentleman. The boy is shown symbolically stretching out his hands to his future adoptive parents, with whom he has clearly got to assimilate himself, as little Fanny Price had to with the inhabitants of the old-style household in *Mansfield Park*. Such a society made no concessions to youthful needs and did not recognize childhood as a different state in itself.

But by the time Jane Austen was a woman, architects and designers were setting to work to change the old authoritarian life-style, debating the problem openly in an attempt, which proved successful, to achieve some freedom, informality and comfort, which should give to members of their society the right to be individuals. They invented new architectural devices and rethought designs for building convenient and congenial homes, and for replanning, or as they called it 'improving' (that is, modernizing by redesigning) old great houses and their grounds – which is one of the subjects of *Mansfield Park*. The Regency style is considered to have come about at the turn of the century, but of course it took time to spread and gain acceptance everywhere, though it at once became the fashion. The revolution that had occurred in Jane Austen's lifetime can easily be proved by comparing with the silhouette of the Austen family in the late 1770s the enchanting painting of the Grosvenor family (in private possession of the Duke of Westminster's family)

by Leslie, painted in 1833, which Jane Austen could have seen if she had lived into a normal middle age [Plate 2]. But anyway she had seen such scenes in actuality and as commonplaces of the new age before she died in 1817, as we can tell from the society portrayed in *Emma*. These Grosvenors were a grand and very wealthy family, unlike the Woodhouses in *Emma*, yet not only are the three generations of Grosvenors shown here as being in the closest contact and on obviously *in*formal terms, but the Marquess of Westminster, the head of the clan then, occupies a comparatively subsidiary place in the composition, while the Marchioness plays the piano for the children to dance to, and the children themselves, from infants upwards, are not merely present and *as* children – engaged in childish pursuits and encouraged in them by the adults, and with the new comfortable hair-styles and clothing – but they are clearly indulged, for the whole interest of the picture is centred on them and their happy faces. This lovely picture surely imparts a totally different conception of family life from the old-style one prevailing in all the Austen novels up to and including *Mansfield Park*. But this picture though child-centred is not *bourgeois*: notice the faces of the men in the painting – they are sensitive, refined and intelligent, particularly the Marquess's, their bearing and expression are aristocratic. But tenderness and such valuable, natural family feelings have now evidently been released and are seen to coexist with humour. Note particularly the child resting its head against its father's knee so confidently and the young husband gazing adoringly at his wife who is playing the harp. The picture is decidedly 'cheerful', one of the Regency aspirations which differentiated it so from the eighteenth century, which was grand; but though the daunting grandeur of a Georgian mansion here has been mitigated, *elegance*, the Regency's summary of its highest values, has not yet been sacrificed to vulgar comfort, as it was to be later in the Victorian age.

From these two pictures alone we can see that the movement of civilization had made a radical change in the family life and social habits of even the highest class, a change that is charted in its various manifestations from *Sense and Sensibility* to *Emma* and *Persuasion*.

Another factor that must have contributed to the absence of warm natural relations between parents and children in Jane

Austen's youth, and significantly in conditioning herself, was that every child in the family of gentry, even such really poor ones as the Austens, was sent to a cottage soon after birth to be wet-nursed and fostered by a cottager. Visited once a day perhaps by the mother though Jane and her siblings were (according to the tradition in the Austen family[1]) – as each child was not brought back to the parental home till it could run about, and talk, often till it was 3 years old – the psychological effect must have been considerable: it seems to me to account for the curious combination in the Austen novels and in many other pre-Romantic writers, of coolness of manner and attitude to others with an evident admiration of, and longing for, warmth of feeling and spontaneity.

The changes that the Regency introduced in its architecture, grounds, interior decoration and furniture were all in accordance with this desire for a new kind of home and family life and were deliberately worked out, not achieved by accident or instinct or gradual change. In its speed and extent it amounted to a revolution. We have seen that the Grosvenors' grand eighteenth-century saloon had somehow become humanized into a multi-purposed living room, fully carpeted, with some convenient pieces of furniture and musical instruments scattered about, and those instruments in use for what an Irishwoman, Maria Edgeworth, noted in 1821 with surprise, on visiting England, in her late middle age, as new to her, though she had been educated in England till she was fourteen, 'joyous playing', that is, playing for pleasure and not to show off the young ladies' accomplishments. In that picture the harp, that characteristic Regency instrument, being at once elegant and portable for informal music-making, figures prominently (for the same reason the Regency gentlemen played the flute). Yet the Grosvenors seem to be making do with their inflexible drawing-room, picnicking in it (as it were) in a habitat not designed for the kind of family life now chosen by its inhabitants; the effect is obviously uncomfortable for both parties to the arrangement and clearly shows why the Regency public desired, and architects were ready to supply, a new style of home. Regency architects accordingly developed the French window (that is, glass doors opening onto a terrace), the bow window, the veranda, the balcony, and the conservatory attached to the drawing-room, whereas previously the conservatory had been situated out in the grounds and therefore inaccessible for much of the year. All these innovations were to allow privacy without seclusion (which would have been unthinkable as yet) and a release from the strict chaperonage of young ladies. Where great houses could be adapted by internal alteration and external additions, this was done; but much wholly new building in the Regency style took place all over the British Isles.

These external changes came about through recognition of the demand for emancipation from the tyranny of eighteenth-century society, represented by the card-table after dinner and the constant but brief morning calls – 'morning' in Jane Austen's time being the whole period before late afternoon dinner. But now, for instance, the drawing-room acquired book-cases built into alcoves designed for the purpose by the architect so that books came out of the master's library and were available for general and casual use. In the earlier Austen novels, we note, Marianne Dashwood who 'had the knack of finding her way in every house to the library, however it might be avoided by the family in general', was unable to procure herself a book otherwise when staying with the Palmers; Elizabeth Bennet when at Mr Bingley's could not find a book in the drawing-room except for a few that happened to be lying on a table – they were the volumes of a book that Mr Darcy was in the course of reading, so Bingley offered to go and get her something from his library. Fanny Price in *Mansfield Park* had to keep her personal hoard of books in an attic. But in *Persuasion* the new informal reading is now apparent: Lady Russell is in this at least up-to-date, and, like her god-daughter Anne Elliot, a great reader; she persists in lending the conservative eldest Miss Elliot, who doesn't read, what the latter resentfully describes as 'all the new poems and states of nations that come out'. The children too were now freely allowed downstairs out of the nursery and school-room, and the old barriers between the generations were thus to some extent broken down. The theory that produced these changes was well understood and generally, though not always, approved. For example, Maria Edgeworth, a novelist seven or eight years older than Jane Austen and mixing in a higher social circle, resisted change in manners, family relations and behaviour, though showing in her letters that she appreciated the Regency *material* innovations, noting in her visit to Badminton in 1820 that though 'the house is a dreary-looking pile' yet 'small conservatories added to the drawing-room and library make both chearful' (sic). She continues: 'How this luxury of conservatories added to rooms opening into them has become general – enlivening thick-walled mansions as well as new-built boxes.'[2] And next year, from the house of the Sheppard family, she writes that 'a delicious conservatory joins to the dining-room, drawing-room and library – a fine rich carpeted suite of rooms', adding: 'People understand the comfort of the inside of houses better now.'

Emily Eden, an amateur novelist of the upper class, who wrote in 1830 an amusing Austenish novel, *The Semi-Attached Couple*, about the Regency society of her own young days, records in it the conflicting style of the two generations still then coexisting, where the two Douglas sisters, though their mother was an heiress and their father is a respectable landed gentleman, and they all live in a country-house in style, have only 'two hard cane chairs' to sit on in their bedroom; and when one of them goes to stay in a thoroughly Regency type of aristocratic family, she writes to her sister rapturously of the room allotted to her there: 'such looking-glasses and sofas and armchairs, mamma would be shocked'. Like Jane Austen, Emily Eden notes also the connexion between material and spiritual in these different generations, remarking that the Douglas girls had 'rather a hard atmosphere at home' while all the ladies of the Regency great house have 'a gentle and caressing manner'. This is the new style that had come in.

Besides redesigning the old, the Regency architects introduced two new types of houses, the *small* country-house and the little villa – designed for convenience, more light, and cheerful informality. In the eighteenth-century-type setting of *Sense and Sensibility* we see that a private conversation could only be carried on under cover of someone's performance on the piano, and a pause in the music allows an observation of Elinor's not intended for the public ear to be overheard, exposing her to malicious comment or jokes from the ill-bred; alternatively, Elinor, to get an opportunity for a confidential talk with her rival, has to employ a ruse – 'address' as we are told it is called – which allows them a brief escape from the obligation to join in the evening game of cards. Courtship and proposals were therefore really difficult in such a situation; no wonder offers of marriage were made through the father or guardian,

and not only because marriage was a family affair and not
considered merely personal – Mrs Charles Musgrove, born the
daughter of Sir Walter Elliot, enunciates the principle when she
says: 'I do not think any young woman has a right to make a
choice that may be disagreeable and inconvenient to the
principal part of her family'.[3] Jane Austen, of course, disassociates
herself from this idea. But now, in the new-style home, the
French window, standing open in warm weather, meant easy
access to the terrace outside, though safely within view, and, like
the other architectural inventions of the kind, was a way of
breaking down the barrier between house and garden and
allowing the sexes to mingle with some privacy and freedom.
Completely carpeted rooms instead of bare boards meant a less
formidable as well as a warmer interior, and the new windows
let in very much more light and a view which was now prized.
The grounds too were completely restyled to suit this new
conception of social life, and views, and liberty to roam, instead
of formal enclosures and high fencing, were at once in universal
demand. For Jane Austen, the novels tell us, a house was
praiseworthy in being 'modern', light and well-placed, and not,
like Sotherton, in *Mansfield Park*, which had been built long ago
in the old style for shelter, down in a hole without any views.
The old type of formal, walled-in, hedged and fenced gardens
were condemned now as imprisoning, which is the effect made
on the visiting Bertrams and Crawfords by Sotherton. We notice
that the young people of both families encourage the new owner
to call in Humphry Repton, the most famous Regency improver,
to give house and grounds a character suitable for a bride like
Maria Bertram, dissatisfied with her own traditional home and
its life-style; and Henry Crawford said that *he* had already
formed plans for the 'improvement' of his own country-house
and grounds when still at Cambridge – plans which were 'at
one-and-twenty executed'; he is in every respect a man of his
age, we gather.

Repton didn't confine his work to the grounds or even the
external architecture of great houses. He deliberately formulated
and propaganded what was needed to bring his world of the
nineteenth century out of its now uncongenial eighteenth-
century setting, for he saw that the forms and furnishings of
living-rooms determined the nature of the social life that could
be lived in them. Jane Austen clearly and constantly uses these

facts to chart and exhibit the accompanying inward changes, showing she understood the Regency revaluation of domestic life. Repton's book *Observations on the Theory and Practice of Landscape Gardening* in 1805, in spite of its title, showed what was being and had been done by the improvers indoors. He there tells us:

Modern habits have altered the uses of a drawing-room: formerly the best room in the house was opened only a few days in the year,[4] where the guests sat in a formal circle, but now the largest and best room in a gentleman's house is that most frequented and inhabited: it is filled with books, musical instruments, tables of every description, and whatever can contribute to the comfort or amusement of the guests, who form themselves into groups, at different parts of the room; and in winter, by the help of two fireplaces, the restraint and formality of the circle is done away.

And in a subsequent work, *Fragments of the Theory and Practice of Landscape Gardening* (1816), he actually published two contrasted drawings he had made to illustrate his point, having them coloured for greater effectiveness. The first is called 'The Ancient Cedar Parlour'[5] [Plate 3] – it is the ancestral or Platonic idea of the drawing-room as seen through the unsympathetic eyes of a new era. The absence of visible occupants is clearly designed to bring out how tyrannical the inherent social principle was, imposing an inescapable routine. The bare highly polished floor might perhaps have a small square of carpet in the middle but no more, and often it was as completely bare as shown here and in the first silhouette picture I mentioned. There are no books in the parlour – they are shut away in the library; no means of making music; no comfortable chairs; no sofa; no convenient little tables; the hearth is not to sit round and the room is dark, gloomy and dull; there are only family portraits on the walls; no visible outdoors, much less a view. It is a room for adults only and designed for but one purpose, the purpose which the eighteenth century thought society was for, general conversation, the chairs being arranged for it in the obligatory circle (we merely aren't shown the people who are in fact there sitting on them). Hence ladies absolutely had to have fans, to whisper behind what was not meant for anyone else to hear, or to hide an expression of countenance not for the public inspection, and in the eighteenth century a *language* of

the fan had necessarily been developed. Repton's 'Cedar Parlour' represents magnificence without comfort, and it is quite uncompromising in its social scheme. As soon as the company has gone, the footman will put the chairs back in their places, tidily against the wall, only to be set out one at a time as required. That's why we know there must be people sitting on them. The side-table is simply for serving refreshments to the visitors. Repton's implied criticism of an outmoded form of domestic life needs no explanation and was really true in essence. We remember for instance that at Mansfield Park though there *was* what was then called a sofa in the drawing-room, it was not meant for reclining on and Fanny is scolded by Mrs Norris for lying on it once when she felt too unwell to sit upright in the usual straight-backed chairs. In the eighteenth century not to sit bolt upright was ill-bred, and in fact no one could fail to do so until the Regency had designed a sofa, with head and foot, and no back, that really could be reclined on (instead of the previous settee that was simply an amalgamation of two or three upright chairs); and the Regency had invented also what they called the 'lounging-chair', which really *was* an armchair in our sense and not merely a straight-backed chair plus wooden arms as previous 'armchairs' were.[6]

But we see in Repton's accompanying drawing to 'The Ancient Cedar Parlour' the ideal that the Regency generation had desired and by then actually enjoyed, thanks to the sympathetic innovations of the Regency improvers. He proudly entitled it 'The Modern Living-Room' [Plate 4], and to make even clearer what he meant it to convey he supplied some verses of his own composition which describe the picture, pointing the contrast with his companion sketch. They begin:

> No more the *Cedar Parlour's* formal gloom
> With dulness chills, 'tis now the *Living Room*;
> Where Guests, to whim, or taste, or fancy true,
> Scatter'd in groups, their different plans pursue...

and so on at great length. As we immediately perceive, it really is for living, multi-purposed. The imprisoning and gloomy wainscoting or panelling is gone; instead walls are hung with charming light papers or delicate silks. The light streams in through windows cut down to the ground which are also doors to the garden. Warmth is suggested by the comfortable carpet,

covering the entire floor, and by the fire with its hearth-rug, beside which you see an elderly gentleman who, no longer secluded in his library, stretches out his legs in his easy chair and studies his books without causing offence by cutting himself off from the company, while the grandmother reclines with a footstool in a private conversation by the windows. The whole family of three generations are present plus visitors; children are being amused and are plainly a usual part of the family circle now. There are abundant books, and busts on the shelves, interesting pictures on the walls, and the books moreover are being freely handled even by small children instead of being shut up in bookcases. We note various tables and centres of interest in the room, the seating is dispersed and there are different kinds to choose from. The new-style conservatory in the usual apsed end of the Regency drawing-room (thus abolishing the old-fashioned imprisoning square room which the drawing-room used to be) – the conservatory makes for additional privacy, and courtship seems to be going on there. The harp is in use too, you notice, being played without interfering with anyone else's occupation – no one need listen unless they wish.

That the case – of a rapid change of a radical kind in the nature of family life – offered thus by Repton for propaganda, to persuade potential clients to adopt the new style, was an actuality, is proved by the evidence to be found in Jane Austen's own novels as well as in letters like Maria Edgeworth's, in family portraits, in conversation pieces and in drawings of actual interiors. Of course the way a family group is arranged for a picture and the family seen by an artist is always revealing, and as a great many portraits of old-style families were painted like this one [Plate 5] by William Pickett in 1811; we see how an old-fashioned family such as the Bertrams of Mansfield Park or the Bennets of Longbourn looked in their unimproved setting. Posed with what to the patron and the artist evidently seemed a suitable formality, they are shown in the library with the master of the house in possession. A mat has been placed for his lady's feet for the occasion as she sits stiffly upright on the settee. Their sons are decorously seated too. The contrast with Leslie's picture of the Grosvenors is complete, and this one might serve as an intermediary between the eighteenth-century silhouette picture of the Austens of a generation earlier and Leslie's painting of the Grosvenors nearly twenty years later than this,

Plate 14 A Formal House and Garden (painted by W. Pyne, c. 1800)

but clearly the painting by Pickett is in spirit closer to the eighteenth-century idea. For the family seem gloomy and constrained; like the young Bertrams and Fanny Price in the presence of the father and Aunt Norris, and like Sir Thomas himself, they all give the impression of being unable to relax or to conceive of being on informal terms with each other. They are evidently admitted to the library for the picture only – the timid wife and children are felt to be there on sufferance – and one remembers the old-style family at Longbourn where Mr Bennet sends for his daughter to the library to rebuke her, and tells his wife when she had for once ventured into the sacred library to consult him in a family crisis that 'I shall be glad to have the library to myself as soon as may be.' But Repton in 1816 wrote that many families *now* liked to use the library as a general living-room; evidently the master of the family had lost his majestic position and his family, no longer in awe or subjection, had taken to browsing among the books.[7]

The sketch of the drawing-room of Bromley Hall [Plate 6], built in 1816, the year before Jane died, shows that there were plenty of incarnations of Repton's ideal 'modern living-room'. Though, like 'The Ancient Cedar Parlour', it has no occupants, it equally implies a mode of living, and how different! Here are the French windows invitingly open with the garden thus almost brought into the house, the signs of achieved comfort and arrangements for individual tastes in different parts of the room, though the architectural features of the room – the draperies and the gracefully designed Regency furniture – are still elegant. This is a typical realization of the Regency idea and was represented in houses of all sizes and types. Thus life became pleasanter and more informal, and more individual. Even Regency Gothic, it should be noted, was cheerful, and Jane Austen's General Tilney, who prided himself on being up-to-date, had put large sash windows into the medieval Northanger Abbey, though, as he said, carefully preserving the pointed arch, and making it altogether too light and unromantic for Catherine Morland's taste, a taste for which Jane Austen had plainly no sympathy whatever, for she ridicules it.[8]

Jane Austen could get quite subtle humour from the contrasts between the manners of the new generation and the old. Even the haughty, conservative Miss Elliot knows that fashions have changed and says of the old family friend, the estimable Lady

Russell: 'I thought her dress hideous the other night. I used to think she had some taste in dress, but I was ashamed of her at the concert. Something so formal and arrangé in her air, and she sits so upright!' The joke is that Miss Elliot herself is 'formal and arrangé' in every respect, but she knows that informality shown by 'lounging' and an unsophisticated girlish style of dress are now the current thing, and so feels superior to Lady Russell. Just as George Eliot's economic data are always correct, so Jane Austen's social detail is always thoroughly well-informed and repays scrutiny since it gives the kind of social history that historians don't. More important, she then uses it as an index of the inward changes that are a more radical part of human history, and shows how they came about. For she was provided by her culture with objective forms to symbolize and incarnate convincingly her preoccupation with the psychological changes she observed, and indeed registers as in part her own. George Eliot wrote of the 'agonising labour' it was for her 'to make out a sufficiently real background for the desired picture – to get individual forms and group them in needful relations, so that the presentation will lay hold on the emotions as human experience', and of 'the severe effort of trying to make certain ideas thoroughly incarnate, as if they had revealed themselves to me first in the flesh and not in the spirit'. Jane Austen did not have that difficulty: the ideas were already dramatically incarnated, as we've seen, and generally current, and 'the real background for the desired picture' attractively and convincingly there.

Thus, the daunting social conventions of Mansfield Park which were still dominated by 'the circle' (that Repton rejoiced to see being superseded), in contrast to the agreeable Regency informality of the new generation, are tellingly incarnated at the opening of the Mansfield ball: when the guests assembled it had to be in 'the gravity and formality of the first great circle,[9] which the manners of neither Sir Thomas nor Lady Bertram were of a kind to do away', but, we are told, 'The entrance of the Grants and Crawfords was a favourable epoch. The stiffness of the meeting soon gave way before their popular manners and diffused intimacies, little groups were formed, and everybody grew comfortable.' 'Fanny felt the advantage', being then able to 'draw back from the toils of civility'. A similar dramatic scene is arranged for *Persuasion* in reverse, when the comfortable 'modern' informality of the Musgrove family's reception at the White Hart is frozen by a formal call from Sir Walter and Miss Elliot 'whose entrance seemed to give a general chill. Anne felt an instant oppression, and wherever she looked saw symptoms of the same. The comfort, the freedom, the gaiety of the room was over, hushed into cold composure, determined silence, or insipid talk, to meet the heartless elegance of her father and sister.' When this 'severe interruption' is over, we are told, 'ease and animation returned'. 'Comfort', which Jane Austen uses so frequently to distinguish the 'modern' from the traditional life-style, covers a great deal more than a material condition.

Anne Elliot goes from the coldness of the unfeeling Elliots in their ancestral hall to visit her younger sister, on whose marriage to a neighbouring landowner's heir we are told 'a farmhouse had been elevated into a cottage for their residence with a veranda, French windows and other prettinesses', in fact an imitation of the cottage orné which was a fashionable Regency invention for an unpretentious home for the gentry. This small house is played off against the great house, Uppercross, where the rest of the Musgroves live, providing an important part of the theme of the novel. At Uppercross the generations are not at variance as in the earlier *Mansfield Park* but are like the Grosvenors where, as we saw, the new ideas had won and the new style had been imposed on the old and enjoyed by all three generations. The Musgrove mansion was 'unmodernized' architecturally, Jane Austen tells us, but Anne, taken on arrival to make the obligatory formal call of 'the full half-hour', notes that in

> the old-fashioned square parlour, with a small carpet and a shining floor, the present daughters of the house were gradually giving the proper air of confusion by a grand pianoforte and a harp, flower-stands and little tables placed in every direction.

'Oh', the novelist continues in her own person, 'Oh, could the originals of the portraits against the wainscot have seen what was going on, have been conscious of such an overthrow of all order and neatness! The portraits themselves seemed to be staring in embarrassment.' Having thus set the scene in terms her readers would recognize, the novelist proceeds to analyse the family correspondingly:

The Musgroves, like their house, were in a state of alteration, perhaps of improvement. The father and mother were in the old English style, and the young people in the new, with more modern minds and manners. [etc.]

There is a punning reference here, in 'improvement', to the Regency Improver, and we notice also that the novelist manifests some amusement at the changing scene – such as the farmhouse 'elevated' into a cottage and 'the *proper* air of confusion' – and more seriously a sensitive appreciation of the difficulties of reorientation for the older people: the family portraits seem 'embarrassed' by the changes, the parents were only 'perhaps' in a state of improvement. Yet she presents the young people with approval as happy, confiding and unaffected, and having wider interests than their elders. A real problem is raised by Anne's own reflections on the Musgrove daughters, whose 'unembarrassed pleasant manners' and evident mutual affection made her envious of what *she* had never known at home; but she decides 'she would not have given up her own more elegant and cultivated mind for all their enjoyments'. This was a dilemma for anyone who, like Jane Austen herself, had grown up in the previous century and been moulded in Augustan manners and values. Must 'elegance' be sacrificed to achieve happiness? And was not the new freedom liable to end in disaster? Jane Austen balances the one against the other and explores by dramatizing these problems. How, for instance, to ensure that daughters should not contract unsuitable marriages now that girls were becoming recalcitrant as to arbitrarily arranged marriages, like Fanny Price who shocks her uncle by utterly rejecting the advantageous match with Henry Crawford that he has promoted. But Jane Austen endorses Fanny in thus exercising her own judgment and shows in the same novel that Maria Bertram's 'suitable' marriage, arranged by their families in the traditional way, almost inevitably resulted in infidelity.

Maria Edgeworth, who can reasonably be compared here with Jane Austen, being also a gentlewoman, a spinster and a witty satiric novelist, shows in her correspondence when over from Ireland (see *Letters from England* by Maria Edgeworth) to make a round of visits at country-houses and in London, that she had much more difficulty than Jane Austen (perhaps because she was seven or eight years older) and could not opt whole-heartedly for these changes in manners and social life and all that this implied – she *felt* them to be sympathetic but she could not *approve* them. She quite agreed with the general Regency complacency in its material achievements, which made Busby (one of the architects largely responsible for Regency Brighton and so entitled to some self-congratulation) write that 'The true impressions of cheerfulness, elegance and refinement are so well understood and so happily united in our domestic dwellings now, that I hesitate not to say that we are rapidly advancing to a state of perfection.'[10] But where *people* were concerned Maria Edgeworth had doubts. Visiting at the older country-houses of the aristocracy, she explicitly remarks (and very valuable confirmation it is) on how like they were to Lady Bertram and the society of *Mansfield Park* and that in other Austen novels. 'The conversation is just like those novels', she writes, 'one wonders how it can be worth their while to live in this way always. I should be extinguished if I lived with them long', but adds significantly: 'I did not know how much I wanted better conversation and more warmth of character till I came here. There is much more *life* here and much more warmth and affection among the young people.'

'Here' was the great house built by David Ricardo the economist for his delightful family, now inhabited by Princess Anne, which was so attractive to Maria that thereafter she was a frequent visitor, though curiously ambivalent in her attitude towards them. It is not surprising that Maria was so struck with the Ricardo household, who opened to her mind, as she admitted, new possibilities in living, with their evident happiness and mutual affection, their genuine musical tastes which were expressed in spontaneous singing and 'joyous' playing, the books open everywhere, and their cordiality and naturalness which, she argued with herself, 'made amends for want of manner', meaning by that their informality and the absence of the conventional life-style to which she had been accustomed. But eventually she came to the same conclusion as Anne Elliot with regard to the Musgrove girls, for though the Ricardos became very dear friends she could not but feel that elegance was wanting (and 'elegance' was the quality in the poor Jane Fairfax that made the rich, conceited and socially dominant Emma Woodhouse feel her inferior and forced to admire her for). Maria Edgeworth could not give up the conviction that social restraint, decorum and strict subordination of the young to their elders, were indispensable marks of good breeding and right conduct – such was the force of an eighteenth-century upbringing even on a witty Anglo-Irishwoman.[11] She felt on principle that the younger Ricardos, even when grown up, had too much liberty, and complains that Mr and Mrs Ricardo 'let their children do as they pleased' in marrying, though all the marriages were happy and all the children creditable – she felt like Sir Thomas Bertram that children even when grown up ought not to be independent of their parents, as the Ricardos' children were allowed to be. And though she wrote home that they had made her realize that there are 'a great variety of modes of being happy and good' (apparently a new idea to her), she concluded:

Notwithstanding all the praises I have in all sincerity poured forth and from which you might think me in love with these people, yet I should not like to live with them...I think I have learned that absolute insipidity, and the affectation of *stillness* of fashion, are still *more* insupportable than vulgarity – but I would rather be without both these defects.

Yet the Ricardos were clearly not vulgar (Mrs Ricardo was the daughter of an English country gentleman and a Quaker), except from the eighteenth-century assumption that to lack the restraint, coldness, repose and indifferent tone of voice (a concept of which Lady Bertram and Miss Elliot are only slight caricatures) was to be vulgar. Sir Walter Elliot and his eldest daughter surely felt the same about the Crofts and their naval friends, but *Jane Austen,* we notice, *did not.* 'Admiral Croft's manners were not quite the tone to suit Lady Russell', the novelist tells us, 'but they delighted Anne. His goodness of heart and simplicity of character were irresistible.' But this is her last novel: one doubts if Elinor Dashwood in her first would have responded to the Crofts like Anne Elliot. No, she would have reacted like Maria Edgeworth to the Ricardos. One feels that Jane Austen, greatly to her credit, had gradually made this revaluation for herself. And Jane Austen I feel was the greater novelist – for Maria was just as witty and lively a writer – but Jane Austen was the greater because she was more open to experience and shows herself able to outgrow and shed, where necessary, assumptions acquired in youth. *She* was not the prisoner of her formative society, as for instance E. M. Forster was of his Bloomsbury and Cambridge environment. As the movement of ideas from *Sense and Sensibility* to *Persuasion* shows us, she was able to reorient herself yet without automatically accepting all the assumptions of the new era either. Anne Elliot, herself an elegant young woman, refuses in the end to remain in the world of the Elliots, against which she had long been inwardly rebellious. She refuses because she has realized they were bankrupt in every sense, as we are shown, and even though to marry her father's heir, who is courting her, would mean being rich and acquiring her beloved mother's title – Lady Elliot – and social position, and Kellynch Hall as her home, to which she is deeply attached. Instead, she chooses to unite herself to a self-made naval officer, brother-in-law to the inelegant Admiral Croft, a Wentworth who, as Sir Walter tells us, is 'quite unconnected; nothing to do with the Strafford family'. 'One wonders how the names of many of our nobility became so common', he fulminates. But Anne has no hesitation in becoming a common Mrs Wentworth and gladly joins a true community of her husband's naval comrades and their wives, people who are not well off, have no estates or family homes, are not much educated, not polished, decidedly inelegant, but warm-hearted, friendly, sincere and not snobbish or worldly-minded, qualities Anne finds preferable to elegance in the long run but which Maria Edgeworth would certainly classify as vulgarity. Moreover, it is important to remember that these men had acquired their position and made their modest fortunes by devoted and heroic service to their country in the Napoleonic Wars, and by proved professional ability, not by inheritance or favour, the traditional sources of fortune and social status[12] – it was therefore a revolutionary choice.

No doubt Jane Austen was assisted to such insights by the accident of having two admirable naval brothers, but it is wholly to her credit that, characteristically, she seized on the suggestions life thus presented to her in order to provide a theory of an alternative society to the traditional one she had inherited and found unsatisfactory. *Persuasion* is almost too evidently schematic, as indeed is also *Sense and Sensibility*, perhaps because the last novel was designed to reverse the teaching of that first novel which argued the case for keeping to the old rules. But Jane Austen shows herself able, unlike

Maria Edgeworth, to distinguish between true vulgarity like Mrs Elton's, and the disconcerting new alternative to traditional ideas of correctness in manners, represented by the Crofts and the Harvilles who were worthy people. Mrs Elton's is a spiritual vulgarity, whereas in the same novel *Emma*, Robert Martin, whom Emma had condemned to social non-existence for being clumsy and unpolished and only a farmer, is shown to be at least good enough for her friend to marry in the end, and Emma ends by admitting Mr Knightley was right when he told her that 'Robert Martin's manners have sense, sincerity and good humour to recommend them, and his mind has more true gentility than a Harriet Smith could understand': by implication, more than an Emma could understand by her own lights.

But the admission Anne Elliot is led to make to herself in the last novel is even more revolutionary. Anne, we are told, as regards the change of family at Kellynch Hall, 'could not but in conscience feel that they were gone who deserved not to stay and that Kellynch Hall had passed into better hands than its owner's. Anne had no power of saying to herself, "These rooms ought to belong only to us. Oh, how fallen is their destination! An ancient family to be so driven away! Strangers filling their place!"' – even though those hands were those of self-made Crofts.[13]

Mansfield Park is the turning point in the Austen enquiry into the value of the movement of social life in her own lifetime, where the profit-and-loss question is quite explicitly the theme. There is no doubt about Jane Austen's rejection of the out-moded life-style, represented by Sotherton and its insufferable Rushworth family. The house is shown as merely a stifling museum where spontaneous life has died and to which the Regency Improver is quite rightly called, to modernize and open a prospect. The novelist conveys all the horrors of an atrophied way of life – the disused chapel, the now meaningless family portraits, the rooms without a view, innumerable, empty and oppressively grand with their bare 'shining' floors and heavy furniture 'in the taste of fifty years back', the only view out being on to 'tall iron pallisades and gates'. We are made to feel how this oppresses the young people obliged to endure it and, by 'politeness', an Aunt Norris and a dowager Mrs Rushworth. Even when the young people escape – to our relief – into the grounds, these turn out to be a series of prisons, and the episode is driven home by Miss Crawford's saying, with all the force of a symbolic statement:

'Here is a nice little wood, if one can but get into it. What happiness if the door should not be locked! – but of course it is, for in these great places, the gardeners are the only people who can go where they like.'

The formality of old-style house and garden is repeatedly used by our novelist to express the corresponding constraints that social forms imposed on ladies and gentlemen. Thus even Lady Catherine de Bourgh, calling at Longbourn in order to forbid the unsuitable Miss Elizabeth Bennet to marry her nephew, finds it impossible to speak her mind in the house among the other members of the family and has to ask Elizabeth to take a turn with her in the garden, where there is a 'little wilderness' and 'a hermitage' (sometimes actually inhabited by a hired hermit or expressly designed as a tribute to the natural state of man). This is the only possible place for a tête-à-tête where politeness and civility could for a while be abandoned.

In contrast to the inhibiting constraints of Sotherton and Mansfield Park, the new style represented by Miss Crawford and her setting in the Rectory, recently modernized by her sister the new Rector's wife, is shown to constitute an irresistible attraction for Edmund Bertram: he escapes from his own house to the freedom of conversation and wit of Miss Crawford and the fascinating novelty of the new idiom of life-style that the novelist sympathetically creates for us in this passage:

A young woman, pretty, lively, with a harp as elegant as herself, and both placed near a window cut down to the ground, and opening on a little lawn, surrounded by shrubs in the rich foliage of summer, was enough to catch any man's heart. The season, the scene, the air, were all favourable to tenderness and sentiment. Mrs Grant and her tambour frame were not without their use – it was all in harmony; and as everything will turn to account when love is once set going, even the sandwich tray, and Dr Grant doing the honours of it, were worth looking at. Without studying the business however, or knowing what he was about, Edmund was beginning, at the end of a week of such intercourse, to be a good deal in love.

The informality of the Rectory is part of the charm we see, in contrast to Mansfield Park where even tea-time is a ritual – 'the solemn procession, headed by Baddeley, of tea-board, urn, and cake-bearers' – life is indeed a ritual there – and the novelist appreciates as much as Edmund the enchanting domestic scene the Regency had created with its relaxation and comparatively emancipated conversation, which are inseparable from the aesthetic charm. Edmund is sufficiently the prisoner of his upbringing to feel that Miss Crawford is wrong, almost immoral, in freely expressing her perfectly just opinion of her uncle, since he feels it improper to criticize the older generation who represent parents; how far the novelist endorses him is arguable. But there is no doubt that in creating the Crawford brother and sister the novelist is expressing her sense of the dangerous side of the Regency desire for the unshackled will and freedom from traditional restraints and in this, of course, she shows wisdom, for Henry Crawford's conduct, in its egotism, reckless self-indulgence and irresponsibility generally (which are carefully documented, including his negligence as a land-owner) was of the kind typical of the man of the new age. One thinks at once of Byron, Shelley, Napoleon, Constant's Adolphe, who of course is Constant himself, Pushkin's Eugene Onégin and Lermontov's Pechorin. Such were the creators of typical tragedies for themselves and others. The Crawfords represent the Regency world in all its brilliance, heartlessness, frivolity and self-indulgence, as opposed to the moral worth, the sense of responsibility, that was the embodiment of what was best in the traditional land-owner, Sir Thomas Bertram who (it should be noted) can still awe a Yates and a Crawford, male or female, into at least the show of respect, however unwilling. Jane Austen asks in *Mansfield Park*: What was the price to be paid for opting for individual pleasure instead of the well-being of the family and society? In this novel she shows she believed the price might be too high. Unlike Maria Edgeworth, she hadn't naturally much sympathy with the 'douce folk that live by rule', yet she saw that formal manners had their uses in restraining impertinence and ill-temper, and that without a code of conduct difficult situations would become intolerable: Lady Bertram, though an apathetic wife and a negligent mother, is in principle treated with punctilious courtesy by her husband and children; Mr Bennet is condemned by Mr Darcy for lacking in respect to *his* far from ideal wife; and Mansfield Park, with all its drawbacks, is shown convincingly to be preferable to Fanny's Portsmouth home because there at least order and civility were imposed on unregenerate human nature.

Yet the blame for the tragic outcome of *Mansfield Park* is

allotted to the older generation more than to what are shown
to be its victims. The household has to be purged of Mrs Norris,
Lady Bertram aroused to real feeling by misfortunes, and Sir
Thomas to contrition and self-blame, as well as the Crawfords
banished, Tom made repentant, and the daughters of the house
consigned to their self-sought dooms, before the Park can be
restored to a hopeful future by the marriage of Fanny and
Edmund, who combine the best features of both ages. Even then
there is the necessary incorporation of the naïve William and
Susan Price into it as well, whose early poverty and strong
characters, developed by the 'consciousness of being born to
struggle and endure', enabled them to supply something the
novelist felt the traditional inert privileged class lacked, fatally
almost. In *Persuasion* it is quite fatal: the Crofts, the equivalents
of the Price children, are wholly triumphant over the baronet,
and the novelist shows them with satisfaction to be superseding
the great-house owners. Sir Walter is bankrupt, Miss Elliot a
withering spinster, and though the heir-at-law is rich, it is true,
yet he has made his fortune contemptibly by marrying a rich
vulgar woman. Nevertheless, when Anne explains her dissatisfaction with her family's values to her cousin, Mr Elliot replies:
'Will it answer? Will it make you happy?' – that is, to be at
war with her environment. The novelist must have felt this
difficulty herself in her youth and we honour her for not
suppressing it.

    It is interesting to observe that this evolution made in the
Austen novels from eighteenth to nineteenth century has nothing
to do with the Romantic Movement except in so far as the new
recognition of children as children is concerned. The work of
the Romantic poets and novelists is something that Jane Austen
shows she knew of but was unimpressed by; she by-passed
it. She was not influenced by the Romantics' extension of
language and subject-matter, and for her the proper study of
mankind is still man, and then only in the form of the gentleman
and lady; for her the legitimate writers for respect and even
enthusiasm are still those of the eighteenth century, not Scott
or Byron, and the congenial mode of writing, as with the
Augustans, is one developed out of satire and irony. And she
holds too the disenchanted Augustan view of human nature
which made Lord Chesterfield recommend his son to study La
Rochefoucauld's Maxims daily in order to know his fellow-men;

and in this realism she is at one with Fielding, Fanny Burney, Maria Edgeworth and the many other novelists from whom she derives, so that it is ill-informed as well as perverse to assert that this feature is unique to Jane Austen and a sign of deep psychological significance. Her attitudes, like those of any eighteenth-century novelist, are always critical, her characters held away from herself, and her vocabulary is that of a system of values which is not emotional but moral, critical and rational; in all this she is like Peacock, and this tradition survived through into the nineteenth century in the novel.

Jane Austen's use of words is also thoroughly that of the eighteenth century, without vibrations and emotional over-tones: Maria Bertram's sense of being trapped in a situation and a social system that is obliging her to make a hateful and disastrous marriage – a horror, forecasting a tragedy, which is unique in Jane Austen's work – can be expressed only through a reference to a then well-known literary source, Sterne's caged starling in *The Sentimental Journey* which he heard crying 'Let me out! Let me out!' and with which Maria feelingly identifies herself. But even so, the author actually makes her tone down the original emotional outburst in Sterne's novel to a merely factual statement: she says 'I cannot get out', and even this instance of poetic emotional symbolism is unique in the Austen novels, I believe. Anne Elliot does not have recourse to the Romantic poets known to her for solace when desolate from her broken engagement; and she explicitly warns Captain Benwick against doing so to console himself for his own broken heart – which heart the novelist, with characteristic un-Romantic realism, shows very soon inevitably healed by another love. In these things Jane Austen did not move with her age, and the strength of her resistance to the *Zeitgeist* in these respects, showing such a radical identification with the culture and literature of her youth, demonstrates the more strikingly, I think, her intelligence in sponsoring, even advancing beyond, the emancipation of the early nineteenth century in domestic and social life from its now uncongenial inheritance.

Talleyrand noted the great difference between his last knowledge of England as a refugee in 1794 and his return as French ambassador in 1830. In that time, 'Never perhaps have thirty-six years effected so complete a change in the outward aspect and in the inward mind of a whole nation. It is hardly too much to say that the complete process of alteration from the eighteenth to the nineteenth century had taken place in that period...' And Talleyrand described London as 'much more beautiful' than he had left it – and this from one essentially eighteenth-century in his tastes. In his biography of Talleyrand Duff Cooper says that this is 'an opinion corroborated by a contemporary American who, on returning to London after an absence of only nineteen years, said that it had become "a thousand times more beautiful"'. The Regency period, during which this change had been thought out, decided on and executed, had therefore good reason for its complacency in material and aesthetic achievement. In 1794 Jane Austen was in her twentieth year and therefore a woman formed by the old order; the revolution in material things, and all that that implied of inward change, had happened in her adult life; the more credit to her then that she was capable of sympathizing with them and eventually, as I've shown, even developing an outlook on those lines in advance of her class.

A critical theory of Jane Austen's writings

It is common to speak of Jane Austen's novels as a miracle; the accepted attitude to them is conveniently summarized by Professor Caroline Spurgeon in her address on Jane Austen to the British Academy:

> But Jane Austen is more than a classic; she is also one of the little company whose work is of the nature of a miracle...That is to say, there is nothing whatever in the surroundings of these particular writers [Keats, Chatterton, Jane Austen, Emily Brontë], their upbringing, opportunities or training, to account for the quality of their literary work.

The business of literary criticism is surely not to say 'Inspiration' and fall down and worship, and in the case of Jane Austen it is certainly not entitled to take up such an unprofitable attitude. For in Jane Austen literary criticism has, I believe, a uniquely documented case of the origin and development of artistic expression, and an enquiry into the nature of her genius and the process by which it developed can go very far indeed on sure ground. Thanks to Dr Chapman's labours we have for some time had at our disposal a properly edited text of nearly all her surviving writings, and scholarship, in his person chiefly, has brilliantly made out a number of interesting facts which have not yet, however, been translated into the language of literary criticism.

Correlated with Professor Spurgeon's attitude to the Austen novels is the classical account of their author as a certain kind of novelist, one who wrote her best at the age of twenty (Professor Oliver Elton), whose work 'shows no development' (Professor Garrod), whose novels 'make exceptionally peaceful reading' (A. C. Bradley); one scholar writes of her primness, another of her 'sunny temper', with equal infelicity, and all apologize for her inability to dwell on guilt and misery, the French Revolution and the Napoleonic Wars. This account assumes among other things that the novels were written in 'two distinct groups, separated by a considerable interval of time...thus, to put it roughly, the first group of three were written between the ages of twenty and twenty-two, and the second group between the ages of thirty-five and forty'[1] and only notices revision where internal dating makes it inevitable – e.g. the mention of *Belinda* (published in 1801) in *Northanger Abbey*, or of Scott as a popular poet in *Sense and Sensibility* (which indicates a revision in 1809). As long ago as 1922 Dr Chapman pointed out[2] – but cautiously, as becomes a scholar, and with a distinct refusal to commit himself to any positive deductions – that 'the chronology of Miss Austen's novels is unusually obscure' and that for 'the great part of this assumption there is little warrant'. But we can go much farther than this. There are, besides the six novels, three volumes of early work in manuscript,[3] and drafts and miscellaneous pieces at various stages, as well as the two volumes of correspondence, which taken together offer the literary detective as well as the literary critic a harvest of clues and evidence; and these writings cover her life from the age of fifteen to her death. Cassandra Austen, besides her notorious work in censoring those of her sister's letters which she did not destroy, left a memorandum of the dates of composition of some of her sister's work; other evidence exists in Jane's *Letters*,[4] and the manuscripts generally tell their own story. Moreover, she had a habit of constructing her novels on the current calendar for her own convenience. From these data we can make out the following table of Miss Austen's working life:

Jane Austen, 1775–1817

Between 1789 and 1793 she turned out for the amusement of her family a mass of satiric work (some dramatic and some in epistolary form), some unfinished stories, and many type epistles. From these she selected a number for preservation by copying them at intervals (to judge by the handwriting, over some years) into three volumes. Of these three, *Volume the First* has been edited and published by Dr Chapman; *Volume the Second* has been published under the title of one of its pieces, *Love and Freindship*; while the third volume has unfortunately never been printed, though a sufficient description of it can be found in the *Life and Letters* published by W. and R. A. Austen-Leigh.

1795 *ca.* *Elinor and Marianne* was written as a novel in letter form.

1796–7. *First Impressions* written as a novel in letter form.

1797. *Elinor and Marianne* was rewritten as *Sense and Sensibility*; the *Memoir* says 'in its present form', which means only that it was no longer in letters; in some respects at least it could not have been the novel that we know.

1797–8. *Susan*, a novel, probably written up from an unfinished story in *Volume the Third* called 'Catharine, or the Bower'.

1803. *Susan* was rewritten and sent to a publisher.

Before 1805, probably in the interval between the two versions of *Susan*, *Lady Susan*, an epistolary *nouvelle*, was written. It is untitled; its paper is watermarked 1805, but what we have is 'not a draft but a fair copy' and, judging by Jane Austen's habits of composition, we can assume that this is a rewrite after a period of years.

Between 1806 and 1807 a new novel, *The Watsons*, was started; we have a fair copy corrected, but not finished. Calendar evidence shows it was located in 1807.

1808–9. *Lady Susan*, on my theory, was expanded into *Mansfield Park* (the 1808–9 calendar was used to construct *Mansfield Park*).

1809. *Susan* probably revised again.

1809–10. *Sense and Sensibility* rewritten or revised, for publication in 1811.

1810–12. *Pride and Prejudice* was rewritten for publication in 1813, radically, beyond all doubt, since it is built on the 'punctilious observance' of the 1811–12 calendar.

1811–13. *Mansfield Park* rewritten as we know it for publication in 1814. Since she spent so long over it, the alterations were probably considerable, and I suspect the 1808–9 version to have been epistolary.

1814–15.   *Emma* written up for publication in 1816 from the earlier story of *The Watsons* (as I hope to show).

1815–16.   *The Elliots* written, but not, I believe, intended for publication as it stands; two of the last chapters towards the final version were completely rewritten, and we have the rejected chapter to compare. The prototype, which exists for every other novel, could hardly have not existed for this work, and as the author's hands were full from 1806 onwards, it can possibly be allotted to the pre-1806 gap. Other reasons can be adduced in support of my theory.

1816–17.   *Susan* was revised for publication as *Catherine*; it was published posthumously as *Northanger Abbey*, with *The Elliots* as *Persuasion*, by Henry Austen, who gave both these books the names we know them by.

Jan.–March 1817.   *Sanditon*, a new novel of which she was writing the first draft when she died. The MS remains for us to see what a first draft of hers looked like.

We can see from this table of what Jane Austen chose to preserve of her work and the records, accidentally preserved, of what she preferred to destroy, that our author wrote unceasingly (we should be unjustified in assuming that nothing was being written in the one period, 1798–1803, for which we happen to have no evidence). She had, it appears, some very peculiar habits of composition, which quite destroy the popular notion of her writing by direct inspiration, as it were. One habit was to lay down several keels in succession and then do something to each in turn, never having less than three on the stocks but always working at any one over a period of years before launching it, and allowing twelve clear months at least for each final reworking. Another was to start writing her novels much further back in conception than most novelists or perhaps than any other novelist; what is usually a process of rapid and largely unconscious mental selecting, rejecting and reconstituting was, in her case, a matter of thoroughly conscious, laborious, separate draftings; in every case except that of *Persuasion* we know, or I hope to show that we know, of early versions which bear little resemblance to the novels as published. Indeed, I propose to argue that her novels are geological structures, the earliest layer going back to her earliest writings, with subsequent accretions from her reading, her personal life and those lives most closely connected with hers, all recast – and this is what gives them their coherence and artistic significance – under the pressure of deep disturbances in her own emotional life at a given time.

This at least is clear, that Miss Austen was not an inspired amateur who had scribbled in childhood and then lightly tossed off masterpieces between callers; she was a steady professional writer who had to put in many years of thought and labour to achieve each novel, and she took her novels very seriously. Her methods were in fact so laborious that it is no wonder that she produced only six novels in twenty-seven years, and the last of those not finally revised, while another (*Northanger Abbey*) was so immature that she despaired of doing anything with it. Another point that emerges is that she was decidedly not precociously mature as an artist. There is no reason whatever to suppose that *Pride and Prejudice, Sense and Sensibility*, and *Northanger Abbey* as we know them agreed in form, tone, content or intention with those versions which were offered earlier to publishers, who (not unnaturally) did not care to publish them. In their original form they were no doubt as thin and flat as *The Watsons*, as sketchy as *Sanditon*, as unsympathetic as *Lady Susan*, and as much dependent for the most part on family jokes as *Northanger Abbey* still is. The novels as we know them are palimpsests through whose surface portions of earlier versions, or of other and earlier compositions quite unrelated, constantly protrude, so that we read from place to place at different levels. Two of the novels, *Emma* and *Mansfield Park*, are the results of an evolutionary process of composition, and bristle with vestigial traits. The novels as a whole, then, cannot be said to be the work of any given date, but the published versions are certainly to be ascribed to Jane Austen at the final date of revision, since before such final revisions they would probably have been unrecognizable to us now. Thus *Pride and Prejudice* was not the work of a girl of twenty-one but of a woman aged thirty-five to thirty-seven, and we have actually nothing as it was written, besides the juvenilia, till *Lady Susan*, a slight but accomplished piece of writing in her thirtieth year, and *The Watsons*, a thin sketch for a later novel, written when she was two years older. Since it is not until *Emma*, written when she was nearly forty, that she brings off a mature and artistically perfect novel, in which the various elements are for the first time integrated, we are justified in concluding that she was artistically a late developer as well as a slow and laborious writer. The wit similarly has a pedigree, so have the characters and much of the plots, and even the details of the intrigue. Much more in the novels is dependent on reference to, reaction against, and borrowings from, other novelists than is commonly realized, I believe. *Northanger Abbey* is generally held to be a 'sport', in its relation to the Gothic novels, but several of her novels were largely, and the others partially, conceived in a similar manner and are as little to be appreciated without at least as much realization of what they are tilting against or referring to. Far from the Austen novels having fallen straight from heaven into the publisher's lap, so to speak, they can be accounted for in even greater detail than other literary compositions, for Jane Austen was not a fertile writer. Her invention except in one limited respect was very meagre; casual jottings on aspects of 'character' and bits of situation and stage business made in her teens turn up at intervals to be worked into the shape required by the story in hand; a great deal of what seems to be creation can be traced through her surviving letters to have originated in life; much of her novels consists of manipulation and differentiation of characters and group relations made long before in cruder and more general or merely burlesque pieces of writing; rarely is anything abandoned, however slight, Jane Austen's practice being rather thriftily to 'make over'. Her inspiration then turns out to be, as Inspiration so often does, a matter of hard work – radical revision in the light of a maturer taste and a severe self-criticism, and under the pressure of a more and more clearly defined intention over a space of years. Her invention consists chiefly in translating the general into the particular; she proceeds from the crude comprehensive outline and the dashing sketch to something subtle and specialized by splitting up and separating out – in fact her tendency is to overdo this process, so that in the end Mrs Norris and Elizabeth Elliot and Miss Bingley and Lady Catherine are each too much on one note, rather monotonous and over-attenuated, whereas the original piece of characterization in the void from which they all derive, Lady Greville in the second MS volume, is more robust in possessing all these facets – she abounds in all these forms of feminine ill nature instead of exhibiting only the one eternally, and is better comedy because she has no such tendency to get on the reader's nerves. But these later inventions were intended to get on the reader's nerves because they were aspects of social intercourse that had got on Miss Austen's.

I will take one illustration, a particularly neat one, of a process common in her work, from the second MS volume (which, like the first, is of the greatest interest to the literary critic). In 'A Collection of Letters' Letter the Third, the only one which is not burlesque, is an account by 'a young lady in reduced circumstances' of a couple of encounters with the local great lady, who first takes her to a ball and then calls next day to invite her to dinner. This letter is probably the best-known piece of Austen 'juvenilia' and it has been noticed by one or two critics that Lady Catherine de Bourgh is descended from Lady Greville and that the incident of Charlotte Collins being called out to the carriage in all that wind is also reproduced from this Letter. But anyone who will turn it up in the *Love and Freindship* volume, however sceptically, will have to admit that it indisputably contains all the following:

1   Lady Catherine's general line of impertinence to Elizabeth and some incidents slightly improved in *Pride and Prejudice*.

2   Mrs Norris's scolding Fanny when she is going out to dine with the Grants – the business about the carriage and walking in spite of the possible rain and the necessity of knowing her place are all there, with just the same tone of voice.

3   The ball which itself produces two balls later on, the one in *Pride and Prejudice* where Miss Bingley is rude to Eliza and the one in *Northanger Abbey* where the situation of being engaged to a partner who turns up at the last minute when the heroine is embarrassed at seeming to have no partner is here first set down. (And this last is borrowed from *Evelina*.)

4   The incident of Miss de Bourgh stopping her carriage, sending for Charlotte to come out in all that wind, 'abominably rude', etc.

5   The conversation between the Bingley sisters on Eliza's indelicacy in taking a cross-country walk is clearly anticipated in Lady Greville's remarks to the letter-writer in similar phrases.

6   The characters of Lady Catherine and Mrs Norris are
         unmistakably delineated in Lady Greville, just as the
         sensitive and down-trodden Maria Williams who writes
         the Letter, with the humble mother, is the original of
         Fanny Price.

To see, however, how such jottings are used item 2 should be
placed beside the relevant passage in *Mansfield Park*. The idea
has not been merely polished or written up or expanded, it has
been worked into an elaborate complex of characters, motives,
plot and so on, so that it is part of the living tissue of the novel
and is given power to move us by all that is behind it and
embodied in it. It comes at the turning point in Fanny's history
when she ceases to be in the general esteem what Mrs Norris
has always represented her, and becomes thenceforward a person
with a position of her own (Mr Crawford is to fall in love with
her at the dinner). Sir Thomas's ordering of the carriage that
Mrs Norris (like Lady Greville) has made a point of denying
her with evident malice is not only employed to affect Fanny
deeply as a mark of his consideration and exhibit both Mrs
Norris and Sir Thomas characteristically, though it is meant to
do all this by the way; the carriage incident in *Mansfield Park*,
unlike the similar incident in the Letter, where it remains a piece
of mere ill-natured rudeness, is a symbol of Fanny's changing
status and a critical, indeed a pivotal, point in the plot. What
was originally simple satiric humour, a piece of external and
isolated observation magnified to the proportions of farce, has
been fused into a work of art. It is this power of seizing on every
trifle at her command, whether drawn from nature or literature
(as we shall see, they were of about equal authority for her) and
making it serve a complex purpose, using it in the one place and
context where it will tell and do exactly what is required of it – it
is this kind of ability that constitutes her genius, rather than any
more mysterious and inexplicable quality.

The large Austen family, well born, but not well off, well
educated, singularly united, with tentacles of kinsfolk reaching
out into great houses, parsonages rich and poor, Bath and
London, the navy and the militia, with its theatricals, dances,
flirtations, marriages and invalids, was a rich source of raw
material for any novelist, but it contributed in two less obvious

respects to Jane's equipment. One was that in her capacity of constant visitor to outlying branches she necessarily wrote letters home, addressed, it is true, to Cassandra, but evidently meant, as Dr Chapman notes, to be read aloud to a group, keeping them in touch with their friends and relatives; similarly, when at home, she wrote to friends, nieces and nephews to transmit family news and give advice. In these letters we can not only find much that later went into the novels, but we can see that material in a preliminary stage, half-way between life and art. The character sketches, the notes on conduct and social functions, were written for an audience, and written also from a point of view that is the novelist's. There is unfortunately no room here to enlarge on this interesting relation of the letters to the novels, but I will summarize my argument by saying simply that without the letter-writing one of the conditions essential to the production of the novels would not have existed: the letter-writing, like the drafting of story into novel at different stages of composition, was part of the process that made possible the unique Austen novels.

   The other service this family unit rendered the future novelist was in providing a literary spring-board in its reactions to novels, which the Austens consumed largely but in no uncritical spirit. In addition to acting among themselves (these amateur theatricals have left, of course, other traces besides the acting in *Mansfield Park*: a preference after epistolary for dramatic narrative, and a tendency to characterization too broad for any medium but the footlights) – in addition to acting plays the Austens by reading aloud and discussing their reading had evidently acquired by the time Jane was fifteen a common stock of conversational allusions, jokes, understandings about the absurdities of their favourite writers, and certain literary criteria. The fruits of this were the contents of the three manuscript volumes – these items have mock dedications to members of the family. Some of these remain private jokes, others are jokes we can understand, while some, though closely related to the rest, are positive pieces of original composition. The trend of this family joke is satiric, but it implies also a habit of discussing the *theory* of novel composition and style. Jane was a sound critic of the novel before she began to be a novelist at all (among other numerous references in the letters to this subject there is a significant one to Cassandra – 'I know your starched notions' in the matter of digressions in fiction). The family joke and writing for a circle which understood her allusions gave her the habit of writing with a side glance at her audience, which though it has in the earlier novels given us some cryptic passages, is nevertheless the source of that intimate tone with the reader that has made her so popular. It is the recollection of such a critical audience liable to pounce that accounts also for her poise – her hold on herself (so disastrously lacking in George Eliot) which constantly evokes self-ironical touches like that in *Persuasion* where, after Anne's indulgence in the poetry of autumn melancholy, she remarks on 'the ploughs at work [that] spoke the farmer, counteracting the sweets of poetical despondence, and meaning to have spring again'.

The Austen family were hard-headed and demanded not poetry but uncompromising fidelity to nature in their fiction. There is hardly anything easier to ridicule in literature than the eighteenth-century novel by contrasting it with daily life, particularly when manners, idiom and social conventions changed as rapidly as they can be seen to have done between *Clarissa* and *Evelina*, and *Evelina* and *Pride and Prejudice*. So the MS volumes are full of burlesques of the literary conventions, the style and the conversations of Richardson, Goldsmith, Sterne, Fanny Burney, and Henry Mackenzie among others, of the novel of sentiment, the language of sensibility and the language of morality. The value of such a start is obvious when compared with the 'sedulous ape' recipe for training an artist of a century later: dead conventions are not propagated thus, and a study of how other novelists wrote, combined with a critical perception of where such writing leads and why and how not to get there, is a tremendous help in finding where one wishes to go oneself. But the burlesque can already be seen in the MS volumes to have a positive side. Though it is impossible here to enter on a detailed examination of *Volume the First* and *Volume the Second* a few main strands are worth following.

There is an unconsciously very funny scene in *Evelina* (a novel the Austens seem to have known by heart) where Evelina visits her hitherto unknown father and experiences the correct emotions on the occasion, a hackneyed enough situation in eighteenth-century fiction to be satirized as a type of the false. Make the father or grandfather and multiply the grandchildren, and the burlesque does itself, as can be seen in Letter 11 of *Love and Freindship*. This device is used again, as we shall see, in *Pride and Prejudice*. Many systematic attempts to prepare booby-traps for the reader and to throw cold water on his expectations are tried out in these pieces for use later in the novels. Many characters in the novels are to be recognized in a certain primitive form; since their origin is an important clue to the way Jane Austen conceived her novels, I will give some illustrations of what I shall call the functional origin of her characters.

The burlesque nature of the early work is visibly the source also of *Northanger Abbey*. Catherine is the anti-heroine of romance, and her family and upbringing and disposition are described entirely in anti-romantic terms. It is essential for the purposes of the joke that the book was meant to be that Catherine should be simple-minded, unsentimental and commonplace, that unsolicited she should fall in love with a young man who snubs and educates her instead of adoring her, and should be launched into the world by an anti-chaperone (for Mrs Allen, like Catherine, is purely functional – hence her concentration on herself and her inability to advise, instruct or watch over her charge). This is generally admitted. But *Pride and Prejudice* was originally the same kind of story as *Northanger Abbey* and it is ignorance of this that has led the critics to debate problems such as whether Darcy is, like Mrs Jennings, an instance of the artist's having changed her mind about the character, whether Elizabeth Bennet is open to the charge of pertness, whether Mr Collins could possibly have existed. But such problems are non-existent. Besides taking its title from the moral of *Cecilia*, *Pride and Prejudice* takes a great deal beside, part borrowed and part burlesqued. One of the absurdities of Cecilia is her behaviour in defeating, out of the morbid delicacy proper to Burney heroines, the hero Delvile's attempts to come to an explanation with her about his feelings and the obstacles to a union with her (like Darcy he is driven to write her a long letter); it is necessary in her rôle of an anti-Cecilia that Elizabeth should be vigorous-minded, should challenge decorum by her conversation and habits, and eventually invite her lover's proposal; she is 'pert' and of a coming-on disposition, just as necessarily as Catherine is green and dense. Darcy is only Delvile with the minimum of inside necessary to make plausible his conduct (predetermined by the object of the novel). For the original conception of *First Impressions* was undoubtedly to rewrite the story of Cecilia in realistic terms, just as *Susan* (or *Catherine*) was both to show up *Udolpho* and *The Romance of the Forest* and to contrast the romantic heroine's entry into the world (*Evelina*) with the everyday equivalent. What would be the reactions of a real girl if, like Cecilia, she was appealed to by her lover's family not to marry him because she was an unsuitable match? In *Cecilia* the hero's mother, a 'noble' aristocratic figure, intended to be impressive, attacks Cecilia with all the appeals of which Lady Catherine's arguments to Elizabeth are a close but comic version (and succeeds in her appeal to Cecilia's higher nature!). Now the character of the intolerable great lady was fished out of Letter the Third in the second MS volume, as I have noted earlier; by putting her into the high-minded Mrs Delvile's place, changing mother for aunt (the old trick of substituting grandfather for father in burlesque), and suppressing the plausible objections to the marriage which existed in the original (the terms of a will which binds the heiress Cecilia), the *moral* situation is exquisitely burlesqued and the incredibly unrealistic tone of *Cecilia* brought down with a jolt to the level of stage comedy. Mr Collins is invented in functional terms for the same purpose; his lengthy proposal is devised to give the author's views on Fanny Burney's preposterous conventions about female behaviour (exhibited by both Evelina and Cecilia) – 'the usual practice of elegant females' – and the stilted, grotesquely Johnsonian, diction of Burney lovers (funnier because the professions in Mr Collins's case are bogus). And the disapproval of Bingley's sisters as a possible bar to his marrying Jane that is put forward by Jane for ridicule by Elizabeth is also part of the anti-*Cecilia* intention: the Bingley sisters underline the Lady Catherine–Mrs Delvile skit. The Austens certainly grasped all this, but unless we realize it too, and a whole order of such literary allusions in the novels, we cannot respond to the novels adequately.

A few more of the sources of *Pride and Prejudice* may be noted here. Mary Bennet, who like Mr Collins has been objected to on the grounds of impossibility, is also a machine for burlesque. She is to be found in isolation in a letter in the second MS volume called 'The Female Philosopher', a mock portrait of 'the sensible, the amiable Julia' who 'utters sentiments of Morality worthy of a heart like her own'. A specimen of her utterances:

Mr Millar observed (and very justly too) that many events had befallen each during that interval of time, which gave occasion to the lovely Julia for making most sensible reflections on the many changes in their situation which so long a period had occasioned, on the advantages of some and the disadvantages of others. From this subject she made a short digression to the instability of human pleasures and the uncertainty of their duration, which led her to observe that all earthly Joys must be imperfect...

On the other hand, there are many positive borrowings from Fanny Burney not in the least in a spirit of satire. The conversation overheard, at the ball where Darcy first appears, by Elizabeth's friend, when Darcy speaks slightingly of Elizabeth, is lifted from *Evelina*, where Evelina's friend overhears the hero speak similarly of Evelina at the ball at which they first meet. Mrs Bennet in her rôle of embarrassing her superior offspring by her vulgar and insensitive conversation, particularly on the subject of matches, is Mrs Belfield in *Cecilia*. Elizabeth's twitting of Lady Catherine both at Hunsford and at Longbourn is an echo of the lively impertinence of the Delviles' niece, a Lady Honoria, whose cool wit at the expense of Mr and Mrs Delvile's convictions of superiority (his on grounds of family dignity, hers on the score of high-mindedness) is quite as amusing and cleverly managed, and rather freer in scope.

But in another function Mrs Bennet was taken from the first MS volume. When *Pride and Prejudice* was expanded from an anti-*Cecilia*, its theme developed from a contrast between sentimental and intuitive human behaviour in a given situation to a general examination of a subject to which Jane Austen was certainly giving much thought at this time, the subject of marriage. We can always see where Miss Austen's interests and preoccupations lie in any novel by observing where the stress falls and where the deepest current of feeling flows. The conversations between Jane and Elizabeth about Charlotte's engagement to Mr Collins, about the disparity between the sexes in courtship and about the sisters' different outlooks on life, and between Elizabeth and Charlotte, and Elizabeth and Mrs Gardiner, about marriage and courtship, are noticed by every reader, I suppose, as differing in tone from the rest of the novel. The obverse to the marriage of love in the face of family disapprobation is the marriage of convenience that is approved by worldly wisdom. This idea is used again later in *Mansfield*

Park and in *Persuasion*, but it is not new in Jane Austen's writings even in *Pride and Prejudice*. Charlotte Lucas's situation, Mr Collins's, and his visit with unspecified matrimonial intent to Longbourn, had already been plotted out in an early story in the first MS volume. This story in letter form is called 'The Three Sisters'.

The situation therein of the mother in the country with £500 a year and three daughters to marry was used later for *Sense and Sensibility* but the action of the story is that of the Collins–Bennet–Lucas intrigue. Mr Watts, a desirable *parti* but disagreeable and ridiculous, proposes like Mr Collins to ally himself with this family, the individual wife being a matter of indifference, and similarly applies first to the eldest daughter, Mary. None of the girls wishes to marry him, but the eldest is anxious to be married and is eventually persuaded by the other two (the second sister is the candid Jane Bennet, the youngest the lively and determined Elizabeth) to accept him for his establishment and from jealous fear that one of her sisters will if she won't. Mary's mamma, like Elizabeth's, engages in battle with her daughters, declaring, 'If Mary won't have him Sophy must, and if Sophy won't Georgiana *shall*.' Like Mrs Bennet's, 'my Mother's resolution I am sorry to say is generally more strictly kept than rationally formed'. (Mrs Bennet's nerves and silliness, however, were a later inspiration.) More interesting still, there is a half-serious discussion between the younger sisters, like that between Jane and Elizabeth where Jane argues that Charlotte has a reasonable prospect of matrimonial happiness, and there is a primitive account of the case for and against a marriage of convenience. But Charlotte Lucas is not Mary Stanhope in disposition (*her* character is used up many years later as Mary Musgrove); though the situation is taken from 'The Three Sisters', her character comes from another early story, 'Lesley Castle', in the second MS volume. This original Charlotte (a family joke from *The Sorrows of Werther*) is another functional character, designed solely to set off by excessive insensibility the conventional delicacy of feeling of her sister Eloisa, the heroine (the contrasted pair provide the Elinor–Marianne relation later). Charlotte Lutterell is wholly taken up with cookery and domestic management (vestigial traits in Charlotte Lucas), the point of this being that, when her sister's betrothed dies suddenly, she is distressed by the waste of wedding-victuals but doesn't understand her sister's sufferings. She has for similar reasons excessively prosaic (though disinterested) views on marriage that naturally acquire an ugly cast when as Charlotte Lucas she puts her views into practice. Colonel Fitzwilliam, who has no necessary part in the plot, was obviously put in to illustrate the theme, and shows signs of having been written down in the final version; his relation to Elizabeth, like that of Wickham and Lydia, Darcy and Elizabeth, Jane and Bingley, Mr Collins and Charlotte Lucas, and the marriages of convenience desired by their families between Georgiana and Bingley and between Darcy and Miss de Bourgh, are all illustrations of the theme of the book. What we have in *Pride and Prejudice*, then, is not simply a subject taken over for ridicule, or a realistic instead of a conventional treatment of a plot, nor is it the simple 'borrowing' for a slightly different purpose that is the only recognition its relation to *Cecilia* has received from Dr Chapman and other scholars. It is the central idea of *Cecilia* given an elaborate orchestration, as it were, sometimes guyed (when Lady Catherine and Miss Bingley stand for the dignified opposition of Delvile's family to his attachment), more often used as an opportunity for self-exploration on the author's part (Elizabeth's outbreak about Charlotte's marriage and her discussion of 'candour' with her sister are spots where the crust of objective comedy visibly cracks). But what I wish to stress here is the way in which the author has secured her materials for constructing a novel which has delighted so many readers, from the severest critics to the least critical. Her writing and reading and living up to the point of the final revision of *Pride and Prejudice* have all tended towards its creation, we might say, and the phases it passed through were necessary to its development into a serious work of art. Many times as much might be written in illustration if there were space, and similar accounts might be given of the other novels. But I have room here only for a short survey of the evolution of two other novels whose origins have been even less realized and which tell an even more interesting story of how miracles in literature are brought about.

It is not surprising that most of the few intelligent critical remarks that have been made about the Austen novels have proceeded from novelists. Mrs Woolf in *The Common Reader* looks with a novelist's eye at *The Watsons* and notes 'The bareness of the first chapters proves that she was one of those writers who lay out their facts rather baldly in the first version...Hence we perceive she was no conjuror after all'; and remarks 'What suppressions and insertions and artful devices' would have been necessary to convert such a version into 'the miracle' of a finished novel of hers! We can, as it happens, study the conjuring in this very case because *The Watsons* became *Emma* by processes that I think can be traced.

The story of *The Watsons* is partly written only, but it was not unfinished, it was only not copied out to the end; a tradition of the rest remained in the Austen family and has been made known. Mr Watson, a poor country clergyman, a widower and an invalid, has a family of two sons and four daughters. One son is a surgeon, the other, Robert, is an attorney in Croydon with a wife Jane and a child Augusta. The daughters are: Elizabeth, a sympathetic old maid, Penelope and Margaret, two unpleasant husband-hunters, and the heroine, Emma, who has returned home at the opening of the story after being brought up from childhood by an aunt, with expectations of being her heiress, which are now at an end owing to the aunt's remarriage. Emma goes to the assembly ball with the Edwards family and there, by her kindness in offering to dance with a little boy whose promised partner, Miss Osborne, throws him over, she gets acquainted with his uncle Mr Howard (a middle-aged cleric) and the rest of the Osborne Castle party. Returning home, Emma has to meet a family party from Croydon, returning with Margaret. During their visit the local lady-killer, the moneyed Tom Musgrave, drops in. There is a scene where Lord Osborne with Musgrave calls on the Watsons to see Emma, at the too early dinner-hour of that humble home. The story was intended to continue with the death of Mr Watson, Emma being thrown in consequence on the Croydon ménage to act as governess to the young Augusta, and after rejecting Lord Osborne she was to marry the mature Mr Howard. As summarized this does not sound at all like *Emma*, but *The Watsons* reads like *Emma* nevertheless. The likeness is in two respects: the tone of the setting, which is what makes each Austen novel distinct and unique, and the details of character and intrigue.

Emma Watson is a refined and superior heroine, but her background is excessively commonplace and belittling – the details of narrow means and management in the story are those that appear in the *Letters* about the Steventon household and which visibly bothered or irritated the writer all along. The theory of the biographer in his *Memoir* is that his aunt abandoned *The Watsons* because she 'became aware of the evil of having placed her heroine too low'; this is probably true, but what she did, in fact, was to make a fresh start with the same materials by shaking the kaleidoscope to make a new pattern. (We have seen her doing this with her materials before, and it can be accepted as one of the means which in combination produced the miracles.) A new Emma was required who should be free from the 'low' circumstances in her immediate person, so Emma Woodhouse becomes a *real* heiress; she is a more pronounced character – frank and decisive – to suit her altered circumstances, and, as we shall see, acquired this shape from life. For the same reason her relatives have to go too, but they are only removed from her home to its threshold – Highbury is Stanton, Dorking and Reigate (though Hartfield is imported to elevate Emma) and the Watson family people the Woodhouse circle. Thus Emma Watson's eldest sister, the spinster Elizabeth, whose situation of old maid is discussed like Miss Bates's, with her simplicity and lack of elegance, her love of company and gossip, turns into Miss Bates (the flowering of her character from a functional one is due to fusing her rôle with the personality and conversational habits of a real Miss Milles who figures in detail in the *Letters* with the same mother as Miss Bates's). The cramped, barely genteel Watson home is relegated to the side of the story and becomes the Bateses', and the petty local society of surgeon-lawyer-country-town gentility of limited means and decided inelegance that distinguishes *Emma* from the other novels is first mapped in *The Watsons* – Mr Weston being developed from Mr Edwards with his whist club at the White Hart, for instance, his kindliness and sociality and seeking out fresh gossip. Tom Musgrave (who dates back in both name and character to the second manuscript volume) undergoes a characteristic change: to fit the new plot he becomes really easy and well-bred, instead of only aspiring to be so; while his attentions to Emma remain, his aimless gallantry is given a specific purpose (to conceal an understanding and secret engagement) and he becomes, in short, by an inevitable process, Frank Churchill, the original stigma still attached to his conduct and a suspicion of the original puppyishness and lack of nice feeling still attached to his character.

Lifting Emma into wealth and refinement required many changes, but another kind of change can be observed which exemplifies what I have found to be a principle of reconstruction in the Austen novels. When drafting a new story this author's tendency is to repeat characters and situations she has already used, as we can clearly see in *Sanditon*, but in her rewritten version she effaces these repetitions and covers her tracks. Thus while Emma Watson's attorney brother Robert gets a lift in the world, from Croydon to Brunswick Square and attorney to gentleman lawyer, his character, which was that of John Dashwood, is abandoned for a new one, that of Mr John Knightley, which was composed to demonstrate part of the real argument of the new novel *Emma* and is a functional one therefore. Similarly, Emma Watson's sister Penelope, who is taken up with trying to marry a 'rich old Dr Harding', is only the outline of the elder Miss Steele again (who, anyway, was lifted from the eldest Miss Branghton in *Evelina*), so she goes too. The assembly ball in *The Watsons* is the first ball in *Pride and Prejudice*, and Lord Osborne is just as evidently Mr Darcy in many particulars of character and conduct and conversation. Obviously this would not do, and the Osborne females could only echo the Bingley sisters, since Lord Osborne was to become a suitor to Emma and Lady Osborne a rival of Emma's for Mr Howard, so the whole Osborne Castle party disappears, to the great improvement of the homogeneous atmosphere of *Emma* (Enscombe is too far away to be felt). The ball does remain, but it becomes a different ball, with all which had been used in *Pride and Prejudice* dropped out and only the new and original incident retained – the act of generosity of one character at the ball taking pity on another who is humiliated and left partnerless. Now this change is significant and beautifully illustrates the kind of revision Jane Austen made when working up her draft to the work of art that her novel eventually became. We may regret, with some critics, the loss of Emma Watson's generosity to little Charles at the ball; but we can console ourselves by noticing, as they have not, that it is rewritten into a much more subtle act of generosity of an artistically and morally superior nature: it becomes the exactly parallel action of Mr Knightley's delicate kindness in sinking his dislike for dancing (and Harriet) to partner her at that other ball where she is publicly slighted by Mr Elton in a far more humiliating way than Miss Osborne had slighted little Charles. The first gesture was invented only to get Emma acquainted with the Osborne-Howard set, and shows only that Emma was an impulsive kind-hearted girl; the second is more significant, rich in overtones, coming as it does when the plot is getting to a critical stage (it gives Harriet the excuse for thinking Mr Knightley means to marry her, with subsequent anguish for Emma that reveals Emma's feelings for Mr Knightley to herself), it reveals Mr Knightley as the moral superior of the world of the novel, and it exposes Mr Elton's character to Emma not only as mean beyond her imagination – the incident is also an ironic comment on Emma's self-deception about Mr Elton's character and about her design of marrying him to Harriet. This, then, like the carriage incident in *Mansfield Park*, is the kind of creation in which Jane Austen's genius manifests itself, not a miracle of inspiration but the maturity of artistic purpose that gives significant direction to a casual piece of social behaviour and co-ordinates it with a complex series of events and shapes of character.

We can get a great deal more out of *The Watsons* yet. We have seen the novelist rejecting characters that were not new,[5] adapting others from life and from her early stock of satiric or first-hand notes, and giving prominence to fresh characterization and intrigue. The original of one of the most acclaimed characters of *Emma* is Emma Watson's sister-in-law Jane, whose over-fine clothes, 'pert and conceited' personality, 'arch sallies', 'witty smile', consciousness of superiority (and daughter Augusta) become with no change but that of situation Augusta Elton. The origin of Mr Woodhouse is more interesting and illuminating. He came into being originally as a purely functional character: Mr Watson had to be an invalid (a real one) in order to keep his daughters at home from balls and to prevent his receiving company and paying calls (so that Lord Osborne's calling at Stanton to see Emma is both an impertinence and an embarrassing event); he had to die in order that Emma might be thrown on the world, have to live with her brother, experience reverses, and refuse Lord Osborne, before happily marrying Mr Howard. Now Mr Woodhouse becomes a valetudinarian – by a brilliant stroke of invention from the point of view of the reader's amusement, but actually, I think, in obedience to an inner compulsion on the author's part that provided the theme of *Emma*, just as from being a specifically sensible and well-informed man he becomes an exasperating clog on his daughter, and his conversation drivel. He keeps his daughter at his side and himself from ordinary social life through *imaginary* invalidism; Mr Watson's basin of gruel is elaborated as Mr Woodhouse's character expands into extravagant fatuity (there is a certain savage heightening of his nuisance-aspect towards the end which suggests that his author enjoyed him less than her critics have done). Poor Isabella naturally follows, and there was 'a poor Honey' of a cousin's wife with Isabella-ish characteristics at the right time (1813) and also a sister-in-law who is described in the *Letters* of the same year taking her children to Southend for the sea-bathing and then paying just such a family visit to the Austens at Godmersham as the Knightleys did to Hartfield – thoughtfully provided by life to give, as Gilbert says, artistic verisimilitude to what might otherwise have been a bald and unconvincing narrative. The *Letters* show that life was often kind in this way, and no doubt the even larger number of missing letters would show even more raw material of the novels. The genius lay not in creating but in using it.

But just as everything was rejected or disguised that was old, so nothing was wasted that was new, a thriftiness characteristic of our author. Mr Woodhouse has to be kept alive to be a problem to his daughter, so Mrs Churchill is introduced to do the dying that alters the course of the plot and the heroine's life, and the story of the original Emma is in fact relegated with her humble circumstances and aunt instead of sister, to a subordinate heroine, Jane Fairfax (note the vestigial vicarage in the background of her family), with her superior upbringing of wealth and education but prospects only of governessing, her confined and trying home, and her exposure to the vulgar familiarity of Augusta Elton (this last not inevitable as in the earlier story, where she was Emma's sister-in-law and later hostess, and a good deal of argument is actually contrived between Emma, Mr Knightley and Mrs Weston solely to make it plausible). The character and position of Mrs Churchill, it may be noted, are remarkably like that of disagreeable Aunt Leigh Perrott in the *Letters*. Thus old and discrete elements were rearranged to make, after assimilation, a new close-knit pattern. One of the rearrangements, perhaps the most important in this case, is the replacing of the somewhat stock heroine (who belongs, as Professor Garrod would say contemptuously, to a land flowing with milk and water) by a faulty and in many ways unsympathetic young woman, who undergoes a steady process of chastening, while the original static heroine and her story are subordinated to contribute to this chastening; while to balance this subordinate story, both artistically and for the moral argument, another and antithetic story, that of Harriet Smith, was invented. Resuscitated rather than invented, in all probability, for, though we do not happen to have the original version of this last, it bears all the marks of an early origin in anti-romance of the kind we may study in the MS volumes and can see somewhat disguised in *Northanger Abbey, Sense and Sensibility* and *Pride and Prejudice*. The Harriet-Emma Woodhouse relation is actually taken from the early *Lady Susan*, though there both parties are sympathetic; linking that up with a burlesque was a characteristic procedure. (*Lady Susan* had just previously been finally rewritten as *Mansfield Park*, and the Harriet-Emma relation was the only feature of the early story that had not been used up.)

The reader will wish to ask, how far was all this deliberate, or, rather, were such processes not unconscious and therefore the result of a kind of taste, an intuition for the right touch, the right character, and not a matter of cold-blooded arrangement and readjustment such as I have suggested? No doubt the artist's sense of what coheres and is in keeping with the general desired effect accounted for much of the very last rewriting, which must have been something like the changes we can see between the rejected chapter of *Persuasion* and the version finally published, and accounted also for the *exclusions* of material not suited to her stylization of life. But the very great difference that we find between an earlier draft of a story and its final form, such as between *The Watsons* and *Emma*, between *Lady Susan* and *Mansfield Park* (so elaborate a change that I cannot, after all, even summarize it here), and no doubt between *First Impressions* and *Pride and Prejudice*, among others, is a proof of the deliberate change of intention which must have impelled the novelist to a radical overhauling of her materials and to evolve in consequence a new technique for reassembling them on each occasion. While we can trace very largely the origin of these

materials, at different times and in widely different circumstances, in quite different relations to reality or to literature, yet
we can put our fingers in each case on a particular combination
of motives that at a given time in her private history caused the
novelist to undertake such a labour. As Mr Harding has
suggested in his valuable essay[6] on Jane Austen, we can often
sense an outbreak of irritation or nervous tension in features of
the novels, but in addition I believe we can in every novel see
the writer exploring her own problems by dramatizing them, or
in this way giving them relief. Thus, to take the case of *Emma*,
whose metamorphosis we have been examining, the central
figure and her problems were taken from the situation of Fanny
Knight at the time the novel was recast from *The Watsons*. Fanny
was left at fifteen by her mother's death the mistress of two large
houses, with many younger brothers and sisters, in a position
of authority and wealth that would develop the qualities of Miss
Emma Woodhouse in an almost similar position, and we find
her actually at the time *Emma* was undertaken corresponding
privately with her aunt to ask for help. She was in the dilemma
that was to be Emma Woodhouse's, of not understanding her
own heart,[7] and this was probably not the first occasion; she
was evidently a handsome, lively and charming young woman,
but it would be unsound as well as unnecessary to assume that
Fanny Knight also embodied Emma's peculiar kind of folly –
that was the *moral* of the book, an intellectual invention, like the
Pride and Prejudice, the Sense and Sensibility morals, all
variations of the Reason versus Romance idea that Jane Austen
never tired of (she was at it again on her death-bed in *Sanditon*).
But besides the moral of the book, which is a mental concept
like the motivating idea in a novel of Susan Ferrier's or Maria
Edgeworth's, there is always a theme proceeding from much
deeper sources of experience, which gives the Austen novels the
resonance lacking in, for instance, Maria Edgeworth's, and
often makes them in effect run counter to the 'moral'. Mr
Woodhouse's valetudinarianism is a useful symbol of the way
he battens on Emma, thwarting her own healthy instinct for
living; and discussions of his claims on Emma, her exaggerated
belief in their validity, and an exasperated picture of what
yielding to parental rights means (so that we feel she *ought* to
have resisted them though she is commended for not doing so),
account for the extravagance with which Mr Woodhouse is

represented and in fact why he is thus substituted for the sensible if irritable, the conversable if unsocial, the intelligent if self-centred father of the first Emma. The *Letters* are full of tart accounts of family invalids who had to be borne with (Mrs Austen herself is one of them) and Jane Austen was not the first daughter who visibly suffered from having lived too long at home with mother. The internal strains and stresses inevitable in any family, however united, and especially if a large one, are more evident in the *Letters* than the novels, but only because undisguised in the former. Another part of the theme of *Emma* is embodied, as I have mentioned, in Mr John Knightley, whose functions are numerous but centre in his much-stressed reprehensible love of domestic privacy which refuses to admit even the reasonable claims of society. This was a standing problem in the Austen family, as we know from the biographies, where we are told that Jane was the member most conscious of the necessity for resisting the family's John Knightley tendency (of hostility to outsiders, and clannish self-sufficiency). It adds to the peripheral comedy that his dislike of going into or receiving mere society should contrast with Mr Weston's too hospitable ways, overflowing confidences and uncritical good mixing, but the contrast is conducted on too tense a note to have been contrived merely for purposes of comedy. Mr Weston is the opposite of his creator in his social character – 'she likes people too easily', we remember of an acquaintance in the *Letters*, and the same criticism is made by Elizabeth Bennet of her sister Jane – and Mr John Knightley is conscience's reply to the Austens' conviction of righteousness in being aloof and despising the undiscriminating. This, like the father–daughter relation and its solution in Emma's relation to Mr Knightley, the moral arbiter of the book and her spiritual regulator who by becoming her husband solves her problems – this and such matters are what *Emma* is *about*. 'Ordination' is what Miss Austen said and no doubt thought was the subject of *Mansfield Park*, but what reader would have noticed the ordination theme unless told of it, or that an important contrast is intended between Dr Grant and Edmund Bertram as clerics, and that the arguments about ordination and the Church were meant to take stress? The reader sees only that the author's emotional capital was invested in the struggle in Mary Crawford's nature and in Fanny Price's sufferings over Edmund, and in the anti-Crawford feeling that animates the moral drama. We can answer the question: At what point in these rewritings does a novel become *the* novel? by saying with confidence that it is when the author changes her treatment so that from being outside she is to be found inside.

A similar account of the origins, alterations and ultimate purpose of each novel can, I believe, be given, with the additional persuasiveness that space for illustration, comparison and detailed deduction allows. But before I give up this hopeless attempt to summarize in a few pages an undertaking that requires several hundred to make it coherent, I should like to give one brief illustration of the necessity for such a critical foundation as a preliminary to any profitable literary account of Jane Austen, to even the smallest and apparently most harmless kind of remarks. It will help to answer the reader's question, what is all this for?

'A woman of such sterling qualities ought surely to have had daughters more attractive than Lady Middleton and Mrs Palmer,' one scholarly critic objects; and it is common to say with Bradley that the author 'wrote herself into a good humour with Mrs Jennings'. These reveal a complete lack of understanding of the novelist's intention in composing *Sense and Sensibility* and the kind of relation to reality that her methods entail. *Sense and Sensibility* is so narrowly symmetrical in its construction, its stylization so artificial and its object so obtrusively evident that there is in the case of this novel, at least, no excuse for not approaching a work of art as such. Marianne is there, like Emma, to be chastened, and the drama leads us through her self-deceptions to her recognition of error and her repentance. Originally, of course, she was the peg on which to hang a literary joke, like Catherine and *Northanger Abbey*, but though the 'Sense versus Sensibility' idea was the moral animating *Elinor and Marianne*, we can see that the superimposed novel has a theme of deeper import. Marianne has lacked 'candour', that key word in Miss Austen's vocabulary, and her sin has consisted in an uncandid attitude to society and a refusal to take her part as a member of society. Mrs Jennings stands for a sample of the social average; we see her first with Marianne's distorted vision (as we first see Darcy through Elizabeth's eyes, and almost the whole of *Emma* through Emma's consciousness) but by the last part of the story the author has written not herself but *us* into a good humour with Mrs Jennings; it is a triumph of her art and not a flaw in it. We have been manoeuvred round from Marianne's original viewpoint to that which makes Marianne's solemn repentance after her illness called for. Mrs Jennings is indelicate in speech, and inelegant in manners, and unrefined in spirit, but from the time of the crisis (Marianne's finding herself deceived in Willoughby) Jane Austen contrives that the absence in Mrs Jennings of the qualities she valued most is seen to be offset by the presence of qualities that must, if only in theory, have been at least as much recommendation to her even when unsupported by elegance and distinction – an unfailingly good heart, a well-judging mind, a shrewd grasp of the essentials of character. It is from Mrs Jennings's mouth that the final verdicts on Willoughby, Mrs Ferrars and her daughter, and other leading characters proceed.

Now the two daughters are not meant to be plausible persons; they have the function of providing contrasts favourable to their mother. Mrs Palmer is good-humoured like her mother without being vulgar, but she is consistently silly, so her mother's good sense stands out, not only in itself but serving as a kind of substitute for taste and delicacy. Lady Middleton has to have the manners and appearance and conversation of a well-bred woman, in contrast to her mother's lack of formality and social decorum (which Jane Austen valued), but her cold-heartedness and insipidity make her mother's lack of elegance seem desirable later on, as Lady Middleton's purely social values lead her from bad to worse (ending with a friendship for Fanny Dashwood and seeking the acquaintance of Mrs Willoughby). If Marianne was deceived in the romantic hero Willoughby, she was equally astray, we gather, in her estimate of the unattractive members of her circle. Once Marianne's judgment is righted, Mr Palmer behaves considerately, Sir John is seen to be not merely a sporting brute, even Mrs Palmer has something to be said for her. But Marianne 'in her new character of candour' goes so far as to reproach herself for injustice even to her relatives-in-law, John and Fanny, who have been exhibited as wholly detestable; this strikes the reader as excessive and betrays that the author is trying to convince herself as well as us that *any* instinctive dislike of people as individuals should be smothered in our obligation to fit in with society. There are plenty of other clues that she was arguing with herself as well as us, and at the end of her life she was to write an anti-*Sense and Sensibility* called 'The Elliots' (which though it was not at her death ready for the press was published by her brother as *Persuasion*).

In short, by examining how she worked we can determine what kind of a novelist she was, by looking to see how she wrote a novel we can discover what her object was in writing it. Without such a preliminary no criticism of her novels can be just or even safe. A small instance of how far astray criticism may go is the treatment that has been given to the problem of the last chapter of *Mansfield Park*. Every reader is puzzled by something odd about it which is felt to jar on the mood created by the rest of the book, and critics have produced various justifying explanations, from aesthetic to psychological, which satisfy no one and are in fact misleading. Actually its ill-assorted tone is vestigial. *Mansfield Park* was written up from *Lady Susan* but much later in life and in a different convention, with a correspondingly different attitude to its material. The early form has a conclusion identical in tone and parallel in content with the concluding chapter of *Mansfield Park*, and in *Lady Susan* it is exactly in keeping with the nature of the original undertaking. It remains in *Mansfield Park* as the least assimilated and most discordant, therefore, of all the parts of that unsatisfactory but instructive novel. The novelist in the early draft was, as always at this stage, outside, and hostile to her material. Either from fatigue or pressure of work (*Pride and Prejudice* still on her hands, *Emma* already imminent), the original conclusion did not receive the necessary transposition. Its spirit remains that of 'Lesley Castle' and *Northanger Abbey*, with the sardonic tone and impatient handling that characterize the earlier stages of her compositions, due to their prevailingly satiric origin.

IIa

Lady Susan into Mansfield Park (i)

Mansfield Park as we know it arrived, I believe, through (at least) three stages, and studying the process of its evolution will help the literary critic in several respects. It will give us an insight into the process of artistic creation, even when that has passed, as in Jane Austen's case, for a miraculous achievement;

it will enable us to account for the unsatisfactory effect and puzzling anomalies of *Mansfield Park* itself; and it will put us in possession of some interesting information about its author which may help us to understand better Jane Austen's other novels. *Mansfield Park*, though published with the latter half of her novels and known to have been written well on in the maturer part of her writing life, is nevertheless generally felt (by those capable of feeling critically about the Austen novels) to be less satisfactory in many ways than any of the others – notably contrasting with a 'pure' work of art like its successor *Emma*. It has many puzzling features, the most pronounced perhaps being its vein of priggishness with outbreaks of a disconcerting kind of cynicism; for instance, characters who are for the most part advanced for our respectful admiration or esteem are also handled at moments with brutality or contempt. There is a marked unevenness in the tone of the narrative, and there is equally a difference in the style; while there is a good deal of the too easy irony of *Sense and Sensibility* and of the lumpy Johnsonese of the two novels previous to *Mansfield Park*, yet here not merely phrases but whole passages are clothed in a new, a religious idiom: the state of mind that numbered Sunday travelling amongst Mr Elliot's vices appears for the first time and in the centre of the undertaking. There is some equivocation in the very heart of the book, in that part of the moral drama represented by Mary Crawford; there is a disparity between what she does and is represented as being, on the one hand, and what she is accused of, the basis for the feelings displayed towards her by the author, on the other – the author is evidently not in this case the detached and impartial presenter that she is elsewhere seen to be. There is a personal animus manifested against Mary Crawford, in fact, which seeps through the book as irritation trying to justify itself on the highest grounds: how does it happen that such an artist is in the power of such an emotion? Then again, *Mansfield Park* is the most upsetting novel to those who give the conventional account of Miss Austen and insist on describing the interest she excites in the usual crass terms.[8] Some other anomalies should be mentioned here: the disparity between the expressed intention of writing the novel on the theme of ordination and the actual theme's turning out to be quite different was cited in the previous instalment of this article, along with the disconcerting last chapter. There is also something odd about the form of the novel altogether, with which I shall deal in its place, as well as an astonishing contrast in form and tone with *Pride and Prejudice*, with the composition of which it overlapped – the one so sparkling and dramatic, the other low in vitality, as it were, and depending very little on dramatic scenes in its narration. The priggishness of the book is of a special kind, not just the occasional school-marmy effects of *Sense and Sensibility* which there are only the result of artistic inexperience (for the same kind of points are made effectively in *Persuasion* without any impression of preaching); in *Mansfield Park* the morality is almost deliberately conventional and the moralizing unbelievably trite, yet there are also savage outbreaks against conventional moralizing and socially approved behaviour. Those who have read in the *Life and Letters* of the Austens' theatricals will have asked themselves why Jane should be so hot in *Mansfield Park* against amateur acting, and that, too, of a play at least as unexceptionable as some of those performed at Steventon Rectory. Another stumbling-block is the heroine Fanny Price; it has been frequently remarked that whereas all the other heroines of our author are young women of character, this one is the approved heroine of the novel of the time – with her ill health, delicate nerves, superstitious respect for authority and conventional moral squeamishness. Yet she is championed by the author as 'my Fanny', a personal relation not accorded even to Elizabeth Bennet or Anne Elliot.

Lady Susan, untitled and undated, survives in manuscript, the paper on which it was written bearing a watermark of 1805. But, as Dr Chapman describes it, this is 'not a draft but a fair copy. It is beautifully written, almost free from correction or erasure' – very different, in fact, from the manuscript of *Sanditon*, which is certainly a first draft. There was apparently a family tradition that *Lady Susan* was a very early composition (mentioned both in the *Memoir* of Jane's nephew and the *Life and Letters* by her later relations), contemporary with *First Impressions* and *Elinor and Marianne*, though this may be merely a deduction from its being composed in letter form. But I think we can decide on internal evidence that it was founded on events of the years 1795 to 1797, and was certainly written before the end of 1797. The manuscript of 1805 or later was the usual revision after a period of years. This we may call the first stage. No explanation has been advanced, I believe, why Jane Austen, who destroyed *First Impressions*, *Elinor and Marianne*, and the earlier versions of the novel finally published as *Northanger Abbey*, preserved this manuscript, though she made no attempt at any time to publish it. I think we may conclude that it was of unique interest for her, like *The Watsons* and the three manuscript volumes of her early writings. No reference to it is to be found in her letters, or anywhere else, but we can form a pretty accurate idea of its conception.

Lady Susan has attracted little attention from the critics, who have been too uniformly repelled by what they have agreed to call its 'bitter' or 'cynical' tone to discover in it the matrix of *Mansfield Park*, though it was first published as early as 1871, appended to the second edition of James Austen-Leigh's *Memoir*. Chesterton seems merely to have voiced an unspoken consensus of opinion when he wrote in his Introduction to *Love and Freindship*: 'I for one would willingly have left Lady Susan in the waste-paper basket.' The general reader has thus been headed off an interesting and frequently very entertaining piece of work. The unpleasant quality so painfully evident in the uneven *Mansfield Park* is actually not to be traced to *Lady Susan*, which is merely stamped (as we may be sure *First Impressions* and *Elinor and Marianne* were, and as *Northanger Abbey* still is even after three revisions) by a perceptible unsympathy with *all* the characters, an impatience to jot them down and rough out their rôles and emotional relations so as to see if the desired total effect has been secured: like *The Watsons*, *Lady Susan* is a novelist's working draft and not meant for print, though like that story, its deceptive appearance of completeness has encouraged its acceptance as an entity, and it has not even such very obvious links with its descendant as *The Watsons* has with *Emma*. A close knowledge of *Lady Susan* can hardly be assumed, therefore, so I will make no apology for a summary. The scene is between a great country-house, Churchill, the home of the Vernons, a wealthy and virtuous couple in the story-book mode, and London, the London of fashionable society in contrast. The link between the two is Lady Susan Vernon. The story is told entirely in letters except for a concluding chapter where the epistolary convention is cast off with explicit satire (we recall the jibes at the convention in the first two MS volumes), and the story is wound up impatiently in the manner of the ends of

Sense and Sensibility, *Northanger Abbey* and *Mansfield Park*. Lady Susan, in the first letter, is inviting herself to Churchill, where she is suspiciously received by her sister-in-law Catherine Vernon and that lady's young brother Reginald De Courcy. We have two sets of correspondence thenceforward, one between Catherine Vernon and her mother and the other between Lady Susan and her confidante in Town, the unpleasant Mrs Johnson. Lady Susan, recently widowed, with a daughter Frederica of sixteen, is a beautiful and well-bred Becky Sharp. Finding Reginald has been 'taught [with justice] to consider her a very distinguished Flirt', she sets about conquering him just as she has already imposed on Mr Vernon in spite of his wife; she attaches any man who comes her way on principle, in case he may come in useful, but she is first piqued by Reginald's hostility and then, after capturing him, thinks he may be worth marrying. Mrs Vernon's sisterly anguishes and laments (she is never for a moment taken in by Lady Susan's 'bewitching powers') are most amusingly sent off to her mother, recording every turn in Reginald's relations with Lady Susan. These soon become involved as Frederica turns up at Churchill to her mother's discomfort, and has to be explained away as intractable and deficient. Actually Frederica is shy, gentle, tender-hearted, pretty in a style contrasting with her mother's beauty, 'totally without accomplishment', but fond of books, and though she has always been neglected by her mother and left to servants is surprisingly endowed with Principles. She soon falls in love with the high-minded Reginald. A foolish young man of great estate, Sir James Martin, whom Lady Susan intends to force Frederica to marry, pursues them to Churchill. Frederica appeals by letter to Reginald to use his influence with her mother to save her from a wretched marriage, and in consequence Reginald has a temporary breach with Lady Susan, soon healed, however, by her artful explanations. She goes off to London, followed by Reginald, whom she has all along managed to persuade into believing her to be what he would like to think her. But she is in a fix. She can hardly make up her mind to sacrifice her liberty for marriage with a man she despises, who is, moreover, dependent on his father; besides, there is another man, Manwaring, with whom she is having an affair, but he is married *à la* Willoughby to Mr Johnson's rich ward, and she would prefer to marry him if only his wife could be disposed of (plaguing her to death from jealousy is the method Lady Susan is actually adopting). Reginald and Manwaring have of course to be kept out of each other's way, and this she manages, but, by an improbable coincidence when Reginald presents his introduction to Mrs Johnson, Mrs Manwaring forces her way in to confide her jealous suspicions of Lady Susan to her guardian. Even after this 'provoking Eclaircissement' Lady Susan still hopes to argue Reginald into believing in her against appearances but, as he writes to her, his 'Understanding is at length restored', and after a brilliant pair of letters to him from Lady Susan she is obliged to extricate herself from poverty and scandal by marrying Sir James Martin, throwing Frederica on the Vernons' hands. This leaves Reginald and Frederica to console each other after a suitable period, ironically looked forward to by the author in her conclusion in the first person.

What are the essentials of the situation noted down in this convenient form for future use? There is first the contrast between London and Churchill, the one, represented by Lady Susan and her set, standing for heartlessness, interested marriages, hypocrisy and vice in general, the other, represented by the Vernons and De Courcys, standing for honesty, heart, 'principles', virtue of the conventional order of the age as exhibited with approval in *Camilla* and *Belinda*, Jane Austen's model novels. Lady Susan's daughter surprisingly belongs to the latter camp, and though as matters stand her possession at sixteen of 'Principles...not to be injured even by her Mother, or all her Mother's friends' is preposterous, we note it as a convenience for signifying that Frederica is to contrast with her mother morally as well as to stand in rivalry with her for the hero's affections, to which she is to succeed. Next, there is roughed out the character of the principal. She is a woman of fashion who despises the country and expects to be bored there and who feels superior to country people with their rustic morality and simple minds; she is a widow still young and very attractive who lives on her charms and intends if possible to make a good marriage, though she values her recently acquired liberty and is in two minds about surrendering it. She is not at all a stock character, as the others are, who are merely indicated in relation to Lady Susan and her intrigues. Thirdly, there is the situation created by Lady Susan's irruption into the life of Churchill: the hero oscillating between doubts as to the reality of his idealization of Lady Susan, his self-deception, and his uncertainty of his mistress's affection for him, is watched by a sister in more than sisterly distress (with the added exasperation of a woman whose husband is being imposed on by a sister-in-law), and whose feelings are set down with more than the requisite exactness; parallel to this sister's, we have reported the feelings of the subordinate heroine, Frederica, who similarly watches the hero deceiving himself all round, but watches with the despair of a hopeless passion. Finally, there is the hero's undeception through a lucky accident, with consolation to hand. To preserve these fruitful notes was clearly the reason why *Lady Susan* was put together, with so much carelessness in regard to plausibility of action and so much care in some other respects.

We must now turn to real life. The biography of Jane's exotic cousin Eliza Hancock received a good deal of space in the *Life and Letters* and it has often been conjectured that she gave some hints for the character of Lady Susan, whom she resembled in a delight in exercising her powers on the opposite sex; she married at the age of twenty the Comte de Feuillide, who was guillotined in 1794. Thereupon she returned to England and at the end of 1797 married Jane's favourite brother Henry, she being then thirty-six (Lady Susan was about thirty-five). The *Life and Letters* hints that Henry's engagement to 'his very pleasure-loving cousin' was unfavourably received by the Austens, particularly as she was ten years his senior (Lady Susan was twelve years older than Reginald De Courcy) and had a son. But they were married immediately; the courtship, according to Eliza's letter to her godfather Warren Hastings, was of nearly as long standing as her widowhood, for she speaks of 'an acquiescence which I have withheld for more than two years'. (Lady Susan had been 'scarcely ten months a widow' when she captured Reginald.) Letters of hers exist showing that she had Lady Susan's (and Mary Crawford's) attitude to the country as opposed to town life, and that she found it hard to decide to surrender her liberty by remarrying. That she was like Lady Susan, an adventuress or an unnatural mother or of bad character has never been suggested, and in fact Jane was a great favourite of hers in her girlhood, which suggests a mutual preference. But the situation of Eliza's flirtations with Jane's much-admired brother[9] (family tradition suggests two brothers, that James Austen's second wife – whom he married in the same year as Eliza did Henry – never forgave Eliza in consequence) was evidently the occasion of the draft for a novel. Originally jotted down in the period of the courtship but before the marriage was decided on, I imagine, it was later preserved in the fair copy we know as *Lady Susan*. An extension of the family tradition on this matter has providentially been made known by a grandson of Jane's elder brother Francis. Incredible as it may seem, in 1928 Mr John F. Hubback writing in *The Cornhill* on 'Pen Portraits in Jane Austen's Novels' is able to record what he heard his mother and aunt tell of their favourite 'Aunt Jane', and the background of her life. He makes an important addition to the story of Eliza: that when she came to England in 1794 she returned to Steventon as a place of refuge and 'it was not long before theatricals were resumed. Eliza's experiences at Versailles, and subsequent changes of fortune, had endowed her character with many new traits, sometimes almost clashing with each other. Their elder brother, Henry, was again Eliza's coadjutor in the play-acting, and the outcome was that he became her husband in 1797. It has been stated that her refusal of James Austen in her youth was on account of his being destined for the Church, but this may be merely family tradition...[10] Henry Austen had also the wish to take orders before he fell in love with Eliza, but we hear no more of this until his actual ordination took place in 1816, three years after Eliza's life ended.' I may add that Henry became a divine of marked Evangelical outlook.

To drag in biography like this is, of course, only justifiable in literary criticism either when it serves to illuminate strictly critical problems or when it helps to show how an artist works on raw material, and in this case biography seems to me to do both. Three of the four aspects of the *Lady Susan* story I have listed are comprised in the situation caused by the Comtesse de Feuillide's irruption into the tranquil life of Steventon Rectory, though the situation has been simplified and her character heightened. One guesses that the alterations were made in order both to avoid an emotional or personal treatment of a sore[11] and delicate subject and to make effective in a brief space something that the still immature writer knew not how to consign to paper in other than bold outline and satiric terms.

The authors of the *Life and Letters* remark that 'strictly

speaking it [*Lady Susan*] is not a story but a study... [of] the one full-length, highly finished, wholly sinister figure which occupies the canvas, but which seems, with the completion of the study, to have disappeared entirely from the mind of its creator'. But as we have seen, such things did not disappear from the mind of their creator. Jane Austen simply put *Lady Susan* by until it could be used as part of a larger and subtler scheme. In 1808 she brought it out again and, just as *The Watsons* was later rewritten as *Emma*, as I have shown, she started to rewrite *Lady Susan* as *Mansfield Park*. *Mansfield Park* as we have it is known with some exactness to have been written between February 1811, and June or July 1813, on Jane's own statement, and I had better say at once that history does not record any previous draft. My supposition of such a version rests on two pieces of evidence. First, the dating of *Mansfield Park* is not that of the time it was 'written', but answers to the years 1808 and 1809. Jane Austen did not construct her novels on a strict calendar basis for any reason but her own convenience (as Dr Chapman observes, the reader is not even expected to notice the clues to the precise dating in the novels) and no writer in these circumstances is going to hunt up old calendars to use when the current ones are handy and will answer equally well. Neither had she reason to bother about changing the date scheme when rewriting for publication.

Secondly, there seems to me quite obviously an overlaid epistolary novel behind the version of *Mansfield Park* that we have. The dimmed and distant effect of much of this novel, the impression it gives of low spirits in its presentation, is due, I suggest, to its being retold from letters. A good deal of *Mansfield Park* reads like paraphrases of letters, and, once the action is launched with the young people grown up, a very great deal actually is letters or summaries of them, and bridge-passages between letters or summaries of letters. There are loose ends due to submerged confidants, confidants who were indispensable to the earlier novel conducted in letters. Among these we may probably class Mary Crawford's London friends Mrs Fraser and her sister Lady Stornaway (the descendants of Lady Susan's correspondent Mrs Johnson) and certainly Sir Thomas's 'old and most particular friend in London', Mr Harding, who is sprung upon the reader as the Mansfield source of information of the Rushworth–Crawford scandal. The flatness of breaking such an event in reports of two successive letters from a hitherto unknown character is such that no novelist could possibly have sat down and thought it up voluntarily, much less the author of *Pride and Prejudice*; it is a device necessitated by the epistolary novel that *Mansfield Park* had been. The same crisis is imparted separately to Fanny partly in a letter from Mary and partly in another letter from Edmund in addition to the paragraph Mr Price reads from his newspaper; nothing is gained from the author's point of view by telling it twice over, once to Mansfield and once to Portsmouth, but repeating a piece of news all round is another disadvantage entailed by writing a novel in letters, as we may see *ad nauseam* in Richardson. (We notice the same clumsiness in the two separate announcements, first of Lucy Steele's engagement to Edmund when it comes out, and then of her marriage to Robert; *Sense and Sensibility*, too, was originally composed in letters.) Sir Thomas then goes up to London himself and sends successive letters home about the affairs of Maria and Julia, duly repeated to Fanny in letters from Edmund. There are two accounts in letters of Henry's first meeting with Mrs Rushworth in Wimpole Street, but no dramatic scene between them at all. Nor is there anything of the other drama conducted in London between Edmund and Mary except retrospectively in Edmund's reports to Fanny. Characters are separated and distributed about the country for little other reason than that they may write to one another. Fanny's going to Portsmouth, which has been condemned by critics on aesthetic grounds as marring the unity of the novel, was I believe, devised for the 1808–9 version as an opportunity for all the Bertram and Crawford complications to be cleared up in letters to and from Fanny, leaving only a Conclusion by the author to wind up, a conclusion differing from that of *Lady Susan* only in having more characters to polish off. And this is precisely what we have in the last chapter of *Mansfield Park*, with the addition of some moral top-dressing in 1813, the irreverence and oddity of which chapter has always worried the more devout Austenites. We can in fact postulate an epistolary form of *Mansfield Park* on internal evidence alone, as we could not have deduced the existence of a similar precursor from *Sense and Sensibility*: yet even though we know such a precursor in letter form did exist, in *Elinor and Marianne*, we cannot make out what that was like, as we can make out an epistolary *Mansfield Park*.

I hope I have established, at any rate, the existence of a precursor in letter form to *Mansfield Park*. But I have still to show that it was an intermediary between *Lady Susan* and *Mansfield Park*, stories whose plot, intrigues and characterization are superficially so different. I hope the reader will bear in mind the demonstration in the last number of *Scrutiny* [vol. x, 1941] of how *The Watsons* became *Emma*. Precisely the same process can be demonstrated here, though much more richly and subtly, but not always so consciously, in action. The quotation from Mr Hubback's important reminiscences links Eliza de Feuillide with *Lady Susan* as regards her personality and the situation she created in the Austen family, but, as the reader may have noticed, it also links Eliza with *Mansfield Park* by way of the theatricals and the ordination business. This, however, is only external and not evidence in the field of literary criticism. Let us now turn to the two documents, *Lady Susan* and *Mansfield Park*.

We have the same antithesis between worldliness on the one hand, comprising deceit, heartlessness, and marriages of convenience, and backed by London and, on the other, Principles, unworldly sincerity and warmth of feeling. Mansfield stands for 'heart' to the worldly Miss Crawford, and though like Lady Susan she comes into the country as a *pis-aller* expecting to be bored, she is impressed in spite of herself by the Mansfield virtues: 'You have all so much more *heart* among you, than one finds in the world at large. You all give me a feeling of being able to trust and confide in you; which, in common intercourse, one knows nothing of,' Mary Crawford confides to Fanny when about to return to her London friends. Lady Susan's set – 'a very bad set' – *is* Mary Crawford's, the description by Edmund of Mrs Fraser and by Miss Crawford of Mr Fraser answering exactly to the accounts of Mr and Mrs Johnson in the earlier book, down to replacing Mrs Manwaring's sister-in-law Maria who was trying desperately to catch the baronet by Mrs Fraser's step-daughter Margaret who was wild to marry Henry. The noble match Sir James Martin, 'under par', 'no Solomon', 'a very weak young man', 'only a fool', becomes Mr Rushworth, both having the advantage of a good appearance and 'person'. Sir Reginald De Courcy, who is represented by a strong paternal letter pointing out (too late) the folly of his son's falling in love with Lady Susan, provides the groundwork for Sir

Thomas Bertram. 'You know your own rights, and that it is out of my power to prevent your inheriting the family Estate. My Ability of distressing you during my Life, would be a species of revenge to which I should hardly stoop under any circumstances. I honestly tell you my Sentiments and Intentions. I do not wish to work on your Fears, but on your Sense and Affection. It would destroy every comfort to my Life, to know that you were married to Lady Susan Vernon. It would be the death of that honest Pride, with which I have hitherto considered my son, I should blush to see him, to hear of him, to think of him.' We recognize the intonation of Sir Thomas blushing for his son Tom, the dignified accents of virtue consciously founded on good sense and right feeling. In addition to the principal situations carried over, which I have summarized earlier, there are many others adapted as we have seen Jane Austen adapting before. For instance, the guilt and vice in the centre of *Lady Susan* are removed to the edge with Maria, the wanton seduction of a married man, Manwaring, by Lady Susan being altered to Mrs Rushworth's seduction by Henry Crawford. Sir James's proposals are forced on Frederica by her mother as a good worldly match and his attentions encouraged against her will as Henry Crawford's are for Fanny by her uncle for the same reason; in both cases the same piece is used when the interested spectator (Mrs Vernon, Edmund) observes that the only possibility of encouragement in the girl's behaviour rests upon embarrassment and consciousness. But we will leave smaller likenesses[12] to grapple with the central changes.

I have said before that in general the point when Jane Austen's immature draft becomes in conception the novel as we know it is when the author changes her treatment so that from being outside, in a relation of satiric superiority to her characters and their involvements, she is to be found inside. What the critics have really meant in calling *Lady Susan* unpleasant is that a general callousness on the author's part, a belittling of *all* the actors in the drama, is apparent. The launching of *Mansfield Park* was when Jane Austen decided to move Lady Susan out of the centre of the picture and adopt the point of view on the drama of the passive Frederica, who had been exhibited only at second hand in other people's letters, a dummy not in the original domestic drama of Steventon Rectory but invented for the novelist to illuminate and offset Lady Susan. We can see how this was inevitable. Instead of adopting the ironical external position of the author of anti-romance, she has to identify herself with the consciousness of a heroine (as she does in every novel but *Northanger Abbey*, which remains primarily a squib); it couldn't be the amoral Lady Susan's, so it must be either Mrs Vernon's (too entirely sisterly to be interesting) or Frederica's (too simple, she being only the consolation prize for the hero). What she did in fact was to combine the two. Frederica had to be the exact opposite to her mother; with her mild eyes and pensive countenance, her 'artless affection' for Reginald, her 'excellent disposition', her 'romantic tender-heartedness which will always ensure her misery enough', her shyness which prevents her 'ever doing justice to herself' ('there cannot be a more gentle, affectionate heart, or more obliging manners, when acting without restraint'), her lack of accomplishments but love of books, and her Principles that Mrs Vernon surprisingly (considering her mother and her upbringing) finds to be her strong point, she is in essentials Fanny Price. But Fanny also inherits Mrs Vernon's position as Reginald's devoted sister who has to hear and see all his ups and downs of feeling, all his doubts and self-deceptions, and who sets down her reflections and forebodings and anger at Lady Susan for her mother's benefit, just as Fanny's reactions to Edmund's similar confidences about Miss Crawford are set down for us. The passive girl in love, with a successful rival always before her, and the exasperated sister are fused in Fanny, who is at once witness and confidante, sister and lover; it is through her sensibility that we feel what passes between Edmund and Mary Crawford, and she inherits from Mrs Vernon 'the perpetual irritation of knowing his [Edmund's] heart'. To make plausible the sisterly part (which is constantly stressed), the background in time was contrived that accounts for the more than cousinly relation between Edmund and Fanny and the peculiar bond of feeling between them. It was necessary for the complicated purposes of this novel to root the Fanny–Edmund relation more deeply than the casual throwing together of Henry Tilney and Catherine Morland or of Reginald De Courcy and Frederica that produces an immediate attachment on the girl's side that can hardly be taken very seriously, so we have the history of Fanny's childhood – the only childhood and growth of a heroine in Jane Austen's work – to account for her unusual position in Edmund's life that combines Mrs

Vernon's interest and Frederica's. It is significant that the hero is saved from marrying the object of his infatuation in both stories, unlike life.

We can see again Jane Austen expanding and enriching her draft by working in material from her early writings and her correspondence. Frederica was, in *Lady Susan*, a victim, abused by her mother; she attracts an earlier victim, the Maria Williams who wrote Letter the Third in 'A Collection of Letters' in the second MS volume, which I described in the previous article. The down-trodden Maria Williams with her poor home combines with Frederica to produce Fanny Price,[13] bringing with her, to do the victimizing, the bullying and nagging aspects of Lady Greville; we have in *Mansfield Park* not only Mrs Norris but the very carriage incident from that early Letter, rooted into the new work as I have shown. Fanny demands our sympathy not only on the grounds that Frederica did but also as being in the situation of Maria Williams.

For Lady Susan was not available as a dragon. The girl of twenty or so who drafted the domestic drama into the crude story in letters had given place to a woman of six and thirty with conscious artistic powers. She was aiming at a record of that experience both truer and nearer to life, and we may see a return to the original source of the story in several important respects, notably in the figure of Mary Crawford, both a more usual and a more subtle character than Lady Susan.[14] In accordance with a tendency we have noticed before in Jane Austen when rewriting, Lady Susan is split up into two characters. The deliberate vice in her character is transferred to Mary's brother – his past career is hinted like hers, with its satisfaction in going about breaking hearts – 'the freaks of a cold-blooded vanity', used of Henry Crawford's conduct, is actually a perfect description of Lady Susan's occupations as we are shown them. Her powers of intrigue and ability to play a part are made over to Henry, while the description of the polished and insinuating Manwaring supplies his personality, combined with Henry Austen's temperament. But the function of Lady Susan, to beguile the hero and torment him, is made over to another version of Eliza de Feuillide and one both more sympathetic and more in keeping with history. From start to finish the courses of Mary Crawford and 'the captivating Lady Susan' are alike in their relation to the hero,[15] except that Mary Crawford is blameless. Edmund is not the dupe of Miss Crawford in the sense that Reginald was the dupe of Lady Susan. Edmund – much more subtly presented – is the dupe only of his own wishes, and though like Reginald he refuses to see what is before him it is not because he has a clever hypocrite to blind him. 'She is clever and agreeable, has all that knowledge of the world which makes conversation easy, and talks very well, with a happy command of language, which is too often used I believe to make Black appear White.' So might Fanny have written to her brother of Miss Crawford, for whom she has the same distrust from the start that Mrs Vernon had for Lady Susan, but it is actually Mrs Vernon's description when writing to her brother of her sister-in-law. Like Reginald, Edmund starts by suspicion and disapproval, but he is won over against his judgment to find himself in the same uneasy position of having to justify a prepossession of which he is ashamed by sophistry: 'But against reason, against conviction, to be so well pleased with her as I am sure he is, does really astonish me...when he has mentioned her of late, it has been in terms of more extraordinary praise, and yesterday he actually said, that he could not be surprised at any effect produced on the heart of Man by such loveliness and such abilities; and when I lamented in reply the badness of her disposition, he observed that whatever might have been her errors, they were to be imputed to her neglected education and that altogether she was a wonderful woman. This tendency to excuse her conduct, or to forget it in the warmth of admiration vexes me...' Thus Mrs Vernon lamented, but so might Fanny have done, and in similar terms she does actually feel and protest to Edmund. We are given identical glimpses of Fanny's feelings: 'But he was deceived in her; he gave her merits which she had not; her faults were what they had ever been, but he saw them no longer. Till she had shed many tears over this deception Fanny could not subdue her agitation...'

Reginald follows Lady Susan to London, as Edmund goes there after Mary, whereupon his sister writes to their mother: 'The probability of their marrying is surely heightened. He is more securely hers than ever...I have done with Lamentation. I look upon the Event as so far decided, that I resign myself to it in despair. If he leaves you soon for London, everything will be concluded.' Fanny reflects: '...the more deeply she recollected and observed, the more deeply was she convinced that everything was now in a fairer train for Miss Crawford's marrying Edmund than it had ever been before. – On his side, the inclination was stronger, on hers less equivocal. His objections, the scruples of his integrity, seemed all done away with – nobody could tell how...It could only be imputed to increasing attachment...He was to go to town...he talked of going, he loved to talk of it; and when once with her again, Fanny could not doubt the rest. – Her acceptance must be as certain as his offer; and yet there were feelings still remaining which made the prospect of it most sorrowful to her, independently – she believed independently, of self.' There are many such close parallels, and it is hardly necessary to point out that the changes show an increased psychological interest on the author's part, both the desire and the ability to probe deeper into feelings and motives and the reasonings of the heart.

A similar change is shown in the *dénouement*. Lady Susan is found out by a clumsy accident which depends on an unlikely combination of circumstances. Edmund is undeceived about Mary by the logical working out of the drama. It is Mary's brother who is guilty like Lady Susan, but in Edmund's eyes Mary is involved almost equally when he discovers she shares her brother's moral outlook; Edmund feels about the revelation of her character as Reginald did on finding out *his* mistress's, there is the same sense of 'seeing through' a beloved object and the same shame at having been taken in. Reginald writes to Lady Susan: 'The spell is removed. I see you as you are.' Edmund says: 'But the charm is broken. My eyes are opened.' Reginald wrote: '...the most mortifying conviction of the Imposition I have been under and the absolute necessity of an immediate and eternal separation'. Edmund said: '...most grievously convinced me that I had never understood her before, and that, as far as related to mind, it had been a creature of my own imagination, not Miss Crawford, that I had been too apt to dwell on for many months past...How have I been deceived!' Both ladies reply with levity and contemptuous resentment instead of contrition. Mary had actually thought Edmund worth marrying only when his elder brother seemed likely to die; Lady Susan had only thought Reginald worth marrying if his father should die quickly. It has been objected that a quick-witted woman like Mary Crawford would not in writing to Fanny expose her desire that Tom should die so that

Edmund will be eligible enough for her, but she does so because Lady Susan had debated in letters with *her* confidante whether Reginald's father's death would decide her to marry the heir.

It is hardly necessary to show that Reginald became Edmund alike in situation and character. Reginald was already the ingenuous (and therefore easily imposed-on) youth required as the siren's victim, and in order to provide the moral drama he has to have a make-up antithetic to hers. Lady Susan writes to her friend of him: 'There is a sort of ridiculous delicacy about him which requires the fullest explanation of whatever he may have heard to my disadvantage, and is never satisfied till he thinks he has ascertained the beginning and end of everything.' She writes with contempt of 'the inquisitive and doubting Fancies of that Heart which always seems debating on the reasonableness of its Emotions', and with irritation of his 'spirit...resulting from a fancied sense of superior Integrity'. She has had, she writes, to 'subdue him entirely by sentiment and serious conversation, and made him I may venture to say at least half in Love with me, without the semblance of the most commonplace flirtation'.[16] He is, she complains, 'comparatively deficient in the power of saying those delightful things which put one in good humour with oneself and the world'.[17] Edmund develops out of Reginald by the addition of the ordination theme, which will be mentioned later, but where did Reginald come from? If Mary Crawford was Eliza he ought to have been Henry Austen, but what we know of the volatile Henry, the brilliant talker, the lively wit, the man of the world of the family, corresponds with the favourable aspects of Henry Crawford (the name is again a clue here),[18] and no one who reads Jane's letter about her brother on losing his wife Eliza ('Upon the whole his spirits are very much recovered. If I may so express myself his mind is not a mind for affliction; he is too busy, too active, too sanguine')[19] can suppose him the original in any respect of Reginald–Edmund. Edmund, it is relevant to remark, has given universal dissatisfaction: he belongs to the least interesting of Jane Austen's classes of character, to which I have referred before. He is not, like Mr Knightley or William Price, probably studied from life and certainly offered as a lifelike person, nor is he, like Mr Collins or Mr Woodhouse, a vehicle constructed for conveying satiric humour or allied effects, but like Darcy he is derived from literature. A novel now unhappily almost unreadable but which from its publication in 1796 made an abiding impression on our author and is constantly alluded to directly or indirectly in her correspondence and fictions – I refer of course to Fanny Burney's *Camilla* – had appeared shortly before *Lady Susan* was, according to my theory, being precipitated from that family drama witnessed by our author to whom it was equally pregnant and painful. If Eliza had to be altered almost out of recognition before it could be safe to use her, it was at least as necessary to make her opposite number plainly *not* Henry. Edgar Mandlebert is the excessively fastidious hero, all delicacy and honour, who makes Fanny Burney's novel so tiresome, but in *Camilla* his speciality takes the form of doubts and hesitations as to whether the heroine is the superior being who alone will satisfy him; so high-minded is he that he drags the book out to five volumes. He is described in these terms to the unfortunate Camilla: 'Mandlebert is a creature whose whole composition is a pile of accumulated punctilios. He will spend his life refining away his own happiness.' The psychology of Edgar undoubtedly impressed Jane Austen, and there he was to hand when a similar kind of hero was needed for the disguised story of cousin Eliza's amours, but he remains quite unrealized and, like Fanny, is composed of conventional attributes. Edgar was spiritually curatic enough to serve even for the ordained Edmund in the revised version. Frederica's unaccountable Principles are also seen by the reader of *Camilla* to have their unmistakable origin in the argument of that novel, a moral lesson which in the more congenial atmosphere of the serious-minded *Mansfield Park* spread over large portions of the book. Thus the principled Fanny is made in the Burney manner to contrast with her female cousins whose education has lacked Principle (brought home to the responsible parent Sir Thomas at the end), and the neglect to instil Principles in females when young inevitably leads to elopements, guilt and misery, as all readers of later eighteenth-century fiction well know.[20] In *Mansfield Park* the idea of 'principles' fills the place that 'candour' had taken in the construction of *Sense and Sensibility* and *Pride and Prejudice* (though in the latter Principle had played a minor part also, with Lydia Bennet illustrating the same moral as Maria and Julia Bertram). The theory of 'principle', ineffectively dragged into *Lady Susan*, is developed from those notes with considerable subtlety. For instance, Sir Thomas and

Mary Crawford are both worldly, but whereas Mary lacks principles Sir Thomas abounds in them, so he is shown to be a good (if erring) man in spite of his worldliness, whereas she is reprehensible in spite of her attractive qualities. Now in *Lady Susan* Sir Reginald De Courcy, as seen in his solitary letter to his son, was preposterously *un*worldly as well as good ('To the Fortune of your wife, the goodness of my own, will make me indifferent' etc.). The clear-cut good-or-bad distinction on which the characters of the immature early story are divided is such a crude reduction of life that even there the author cannot take it seriously (hence the fun poked at the Vernons, all the brains allotted to the bad side and diffused scorn directed at the good people). Sir Thomas differs from Sir Reginald not only in being more plausible but in being a really subtle, sustained study of a type, the upright worldly man, whereas his original belongs to the too-good-to-be-true world of the conventional moral novel of the age. Just as instead of the unblenching villainess Lady Susan, exhibiting cold-blooded malignity, we have Mary Crawford's complex character always trembling in the balance. The theory of Principle is even more present, but it gives us this time, instead of a précis of a melodrama, an involved psychological study we must take with respect.

But we can observe some confusion here. Mansfield, according to one theme, as I have shown, was to stand for right feeling, as opposed to London; this is quite clear in *Lady Susan*, and remains so for the Crawfords (Henry learns a moral lesson at Mansfield from contemplating William and Fanny, as Mary does from associating with Sir Thomas, Edmund and Fanny, and her own sister, Mrs Grant). But Maria and Julia confuse the contrasted values. They ought to belong to the London set, who are heartless, unprincipled and end badly, instead of being Mansfield products. The fact is, they compose another strand of the novel, and one derived from quite another source. They come from an early piece of Jane's fiction, absorbed into *Mansfield Park* in the way we have seen her amalgamating extraneous matter in her other novels. In 'Lesley Castle', in *Volume the Second*, the principal characters are a vain, worldly, 'dissipated' Susan, who marries Sir George Lesley, and her almost equally unpleasant step-daughters, Margaret and Matilda, who, however, are country-bred girls just enjoying their first taste of London society. No doubt our Lady Susan was derived in name from the earlier one, connected as they were by the worldliness and ill feeling common to them both, and both being, by description, extravagant and dissipated. By means of this link already existing, when the author was looking for more characters to fill out the new story *Mansfield Park* in 1808, the conceited Lesley step-daughters, with their mutual jealousy, would easily suggest themselves for the two sisters needed to work in with the Lady Susan, i.e. Crawford, part of the plot, bringing with them their rivalry in love and their delight in escaping from the country into Society. The Lesley sisters were tall, fine young women, in contrast to their 'lively', 'pretty little Mother-in-law', the contrast being a source of spite on both sides, and here we have the origin of one of the characteristic bits of caustic insight into human nature of our author, even though it is gratuitous in *Mansfield Park*. It was too good a shaft to waste:

Miss Crawford's beauty did her no disservice with the Miss Bertrams. They were too handsome themselves to dislike any woman for being so too, and were almost as much charmed as their brothers, with her lively dark eyes, clear brown complexion, and general prettiness. Had she been tall, full formed, and fair, it might have been more of a trial; but as it was, there could be no comparison, and she was most allowably a sweet pretty girl, while they were the finest young women in the country.

There has been a slight improvement (to judge by the first two sentences) in the author's opinion of feminine nature since 'Lesley Castle' was written.

To expand the simple and consistent *Lady Susan* into a complex novel entailed the sacrifice of consistency in several other important respects. We have seen that the original function of Mansfield was in the end supported only by Fanny, Edmund and Sir Thomas, all of whom were represented in the original draft, *Lady Susan*. But even Sir Thomas has been refined into a study on his own, and his realistic character is partly at variance with his theoretical function. As we have also seen, the Bertram sisters, like Mrs Norris, come from different sources. While Mrs Norris, who is offered only in her original form, remains outside the drama, the Misses Bertram are welded into it, yet don't fit in with the original moral argument. They illustrate another of a conflicting and quite conventional kind. That it is conventional and not, like the story of Mary

Crawford, deeply realized by the author, is shown by the relief with which she abandons it when she has done her duty by it; hence the much debated opening of the conclusion – 'Let other pens *dwell* on guilt and misery' etc. There is still another inhabitant of *Mansfield Park* who has even less to do with 'heart', and we may well ask how she got there: Lady Bertram.

I am afraid she comes under the head only of self-indulgence on Miss Austen's part, though she has probably given more pleasure to the reader than any other of the Austen 'characters' except Mr Woodhouse. *Susan*, the earlier form of a novel which became *Catherine* when revised for publication in 1816–17 (we know it as *Northanger Abbey*) had been refused publication and the author seems by the time of the 1811–13 revision of *Mansfield Park* to have given up hope of ever bringing out so dated a tale as an anti-Gothick burlesque. Mrs Allen, the anti-chaperone, who had been conceived in the burlesque spirit for Catherine's anti-romantic début was 'much too good to be lost', as her creator writes of another episode, and she could be used in relation to Fanny much as Mrs Allen had been used with Catherine. Hence the recurrence of pieces of the same kind as those in *Northanger Abbey* which illustrate Mrs Allen's concentration on her own dress and well-being, her moral and mental apathy, her omission to guard her ward's manners and conduct and to give moral advice. Everybody recollects the episode of sending Chapman too late to dress Fanny for the ball, but the reason for the following has perhaps been less evident:

'No, my dear, I should not think of missing you, when such an offer as this comes your way. I could do very well without you, if you were married to a man of such good estate as Mr Crawford. And you must be aware, Fanny, that it is every young woman's duty to accept such a very unexceptionable offer as this.'

This was almost the only rule of conduct, the only piece of advice which Fanny had ever received from her aunt in the course of eight years and a half.

This use of a character conceived in burlesque terms suggested, I believe, relating her with a typical Austen joke. In 1791 Mrs Inchbald's[21] immensely popular novel, *A Simple Story*, appeared; there had been four editions by 1799, and a family of shameless novel-readers[22] like the Steventon household would hardly have failed to get hold of it. It is, moreover, in the first half at any rate, one of the outstanding pieces of fiction of the later eighteenth century, remarkably well written and unusually subtle in its analysis of feelings, and built round a lively and witty heroine who might have suggested some hints for Elizabeth Bennet (and like *Pride and Prejudice* it is wholly dramatic in form – Mrs Inchbald had been an actress). Unfortunately Mrs Inchbald felt obliged to support morality by tacking on two final volumes which show the heroine justly punished for her lack of 'A PROPER EDUCATION' (the moral tag with which the story closes). Volume three opens with her flight from her home and child, briefly accounted for in these preposterous terms – that her husband, Lord Elmwood, after a few years of perfect matrimonial happiness, had to leave her 'in order to rescue from the depredation of his own steward, his very large estates in the West Indies. His voyage was tedious; his residence there, from various accidents, prolonged from time to time.' In consequence, Lady Elmwood became dissipated: 'at first only unhappy...she flew from the present tedious solitude to the dangerous society of one who', etc. The absurdity of this device to secure a moral was exactly in the Austen taste – there is much humour about similar absurdities in fiction in the *Letters* and the MS volumes. It may have been at first an independent joke, but for the reconstruction of *Mansfield Park* it was obviously useful to send Sir Thomas, like Lord Elmwood, on a prolonged voyage to the West Indies in order to have him out of the way of the young people, and the joke of the already apathetic Lady Bertram's extreme insensibility to his absence could be worked in as well. Thus it is referred to repeatedly, but well rubbed in on the occasion when Edmund remonstrates with Tom about the theatrical project:

'...And as to my father's being absent, it is so far from an objection, that I consider it rather as a motive; for the expectation of his return must be a very anxious period to my mother, and if we can be the means of amusing that anxiety, and keeping up her spirits for the next few weeks, I shall think our time very well spent, and so I am sure will he. – It is a *very* anxious period for her.'

As he said this, each looked towards their mother. Lady Bertram sunk back in one corner of the sofa, the picture of health, wealth, ease and tranquillity, was just falling into a gentle doze, while Fanny was getting through the few difficulties of her work for her.

Edmund smiled and shook his head.

'By Jove! this won't do' – cried Tom, throwing himself into a chair with a hearty laugh. 'To be sure, my dear mother, your anxiety – I was unlucky there.'

Lady Bertram, in fact, serves as a hold-all for burlesque purposes. Her epistolary style is another self-indulgence of the author, inserted first, perhaps, in the version of *Mansfield Park* in letters of 1808–9. The whole passage (in ch. 13 of vol. III) strikes a different note from all that precedes it and all that follows; it is in the same unfeeling tone as the spiteful descriptions of Mrs Allen and of Lady Middleton and of much in the early writings (for instance, it implies that the dangerous illness of her eldest son was a source of pleasure to his mother because it 'was of a nature to promise occupation for the pen for many days to come'). It is only an opportunity to work in a satiric account of conventional letter-writing, and belongs with the early satiric letters, whence no doubt it was taken.

> ...Lady Bertram rather shone in the epistolary line, having early in her marriage, from the want of other employment, and the circum-stance of Sir Thomas's being in Parliament, got into the way of making and keeping correspondents, and formed for herself a very creditable, commonplace, amplifying style, so that a very little matter was enough for her...

serves as a pretext for inserting a number of pieces in the style described. But the thinness of the device is exposed by the inconsistency it imposes on the character: no one can imagine the Lady Bertram described in every other part of the book taking the trouble to write such letters, when she requires a niece to manage her 'work' and write her notes for her and a son or husband to direct and seal her letters. It is not greater than the impossibility of a Sir Thomas ever marrying such a woman, but that glaring improbability is due to the author's self-indulgence in replacing the worthy and sensible Lady De Courcy by a burlesque character. Other expansions from the original *Lady Susan* can be accounted for in other ways with equal satisfaction to the critic, I think. Thus a stiffening of incident from real life was used, as in *Emma*: William Price has long been admitted by the Austen family to have been drawn from one of the sailor brothers in his youth, while Fanny's amber cross derives from the topaz cross and gold chain Charles bought for each of his sisters in 1801 with his prize-money – deprived of the chain for dramatic purposes naturally, but why converted from topaz to amber unless in accordance with a habit of altering on principle whatever she took from life for use in her work? A similar use of relevant copy which had some place in the author's emotional history is the linking up of Maria's elopement with that of an actual acquaintance. Maria's misconduct had originally, as we have seen, been introduced to illustrate a conventional moral theory, and would have been as insubstantial or remote from the author as Lydia's or Mrs Brandon's or Eliza Williams's 'fall' evidently was – there is no personal feeling betrayed in their case. But in June 1808 an acquaintance, Mrs Powlett, eloped with a peer, and Jane wrote to Cassandra: 'This is a sad story about Mrs Powlett. I should not have suspected such a thing. – She staid the Sacrament, I remember, the last time that you and I did. – A hint of it, with Initials, was in yesterday's *Courier*.' The mixture of shock and disgust at a near acquaintance outraging one's moral code is a not unusual phenomenon in those who can accept violation in theory with equanimity or even amusement. The unpleasant feeling attached to Jane Austen's handling of the episode of Mrs Rushworth's infidelity, which has been so often adversely commented on, has its origin, I think, in her reaction to Mrs Powlett's history (occurring in 1808, it must have been a very recent shock), just as the account of the elopement read out by Mr Price to Fanny is based on the 'hint of it, with Initials, was in yesterday's *Courier*'.

Sotherton, I believe, was suggested by the visit Jane and her mother paid to the old mansion of Stoneleigh in 1806, when it descended to Mrs Austen's relatives. We notice that in the case of other great houses Jane thinks it sufficient to describe the mansion as handsome, modern, and well placed, having no particular seat in mind for Pemberley or Rosings or Mansfield Park or whatever it is, and these being the qualities she admired in a house, with her thoroughly pre-Romantic taste. But there is a whole background to Sotherton. Now there is a letter extant from Mrs Austen while at Stoneleigh during this visit which describes just such a mansion and way of life as that described for Sotherton. We have no knowledge of any such basis for the Portsmouth household, but we may safely conclude that like the Watson household and the Bateses' home it is an exaggeration of the element in the author's surroundings that, as we see in her letters, irritated and depressed her at times, a nervous outlet for a life of trivial preoccupations due to narrow means contrasted, as Portsmouth was contrasted by Fanny with Mansfield, with the ideal life of elegant propriety based on ample means which, through the *Letters*, we see her pathetically savouring at Godmersham and other such places.

The use of *Lovers' Vows* in the first volume is equally characteristic of her method of working. She uses it as a reference that the reader could be expected to follow, just as she elsewhere uses *Evelina*, *Cecilia*, *The Romance of the Forest* and *Udolpho*, and probably other contemporary writings. As Mr Reitzel says: 'Jane Austen was intent, as she composed this section of her novel, on a fulness of meaning that is no longer entirely understood.'[23] *Lovers' Vows* in fact, as Mr Reitzel demonstrates, was very well known at the beginning of the century, even performed a number of times at Bath while the Austens lived there, and had aroused hostile criticism by its 'advanced' Romantic morality. The subject was sufficiently in the air to suit her purpose, which was for personal reasons a narrowly moralistic one. The play, moreover, gave her an opportunity to justify her personal disapproval of amateur theatricals – it would occasion undesirable situations among the performers, such as acting love-making, which in her own family had led to Henry's engagement, and enough dubious matter both to expose Mary Crawford as lacking delicacy in being willing to act the part of Amelia and to justify that censure by Sir Thomas and Edmund of private play-acting which it is one of the author's purposes to proclaim. It is certainly as a hit at the new morality that we are to take Sir Thomas's 'That I should be cautious and quick-sighted, and feel many scruples which my children do *not* feel, is perfectly natural'. The theatricals got into *Mansfield Park* owing to the performances at Steventon, as Mr Hubback describes them. It is interesting that they are not even sketched in *Lady Susan* though apparently an important part of the total situation which inspired that story. Raking up the whole episode in 1808, when *Lady Susan* was first expanded, offered the now mature artist the opportunity to use material such as this which had before been beyond her scope. *Lovers' Vows* was handy and something more: like other literary pieces she had used in her previous novels, it provided a hint for pattern as well as a source of reference, though the reader can understand the novel quite well enough without a knowledge of *Lovers' Vows*, just as *Pride and Prejudice* can be enjoyed without a knowledge of *Cecilia*, though not perhaps fully understood in either case.

All these varieties of fresh material have not successfully been fused with the old story, as we have seen, but *Mansfield Park* represents a much more ambitious undertaking than anything before, and shows new technical devices, a new kind of seriousness, and an attempt at a more sensitive, if less immediately successful, style of writing. We may explain this sudden access of ambition and confidence as an artist. By 1808 she had drafted five novels, and in the following year she was able to rewrite *Sense and Sensibility* for publication, which met with more success than she had expected. From then till the end her life was taken up with the overlapping production of novels for the press. A sense of power as a writer must have possessed her at this period, and a sense also that her real life lay in the past – like her sister, she had lost her lover by death, she had deliberately rejected a conspicuously eligible offer in the following year, and had now long passed the age of twenty-seven, an age that in her novels is taken as marking a period, as she would say.

She had lost her father and her early home and some of her closest friends. It is not surprising that the revision of *Lady Susan* at this date should produce a revival of painful memories and poignant feelings. But she again put the story aside, and returned for the third time to *Sense and Sensibility*, then to rewriting *Pride and Prejudice*, after which she devoted more time to turning the epistolary *Mansfield Park* into the narrative we know.

IIb

Lady Susan into Mansfield Park (ii)

What kind of change did she make beside that of form, that will account for the length of time she is said to have spent on the third version of this episode in Eliza's history? I have hitherto investigated the elements of character, plot and setting that went to constitute *Mansfield Park*. We must now examine it for evidence of another kind. When *Pride and Prejudice* appeared she wrote of it to her sister:

The work is rather too light, and bright, and sparkling; it wants shade; it wants to be stretched out here and there with a long chapter of sense, if it could be had...

The letter then goes off into characteristic humour, at the expense of the idea she has started, which need not prevent our seeing a serious self-criticism intended and no doubt long since made. For the week before (29 January 1813) she had written to her sister: 'Now I will try and write of something else; and it shall be a complete change of subject – ordination.' Since *Mansfield Park* was entirely finished by the summer of the same year, according to the received account, she had been at this final revision for two years (though it is evident that *Pride and Prejudice*, which was substantially rewritten between 1811 and 1812, must have made a hole in the first of these years at least). Yet mention of the subject in this way suggests that she must be breaking to Cassandra the fact of *Mansfield Park*'s existence. With its treatment of an old family sore and its new serious tone and theme she perhaps feared it would be a shock to her sister as well as to admirers of *Pride and Prejudice*. (Actually, *Mansfield Park*, owing to its high moral tone, was more popular than its predecessor, even in her own circle – though not with her brothers.) But in this same letter she is enquiring of Cassandra 'whether Northamptonshire is a country of hedgerow'. Mansfield is in Northamptonshire, and, according to tradition, she intended to employ in this novel a scene such as (with her thrifty habits) she used up later (Northamptonshire apparently not being a country, like her native Hampshire, of double hedgerows) in *Persuasion*. There Anne overhears the pregnant conversation between Captain Wentworth and Louisa in the hedge; Fanny was probably to overhear Edmund and Miss Crawford by means of the convenient hedgerow, instead of the less dramatic manner in which she gains all her knowledge of Edmund's progress in Miss Crawford's esteem. But what is interesting in this is that in January 1813 the novel was still apparently in a fluid state.[24] May we not conjecture that it was merely being turned over in her mind while *Pride and Prejudice* was on the stocks, and at last rewritten from the epistolary version only in the spring and summer of 1813? I think we can find more evidence to this effect. Henry's wife Eliza, formerly the Comtesse de Feuillide, died in April 1813. The Austen-Leighs say: 'She had suffered from a long and painful illness, and the end was "a release at last".' The knowledge that Eliza was dying – Jane herself writes of 'her long and dreadful illness' – would revive all those earlier feelings about her disposition and conduct which make Mary Crawford at once so subtle and realistic a study and yet so loaded with the author's animus. And her death would make it permissible to publish such a novel, Henry not having any inconvenient delicacy and no other member of the family being recognizably in the text except the flattering portrait of Charles as William Price. The solemn circumstances of Eliza's wretched end, contrasting so markedly with the memory of her coquettish youth, must have helped to weigh down the treatment on the side of solemn moral and horror of worldliness, associating well with the artist's sense that *Pride and Prejudice* was a kind of success she would not care to repeat. I think the haste with which the novel must have been put together, assuming my theory that it was in effect 'written' in the spring and summer of 1813, accounts for the disparities in style and tone and treatment mentioned at the beginning of this article. She had no time to assimilate all the elements we have noticed, as she had had in the novel which had just left her hands and was to have in the next; we may see the same kind of thing in *Persuasion*, where the business of Mrs Smith, so clumsily patched on, of Mrs Clay's unconvincing intrigue with Mr Elliot, and the episode of Dick Musgrove which sticks out so unpleasantly (it came from the life, if I have interpreted the *Letters* correctly) had not the chance, owing to her premature death, of getting worked in smoothly.

For I think it evident that the epistolary version of 1808–9 differed very considerably from *Mansfield Park* as we know it. If the ordination theme was a final addition, then Dr Grant was too, for he is there to show what a priest ought not to be, in contrast with Edmund; and Tom's profligate debts and similar episodes must have been patched on at the same time. The discussions with Henry Crawford and Mary that Edmund has at different times on ordination, the conduct of church services, etc. could more easily have been written in, and Mary's original hesitations about accepting Edmund may have been due only to his not being the heir (as in *Lady Susan*). We may remark that all these conversations are dramatic, and what could hardly have been managed in letters. And the moral tone is equally seen to have been 'written in'. What is the natural, the instinctive tone, of the author? Is it not that felt in such passages as these?

I believe there is scarcely a young lady in the united kingdoms who would not rather put up with the misfortune of being sought by a clever agreeable man, than to have him driven away by the vulgarity of her nearest relations.

She could not, though only eighteen, suppose Mr Crawford's attachment would hold out for ever; she could not but imagine that steady, unceasing discouragement from herself would put an end to it in time. How much time she might, in her own fancy, allot for its dominion, is another concern. It would not be fair to enquire into a young lady's exact estimate of her own perfections.

Sir Thomas was most cordially anxious for the perfection of Mr Crawford's character in that point. He wished him to be a model of constancy; and fancied the best means of effecting it would be by not trying him too long.

I purposely abstain from dates on this occasion, that every one may be at liberty to fix their own, aware that the cure of unconquerable passions, and the transfer of unchanging attachments, must vary much as to time in different people. – I only intreat every body to believe that exactly at the time when it was quite natural that it should be so, and not a week earlier, Edmund did cease to care about Miss Crawford, and became as anxious to marry Fanny, as Fanny herself could desire.

This is recognizably a similar tone, with its combination of acid amusement and cynical estimate of motive, to that of *Sense and Sensibility* and all the work up to and including *Pride and Prejudice* – we think at once of the picture of the united Ferrars family at the end of the last sentence of the same novel, of Edward's coming to Barton Cottage to propose to Elinor:

... it is to be supposed, in spite of the jealousy with which he had once thought of Colonel Brandon, in spite of the modesty with which he rated his own deserts, and the politeness with which he talked of his doubts, he did not, upon the whole, expect a very cruel reception. It was his business, however, to say that he *did*, and he said it very prettily. What he might say on the subject a twelvemonth after must be referred to the imagination of husbands and wives.

And in fact the last quotation I have made above from *Mansfield Park* is in the whole tone of *Lady Susan* and particularly in that of the passage of which it is an echo:

Frederica was therefore fixed in the family of her Uncle and Aunt, till such time as Reginald De Courcy could be talked, flattered and finessed into an affection for her – , which, allowing leisure for the conquest of his attachment to her Mother, for his abjuring all future attachments and detesting the Sex, might be reasonably looked for in the course of a Twelvemonth. Three months might have done it in general, but Reginald's feelings were no less lasting than lively.

It is from *Lady Susan* that the early habit of not taking too seriously the puppets' feelings is carried over into *Mansfield Park*. But there is a new habit of taking them very seriously indeed, at their own valuation, or rather with the conventional attitude to them, and the more subtle kind of irony in the book is bound up with this new attitude, occurring as a relief from it, slipping in in spite of the author.

For the tone of the new *Mansfield Park* that belongs with the moralizing about the worldliness and lack of principle, is not to be found in *Sense and Sensibility* or *Pride and Prejudice* or any of the earlier stories or fragmentary writings, or in the letters that survive. I mean the passages of this kind:

In their very last conversation, Miss Crawford...had still been Miss Crawford, still shewn a mind led astray and bewildering, and without any suspicion of being so; darkened, yet fancying itself light.

...the purity of her principles added yet a keener solicitude, when she considered how little useful, how little self-denying, his life had (apparently) been.

There are many such. We may compare Anne Elliot meditating on Mr Elliot's past life: 'How could it ever be ascertained that his mind was truly cleansed?' This is the language of a religious change of heart, and conflicts strikingly with the tone and implications of the delicate cynicism of

In this world, the penalty is less equal than could be wished; but without presuming to look forward to a juster appointment hereafter, we may fairly consider a man of sense like Henry Crawford, to be providing for himself no small portion of vexation and regret...

Such deeply felt passages contrast just as strongly with the perfunctory attention given to the conventional moral, as instanced by the famous 'Let other pens dwell on guilt and misery.' Now when did this change in the author occur? It was after the 1808–9 version of *Mansfield Park* had been made, because in 1809 there is a letter to her sister declaring she knows she will not like Hannah More's improving new novel, *Cœlebs in Search of a Wife*, that her disinclination for it which, before Cassandra's description, was affected is now real: 'I do not like the Evangelicals.' But in 1814 in the letter to Fanny Knight concerning the suitor her niece cannot make up her mind about, she defends him against Fanny's objection of his intolerable religious earnestness, saying: 'I am by no means convinced that we ought not all to be evangelicals, and am at least persuaded that they who are so from reason and feeling must be happiest and safest.' The choice of ordination as a theme, then, may be taken as indicating a conscious change about 1813. (There are unfortunately no letters of 1812.) *Pride and Prejudice* is a pagan work, so to speak, with its ridicule of Mr Collins's advice about the proper attitude towards the erring Lydia; I don't know how many readers notice that Sir Thomas actually adopts the Christian attitude to his fallen daughter that Mr Bennet rejected for himself, and that this time the author evidently thinks it the right one. This upset to the author's poise (associated no doubt with the subject of Eliza which goes back into her own youth) and which has shaken the sound moral taste she had hitherto possessed, is visible only in *Mansfield Park*. In *Emma*, a year later, we see her at the climax of her art and in the completest possible state of control over her writing. The collapse of control at times in *Mansfield Park* is unprecedented in her literary career.

A deeply religious outlook, even if concealed (and, with such a family code of unfailing jesting to live up to, her tendency would be to conceal it from her coevals as far as possible), would account for the castigation of worldliness in the novel, not only of the reprehensible kind but of varieties which in her previous novels she approves as worldly prudence. Though the noble match Sir James is pressed on Frederica by her mother, yet that is not part of the theme of *Lady Susan*, though an antithesis between heartless ambition and artless affection is just indicated in the early story, for future use no doubt. But prudential marriage (made by Maria with disastrous results, discussed by Mary Crawford with illustrations from her London set, advocated for Fanny by everyone, and finally renounced by Sir Thomas for his son, with dust and ashes self-heaped on that worldly head) is decidedly part of the main theme of *Mansfield Park*. The most striking and technically remarkable part of the novel is that telling of Maria's engagement and wedding, something unprecedented in Jane Austen's art as a sustained effect. These are reported with the detachment of a looker-on, with a skilfully implied disgust at such a heartless mockery of courtship and marriage. But if these effects are sincerely achieved, there are others that ring dubiously. Everyone remembers the hollow moralizings of Fanny and Edmund. And for the first time in her writings Victorianism makes its appearance. The kind of thing I mean is what comes to a head in Edmund's horror at Mary's indelicacy: 'Guess what I must have felt. To hear the woman whom – no harsher name than folly given – So voluntarily, so freely, so coolly to canvass it! No reluctance, no horror, no feminine – shall I say? no modest loathings!' This is quite unaccountable to the reader of the *Letters*, where there are certainly no modest loathings.[25] There is an element of self-flagellation here. Loathing of one's former self may quite sincerely be overdone in the first heat of reaction; I do not think we need accuse Miss Austen of paying deliberate lip-service to the theory of feminine propriety. A very revealing instance of something related to this is the censure heaped on Mary Crawford for her freedom in speaking of her dissolute uncle and ill-tempered clerical brother-in-law. Mary's criticism is certainly justified, and harmless besides, yet we are told it denotes an improper way of thinking and speaking. But Mary merely exercises the same freedom in criticizing her relations as her creator manifests towards her own far less exceptionable relations in her correspondence. This attack on Mary seems to be due to a sense of guilt, and is inspired, I imagine, by a sense that it is that part of her earlier self which she had in common with her cousin Eliza. We know from her letters that Jane, too, flirted enthusiastically (it is a happy hit of Mr Forster's to have remarked that 'in the earlier letters Lydia Bennet is all-pervading'), talked lightly and joked censoriously. She displays impatience with her youth in the other novels prepared for the press about this time. The business of the theatricals is all in keeping with the theory I have advanced. Theatricals were not frowned on at Steventon as they were at Mansfield, the young Austens had their theatre in the barn; instead of Sir Thomas to ban there was Mrs Austen to encourage;[26] and *Lovers' Vows* was improper only on theoretical grounds, whereas *Bon Ton* and *High Life Below Stairs* and the farces in the Steventon repertoire were vulgar and possibly worse. Jane seems to have enjoyed the theatre without any qualms, if only with modified rapture, throughout her life. But amateur theatricals were connected for her with those that at Steventon culminated in her cousin's engagement to her brother. So her distaste for them is made out to be justified on moral grounds in the novel that embalms this early experience. She makes Tom's repentance include 'self-reproach arising from the deplorable event in Wimpole Street, to which he felt himself accessory by all the dangerous intimacy of his unjustifiable theatre', and Sir Thomas condemns the acting as an 'unsafe amusement'.[27]

The censure Mary Crawford comes in for is so much heavier than there is any occasion for, as matters stand in *Mansfield Park*. She stands in Fanny's way chiefly, and the author has identified her interest with Fanny's, but she stands there innocently. She has done nothing deliberate to attract Edmund, but her mere attractiveness somehow appears reprehensible. She does not make herself out to be other than she is – in fact she shocks him constantly by refusing to subscribe even by lip to his idealism and standards of propriety. Where Edmund is concerned she struggles between following the instincts of her heart and the promptings of ambition, and though it is no doubt reprehensible in her that the latter win, from Fanny's point of view this is all to the good. She is not, like Lady Susan, a siren, a hypocrite or a villainess of any kind, but she incurs about as much blame from the author. This is unjust morally and unsound enough artistically to strike the reader as a serious flaw. Why did not so acute a writer as Miss Austen notice this herself? The answer, as I have shown, is partly autobiographical and partly a matter of literary history. In rewriting any book it is hard to keep clear altogether of the spirit of the original: Lady Susan's culpability is carried over to her successor. Lady Susan, moreover, as Mrs Craven, was particularly culpable in her conduct towards her daughter, the original of Fanny, and though Miss Crawford has no obligation to Fanny the relation between them is the same mixture of fearfulness on the one side and cruelty (unconscious on Mary's part) on the other – there is a great deal of analysis, quite unnecessary to the plot, devoted to the nature of the intimacy between the two girls, something unknown to the English novel before and not paralleled anywhere else in this author's work. The subject must have deeply interested her. We may conjecture that Jane's attitude in her youth towards Eliza was the same mixture of personal fascination and moral repulsion that we find fixed in not merely Fanny's but also the author's attitude to Mary Crawford. The tone of Mary's ordinary conversation is seen to be something that the author cannot stomach. Though in the other novels the conversation of several characters is felt to be insufferably silly or vulgar or conceited or otherwise disagreeable, there is nothing that arouses the same sense of moral distaste as Mary Crawford's clever playfulness. Mary differs from Lady Susan in being something of the author herself as well as much that she was not. There is even a momentary defence put up for her wit, by Edmund, who is in love with her – 'The right of a lively mind, seizing whatever may contribute to its own amusement or that of others; perfectly allowable, when untinctured by ill humour or roughness.' This is certainly the defence the author of *Pride and Prejudice* would have advanced if her right to criticize had been questioned, and such a self-justification must have satisfied her up to the date of rewriting *Mansfield Park* for publication. Then, with so much else in herself, it came up for reconsideration.

This unnatural censure, to be found only in this novel, of Jane Austen's own standards of judgment, of her independence of outlook and her own instinctive values, is what the discerning reader finds intolerable. To deny his own light is the worst offence of which an artist can be guilty. But we can now understand how it came about. It was the delightful but not admirable cousin, the friend of her girlhood but now, after a phase as comtesse at Versailles, revealing a character less congenial, who was leading the favourite brother into a wholly unsuitable marriage. Therefore what she admired in that cousin must also be wrong, even when it was something they had in common. Everything that Mary says, however witty or intelligent, and everything that she does, however kind it may at first appear, is exposed as unfeeling, selfish or worse.[28] One recent critic[29] has complained that Jane Austen is 'incapable of appreciating such pleasant worldlings as Mary Crawford'. This is to accuse himself and not the author: she takes care that we shall have no excuse, if we read carefully and relate the scattered passages that are meant to be dovetailed, for finding the Crawfords pleasant. Lady Susan, in whom they first took shape, was an entirely unpleasant worldling; she has been toned down to match a setting of everyday life, that is all. We get a glimpse of the 'knowledge of the world' that Eliza de Feuillide brought to the rustics at Steventon, and which is so alien to the feeling and sentiment of Jane Austen's world, in Mary's speeches to Henry and Fanny about Henry's courtship:

'...I know you, I know that a wife you *loved* would be the happiest of women, and that even when you ceased to love, she would yet find in you the liberality and good-breeding of a gentleman.'

'But this I will say, that his fault, the liking to make girls a little in love with him, is not half so dangerous to a wife's happiness, as a tendency to fall in love himself, which he has never been addicted to. And I do seriously and truly believe that he is attached to you in a way that he never was to any woman before; that he loves you with all his heart, and will love you as nearly for ever as possible. If any man ever loved a woman for ever, I think Henry will do as much for you.'

This style of talking, reasonable as it is and based as it is on knowledge of one order of life, is distasteful to our novelist; we are made to feel that she considers it offensive and revealing a shallow nature. She loathes the society where such wisdom is current, but she is not content to make it seem odious, she must claim moral sanctions for her instinctive distaste. She must prove it to be wicked as well as cheap. We are instructed to regard the world of the Crawfords with horror, not merely dislike.

An assumption of the conventional outlook on morality and the sentimental commonplaces it carries with it too easily accompanies religious convictions and at that date perhaps was an inevitable accompaniment of them in a country lady. To this we may ascribe the passages where the acute observer of human nature, the shrewd analyst of motive, gives place to a Charlotte Yonge, for instance that piece, so sentimental and unrealistic, the moral explanation of Henry Crawford's falling in love with Fanny (ch. 12, vol. II). How it contrasts with the flashes of genuine psychological understanding elsewhere in the book. But the old Adam breaks out from time to time, as in the piece about cant at the end of ch. 13, vol. III, and the sly digs at the good Sir Thomas,[30] where we see the author rounding on herself in spite of herself. This accounts for some of the most subtle bits of irony, changes of moral direction or abysses of cynicism opening under the reader's feet, which are thoroughly disconcerting if the reader has not this account of the novel's evolution in his possession. The author sometimes takes a holiday from trying to persuade herself that she feels as she believes she ought to feel. She reverts to her unregenerate youth, with the example of *Lady Susan* before her, no doubt.

But she has sacrificed some of the advantages of the simple and consistent story with which she started. She has, of course, been led into inconsistencies of character – such as Henry

Crawford falling in love with Fanny because that, however improbably, is necessary to balance the Mary–Edmund affair and to complicate Fanny's sufferings. Mary is so involved with the author's emotional and moral life that she is only made possible by abandoning the letter form of novel: we are deprived thus of Mary's confidence, and if we are left to conjecture for the most part the springs of her impulses – 'she would try to be more ambitious than her heart would allow', for example – that suits the author; Mary does not have to be so consistent and logical as Lady Susan. But the author has sacrificed also a moral advantage; her hands in *Mansfield Park* are tied where in *Lady Susan* they were free, and in this respect the earlier story is more lively than the later novel. In the first version the virtuous people are presented from the devil's point of view, as well as from their own, and we are not meant to be shocked, as we are later with Edmund and Fanny; we are permitted to be exhilarated, for there is some truth in both accounts and we have a sort of wisdom offered us which in *Mansfield Park* is only allowed to flourish on the edges of the scene (as in the summing-up on Mr Rushworth). Vestiges of Lady Susan's refreshing outlook on the unco' good we have in Mary's levity, but it is allowed to play only upon the Admiral, Dr Grant, family prayers and such, and we are at once told by the author, speaking through Edmund, how to look upon even this mild irreverence. Mary is awed by Edmund's superiority as Lady Susan never is by the Vernons and De Courcys, and even Henry is never allowed to ridicule Edmund. But we see there is something to be said for Lady Susan's point of view – Mr Vernon is indeed foolishly credulous and the author herself has no patience with him nor much respect for Reginald; there is undeniably something in Lady Susan's ill-natured account of the interest Mrs Vernon has in Frederica:

She is in high favour with her Aunt altogether – because she is so little like myself of course. She is exactly the companion for Mrs Vernon, who dearly loves to be first, and to have all the sense and all the Conversation to herself; Frederica will never eclipse her.[31]

Now in *Mansfield Park* the hatches have been battened down on the insight of the lower nature. Fanny is specifically protected by the author as 'my Fanny'; the author is aware that such protection from criticism is necessary. Hence a certain uneasiness that one senses. Though *Lady Susan* was a remarkable feat, there is no sense of strain apparent in it anywhere. Lady Susan is the character in the story with the brains, and Jane Austen was not the woman to undervalue that distinction (Fanny has to be made out most unconvincingly to be Mary Crawford's 'mental superior' to enforce her claims as heroine). The earlier story had the advantage of reproducing real life in this respect, where the fascinating worldly cousin had the field to herself. All the reality remains with Mary Crawford; and Fanny, like Edmund, has no substance, the good cousins are only a stance for moral disapproval. Yet, as we have seen, in spite of Jane Austen's determination to sponsor the conventional moral outlook, wisdom, the report of experience, will not be smothered: it breaks out in ways calculated to defeat her intentions.

But to this very inconsistency we owe some of the most interesting portions of the later novel. The original theme of Mansfield (or Churchill) standing for 'heart', a simple one and not argued in the first book, merely assumed, is whittled down by the circumstances of the novel's evolution, as we have seen, until when the mature woman comes to consider it she cannot flourish it wholeheartedly as a banner, as she could in her youth. The Portsmouth episode corrects the theory by bringing it down to the touchstone of the practical test: what is valuable in Mansfield for Fanny turns out not to be 'heart' – strong instinctive feelings freely expressed – of which there is a crude superabundance in her Portsmouth home, but the virtues of civilized existence which, so Fanny discovers with Jane Austen's backing, are a preferable alternative even when 'heart' is mainly absent:

Yet she thought it would not have been so at Mansfield. No, in her uncle's house there would have been a consideration of times and seasons, a regulation of subject, a propriety, an attention towards everybody which there was not here...At Mansfield, no sounds of contention, no raised voice, no abrupt bursts, no tread of violence was ever heard; all proceeded in a regular course of cheerful orderliness; every body had their due importance; every body's feelings were consulted. If tenderness could ever be supposed wanting, good sense and good breeding supplied its place.

By the time *Mansfield Park* was rewritten, the author has to admit that either the original structure of the story was crude and unrealistic or that she herself has changed her outlook; she is too sincere an artist to allow it to stand, and, as in so many other respects, the later novel is a more subtle, illuminating experience for us, though so often also contradictory and confusing. We see that at this period the kind of life that was organized to run smoothly was what seemed to her the best. *Sense and Sensibility* had been made into a plea, two years before, for that 'candour' and 'address' without which society cannot function; the discussion between Edward, Elinor and Marianne on these lines, and the frequent admonitions to the reader to the same effect that stick out of the book, belong clearly to the final revision of *Sense and Sensibility* for publication in 1811: they are written in the same easy but serious colloquial style as the similar serious discussions in *Pride and Prejudice* and *Mansfield Park*, and have no equivalent in the early work, which is all satire and character-revealing dialogue. I make no apology for calling attention to what should be so obvious, since I have found that these are precisely the passages, with their important implications, that the devoted reader of the Austen novels overlooks. Apparently Mrs Norris and Lady Bertram are now generally felt to be the *raison d'être* for *Mansfield Park*. This would have made its author feel that the novel was a failure, for they are only ornamental additions to the structure, and it is the structure that she laboured over so many years.

Then, is the book a failure, into which Jane Austen had put so much of herself? Posterity has agreed to place it below *Pride and Prejudice* (though many of her contemporaries, like her own sister, preferred it to all her previous writings when it appeared), and this for her would have been failure, for she was trying to improve on *Pride and Prejudice*, as we have seen. She had most brilliantly written that novel out of a previous immature version[32] by the use almost entirely of dramatic scenes. But *Pride and Prejudice*, for that and other reasons, leaves a taste of the stage; not only is the wit too uniform, especially in the dialogue, which is never without point, but the convention in which it is written has no place for the subtler and finer effects the author must have felt herself capable of when she embarked on the last version of *Mansfield Park*. There, as in *Emma* and *Persuasion*, we see her forgoing the immediate effect of witty rejoinder and humorous character to analyse motive and to build up total effects; in this new manner the human heart is investigated in a new way, every impulse noted and considered with respect, instead of inspiring the easy comments of the earlier automatic and rather unfeeling sprightliness. If the analysis in *Mansfield Park* annoys us by its ejaculatory and panting manner, we must bear in mind that it was the forerunner of a new technique, which made possible the sensitive reflection of the emotions of Emma Woodhouse and Anne Elliot, and that even at its worst it offers us something more interesting than the brief summaries of Elinor Dashwood's and Elizabeth Bennet's states of mind that we are presented with from time to time. In those conversations between Edmund and Fanny, those broken musings of Fanny's and her agitated communings with her heart, something deeper is being attempted than ever before. There is a real, difficult fidelity to experience. There is an internal glow that proceeds from those palpitating feelings, which is what is lacking in the cold formality of *Sense and Sensibility* and even in the hard bright light that illuminates the players in *Pride and Prejudice*.

The irony that is characteristic of the later work is not underlined as in the earlier, it is part of the larger effects and can be quite easily overlooked. For instance, Edmund writing to Fanny at Portsmouth of his visit to Miss Crawford in London and the bad effect her friends there have on her character, is ready to give her up, but: 'When I think of her great attachment to you, indeed, and the whole of her judicious, upright conduct as a sister, she appears a very different creature, and I am ready to blame myself...' etc. Her 'attachment' to Fanny is subtly shown in various passages to be worthless, and the judiciousness and uprightness of her conduct as a sister culminate in keeping Henry in London out of curiosity to see his meeting with Mrs Rushworth, which Fanny feels to be 'grossly unkind and ill-judged' and which in fact launches him on the fatal intrigue. The total difference between the early and the later work is that the classical account of her novels as Comedy does not apply to the last three.

In this succession of novels *Mansfield Park* marks the turning point, and it is like most works of transition in an artist's career in that its most obvious quality is that of not succeeding. In deliberate opposition to its predecessor, it is exaggeratedly undramatic; the contrast to *Pride and Prejudice* is overdone. And though the author wishes to do something different and in a different medium, she is uncertain how to set about it. The letters in *Mansfield Park* are not even successful as letters on the whole, as those of the two earlier novels always are. This is evidently because she is trying to do many things through them, not merely the one simple thing which the letter of a Mr Collins or Lucy Steele does (reveal the character of the writer in a characteristic attitude) or the letter of a Mrs Gardiner or Darcy (put us in possession of some necessary information). The letters in *Mansfield Park* are made to serve as devices for forwarding plot and revealing character, as they must have done in the epistolary version, as they do in *Lady Susan*; but this is possible only when the characters are simply conceived and expressed in a bold convention, it becomes impossible if the author has a psychological preoccupation, and these letters are in addition overloaded by having to fill in background, report experiences, and convey the emotions of their writers in very complicated relationships. It is no wonder that Mary Crawford's letters to Fanny fail to be plausible even by the standards we apply to the epistolary novel of the eighteenth century. Yet we can see how these unsatisfactory letters made possible the wonderful achievement that *Emma* is, for it is the experiments made therein that taught their author how to convey through Emma's consciousness, without any but implicit criticism, the whole of that subtle and complicated work. *Emma*, if one thinks only of the English novels that preceded it, is a dazzling achievement. Its author, entirely on her own and without the benefit of theory or of the practice of others, is seen to have somehow discovered the technique of Henry James. In the evolution of *Mansfield Park* we can see her discovering it. *Emma* is the first of her novels *not* to have been drafted in letter form; after *Mansfield Park* this preliminary became unnecessary. *Lady Susan* was a *tour de force*, like *Jonathan Wild*, and its author was justly proud of it, as of the three volumes of earlier work she cherished, but *Mansfield Park*, with all its confusions, discrepancies and unevenness of tone and intention, is something more remarkable in English fiction. If *Mansfield Park* had been only the stodgy setting for the comic characters Lady Bertram and Mrs Norris, with lively patches where 'those pleasant worldlings' the Crawfords make a diversion, and spoilt otherwise by an out-of-date morality, an account of the book which most readers would now subscribe to, I gather – if *Mansfield Park* were only this, Jane Austen would not be the great novelist she is. For what is the difference between her novels and those of the most accredited of the Bloomsbury novelists of the 'twenties? Is it only in a greater degree of accomplishment that her novels differ from those of David Garnett, from *Lolly Willowes*, *Crome Yellow* and so forth? I mention this because there was at one time noticeable, in the golden age of Bloomsbury, an attempt by Bloomsbury products to pass Jane Austen off as one of themselves. They alleged she possessed the same kind of witty outlook and the same sophisticated cynicism as they endeavoured to exhibit. Nothing could be further from the truth. It is, to take a much less flagrant instance of critical confusion, like classing *South Wind* and the imitations of Norman Douglas with the novels of Peacock. Peacock's entertaining surface and occasional frivolity proceed from a mind that is fundamentally responsible, that takes living and the problems of life and society seriously. The novel with no inside, so strikingly illustrated by *The Sailor's Return* and *They Went*, is something with which neither Peacock nor Jane Austen would have had the slightest sympathy. They do not have to put in Significance, it is implied in the nature of their undertakings. And their technique is something that grows out of their work, like their style. What is now generally felt to be Jane Austen's boring preoccupation with morals and propriety is nevertheless a prerequisite to that view of character which diverts the reader who dislikes its roots so much that he tries to allege that those delightful flowers have none. Jane Austen's novels cannot be assimilated to a taste for P. G. Wodehouse's, and the pretence that what is not humour can be disregarded will not stand investigation. The patronizing cult that has frequently accompanied this attitude is as offensive to the literary critic as it would have been to Miss Austen.[33]

If my account of how Jane Austen composed her novels is still felt to be unconvincing, I can only say that it seems to me not merely borne out by all kinds of evidence, and that it explains what is otherwise inexplicable, but is very much less improbable than the classical account of the Austen novels. It saves us from the contortions that aesthetic criticism (on the *Craft of Fiction* model) has to exhibit in discussing her novels. And it explains her contemptuous allusions to hasty work elsewhere – e.g. in the *Letters*, she says of *Ida of Athens* that it 'must be very clever, because it was written, as the authoress says, in three months'; to read the text-books you would think *Pride and Prejudice* was composed even more lightly. This account agrees, too, with a piece of evidence that has been quite overlooked, but is of the utmost value since it is the only document by a member of her own generation and by one who knew her literary life intimately: I refer to her brother Henry's Biographical Notice prefixed to the posthumous novels. He says:

From this place (Chawton) she sent into the world those novels, which by many have been placed on the same shelf as the works of a D'Arblay and an Edgeworth. Some of these novels had been the gradual performances of her previous life...[34]

It is not for nothing, though playfully, that in writing to her nephew she compares her manner of composing to brushwork 'so fine as to produce little effect after much labour' – the last three words are the clue, since we know she was actually very proud of her effects. Another corrective to the complacent account of her 'comedy' is her complaint that her kinsman Egerton Brydges in his novel draws characters 'for the sake of delineation'. Her own aim, it is apparent, was to have no loose ends, no padding, no characterization for its own sake; she was the opposite kind of novelist to Scott, and had at any rate the intention of putting in nothing except for a clearly defined reason – to contribute to the plot, the drama of feelings, the moral structure, or the necessary psychology. Her own practice is meant to be in accordance with Cassandra's 'starched notions', and if these principles of composition are violated I conclude that it is reasonable to assume that there is some reason for this. And I have tried to show in many cases what the reasons were. There is unfortunately not room here to recapitulate those reasons and what they imply about her methods of composition. But I must guard against one misapprehension. I have been accused of trying to write a *Road to Xanadu* about the Austen novels. On the contrary. Jane Austen was not a poet, least of all a poet like Coleridge, she was a novelist like Henry James and Joseph Conrad, who had a very high degree of awareness of the origin and adaptations of their material, and who took an intense interest in the deliberate shaping of their novels. What a preface to *Pride and Prejudice* Jane Austen could have written! Whereas all that Coleridge knew about *Kubla Khan* was that he had dreamt it. The change from the simple technique of *Lady Susan* to the final, complicated, laboriously achieved

Mansfield Park was something she could have accounted for better than we can. The shift from composing with the separate points of view of Lady Susan and Mrs Vernon to producing the novel through Fanny's consciousness almost entirely, is a technical change quite in accordance with Henry James's theory and practice.

I will not end therefore on a consideration of the failure of *Mansfield Park*, but on its achievement. I have appeared to contradict myself, to describe the creation of *Mansfield Park* as laborious but to advance a theory that it was in effect written in the spring and summer of 1813. But in view of her regular process of writing a novel in versions which grow like snowballs as they advance, gathering in earlier oddments and satiric experiments and sketches from the life already jotted down in correspondence, there is no inconsistency really. We may even generalize now about how the Austen novels came into print. Once all the necessary elements were present, the essentials of what material was to be used, how to use it, with what intention and through what form of treatment, and when life had presented her with the right centre of interest (Eliza's death-bed, Fanny Knight's love affairs, her own views and emotions about marriage at a critical time in her life), she could undoubtedly work at speed under pressure, perfecting details, inventing alternative situations and speeches where she felt it necessary for getting the right effect (as she rewrote overnight the scene of Captain Wentworth's proposal when dissatisfied with her first version of it in utterly different circumstances, having led up to this crisis slowly enough, no doubt). What originally was owing to accident in denying publication to her first three novels in their early forms, brought about a method of composition which enabled her to put all her powers into everything she published. Later in the century these first-stage stories like *Lady Susan* would have been prematurely rushed to the press for periodical publication, and the intricate process by which her immature conceptions and experiments became works of art of great value would have been destroyed half-way. Henry wrote in his notice, 'everything came finished from her pen', and we may see that this is true in one sense by reading her letters, which have on occasions as lively a surface as the novels and abound in happy expressions. But Henry's epigram needs interpreting if it is not to mislead. Almost everything did come out finished in the end (except a few botched jobs like Willoughby's past, Nurse Rooke and Mrs Smith), but the whole was not put on paper in one stroke. Any one of the novels took years to reach the finished stage, and many pens must have been worn out on that novel before it came finished from the last one.

The final novel, *Mansfield Park* let us say, differs, then, from its earlier form or forms not simply in greater abundance of detail, richer plot and characterization and added finish of surface, as we should expect. It differs utterly in kind. The original material has not only been added to, but put to a different kind of use; the use of the carriage incident in *Mansfield Park* is representative. In *Lady Susan* and *Mansfield Park*, as in *The Watsons* and *Emma* and, no doubt, in *First Impressions* and *Pride and Prejudice*, we have an illustration of the difference between a low-level success and a high-level one, between the efficient and the unique in art. As an illustration of what I mean by this different use of the same material, the exposure scenes of *All's Well that Ends Well* and *Measure for Measure* suggest themselves. The one play followed the other after a couple of years, and a comparison of the exposure scene in each, which elucidates the plot and winds up the play, shows that the dramatist used exactly the same pattern in the later as in the earlier play for this purpose, with a similar pair of women, the same situation, the same perplexing and teasing way of letting out the secret in bits and baffling or checking first one party and then the other. But *All's Well* is quite uninteresting, and the exposure scene might have come from any well-made play of the kind – we only feel about it that it does all that is required of it and rounds off the comedy neatly. But in using it again for the later play the dramatist has made it the culmination of the whole work, an epitome as well as an explication. All our bewildered feelings and doubts about what the dramatist has intended by the play till then, about what to think and how and whom to judge, are resolved for us, everything is revealed with marvellous economy and every phrase becomes pregnant (I assume the reader is in agreement with Professor Wilson Knight's interpretation of *Measure for Measure* in *The Wheel of Fire*, which alone makes sense of the play).[35] Jane Austen's method of creating works of art is not unique, it has been practised by many poets, but it has never, I believe, been *habitually* practised by any other great writer as a regular method of composition. But if we think of the conditions in which she of necessity wrote – the lack of privacy of her life generally and the frequent visits and changes of house, common sitting-room, the domestic duties, the callers against whom she was warned but not protected by the creaking door, the jottings on little slips of paper that could be concealed under a blotting-pad – we can see that only by such a method could she have translated the product of an intense and sustained private life into substantial works of art.

III

The Letters

The first thing to be said about Jane Austen's letters is that we have comparatively few of them and those certainly not the more personal ones. Cassandra her sister, to whom the bulk of the novelist's correspondence seems to have been addressed, destroyed all except those which seemed to her trivial,[36] distributing among the family as mementoes what she did not burn. Some of a more intimate kind which were written to the sailor brothers and the favourite nieces and nephews, and to one or two close friends, survived independently. None of those has been found which were written to the peculiarly congenial brother, Henry, who managed her literary business, though this series of letters might well have been the most interesting of all to us. We have no letters before 1796, when she became twenty-one, none for 1797, when Cassandra's fiancé died, nor any between 1801 and 1804, the period when a number of important events occurred in Jane's emotional history. It is therefore not surprising that they have generally been described as disappointing. Bradley alone praises them, declaring, 'I do not find the letters disappointing, [because] the Jane Austen who wrote the novels is in them...And the attitude of the letter-writer towards the world she lives in is the attitude of the novel-writer towards the world she creates.' This is very just but he does not really mean by this all he seems to say, for he had in front of him only Lord Brabourne's selected edition of the Letters, so edited that Bradley can reconcile his complacency in them with his statement that 'her novels make exceptionally peaceful reading. She troubles us neither with problems nor with painful emotions.' Quotations from her letters in the 1870 *Memoir* by Jane's nephew, the Rev. J. E. Austen-Leigh, and in the *Life and Letters* published in 1913 by the next two generations of Austen-Leighs, were tactfully made in accordance with the Victorian feeling for presenting one's relative in the most favourable light in a biography, that is, as a conventionally estimable person. The same principle evidently decided Lord Brabourne to edit with a blue pencil the letters that he published in 1884 – from his great-aunt Jane to his mother (when still Fanny Knight), to his mother's cousin Anna, and to his great-aunt Cassandra. The family biographies of Miss Austen, from her brother Henry's Biographical Notice onwards, show a similar bias. When Dr Chapman in 1932 printed for the first time in its entirety every letter of Jane Austen's he could find, the reaction of even Bloomsbury critics was one principally of shock and distaste (best seen in *Abinger Harvest*, where Mr E. M. Forster reprints his review); it looked for the moment as if there would be a similar slump in her reputation to that in Trollope's in consequence of the publication of his disillusioning *Autobiography*, which proved too much for an age committed to the Romantic theory of artistic Inspiration. But Janeites rallied round, declaring that the objections rested only on two or three jokes, lapses of taste and ill humour such as we are all liable to in our correspondence,[37] and that far from these representing the tone of the Austen household it was probable that Cassandra wrote back reproving Jane.[38] The Austen stock recovered, and the Victorian account of her character and personality was reinstated.

Cassandra did not write back reprovingly, we may be sure, because it never occurred to her that such passages might be objectionable when she was censoring Jane's correspondence after her death or she would have destroyed such letters. Moreover, the jokes are only the most striking examples of a tone and an attitude regularly adopted in Jane's correspondence with her sister. The letters, far from suiting with the Victorian notion of the Austen novels and their author's character, finally destroy that myth. They are therefore of real value to the literary critic, confirming the impression of the author he deduces from the novels and the interpretations he makes of the novels as works of art. The Letters emphasize the underlying intentions of the novels that have been ignored by literary criticism; that they are not 'good' letters, as Mr Forster and others have decided, is beside the point. Great letter-writers are mostly great bores. The letters that the literary critic is interested in are those that reveal an interesting mind.

Let us start with the simplest and most easily demonstrated point. Though no one any longer believes in the old account of her as a practically uneducated genius, yet the conventional account of Miss Austen as prim, demure, sedate, prudish and so on, the typical Victorian maiden lady, survives. This ignores the fact that she spent the first twenty-four years of her life in the eighteenth century and the rest in the Regency period. But the collected edition of the *Letters* brings this fact home to us, even if the novels have not done so already. Miss Austen is seen to have had no innate sense of propriety, as a clergyman's daughter of the next age could be expected to have. She jokes in the letters to her sister about having got tipsy last night, about fleas in the bed, about perspiring:

What dreadful Hot weather we have! It keeps one in a continual state of Inelegance [1796];

about sexual relations:

We plan having a steady Cook, and a young and giddy Housemaid, with a sedate, middle-aged Man, who is to undertake the double office of Husband to the former and sweetheart to the latter. – No children of course to be allowed on either side [1801];

and gives her sister a hint to see that the maid is kept from making advances to visiting nephews. The sisters still like to make the eighteenth-century joke that any female acquaintance who has been ill must have been lying-in of an illegitimate child, and if a lady and gentleman are both absent from a party it is humorous to assume they are meeting secretly instead. The freedom of humour, in its separation of feeling from the occasion for a joke, is even reminiscent of Smollett, as in the well-known example that pained Mr Forster, though it scarcely stands out in the letters:

Mrs Hall, of Sherbourne, was brought to bed yesterday of a dead child, some weeks before she expected, owing to a fright. I suppose she happened unawares to look at her husband [1798].

The free play of her mind on whatever came to her notice constantly produces unpredictable results; for instance, in 1813 she calls on a friend's daughter at a London finishing school, and tells Cassandra:

I was shewn upstairs into a drawing-room, where she came to me, and the appearance of the room, so totally unschool-like amused me very much; it was full of all the modern elegancies – and if it had not been for some naked Cupids over the Mantelpiece which must have been a fine study for Girls, one should never have smelt instruction.

The sisters inherited from their mother what Mrs Austen herself described as her 'sprack wit', a mental liveliness that evidently went with a preference for outspokenness and a contempt for prudery. Thus Jane writes:

Your Anne is dreadful. But nothing offends me so much as the absurdity of not being able to pronounce the word *Shift*. I could forgive her any follies in English, rather than the Mock Modesty of that French word [1817].

And she writes casually and characteristically of a sister-in-law who 'neither looks nor feels well': 'Little Embryo is troublesome, I suppose.' Obviously she was neither puritanical nor Victorian – she thought freely and knew no reason why she should conceal what she thought. The idea of Good Taste for ladies with its paralysing effects had not yet been invented. This is the more apparent when we remember that these letters were meant to be read aloud by the recipient to whatever branch of the family she was staying with, or to the home circle if the writer was on a visit; there are many indications that this was so in the text.

Miss Austen's absence of squeamishness on such subjects as sex is not, however, the conscious uninhibitedness cultivated by twentieth-century lady novelists. It evidently arose quite naturally from acquaintance with life in a large and proliferating family, where friends and sisters-in-law produced a child a year and not infrequently died of it.[39] Life can only be taken as it comes and doesn't bear much thinking about. We get two good examples of this sobering knowledge of life in the *Letters*. The first is in 1798, when Jane, not yet twenty-three, has visited a sister-in-law expecting her first baby:

I went to see Mary, who is still plagued with rheumatism, which she would be very glad to get rid of, and still more glad to get rid of her child, of whom she is heartily tired...I believe I never told you that Mrs C. and Anne, late of Manydown, are both dead, and both died in childbed. We have not regaled Mary with this news.

The second is in 1817, when she writes advising her favourite niece Fanny against marrying someone she is not sure about:

Single women have a dreadful propensity for being poor – which is one very strong argument in favour of Matrimony, but I need not dwell on such arguments with *you*, pretty Dear, you do not want inclination...And then, by not beginning the business of Mothering quite so early in life, you will be young in Constitution, spirits, figure and countenance, while Mrs — [of the same age] is growing old by confinements and nursing...Anna [another niece] has a bad cold, looks pale, and we fear something else. She has just weaned Julia.

Ten days later she writes again on the same subject to Fanny:

Anna has not a chance of escape...Poor Animal, she will be worn out before she is thirty. – I am very sorry for her. – Mrs Clement too is in that way again. I am quite tired of so many Children. – Mrs Benn has a thirteenth.

The advantage of seeing life unprotected by blinkers is apparent in the faculty it developed in her, that of taking stock of all kinds of experience and absorbing new kinds not only without being disconcerted or repelled but without having even to brace herself. We see her, for instance, taking even Don Giovanni in her stride when, up from the country on a visit to her brother Henry's household, she has been on a round of theatres including Covent Garden opera:

The girls still prefer 'Don Juan'; and I must say that I have seen nobody on the stage who has been a more interesting character than that compound of cruelty and lust [1813].

Or she visits a prison:

He went to inspect the gaol, as a visiting magistrate, and took me with him. I was gratified, and went through all the feelings which people must go through, I think, in visiting such a building.

It is this poise that is behind the novels. What she can have found objectionable in *The Spectator*[40] is beyond conjecture.

Nor, after reading the *Letters*, can we fall into the common error of believing her to have lived the life of the country parsonage cut off from society and knowledge of the great world. Wherever she was she mixed with all kinds of society. She lived in Bath for four years besides paying earlier visits to her uncle resident there, she lived for two years in Southampton, and

visited Lyme, Canterbury, Winchester and other frequented
social centres as well as staying in London, where her brother
Henry lived with his banking connections and whose wife,
widow of a French count, collected round her a circle of French
emigrés and cultivated musical society. The *Letters* tell us a good
deal about all this. Many, besides, are written from great houses
in the country or mention visits to them, the establishments of
relatives or connections; and visits in those days, as we see in
her novels, were of some duration. There is no sign that she led
what is called a sheltered life. She knew very well what went
on behind the façade of social decorum. The casual and
indifferent references in the letters are more impressive evidence
of this than greater stress on single incidents would be.
Eccentric or merely immoral peers flit through the pages of these
volumes – like their connection Lord Craven, whom Henry's
wife reports on:

> She finds his manners very pleasing indeed. The little flaw of having
> a Mistress now living with him at Ashdown Park seems to be the only
> unpleasing circumstance about him. [But they are all] on the most
> friendly terms [1801].

Calm notes on impropriety constantly appear:

> Mrs W. has another son, and Lord Lucan has taken a
> Mistress...[1808].

> Mr S. is married again...the Lady was governess to Sir Robert S.'s
> natural children...[1808].

> *He* is as raffish in his appearance as I would wish every Disciple of
> Godwin to be [1801].

> I am proud to say that I have a very good eye at an Adultress, for...I
> fixed upon the right one from the first...She was highly rouged, and
> looked rather quietly and contentedly silly than anything else. Mrs.
> B. and two young women were of the same party, except when Mrs.
> B. thought herself obliged to leave them to run round the room after
> her drunken husband. His avoidance, and her pursuit, with the
> probable intoxication of both, was an amusing scene [1801].

There is the drama of Earle Harwood, R.N., one of the family
of a neighbouring rector. He marries a low young woman of
alleged improper life and 'lives in the most private manner
imaginable at Portsmouth, without keeping a servant of any
kind. What a prodigious innate love of virtue she must have,

to marry under such circumstances' [1798]. He then gets 'the appointment to a Prison ship at Portsmouth...he and his wife are to live on board for the future'. In 1799 Cassandra apparently sent Jane a description of Earle's wife, to which Jane replied: 'I cannot help thinking from your account of Mrs E. H. that Earle's vanity has tempted him to invent the account of her former way of Life, that his triumph in securing her might be greater: I daresay she was nothing but an innocent Country Girl in fact.' Next year, 'Earle Harwood has been again giving uneasiness to his family, and talk to the Neighbourhood' by shooting himself, but not fatally and it is hoped not on purpose.

The world of the novels was not the world of Miss Austen's life but only a selection from it, made in order to facilitate certain intentions of the novelist; that is the interesting and indisputable fact that emerges from the *Letters*. In these letters people have executions in the house owing to failure in business, or leave the neighbourhood because they can't pay their bills; there are disputed wills and all kinds of lawsuits; women constantly die in childbed and when alive are shown to be preoccupied with nursing and educating their children, or, if spinsters, with helping to rear and teach their little relatives, assisting the poor, and nursing the sick and aged of their own family; the Austens are on intimate terms with people of all classes and are not snobbish; Jane herself is always anxious about money and the cares of a household where the strictest economy was necessary – 'vulgar economy' she calls it, having to worry because the bread and tea are not lasting as long as they should, because the only cooks they can afford can't make a tolerable meal (Jane is ashamed because Capt. — who dropped in to dinner couldn't eat the underdone mutton), because the sweep is coming ('Depend upon my thinking of the chimney sweeper as soon as I wake tomorrow') or company, which means torment:

I wanted a few days quiet, and exemption from the Thought and contrivances which any sort of company gives...how good Mrs West could have written such Books with all her family cares, is still more a matter of astonishment to me! Composition seems to me Impossible with a Head full of Joints of Mutton and doses of rhubarb.

In the letters there are many jottings of what might well have been material for novels, such as the story told above of Earle Harwood, or that of Mrs Gunthorpe:

Miss Jackson is married to young Mr Gunthorpe, and is to be very unhappy. He swears, drinks, is cross, jealous, selfish and Brutal; – the match makes *her* family miserable, and has occasioned *his* being disinherited [1807];

but they are the kind of novels she did not choose to write (unless she used the extract above for the history of Mrs Price in *Mansfield Park*, where it is conspicuous and indeed unique in her work).

In her life, too, there were many tragic or dramatic incidents. As children she and her sister nearly died of 'a putrid fever' and her aunt who caught it from them did die; her cousin and playmate Lady Williams, who had been married from Steventon Rectory, was killed six years later in a carriage accident; her beloved friend Mrs Lefroy, whose 'partial favour from my earliest years' Jane's touching verses four years after the disaster lovingly record, was thrown from her horse and killed on Jane's birthday; her sister's fiancé died in the West Indies and Jane is conjectured[41] to have suffered a similar bereavement herself; one night in her twenty-seventh year she accepted the proposal of the brother of her best friends, and in great agitation next morning broke off the engagement, though he was heir to a good estate; her favourite sister-in-law died leaving an enormous family of young children, four other brothers lost their wives, one after her 'long and painful illness'; her closest companions (later they became her sisters-in-law) were grand-daughters of the famous beauty, 'the cruel Lady Craven', whose unnatural behaviour drove her daughters into eloping from their home; her rich aunt was the victim of a blackmailing charge of theft and spent nine months in custody awaiting trial, where Jane (aged twenty-three) and Cassandra might have joined her, it appears, if Mrs Leigh Perrot had not decided to refuse their mother's offer since she could not 'let those elegant young women be inmates in a prison'; her cousin Eliza, of Anglo-Indian origin, married a French count in 1781, and led a romantic life at the French court till the Revolution when she escaped to England and took refuge at Steventon Rectory while her husband was guillotined; three years later she married Henry Austen, against the wishes of his family. There was certainly plenty of incident in Jane Austen's life and many varieties of experience for her to draw on in her family. Besides her own travels in the south and west of England she knew Oxford and the university world from her two brothers who were Oxonians, as well as from other connections there; another brother had made the grand tour and there were several well-travelled relatives; an aunt came from the West Indies, and a cousin went there; another aunt went out to India as a girl and married there, returning with her little daughter to remain in close contact with the Austens and to connect them with the trial of her benefactor, Warren Hastings; one brother was a London banker, two were naval officers; and so on.

None of this tempting subject-matter is used by the novelist, and this is all the more remarkable when we remember that our knowledge of all other women novelists shows that the strength of their stories lies solely in being personal and reminiscent of the lives they saw around them, often closely autobiographical. There was a century's tradition of women novelists to keep her in countenance if she had wanted to write novels around such subjects. And that she could write well on almost anything, the *Letters* prove. To ascribe the lack of dramatic incident in the novels to the author's humdrum experience and confined outlook is clearly wrong; the novels are limited in scope and subject by deliberate intention. The *Letters* therefore prove that Jane Austen was the kind of novelist she was because she was consciously restricting her work for a given purpose, in order to concentrate on what seemed to her most worth writing about, to convey her deepest interests, and to express some things that seemed to her important.

There is a similar difference between the vocabulary and idiom of the *Letters* and that of the novels, which shows that the latter were not dashed off as gaily as is generally assumed. There is much greater freedom of expression in the correspondence, while the language of the novels, though depending a good deal on having speech forms behind it and making frequent use of colloquialisms, is always restrained – the 'trollopy-looking servant-girl' at Mrs Price's in *Mansfield Park* stands out as if an oversight, certainly it is the only such phrase in all the novels, though in the *Letters* it would not attract attention. The vivacity of the novels is controlled, it is art, whereas that of the letters is the careless high-spirits of conversation – as when she writes to her niece, urging her to reject a suitor: 'Think of his Principles, think of his Father's objections, of want of Money, of a coarse Mother, of Brothers and Sisters like Horses, of sheets sewn across,' etc. or of a disagreeable sister-in-law: 'But still she is in the main *not* a liberal-minded Woman, and as to this reversionary Property's amending that part of her Character, expect it not my dear Anne – too late, too late in the day.' She withheld from the novels the licence of language and prose style and the range and strength of feeling that we see her to have had at her disposal in her correspondence. Similarly we learn with surprise from the *Letters* that she had many interests which do not appear in the novels – for example, she was fond of history and even such subjects as military history and tactics.

But the questions raised here must be left for consideration in a later essay. We must go on to enquire what the letter-writer and the novelist have in common. The letters, I said in the first of these essays, were an indispensable stage in the production of the novels. We see in the *Letters* the novelist writing steadily and for an audience, and an audience which had imposed a certain attitude and tone on the writer and which demanded certain kinds of information. When Jane Austen writes to the next generation, her nieces or nephews, she writes warmly, kindly and sympathetically: their reminiscences all agree that she was the ideal aunt, and her letters to them (though not all those about them) corroborate this. The letters to her friends are also ordinarily pleasant and imply an amiable outlook. Those to Cassandra and sometimes to her brothers are notably different. There is little affectionate sentiment – that was understood, no doubt, and left for personal intercourse; the letters, on which the not inconsiderable postage had to be paid by the recipient, were to convey information and it is information about social matters they wanted and received, about functions, family events, and personalities, especially new ones. Characterization of new acquaintances plays a prominent and obviously acceptable part in their letter-writing. In analysing the novels before, I showed that the characteristic vein of the writer is marked by acid comment on character and cynical estimate of motive. Now these give the distinguishing tone of the letters to Cassandra and the Steventon circle; no doubt it was the tone of family intercourse, arising in the schoolroom over the family jokes (as we can see in the manuscript volumes), and not surprising in a family conscious of unusual gifts[42] and cherishing a clannish spirit.[43] Their sense of difference was intensified by their all being educated at home, by their highly critical and vigorous-minded mother,[44] and by their pronounced taste for literature (to which two of the brothers added a scholarly-critical attitude to the use of language). The sisters, without husband or child to mitigate the adolescent hardness and sharpness of outlook, were still more conscious of being different and superior; they formed a clique within an élite.[45] And Cassandra was the dominating character in this alliance. Their nephew wrote in his *Memoir of Jane Austen*:

Their sisterly affection for each other could scarcely be exceeded. Perhaps it began on Jane's side with the feeling of deference natural to a loving child towards a kind elder sister. Something of this feeling always remained; and even in the maturity of her powers, and in the enjoyment of increasing success, she would still speak of Cassandra as of one wiser and better than herself... They were not exactly alike. Cassandra's was the colder and calmer disposition; she was always prudent and well-judging, but with less outward demonstration of feeling and less sunniness of temper than Jane possessed.

His sister Anna contributed the information that Cassandra was the more equable while Jane, who could be very grave as well as uproariously funny, was given to ups and downs. None of Cassandra's letters to her sister are known, but it is suggestive that Jane writes in the one tone to her and that, acknowledging a letter from her sister, declares: 'You are indeed the finest comic writer of the present age.' The letter Cassandra wrote on the second day after Jane's death, to their niece, reveals an extraordinary nature whose iron quality perhaps explains something in the younger sister's attitudes (e.g. 'I *have* lost such a treasure, such a sister, such a friend... I loved her only too well – not better than she deserved, but I am conscious that my affection for her made me sometimes unjust to and negligent of others; and I can acknowledge, more than as a general principle, the justice of the Hand which has struck this blow. You know me too well to be at all afraid that I should suffer materially from my feelings... ').

The novelist's tone is seen, through the *Letters*, to be not simply the self-protection of the sensitive person against the world, but something shared and expected, a matter of common assumptions that could not be revised and that she could only escape in relations that started on a different basis, as those of an aunt to children or grown-up nieces. So much a habit was this tone and manner that she adopts it even when completely unsuitable, where only our knowledge of the facts from other sources shows that she intended to be playful merely or even to express gratitude or admiration in such an awkward convention as to convey the opposite sense. She was not unconscious of this and sometimes pulls herself up when she has fallen into it to an unsuitable recipient, as when in a letter to a brother at sea, after such a piece of characterization of a cousin's wife as would be natural in a letter to Cassandra, she adds, 'This is an ill-natured sentiment to send all over the Baltic.'

The assumptions were, first, that the outside world was inferior to Steventon Rectory and their circle. Contempt is freely implied for their neighbours' lack of intellectual interests, the latter's stupidity being always assumed:

The C.s are at home, and are reduced to read.

The Miss M.'s are as civil and as silly as usual.

She has an idea of your being remarkably lively, therefore get ready the proper selection of adverbs and due scraps of Italian and French.

Miss Beaty is good-humour itself, and does not seem much besides.

...among so many readers or retainers of books as we have in Chawton...

I cannot anyhow continue to find people agreeable...

As to Agreeableness, she is much like other people.

Inferiority of manners is constantly noted too, as implying something more radical:

Mrs B. called here on Saturday. She is a large, ungenteel Woman, with self-satisfied and would-be elegant manners.

They (male visitors) are very good-natured you know and civil and all that – but not particularly superfine.

Like other young ladies she is considerably genteeler than her parents; she is very conversable in a common way; I do not perceive wit or genius, but she has sense and some degree of taste, and her manners are very engaging. She seems to like people rather too easily.

and, still more, inferiority of standards – other people are snobbish, ill-humoured, affected or insincere, purse-proud or mean about money, meddlesome or overbearing, effusive or heartless:

I rather wish they may have the Curacy. It will be an amusement for Mary to superintend their Household management, and abuse them for expense.

I would not give much for Mr Rice's chance of living at Deane: he builds his hope, I find, not upon anything that his mother has written, but upon the effect of what he has written himself. He must write a great deal better than those eyes indicate if he can persuade a perverse and narrow-minded woman to oblige those whom she does not love.

If not guilty of any of these defects, then they fail to satisfy the Austens' high standard of cheerfulness and stoicism in the face of tribulation. The scrutiny the *Letters* show directed on outsiders (even on sisters-in-law and aunts-by-marriage) is more than critical, it is hostile, disapproving, and incipiently contemptuous:

My Aunt...looks about with great diligence and success for Inconvenience and Evil.

Miss Holder and I adjourned after tea into the inner Drawing room to look over Prints and talk pathetically. She is very unreserved and very fond of talking of her deceased brother and sister, whose memories she cherishes with an enthusiasm which tho' perhaps a little affected is not unpleasing.

are fair samples. Even a brother may degenerate under the influence of marriage, as Jane suggests in this reference to her brother James:

I am sorry and angry that his Visit should not give one more pleasure; the company of so good and so clever a Man ought to be gratifying in itself; – but his Chat seems all forced, his Opinions on many points too much copied from his Wife's, and his time here is spent I think in walking about the house and banging the doors, or ringing the bell for a glass of water.

The fact that outside her own circle there was immorality of various kinds fitted in here – being immoral was part of other people's inferiority. The unfeeling treatment of a Lydia Bennet or a Maria Rushworth that readers of the novels complain of is the result of the letter-writer's unsympathetic attitude to all who lapse from an implied standard of great severity. She could believe it a reasonable standard because it was shared by her own group. Inside that group she was evidently the lovable and sweet-natured person the family traditions agree in describing.

Finally, the hostility of this world to the Austens and what they stand for is also assumed – the world is inferior and therefore malicious. We have probably all noticed that conversation is liable to be spiced with malice, especially in a confined society, and that it is a tendency of human nature to enjoy the misfortunes of others. Nevertheless, there are opposite impulses and counterbalancing virtues. It is not normal to believe only in a malicious and hostile attitude on the part of our immediate neighbours and of indifferent strangers alike. But this is an understanding between Jane Austen and her sister abundantly witnessed by the *Letters*:

Mrs Portman is not much admired in Dorsetshire; the good-natured world, as usual, extolled her beauty so highly, that all the neighbourhood have had the pleasure of being disappointed.

Ch. Powlett gave a dance on Tuesday, to the great disturbance of all his neighbours, of course, who, you know, take a most lively interest in the state of his finances, and live in hopes of his being soon ruined.

…his wife is discovered to be everything that the neighbourhood could wish her, silly and cross as well as extravagant.

Whenever I fall into misfortune, how many jokes it ought to furnish to my acquaintance in general, or I shall die dreadfully in their debt for entertainment.

Of her friends' father who is ill:

Poor man! his life is so useful, his character so respectable and worthy, that I really believe there was a good deal of sincerity in the general concern expressed on his account.

The lack of sincerity in ordinary social intercourse is clearly one of the sources of irritation in her relations with the outside world. New acquaintances are looked upon with suspicion and 'civility' is a term of pejorative implications because it is assumed to impose hypocrisy. For instance:

In consequence of a civil note that morning from Mrs Clement, I went with her and her husband in their Tax-cart – civility on both sides; *I* would rather have walked, and no doubt *they* must have wished I had.

Similarly she writes with characteristic irony of an acquaintance: 'We were all delight and cordiality of course.' This extract

about callers in 1807 is representative of a good deal of the kind
scattered throughout the *Letters*:

I suppose they must be acting by the orders of Mr — in this civility,
as there seems no other reason for their coming near us. They will not
come often, I dare say. They live in a handsome style and are rich
and she seemed to like to be rich, and we gave her to understand that
we were far from being so; she will soon feel therefore that we are not
worth her acquaintance.

And the continual irony at clichés of feeling and expression, at
conventional exaggerations, the impatience with anything that
might be related to cant, is associated with this irritation.[46] It
is always coming up in the novels.

In all these respects the *Letters* chime in with the novels. These
feelings are the groundwork of the novels and after reading the
Letters we can see more distinctly the part the Austen attitude
played in making the novels what they are. The letters between
the sisters show them to have had a sense of difference from the
world outside their immediate family and few chosen friends;
it was not that they were ignorant of it or shy of it, but that
they had too much penetration to be comfortable in society and
knew too much about the people they had to live among. There
was not enough elbow-room, they could leave home only to pay
a visit to another home, and social decorum imposed intolerable
restraints and hypocrisies on their intercourse with others, they
felt. The blessedness of having a few people who endorse one's
standards, speak one's language and can be counted on, the
necessity for making one's own private society, was well
understood by Jane Austen, and the *Letters* prove that in this
respect she was happy. Her immediate family, Martha Lloyd,
the favourite niece Fanny, when she grew up, the three Misses
Bigg of Manydown formed such a refuge for her:

In another week I shall be at home – and then, my having been at
Godmersham will seem like a Dream – The Orange Wine will want
our Care soon. – But in the meantime for Elegance and Ease and
Luxury; the Hatters and Milles' dine here today – and I shall eat Ice
and drink French wine, and be above vulgar Economy. Luckily the
pleasures of Friendship, of unreserved Conversation, of similarity of
Taste and Opinions, will make good amends for Orange Wine [1808].

and five years later she writes to Cassandra:

In a few hours you will be transported to Manydown and then for
Candour and Comfort and Coffee and Cribbage.

'Candour', that key word in the novelist's vocabulary, is, strictly speaking, the opposite of censoriousness, putting the best interpretation on everything (it was to reverse its meaning by George Eliot's time). But in the Austen letters and novels it implies much more, it is an ideal that ordinary society is incapable of in its intercourse. To be candid is to be charitable, sincere and one's real or best self. In Jane Austen's scheme her élite of family and friends are the ideal of the society she belongs to, in which Candour and not malice is the regulating impulse, where warm affections reign ('Tenderness' is another key word) and good conversation is the chief pleasure; we remember Anne Elliot's definition of good society, to which her cousin objects: 'That is not good company – that is the best.'

For the interesting point for literary criticism is that the letters led to the novels. Her taste for sharing her observations on human nature with her family did not stop at letter-writing and conversation or even at the satires and parodies of the manuscript volumes and the early form of *Northanger Abbey*. And the kind of interest in people and life that the letters show did not even produce the kind of novels we should deduce from the *Letters*. She had this passion for examining people's lives and in every detail – as she notes in the *Letters*:

Mary and I went to the Liverpool Museum and the British Gallery and I had some amusement at each tho' my preference for Men and Women always inclines me to attend more to the company than the sight [1811];

and a few years earlier, demanding exact details of some affair from her sister:

You know how interesting the purchase of a sponge-cake is to me.

Thus the *Letters* are full of character sketches made for their own sake and for the amusement of the home circle, but they often reappear in a recognizable form in the novels; such little studies as that of the M.P. she met on a visit in 1813:

Now I must speak of *him*, and I like him very much. I am sure he is clever, and a man of taste. He got a volume of Milton last night, and spoke of it with warmth. He is quite an M.P., very smiling, with an exceeding good address and readiness of language. I am rather in love with him. I dare say he is ambitious and insincere. He has a wide smiling mouth, and very good teeth.

which suggests Mr Walter Elliot, or Harriet Moore's husband, who suggests Mr John Knightley, or Miss Milles and her mother, who suggest Miss Bates and hers – the list is endless.

This interest in how other people felt, behaved, passed their time, looked and spoke, what they thought and said about each other, was her great asset as a novelist. But when such an interest goes with a fundamental irritation with the social actuality and a habit of looking for its shortcomings only, we should expect works of fiction in the vein of Mr Somerset Maugham. That Jane Austen's novels are so thoroughly different from Mr Maugham's is a tribute to the congenial circle she was born into and gathered round her and to the strength of the positive standards they shared with her.

Sense and Sensibility

A month before the announcement of *Sense and Sensibility* in 1811, Jane Austen's favourite niece recorded in her diary: 'Letter from Aunt Cass to beg we would not mention that Aunt Jane wrote *Sense and Sensibility*.' In this unprofessional spirit did Jane Austen embark on her literary career. Publishing at her own expense and anonymously, she yet cleared £140 on the first edition, which was exhausted in two years, and she was encouraged by its success to prepare for publication other early works. Yet in the twentieth century *Sense and Sensibility* seems to be the Cinderella of the Austen novels – it has had the lowest sales to the general public and the least attention from literary critics. Obviously it is less lively than *Pride and Prejudice*, less *sympathique* than *Persuasion*, less amusingly satiric than *Northanger Abbey* and less like a modern novel than *Mansfield Park* and *Emma*. But each of Jane Austen's novels has its unique attractions and its own centre of interest. One of the special features of this one is that we can by inspection see how it was evolved, for its successive layers of creation are still perceptible and reveal how the 'miracle' (as it has been called) of an Austen novel was achieved.

We know that the young Jane had written a story in letters called *Elinor and Marianne* which she read aloud for family entertainment, and her sister recorded that *Sense and Sensibility* in its present form (that is, not an epistolary novel) was begun in 1797, when Jane was twenty-two, though it must have had a good deal of rewriting by 1811, for parts of it are plainly as mature as her next two novels and the use of Scott as a popular poet, for instance, would have been impossible before 1805. Like *Northanger Abbey*, *Elinor and Marianne* must have been a satire, in this case against 'romantic' ideas, and, like the early unfinished tale in letters, *Lesley Castle*, striking outward from the contrast between a romantic and an unromantic sister. The satiric matter has been abbreviated in our novel but even so we can still see that Marianne has Rousseauistic ideas, rejects the conventional social code and cultivates intense sensibility to the arts and the events of her life; whereas Elinor represents the good sense of the eighteenth century which, without being insensitive, recognized the claims of society on the individual and held that traditional experience and not theory is the sound basis for conduct.

Elinor and Marianne was followed up by another novel, *First Impressions*, also lost to us except in its revised form, *Pride and Prejudice*, but from this last we can tell that *First Impressions* also must have had as basis a contrast between two sisters united by a deep affection but opposed in temperament and social theory. Elizabeth Bennet, though not addicted to uncontrolled sensibility, is a much more sympathetic Marianne who gets off more lightly though she makes similar mistakes, and Jane an ineffective Elinor who is not nearly so completely endorsed by the author. We can deduce that the contrasting sisters began (typically) as a family joke, for the differences between the Dashwood sisters correspond in an exaggerated form to what we know about the Austen sisters. Their nephew in his *Memoir of Jane Austen* wrote that Cassandra (like Elinor) drew well but that Jane (like Marianne) was literary and musical in her tastes and read French and Italian, while 'even in the maturity of her powers, and in the enjoyment of increasing success, she would still speak of Cassandra as of one wiser and better than herself...Cassandra's was the colder and calmer disposition; she was always prudent and well-judging, but with less outward demonstration of feeling and less sunniness of temper than Jane possessed.' A favourite niece contributed the information that Cassandra was more equable, while Jane was given to extremes of feeling. We have besides the letter Cassandra wrote directly after Jane's death, expressing the strongest sense of loss but concluding, exactly like an Elinor Dashwood: 'You know me too well to be at all afraid that I should suffer materially from my feelings.'

Marianne's impassioned farewell to Norland, her amazement that Edward should be better pleased by 'a troop of happy villagers than the finest banditti in the world' and insensible to the poetry of Cowper, and that he should 'like a fine prospect, but not on picturesque principles' are deposits left by the original satire. And in keeping with this satiric conception is the presentation of Willoughby as a romantic hero who turns out to be contemptible in practice, while the dull, middle-aged Colonel with his flannel waistcoat proves to have in truth the chivalrous nature, the moral delicacy, and the passionate emotions that Marianne had denied him on theoretical grounds. Edward Ferrars is also placed, by his youthful follies and commonplace tastes, in the most unromantic light, but he shows, when tested, and in studied contrast to Willoughby, a high standard of rectitude and is thereby enabled (as Willoughby, we learn, might have been) by behaving honourably to extricate himself from his difficulties and be happy. Marianne's marriage crowns this satire, when marrying without love and against her principles she finds that love and happiness follow.

This crude satiric base is overlaid in the novel by the much more interesting and thoroughly mature discussions it occasions, arising from what was to remain Jane Austen's abiding interest: the relation between the individual and the society he and she must live in. Miss Austen was caught between two worlds – the stable, traditional one of her birth in 1775 at Steventon Rectory, and the New Age which she encountered when growing up, in the form of John Dashwoods enclosing the commons, and disciples of Godwin and Rousseau, as much as in poetry and letters and the French Revolution and Napoleon. A changing attitude to society and the family was questioning the old assumptions that we find in Richardson and Fanny Burney, bringing about a revolution in *moeurs*. The peculiar province of the novelist seems to be the family tie, the relative obligations of parents and children, the proper basis for marriage and the rights, if any, of passionate feeling and spontaneous judgment in a civilized state of intercourse. When there is unrest and reorganization in this department of life a novelistic talent is most likely to be impelled into significant creation. We can see that here was Jane Austen's stimulus: her novels are discussions and dramatizations of problems in what we should call psychology and sociology – terms with which she was of course unacquainted. The problems had been debated by earlier novelists who had made the answers standardized by convention, but these answers seem to have increasingly failed to satisfy Jane Austen. In each novel we see her trying to find out what she really thinks and feels about the problems life pressed on her and what solutions are, for her, workable. The spirit of her enquiry is what Henry Tilney says when Catherine Morland admits that she does not feel as she assumed she ought to feel in a given situation: 'Such feelings ought to be investigated, that they may know themselves.' And all her novels are different because they are projections of different positions as Miss Austen matured and altered. The differences between the positions of Elizabeth and Jane Bennet in comparison with those of Marianne and Elinor Dashwood, and the relation of Marianne to Elinor compared with that of Elizabeth to Jane, and their creator's attitudes to them all, are revelatory of the general development in her inner life that led her from *Sense and Sensibility* to *Persuasion* – to a complete reversal of the inherited assumptions with which she began (those which had caused her to exaggerate playfully and pillory her own anti-social impulses in the person of Marianne) until she ends with a heroine, Anne Elliot, whose unhappiness and mistakes before the novel opens were entirely the result of following the prudential counsels of an older Elinor, Lady Russell.

The plot of *Sense and Sensibility* is almost entirely dramatic, managed so as to hold the reader's interest while illustrating an abstract argument. I will first analyse this plot, for it has not had the recognition its economy, drive and original use of symmetry and surprise deserve. George Moore said with truth that it was the first novel in English to be shaped like a vase instead of a wash-tub. Not unrelated to its formality of plot, which has the symmetry of a formal garden, is the weighty structure of the sentences. *Sense and Sensibility* is in fact the most Johnsonian of the Austen novels in style; its characteristic sentence has a heavy balance and counterpoised effect, even in Marianne's conversation – e.g.: 'Do not, my dearest Elinor, let your kindness defend what I know your judgment must censure.'

The first four chapters set out the characters and background of the Dashwood–Ferrars clan who between them represent all shades of the positions from the 'romantic' to the 'prudential'. Elinor Dashwood becomes attached to Edward Ferrars. The Dashwoods move to Barton and there Marianne becomes attached to Willoughby, while Colonel Brandon becomes interested in both sisters apparently – attracted by Marianne but intimate only with Elinor. An uncertain quantity, he might ultimately marry either. Willoughby soon turns out to be an unknown quantity too. The first complication in the plot follows: Marianne's love-affair is not going straightforwardly. The Colonel leaves suddenly, wrapped in mystery. Willoughby leaves suddenly, also wrapped in mystery. The vacuum left by these two is filled by the arrival of Edward but he also is mysterious in his behaviour to Elinor and as unsatisfactory as Willoughby. He too leaves unanswered questions behind him – the second complication. Both sisters are dispirited for good reason.

There is a lull here while we wonder, and make the acquaintance first of the Palmers and then of the Steeles (both families are needed for the action). Then the first trap is sprung: Elinor's attachment is hopeless because Lucy Steele has been engaged secretly to Edward for years and means to hold him to it. (Dramatic close to volume one.) Elinor, on reflection, has nothing to reproach herself with, and for the sake of her family and from pride in not letting Lucy triumph, keeps her composure and Lucy's secret.

Mrs Jennings has to go to London for Mrs Palmer's confinement, so is able to take the Dashwood girls there to meet Edward and Willoughby again. In town the second trap is sprung: Marianne's attachment is also hopeless because Willoughby, like Edward, is engaged. She discovers then she had been totally mistaken in Willoughby, for he behaves to her like a cad; giving 'sensibility' its head, Marianne abandons herself to misery instead of exercising self-control like Elinor. The difference between the way the sisters bear their disappointment is essential to the moral burden of the novel, but a more subtle contrast lies in their social attitudes: Elinor is primarily conscious of the outside world, Marianne ignores it. When Elinor begs her sister to bear up by remembering that people are watching and commenting maliciously (Elinor's attitude to society seems to be Jane Austen's, one of polite distrust), Marianne, who knows no medium between loving a few people and despising all the rest, retorts: 'No, no, misery such as mine has no pride.' We have now reached the centre of the book, when, Colonel Brandon having told his own history and 'opened Willoughby's character', that of a vicious waster, we can expect no more surprises and think we can foresee the end – that the Colonel will find consolation in Elinor, who is increasingly drawn to him. Willoughby's marriage actually takes place. The nadir is reached.

But now, to change the simile, the pendulum starts to swing back. Immediately Marianne is really injured we get a psychological surprise. People on the whole behave well to Marianne, and Mrs Jennings, who has been hitherto seen from the social surface as a vulgar gossip, becomes known to us as a truly motherly, well-judging woman. It is from her mouth that the final verdicts on Willoughby, Mrs Ferrars and her daughter are delivered, verdicts which are evidently endorsed by the author. An additional and parallel surprise for Marianne is to learn that it was not Willoughby but the Colonel who was the man of feeling, the hero in real life.

On this follows a fresh set of dramatic surprises parallel to those in the first half of the novel but all making in the opposite direction. First there is the *éclaircissement* in the Dashwood–Ferrars household, followed by Marianne's enlightenment about Edward, Fanny's hysterical reaction anticipating Marianne's but on totally different grounds. Marianne is first broken down by the parallel between her own and her sister's case and then shamed by Elinor's fortitude and unselfishness into an effort to emulate her – the beginning of maturity for her. Her 'putrid fever' following, we are given the impression that she will die. The news of this coming to Willoughby enables him to deliver his apologia – a new surprise for us: he was not so bad after all, if not a romantic hero he was not a villain either. Another surprise: Marianne recovers. The girls' return to Barton then produces an apparently final blow for Elinor, corresponding to the announcement of Willoughby's marriage for Marianne – 'Mr Ferrars is married' to Lucy. Now we can only conjecture whether it is Elinor or Marianne whom the Colonel will marry. But on this follows Edward's own appearance at Barton and the greatest surprise of all, the height of the drama: it was Robert that married Lucy, so Edward is honourably free for Elinor and happiness. Lastly, the ultimate surprise: Marianne is persuaded to marry the Colonel 'with no sentiment superior to a strong esteem and lively friendship' in spite of her recent passion for another and in spite of her belief that there can be no second love, to find that she was wrong and must be happy after all.

Besides dramatizing an argument, the plot gives many

opportunities for investigating the social attitudes of the new and the old woman, and discovering how, when put into practice, the former compare with these latter. We see this exemplified in the neat interchange between the sisters at the end of ch. 13 when Elinor is trying to prove to Marianne the impropriety of having allowed Willoughby to show her over the mansion he expects to inherit. Elinor is unsuccessful because Marianne's reasoning is quite as good as her own: only Marianne's premises are mistaken. (Both sisters are logically minded; Marianne, we are explicitly told, is 'sensible and clever', and only less decidedly John Dashwood's half-sister than Elinor, whose argument with him in ch. 41 parallels that between the sisters in ch. 13.) Again, when 'Elinor ventured to doubt the propriety of her receiving such a present from a man so little, or at least so lately known to her', 'This was too much', and Marianne retorts with the Romantic argument: 'It is not time or opportunity that is to determine intimacy; it is disposition alone...of Willoughby my judgment has long been formed.' The fallacy is not recognized by Marianne until her intuitive judgment of the man is proved wrong. Marianne is decidedly not silly, like the heroine of *Northanger Abbey*, she is merely misguided and inexperienced – 'everything but prudent'. Prudence was the grand female virtue of the pre-Romantic system, so in flouting it (it is the old-fashioned moral) Marianne comes to grief. However, Jane Austen came to think less well of the prudential outlook as we can see in *Persuasion*. But Elinor is not 'prudent' from any meanness of nature – her brother is there to show the soul eaten away by prudence – she is on the contrary a fine, superior creature whose intelligent insight into the motives and ideas of her acquaintances has driven her to adopt something like the disillusioned attitude of a Chesterfield. Indeed, some of the discussions in *Sense and Sensibility* appear to me to have been inspired by passages in Chesterfield's *Letters*.

The 'sense' of the title is not opposed to 'sensibility' as has generally been assumed, for each sister has both – the contrast is in the way each directs these qualities. Marianne constantly exposes herself and her sister to vulgar comment by laying herself open to 'the ridicule so justly annexed to sensibility': the irony here is directed against those who think sensibility a joke. 'Sensibility' is not meant to convey any suggestion of affectation or exaggeration, that is done by the word 'romantic' – 'her opinions are all romantic', says Elinor. The Austen code respected sensibility, that is, profound feeling, but expected a stoic surface. When the stricken Marianne cries: 'The Middletons and the Palmers – how am I to bear their pity?' we are to rejoin that she would not have been exposed to it if she had not imprudently shown her love for Willoughby before he had engaged himself to her. 'Her systems', Elinor the realist observes, 'have all the unfortunate tendency of setting propriety at nought', but 'A few years however will settle her opinions on the reasonable basis of common sense and observation', which is what happens by the end of the novel. The point of the satire is that Marianne is so young that she has formed her 'systems' in the schoolroom from books. Jane Austen was a reliable observer and that she had hit a contemporary target when launching Marianne Dashwood as the Young Idea of the period is confirmed by much evidence; Princess Charlotte's papers show that the Heiress Presumptive reading *Sense and Sensibility* when it appeared, at the same age as Marianne, was struck with the likeness between herself and Marianne 'in disposition'.

'Prudence' for Elinor seems to mean discovering a *modus vivendi* by which the sensitive and superior can protect themselves from society – the Middletons and Palmers, the Misses Steele, Robert and Fanny and their mother, a society where an Edward and a Colonel Brandon are exceptional. Along with Marianne's rejection of prudence goes her 'inattention to the forms of general civility'. 'Civility' is the handmaid of prudence; it means a sort of dishonesty imposed on one by the demands of polite intercourse. In Miss Austen's letters 'Civility' is mentioned with distaste or contempt, and its opposite is 'Candour', a word made much of in the Austen novels. To be candid is to be not only sincere but charitably so. Marianne is not candid either, and consequently undervalues worthy people like the Colonel and Mrs Jennings. Elinor's 'system' enables her to combine 'candour' and 'civility' though this obliges her to practise 'address' which Marianne scorns. The discussion between the sisters about Elinor's 'plan of general civility' to which Marianne won't subscribe is important because it makes clear the position the author supports. Against Marianne's ironical caricature of what she takes to be her sister's position Elinor protests:

'My doctrine has never aimed at the subjection of the understanding. All I have ever attempted to influence has been the behaviour. You must not confound my meaning. I am guilty, I confess, of having often wished you to treat our acquaintance in general with greater attention; but when have I advised you to adopt their sentiments or to conform to their judgment in serious matters?'

Elinor, that is, is concerned to maintain a civilized form of social intercourse and thinks it can be done without sacrificing integrity. Ought one to fit in? What is the price of not deferring to society? What is the minimum or necessary degree of social conformity? Posing and answering such questions in the concrete terms of every-day living as she knew it, Jane Austen created in *Sense and Sensibility* a novel that must always have value for us. A related enquiry is the rights of parents over children and their mutual obligations, a theme which had preoccupied the novelists ever since Richardson faced his age with the dilemma of Miss Clarissa Harlowe and aroused the interest of all Europe. In our novel it is described as 'the old, well-established grievance of duty against will, parent against child'. By choosing a Mrs Ferrars as the parent Jane Austen seems to leave us in no doubt where her sympathies lie; but we must realize that the too sympathetic and ductile mother, Mrs Dashwood, is meant to be equally reprehensible. The two mothers are balanced against each other as part of the symmetrical scheme.

The scheme of this book, as we have seen, rules out a hero. It also rules out romantic 'only love', for the Colonel, Marianne and Edward are all shown to change successfully the objects of their first affections. No hero, the insubstantiality of first love, and a moral of Prudence, Reserve and Civility, are not in themselves attractive in fiction. But there is much of a different kind in this one. It is full of touches of nature, some of them memorable and exquisite moments such as Marianne's 'strong impulse of affectionate sensibility' towards Elinor at the dinner-party, and when Edward, in the awful family tenseness, breaks the news that he is free: 'Elinor could sit it no longer. She almost ran out of the room, and as soon as the door was closed, burst into tears of joy, which at first she thought would never cease.' One can well understand Jane's writing from her brother's house in town, protesting against Cassandra's thinking that the distractions of London have made her forget her novel (then in the press): 'No indeed, I am never too busy to think of S. & S. I can no more forget it, than a mother can forget her sucking child.'

The liveliest parts are really stage comedy, as when Edward calls on Elinor and finds Lucy there, the last touches to his and Elinor's discomfort being added by Marianne's joining the party and in her innocence treading on everyone's toes. Mrs Jennings's account of the scene in Harley Street when Lucy's secret came out, is another that springs to mind, like the further comic scene when John Dashwood gives his sisters *his* version of it, and the farcical misunderstanding when Mrs Jennings thinks the Colonel has proposed to Elinor. Robert Ferrars belongs to this world – the stage fop whom few of the women novelists could do without; here he is given a contemporary appeal in his folly about cottages (a satire on the vogue of the preposterous 'cottage orné' in the Regency period). But the deeper comic level is that struck at the opening of the novel, by the masterpiece of meanness in the dialogue between John Dashwood and his wife: this is comedy in the line of Ben Jonson, and *Sense and Sensibility* links Jonson with Dickens.

We end, as nearly always in an Austen novel, with an ideal society. Here it is at Delaford, and Elinor and Marianne and their husbands are content to leave social and material success to Fanny, John, Lucy, Robert and Willoughby. The scrupulous couple, Edward and Elinor, do not even get their rights, a point Miss Austen stresses. This is not a comforting conclusion, but it is the truth of life, and we must not expect comfort from Miss Austen. We go to her to be alerted and braced.

Lady Susan, untitled and undated, survives in manuscript on paper watermarked 1805, but as it is a fair copy and not a first draft like *Sanditon* it may have been composed much earlier, which indeed its old-fashioned epistolary form and general immaturity suggest. It may have been written soon after *First Impressions* and *Elinor and Marianne*, and there was actually an Austen family tradition that *Lady Susan* was a very early work, though it is obviously much more accomplished than anything in the three volumes of Jane's juvenilia. In fact, it is an important link between the juvenilia and the published novels, giving us some idea of what the first two novels were like in their original form. It was first published by her nephew, with some misgivings, and Chesterton seems to have voiced a common opinion when he wrote: 'I for one would willingly have left *Lady Susan* in the waste-paper basket.' The general reader has thus been headed off an interesting and often very entertaining piece of work. Nobody like the heroine figures in any other Austen novel – unscrupulous, plausible, completely lacking in any maternal affection, enjoying nothing so much as tormenting women and knowing how to turn all men round her finger. She is a beautiful and well-bred Becky Sharp and could hardly have been invented by young Miss Austen. An original may be found in 'the beautiful and fashionable and utterly neglectful mother', the Mrs Craven who was notorious for her unnatural behaviour to her daughters (who eloped) and who was the grandmother of two of Jane's friends and later sisters-in-law. Another, more direct contribution from the Austen annals is that of the courtship of Jane's cousin Eliza de Feuillide by her favourite brother Henry. Eliza was the widow of a count guillotined in the Revolution; she was ten years older than Henry (Lady Susan was a dozen years older than Reginald), she was the same age as Lady Susan and like her recently widowed when the courtship started, and like her reluctant to surrender her liberty by remarriage. Eliza's letters show too that she had the same preference for town life as Lady Susan. Henry's engagement to 'his very pleasure-loving cousin' in 1797 was unfavourably received by the Austens and was very likely a sore point with Henry's sisters, as Reginald's infatuation was with *his* sister, who writes to her mother, expressing no doubt the experience of Jane and Cassandra: 'I have never yet found that the advice of a Sister could prevent a young man's being in love if he chose it.'

We may therefore guess why Jane kept the manuscript 'locked up in her desk'. When she made use of it for publication, as we can see she did in *Mansfield Park*, she took care to remove all traces of the domestic drama. Frederica, so highly principled, so full of feeling, fond of books and unkindly treated, with a rich suitor she dislikes forced on her and falling in love with the good young man who is infatuated elsewhere, needed little alteration to become Fanny Price. In Reginald we have Edmund Bertram minus only Ordination. Does not Lady Susan complain of him, very much as Miss Crawford does of Edmund:

'There is a sort of ridiculous delicacy about him which requires the fullest explanation of whatever he may have heard to my disadvantage, and is never satisfied till he thinks he has ascertained the beginning and end of everything. This is *one* sort of Love – but I confess it does not particularly recommend itself to me, I...look with a degree of contempt on the inquisitive and doubting Fancies of that Heart which seems always debating on the reasonableness of its Emotions'?

(That heart, by the way, had been put into circulation by Fanny Burney in 1796 as Edgar's, the hero of *Camilla*, a novel whose original subscription-list contains Miss Austen's name and which she cites in *Northanger Abbey*, along with the same author's *Cecilia* and Maria Edgeworth's *Belinda*, as outstanding examples of the novelist's art.)

Sir Reginald De Courcy certainly suggests a basic Sir Thomas Bertram in his letter pointing out (too late) the folly of his son's succumbing to Lady Susan; he blushes for his son with the same accent as Sir Thomas does for Tom, the dignified voice of virtue consciously founded on good sense and right feeling. Lady Susan, having an affair with a married man, produced Henry Crawford, while softened down and with the vice removed, still bewitching and unprincipled and somehow bad, still showing a reprehensible prejudice in favour of town life, she became the more innocent and commonplace Mary Crawford. But the crude plot of *Lady Susan* is immensely improved in *Mansfield Park*: whereas Reginald finds out Lady Susan's duplicity by a clumsy accident, Edmund Bertram is undeceived about Mary by the logical working-out of the drama. Both young men are ashamed at having been taken in and find consolation in a young lady who is very ready to give it. The cynical end of *Lady Susan*, following naturally from the very nature of the little comedy, is repeated in the conclusion of *Mansfield Park*, where it is hardly in place, for the latter is not in the least comic. We can learn something of what Jane Austen's nephew called 'the filing and polishing process by which she was accustomed to impart a high finish to her published works' by juxtaposing the two passages:

Frederica was therefore fixed in the family of her Uncle and Aunt, till such time as Reginald De Courcy could be talked, flattered and finessed into an affection for her – which, allowing leisure for the conquest of his attachment to her Mother, for his abjuring all future attachments and detesting the Sex, might be reasonably looked for in the course of a Twelvemonth. Three months might have done it in general, but Reginald's feelings were no less lasting than lively.

Edmund had not to wait and wish with vacant affections for an object worthy to succeed her in them. Scarcely had he done regretting Mary Crawford, and observing to Fanny how impossible it was that he should ever meet with such another woman, before it began to strike him whether a very different kind of woman might not do just as well, or a great deal better...I purposely abstain from dates on this occasion, that every one may be at liberty to fix their own, aware that the cure of unconquerable passions, and the transfer of unchanging attachments, must vary much as to time in different people. I only entreat everybody to believe that exactly at the time when it was quite natural that it should be so, and not a week earlier, Edmund did cease to care about Miss Crawford, and become as anxious to marry Fanny as Fanny herself could desire.

We can see from *Lady Susan* how *Elinor and Marianne* must have been managed in its letter form – the sisters could of course write to their mother at Barton when they were in London, but when they were all at Barton, Elinor must have had a friend from her Norland days to confide in by post, as Lady Susan has Mrs Johnson; Mrs Dashwood would correspond with Colonel Brandon as the family friend, Mrs Jennings would sometimes write to Elinor, Lucy and Edward being engaged could with propriety correspond, and Marianne the imprudent corresponded with Willoughby, as we know, though she was not sanctioned to do so by an engagement. And no doubt dreadfully characteristic letters came to Barton from brother John.

In reworking *Lady Susan* for *Mansfield Park* the major change was to make Frederica, instead of being passive, the sensitive observer and the pivot of the whole action as Fanny, inheriting also Mrs Vernon's position as the exasperated commentator on Lady Susan's intrigues. We see that the plan of *Mansfield Park*, where the Country is contrasted with the Town and the latter is defeated, was already present in *Lady Susan*. There London is opposed to Churchill, the former standing as in *Mansfield Park* for heartlessness and immorality, the latter, in the person of the honourable De Courcys and Vernons, for Principles, and Churchill wins. This feeling for formal pattern and for order in the moral universe seems to have been so early a feature of Jane Austen's work that it must have been radical; it is what made her find Dr Johnson's work so congenial. There is, however, nothing simple-minded about such pattern-making in her case; as we have seen, there is genuine subtlety about her insights.

In *The Common Reader* Mrs Woolf looks with a novelist's eye at *The Watsons* and notes, 'the bareness of the first chapters proves that she was one of those writers who lay out their facts rather baldly in the first version' and remarks 'what suppressions and insertions and artful devices' would have been necessary to convert such a version into 'the miracle' of a finished novel of hers! Fortunately we have *Emma* to show us what kind of alterations and additions were necessary – for there seems to me no doubt that *The Watsons* was used for *Emma* as *Lady Susan* was for *Mansfield Park*. Though *The Watsons* is only a fragment, it was not unfinished in conception because the Austens knew that Emma was to marry Mr Howard after her father's death, when she was to be reduced to living with her married brother. She was also to refuse Lord Osborne and thwart Miss Osborne's passion for Mr Howard. Why Miss Austen grew bored with writing it out we don't know: we may conjecture she saw it would not do and that it would be better to start again from a fresh centre, retaining the gist of *The Watsons* for the sub-plot. Thus Emma Watson becomes Jane Fairfax in her circumstances, her talkative inelegant spinster sister was worked up into the aunt Miss Bates, Dorking and Stanton became Highbury, and one of the most famous of Jane Austen's characters, the insufferable Mrs Elton, was elaborated from the first Emma's sister-in-law with her finery, 'arch sallies', 'witty smile', and 'pert and conceited nature'. Emma Watson's father, the invalid, was expanded into extravagant fatuity as the valetudinarian Mr Woodhouse. The most striking incident in *The Watsons*, the delightful impulse of kind Emma to dance with the little boy who has been humiliated by Miss Osborne, becomes the much more subtle, and morally superior, act by which Mr Knightley, overcoming his dislike of dancing and Harriet Smith, partners her at the ball when she has been publicly slighted by Mr Elton. These are the kinds of creation by which Miss Austen's genius manifests itself.

Mansfield Park

Though in 1815 a Court physician was able to inform Miss Austen of the Prince Regent's admiration for her novels, that 'he read them often, and kept a set in every one of his residences', yet her works have been popular classics for less than a century and have only recently been accepted as great masterpieces. To give them their due means reading them with a fuller attention than was customary when they were considered to be nothing more significant or profound than tales written with artless facility, designed to make us laugh at the follies of Miss Austen's contemporaries. Yet to appreciate her duly we must not credit her with too much, with originality when she is only drawing on traditional subjects, themes already discussed, stock patterns of dialogue and types of characterization in use. To know where she adds to the tradition and where she departs from it we need the relevant facts about her literary heritage. We must know where her work stands in relation to that of her predecessors, and where any particular work stands in relation to her other works, before we can decide what is the purpose and achievement of this particular novel. In the case of *Mansfield Park* we want to discover why it is now recognized as the most interesting and important of the Austen novels, and for this we must know something about Miss Austen's private life and disposition.

The relevant facts of her life are few but they are decisive. Born in a Hampshire village in 1775, daughter of an amiable, scholarly rector and of a woman of pronounced character of educated family, she died a spinster at the age of forty-one, having lived mostly in the country, with a spell at Bath, varied by visits to London and the homes of her friends and relatives. She is known to have refused offers of marriage and thought by her sister to have been attached to a man who died before their relations ripened. Her immediate family included besides the inevitable clerical brother a beloved sister, two sailor brothers (one of whom was recognized by the Austens as the original of William Price), another brother who by adoption became a squire and owner of a fine country-house where she enjoyed staying, and a fourth brother, her favourite Henry, who managed her literary business. He contributed most to the family chronicles, serving in the militia, then becoming a banker and living in suitable style in Town, going bankrupt when his firm collapsed, and ending as an Evangelical clergyman. Evidently it was a serviceable family for a novelist, and Jane had plenty of vicarious experience of different kinds of life. All around her she had the large, well-connected, well-bred, well-educated, and in some branches well-off, Austen clan, its tentacles reaching out into great houses, parsonages rich or, like her own father's, poor, Bath, London and many parts of the countryside, India and the Mediterranean, the universities, the services and the law, the aristocracy and the literary world. With its dances, theatricals, flirtations, marriages, invalids, births, deaths and disasters it provided a rich source of materials for any novelist, and it did Jane a particular service by making her, in her privileged position as popular visitor, into a practised letter-writer, whose correspondence, generally meant to be read aloud, kept friends and relatives in touch; as valued aunt and sister she had to transmit not only news but advice, opinions and insights into character and motive – all good training for a novelist.

And the Austens, besides, were great novel-readers and poetry-lovers and highly critical of what they read; they read aloud, acted (the Rev. George Austen seems to have had none of Sir Thomas Bertram's prejudices) and formed a stock of literary jokes and references which launched Jane into attempting mock fictions herself. These she collected into three treasured manuscript books, published by Dr R. W. Chapman in the volume *Minor Works.* They are prevailingly satiric (largely in the form of letters but with some dramatic scenes), and meant for the family ear; for like *Northanger Abbey,* they are full of private jokes. Soon, tired of skits no doubt, she made a novel in letters, *Elinor and Marianne,* which after years of rewriting was published as *Sense and Sensibility,* and the next novel we know, *Pride and Prejudice,* now so dramatic in form, was probably also originally told in letters. This preference for the epistolary form was not only because of her experience of letter-writing, but because some of the fictions she most admired – *Sir Charles Grandison* and *Evelina* above all – were so written, though the form was already old-fashioned by her time. It has obvious disadvantages, and she gradually worked out her own form, which combines dramatic presentation (owing something to the rectory theatricals and something to her frequentation of Shakespeare) relieved by moral reflection and satiric comment from the author, and interspersed by as many letters as her critical sense would allow (these are always gems, written with obvious zest and each embodying the very soul of its assumed writer). The last work we know her to have written in letter form was a novelette, *Lady Susan*, which I believe to have been the matrix of *Mansfield Park* – there is a close relation between the plot and theme, and there are many parallel passages.[1] An unfinished tale, *The Watsons*, which I have no doubt was the nucleus of her next novel *Emma*, was *not* drafted in letters, so that by then (1806) she no longer thought of the epistolary novel as the natural technique of the story-teller, and was emancipated at last from her early models.

Lord Justice MacKinnon, who applied his legal talents to an analysis of the chronology of the Austen novels, discovered that she used a calendar – presumably the current one – when composing, and that *Mansfield Park*'s chronology corresponds to the year 1808–9. But she must have rewritten it yet again for publication in 1814, for though we know it was finished by the summer of 1813, we find her writing to Cassandra – the sister from whom she had no secrets – as late as January 1813 that she is now writing something on 'a complete change of subject' (from *Pride and Prejudice*) '– ordination'. On inspection we can see that all that bears on the ordination theme could have been inserted in a final rewriting, and that of the two themes mentioned in the novel, 'ordination and matrimony', only the second is radical. We have here in the composition of *Mansfield Park* an example of Miss Austen's literary method, which I have found to be her almost invariable practice and which justified her brother Henry in stating, in his Biographical Notice, that 'some of these novels had been the gradual performances of her previous life'. She worked into her novels incidents and characters adapted from both life and literature, and starting at first, we may conjecture, by a satiric sketch, unsympathetic in tone, of what had amused her or irritated her – the remains of these first studies still obtrude through the texture of the later, subtler forms – she worked that over in the light of her deeper thoughts and feelings, under the pressure of her intimate experience and in response to her own problems and self-questionings; so that what we have in the final version is a work of art, proceeding from the deepest layer of her personality, the product of a sustained private life. No wonder she thought highly of the novel as a criticism of life and would have claimed for her own work what she implies when, in *Northanger Abbey*, defending novels from detraction: 'there seems almost a general wish of decrying the capacity and undervaluing the performances which have only genius, wit and taste to recommend them... "And what are you reading, Miss — ?" "Oh, it is only a novel!"...It is only *Cecilia*, or *Camilla*, or *Belinda*, or, in short, only some work in which the greatest powers of the mind are displayed, in which the most thorough knowledge of human nature, the happiest delineation of its varieties, the liveliest effusions of wit and humour, are conveyed to the world in the best-chosen language.'

Pride and Prejudice in the making had filled her with delight, but when it had at last been published she wrote to Cassandra, with characteristic self-criticism: 'The work is rather too light, and bright, and sparkling; it wants shade; it wants to be stretched out here and there with a long chapter of sense, if it could be had.' What makes *Mansfield Park* so very different from its predecessor is not only the artist's sense that *Pride and Prejudice* was a kind of success that she would not care to repeat, or that it was slighter and less mature in content than what she was now capable of; it was that she had become a different person. In *Pride and Prejudice* a marriage is patched up between Lydia and the man with whom she had been living in sin, and Miss Austen makes this the occasion for two separate attacks on the conventional moral attitude of her age:

The good news quickly spread through the house, and with proportionate speed through the neighbourhood. It was borne in the latter with decent philosophy. To be sure, it would have been more for the advantage of conversation, had Miss Lydia Bennet come upon the town; or, as the happiest alternative, been secluded from the world, in some distant farmhouse.

This is the voice of Fielding, whose humane, large masculine stance and generous scorn of moral spite was altogether outside the feminine world, and the passage is one of the clearest proofs I know that Miss Austen was ever seriously influenced by him. And later in the book the Rev. Mr Collins writes to express horror at Lydia's being received at home:

'It was an encouragement of vice; and had I been the rector at Longbourn, I should very strenuously have opposed it. You ought certainly to forgive them as a Christian, but never to admit them in your sight, or allow their names to be mentioned in your hearing.'

'*That* is his notion of Christian forgiveness!' comments Mr Bennet – and presumably the author. Yet the banishment proposed for the fallen woman by the neighbourhood, and the paternal attitude recommended by the professional Christian, are in *Mansfield Park* actually the fate meted out to Maria, and this time the author evidently thinks it the right one. What accounts for such a change?

The Austen Letters reveal that whereas Jane was hostile to 'the Evangelicals' in 1809, by 1814 she has changed and is 'by no means convinced that we ought not all to be evangelicals'. The change-over to sponsoring a conventional moral outlook must be associated with this change of opinion about Evangelicalism, which must have dictated her choice of what strikes us as a most unlikely subject for an Austen novel: 'Ordination'. In 1813 Jane Austen was in her thirty-eighth year and had gone through a great deal. She had, like her sister, lost by death the only man she could care for; she had lost her dearly-loved father and her early home, and lost some of her closest friends in tragic circumstances. She had rejected on second thoughts a conspicuously eligible offer of marriage after accepting it, and had now long passed the age of twenty-seven when that offer occurred – an age which in her novels is taken to mark, as she would say, a period. She must have had a sense that her real life lay in the past, and that the time had come to reconsider it. She seems to have felt that hitherto she had set too high a value on liveliness of mind, had lacked Jane Bennet's virtue 'candour', and had differed from conventional moral theory too confidently. Why otherwise should she endorse Sir Thomas's and Edmund's objection to private theatricals? The Austens and their friends had performed questionably decorous plays in their barn without any ill effect on their conduct. Fanny Price ('my Fanny' she calls her) is merely the over-delicate, timidly feminine type of heroine who had been evolved by the women novelists of the last third of the eighteenth century and is marked by their almost superstitious respect for authority, while the lively, talking, arguing heroine who resists convention – the girl that we associate with Jane Austen – is in this novel, and this only, the heroine's rival and marked with the stigma of being next thing to a bad woman (which is what her original, Lady Susan, actually was).

It belongs to this new moralistic phase that Miss Austen should fix on Kotzebue's *Lovers' Vows* as a target; in translation the play was so popular that it had aroused hostile criticism. Its 'advanced' Romantic morality, like Lydia Bennet's rehabilitation, was felt to constitute a threat to the moral basis of society. Some knowledge of this play is essential for understanding *Mansfield Park*, so I will give the briefest outline. The menace to morality lay in the fact that the Baron Wildenheim, who in youth had seduced the village maiden Agatha under promise of marriage and then abandoned her, decides, on meeting their now grown-up son Frederick, to satisfy his conscience by recognizing the bastard as his heir and marrying Agatha. This too with the encouragement of his chaplain Anhalt and his legal daughter Amelia! Besides this, Amelia has fallen in love with her tutor, the poor chaplain, in defiance of the Richardsonian canon that a lady cannot with propriety entertain a sentiment for a man until he has made her an offer; worse, she proceeds to make him the offer of her hand, rejecting the silly fop Count Cassel, and succeeding in converting both the chaplain and her father to her wishes. The extreme indelicacy of Miss Bertram's playing the part of the fallen Agatha is obvious, while the distress of Edmund at finding that the lady he wishes to marry is willing to make Amelia's shameless avowals is well grounded in conventional notions of decorum. We should be resigned to this in Fanny Burney, but Miss Austen is elsewhere noticeably in advance of the conventions – not of course 'advanced' like a novelist–*philosophe* such as Bage, but compared with novelists within the pale – and likes to represent such features of the age as cant or unwholesome affectation, as she had in *Pride and Prejudice*.

But being a great artist she contrives a serious function for the play within the play: the prophetic irony of casting Maria for the tragic rôle of a seduced woman and Miss Crawford for the part of a woman lacking in feminine decorum, is a less obvious but more important contribution to the meaning of *Mansfield Park*, and a technique that Miss Austen could have found only in Shakespeare. We should indeed know, even without Edmund's and Mr Crawford's telling us, that our author was soaked in Shakespeare. Fanny's poets are Shakespeare, Cowper and Crabbe, her favourite prose-writers Johnson and Goldsmith, reflecting her creator's taste. While the mould and moral tone of the Johnsonian sentence can in *Mansfield Park* be found decisively influential, it is the frequentation of these poets which seems to me to have enabled Jane Austen to have risen, as an artist, out of the class of the Fanny Burneys, Maria Edgeworths and Mrs Inchbalds of the age she grew up in. That age, we must remind ourselves, was the fag-end of the eighteenth century, the literary inheritor of Richardson, Fielding, Fanny Burney; at the turn of the century it became in effect Regency, for the Regency style in architecture and interior decoration is considered to have begun with the nineteenth century, and we can see from Jane Austen's novels alone how a corresponding change had begun in letters and life. *Mansfield Park*, in technique and subject and prose style and in its thoughtful inquiries into human relationships, looks forward to George Eliot and Henry James; so *Mansfield Park* is the first modern novel in England.

Before going into this assertion I must mention what is not original. Jane Austen did not invent the kinds of satire she uses, even when she is not feeling like Fielding. As Miss Tompkins points out in her invaluable book *The Popular Novel 1770–1800*, the women novelists among her predecessors had specialized in a satiric approach to the opposite sex in order to castigate masculine selfishness and conceit, and had often and roughly handled feminine affectation and malice; they particularly aimed at snobbish or vulgar women who make sensitive heroines suffer, and in these respects they were by no means always inferior to Miss Austen. They had provided her with a moralistic tradition – with crude models for those subtle discussions of matrimonial relations, filial obligations, right feeling and so on, which take up a good deal of space in *Mansfield Park*. They had endowed her with a vocabulary, based on conventions which we no longer understand, for criticizing character and personality – it contains such terms as 'principled', 'address', 'air', 'temper', 'countenance', 'well-regulated mind'; everyone was expected to be a connoisseur of character – when Edmund wants to praise Miss Crawford to Fanny he says: 'She has great discernment. I know nobody who distinguishes character better.'

What is really new is the attempt to work out a psychological analysis of feeling, which creates a new style; the very movement of thought and feeling is caught in the panting, ejaculatory sentences, often only disordered phrases, which register Fanny's emotions and Edmund's hesitations and doubts. This new sensitiveness to the complexities of experience has upset the original symmetry of the theme, which in *Lady Susan* was Town against Country, worldliness in opposition to 'heart', 'domestic happiness' and 'principles'. The theme is still there, and Miss Crawford, like Lady Susan descending from Town to destroy the peace of mind of the Great House, is softened and moved, to declare: 'You have all so much more *heart* among you.' Actually, though, it is only to Fanny and Edmund that this really applies – and perhaps to Mrs Grant. However, in the end Mansfield is purged of worldliness and an ideal order established. For what we are offered is a parable, something that no English novelist had attempted before.

Jane Austen shared with Pope the Augustan vision of the place of the great country-house in the life of the nation, duly related, she shows, to the parsonage, farm and cottage. Mansfield Park seems to be an Adam-type mansion with grounds laid out by 'Capability' Brown, since Sir Thomas certainly belongs to that phase of our cultural history; his children, however, like the Crawfords, are of the new age, rebelling against the traditional proprieties and the restraints of country life and hankering after the dubious pleasures of the gay Regency world of Brighton and London (we hear too of Cheltenham, Bath, Weymouth, Tunbridge, Richmond and Twickenham to build up an impression of a round of dissipations from which the Park is isolated). Which is right? is not Miss Austen's subject, but: What is to be said for and against each? Our author holds no brief for the Past – Fanny is well laughed at for her Gothic yearnings at Sotherton Court, and that Elizabethan mansion is represented as a stifling museum where spontaneous life has died and to which the Regency improver is quite rightly called, to modernize and open a prospect. She conveys all the horrors of a dead way of life. The disused chapel, the now meaningless family portraits, the rooms without a view, and the antique furniture – all oppress the young people obliged by 'politeness' to endure an Aunt Norris and a dowager Mrs Rushworth. When they find a way of escape into the grounds our sympathy is with them; we share their relief until we find that even the grounds are prison within prison, and the intense impression thus created culminates with Maria identifying herself with Sterne's caged starling that called 'Let me out – let me out.'

The Sotherton episode is the finest and most original in the Austen novels, and I know nothing of the kind more remarkable in any English novel; if we met it in Kafka or Henry James we should at once recognize its wonderfully sustained but never obtrusive symbolism – perceive that its action is a pregnant microcosm. Yet there is not a phrase or image in it which is not meaningful, giving a forecast of the rest of the action (again a Shakespearian technique). All the action is symbolic – we have Maria contriving to slip round the locked gate with her lover, to Fanny's horror ('You will hurt yourself against those spikes', etc.), Julia scrambling after her, Edmund deserting Fanny for Miss Crawford, with whom he has a significant debate before he returns to his desolate cousin, and so on. At the time it reads like a bad dream, and we see its point when we find the pattern of events so exactly and awfully repeated, when Maria, imprisoned in matrimony, forces Mr Crawford to elope with her. The novel is as full of prophetic ironies as *Macbeth*: only on second reading do we note Henry Crawford's boast, 'I never do wrong without gaining by it'; and Tom's, that *he* can be trusted to 'take care that Sir Thomas's daughters do nothing to distress him'. And there are effects for which there is no name, such as Sir Thomas's dramatic return which closes the first volume, giving an excellent comic effect that is repeated with more point when he walks out onto the unimagined stage on which a stranger is ranting, and which nevertheless also serves a serious purpose in underlining the repressive nature of Sir Thomas's personality.

With his return not only the play-acting, which may be undesirable, but also the merriment and the spontaneity, which cannot be, are at an end – 'all was sameness and gloom'. With all his virtues Sir Thomas has been culpable towards his children; in forcing on them an appearance of conformity and leaving no outlet for their tastes, he has precipitated the tragedy – for *Mansfield Park*, alone of the Austen novels, is tragic (in spite of the appearance of a happy ending). The Mansfield stage is finally as strewn with corpses of ruined lives as the stage at the end of *Hamlet* with dead bodies. The tragedy of the Crawfords is of their own making, though involving Mansfield; they are the dangerous side of the new age (the age of Byron and Constant), and Crawford anticipates the latter's Adolphe in 'indulging in the freaks of a cold-blooded vanity too long'. His punishment, like Byron's, is to have outlawed himself from Mansfield Park. Maria seems to belong to the tragic world of Racine, a repressed but passionate woman tormented first by vanity and pride, and then by jealousy, into her own destruction. We are not spared the Dantean sequel, that they become each other's torment until they break apart and Maria is consigned to a yet lower circle in hell shared with Mrs Norris. The means Maria took to escape from the confinement of Mansfield has ironically produced a sentence of life imprisonment.

The brilliance, the heartlessness and the frivolity of the Regency world are presented in contrast to the moral conservatism, the formality and decorum of the Age of Adam that lingers on in Northamptonshire and can still awe a Crawford, male or female, into at least the show of respect. At the end a purged and revitalized Mansfield is provided for a significant trinity – a humbled Sir Thomas, an undeceived Edmund, and a Fanny who has matured out of submissiveness into someone who can judge, resist and act on others. William and Susan Price, whose early poverty has made them strong with 'the consciousness of being born to struggle and endure', are grafted onto Mansfield, to its advantage as well as to theirs.

The Portsmouth episode makes its own contribution to the enquiry into the question of what kind of society maintains a life where 'heart' can be the criterion. Fanny's natural family live in a more primitive state of unrepressed feeling than the Bertrams, but Fanny soon realizes that 'heart' is not the inevitable opposite of elegance either. Portsmouth is even less the home of the ideal society than Mansfield, where 'there was a propriety, an attention towards everybody which was not here', where 'If tenderness could ever be supposed wanting, good sense and good breeding supplied its place.' 'Self-knowledge, generosity, humility' are the qualities Jane Austen stipulates in *Mansfield Park* as even more essential than 'elegance', that concept which for her sums up the achievements of a fine civilization.

It is characteristic of Jane Austen that she collected all the opinions she could obtain of *Mansfield Park* and transcribed them, whether fatuous or discriminating. Posterity is likely to agree with that lady who tersely replied: 'All who think deeply and feel much will give the Preference to *Mansfield Park*.'

Jane Eyre

The life of the author of *Jane Eyre* must be read in Mrs Gaskell's *Life of Charlotte Brontë* (1857), one of the great English biographies. Though Mrs Gaskell had to make concessions to the prejudices and feelings of the living, though she did not know Charlotte personally till late in Charlotte's life after the deaths of all her relatives except old Mr Brontë, though her Victorian outlook and training made her excise and mollify a good deal, and though, most serious of all, we must doubt if she really understood in what the importance of *Jane Eyre* consists, still the biography remains essentially valid. And it has the great advantage of Mrs Gaskell's intimate friendship with her sister-novelist, visiting each other and exchanging confidences as they did. A long, fascinatingly detailed letter Mrs Gaskell wrote in 1853 during her first visit to Haworth is indispensable (it is printed in the Introduction to the 'World's Classics' edition of the *Life*). In it she remarked on the 'pestiferous churchyard' which overhung the gloomy parsonage and into which 'one by one they [the children] had dropped off' – disease and premature deaths being only part, however, of the tragic story of the Brontës.

'A little, plain, provincial, sickly-looking old maid', is how George Lewes described Charlotte to George Eliot, 'yet', added the latter in her Journal, having been overwhelmed by the novels, 'what passion, what fire in her!' Mrs Gaskell saw deeper. She remarked the beautiful eyes and the sweet voice that counteracted the impression of plainness, and was profoundly moved by her personality:

In general there she sits quite alone thinking over the past... She has the wild strange facts of her own and her sisters' lives, – and beyond and above these she has the most original and suggestive thoughts of her own: so that, like the moors, I felt on the last day as if our talk might be extended in any direction without getting to the end of any subject.

Charlotte's most intelligent school-friend (who figures in *Shirley* along with her extraordinary family 'the Yorkes') wrote to Mrs Gaskell after reading the *Life*: 'Though not so gloomy as the truth, it is perhaps as much so as people will accept without calling it exaggerated', adding that the reviewers do not seem 'to think it a strange or wrong state of things that a woman of first-rate talents, industry and integrity should live all her life in a walking nightmare of poverty and self-suppression'. One might cite, as an instance of the kind of manly crassness Mary Taylor complains of, Kingsley's tribute to Mrs Gaskell: 'Well have you done your work, and given us the picture of a valiant woman made perfect by suffering.' It was just such Victorian attitudes about women, and such an assumption about the improving effects of filial duty, unhappiness, and deprivation, that made Charlotte write her novels, which all spring from the passionate need to demonstrate that a good life for a woman, no less than for a man, is a satisfied one.

Charlotte was born in 1816, and was therefore by no means the 'Victorian' product she is generally thought of as being. The third daughter of an Ulsterman who had gone to Cambridge University and settled as a parson in Yorkshire, she was motherless from early childhood, and by the premature deaths of her two elder sisters was left henceforth in charge of her younger sisters Anne and Emily and the brother Branwell. The four children doomed to isolation, constraint, and precocity because turned in on each other, were made companions in his reading by their father. When Charlotte went to her second boarding-school in 1831, aged fifteen, it was noted that she spoke with a strong Irish accent and that 'she said that she had never played and could not play' when the girls invited her to join in their games. An earlier, unhappy experience of school at a religious foundation provided the material for the Lowood section of *Jane Eyre*: from this school the nine-year-old Charlotte was withdrawn after the deaths of her elder sisters, also pupils there. She remembered it all so faithfully that, when the novel was published anonymously, many Yorkshire readers recognized the teachers, the 'black marble clergyman' its founder, and 'Helen Burns' the suffering Maria Brontë. The four surviving children comforted themselves with a life of corporate fantasy in which their favourite hero Wellington figured with other real and invented characters (aristocratic and royal) in a Byronic ethos. Their father discussed politics (Tory) with them: they read his newspapers and his books, so they early took to literature; they wrote tales, fantasies, poems, journals, serial stories, and brought out a monthly magazine, like so many children. But with the Brontës the practice of creating a fictional daydream world persisted into adult life, so that from being the most precocious of children they became retarded adults. Eventually Emily and Anne combined to produce a saga of the Gondals (of which only the poetry Emily wrote for the characters to declaim survives), while Charlotte and her brother had their own country, Angria. Miss Fanny Ratchford has edited what survive of Charlotte's Angrian manuscripts; they show a feverish imagination providing what was lacking in the life of the parsonage, no doubt, but drawing on no first-hand experience whatever. In fact, they seem to me utterly without promise. Yet Charlotte was writing the latest of them not much before her first novel *The Professor*, half at least of which is strikingly realistic and founded on her own experiences (even though the narrator is a man) – *The Professor* is the authentic voice of the author of *Villette*, into which novel indeed it was later transformed.

What precipitated Charlotte into writing fiction that was based in real life was evidently the earthquake that going to study at Brussels occasioned. For after attempts to earn her living as a governess (for which she was peculiarly unfitted by her ignorance of normal children, her disabling shyness, and her yearning to be with her sisters), she persuaded the aunt who presided over the Haworth home to subsidize Emily and herself for a spell abroad to qualify them in French and German. Reading *The Professor* and *Villette* we may conclude that the shock for these very Protestant and Yorkshire-bred sisters at encountering the unimaginable culture of a Catholic boarding-school for the wealthy and aristocratic young ladies of Brussels, was what forced Charlotte out of her melodramatic, Byronic daydreams into examining her own identity and problems. She told Mrs Gaskell 'of her desire (almost amounting to illness) of expressing herself in some way'. When the sisters were home again and their plan of keeping a school in the parsonage proved hopeless, they turned first to publishing their poems in a joint volume and next to writing a novel each; *Jane Eyre* seems to have been started in August 1846 after *The Professor* had been rejected by several publishers.

Charlotte was the ambitious and energizing member of the sorority. She thought of literary fame as 'a passport to the society of clever people', her school-friend said, but 'When at last she got it, she lamented that it was of no use' – her sisters and brother were tragically dead and her sufferings had left her unable to bear society: 'She never criticized her books to me further than to express utter weariness of them, and the labour they had given her.' We can see that to write *Jane Eyre*, at least, must have been at the time a great joy as well as a relief of the pressures of her inner life and her aspirations. But, with that recurrent tragic pattern that made up her life, even the encouraging reception of *Jane Eyre* was spoilt for her, for *Wuthering Heights*, Emily's bid for fame and fortune, got no recognition at that time: 'But Emily – poor Emily – the pangs of disappointment as review after review came out about *Wuthering Heights* were terrible', wrote Mrs Gaskell in her letter from Haworth. 'Miss B. said she had no recollections of pleasure or gladness about *Jane Eyre*, every such feeling was lost in seeing Emily's resolute endurance yet knowing what she felt.' And within the year Emily died.

When *Jane Eyre* was published under a pseudonym ('Currer Bell') in October 1847, it attracted a great deal of admiration: Thackeray described it as 'the masterwork of a great genius'; next year, when it was in the third edition, the *Quarterly Review* referred to 'the equal popularity of *Jane Eyre* and *Vanity Fair*'. The critic G. H. Lewes thoughtfully advised Charlotte to study Jane Austen's novels and correct her shortcomings in the light of that great artist's practice. Charlotte had never read any Jane Austen, it appeared, but she was willing to learn. Having read *Pride and Prejudice* she wrote to explain to Lewes with admirable spirit why such a novelist could be of no use to her, indeed, by the light of what she was trying to do, was not a novelist at all. Her side of the correspondence between them is given in an abridged form in the *Life*. Charlotte rejects Miss Austen's work as 'only shrewd and observant', 'sensible real (more *real* than *true*) but she cannot be great'; one sees there only 'a highly-cultivated garden but no open country'; she is 'without poetry'; 'Can there be a great artist without poetry?'

Obviously, in those two-hourly walks that the Brontë sisters took every night round the parlour table, 'like restless wild animals', while they discussed their plans and projects, a revolutionary theory of what a novel should be and could do had been arrived at by the authors of *Jane Eyre* and *Wuthering Heights*. We may guess that it was the experience of the poetry of the Romantics and Shakespearian tragedy that had enlarged for them the idea of the novelist's function. I give this significant extract from Charlotte's correspondence in 1850 because Mrs Gaskell doesn't (she probably thought it would alienate the Victorian reader, with whom she was pleading Charlotte's case):

She does her business of delineating the surface of the lives of genteel English people curiously well... What sees keenly, speaks aptly, moves flexibly, it suits her to study; but what throbs fast and full, though hidden, what the blood rushes through, what is the unseen seat of life and the sentient target of death – this Miss Austen ignores. She no more, with her mind's eye, beholds the heart of her race than each man, with bodily vision, sees the heart in his heaving breast. Jane Austen was a complete and most sensible lady, but a very incomplete and rather insensible (*not senseless*) woman. If this is heresy, I cannot help it.

As always, criticism has preceded and fostered creation. Here the idea of a novel, the novelist's ambition and the expression of it, are all curiously suggestive of D. H. Lawrence. Charlotte and Emily Brontë were evidently united in their determination not to write novels which give merely a surface imitation of life ('more real than true') nor to be satisfied with studying people in their social and intellectual character. They aimed at achieving through prose fiction something as serious, vital, and significant as the work of their favourite poets, which should voice the tragic experience of life, be true to the experience of the whole woman, and convey a sense of life's springs and undercurrents. To envisage such a possibility for the novel was at that date a critical achievement of the first order; to succeed, however unequally, in carrying it out was surely proof of great creative genius. In order to be great art their novels, these girls realized, must include 'poetry', necessarily employing a poetic method and evolving new prose techniques. This effort in due course led to the novel's becoming the major art form of the nineteenth century.

Yet though *Wuthering Heights* and *Jane Eyre* have always been accepted as powerful and impressive, it is not as works of art that they are commonly thought of, rather as artless concoctions of uncontrolled daydreams. In the standard work *Early Victorian Novelists* Lord David Cecil describes Charlotte Brontë's novels as 'incoherent', alleging 'She has no gift of form, no restraint, little power of observation, no power of analysis' and that she holds up the 'narrative' to insert passages of poetic prose which have no function. This reaction to *Jane Eyre* seems to me to show an inability to read, to see what is in fact staring one in the face, for the novel is strikingly coherent, schematic (like *Wuthering Heights*) and, with a few lapses, thoroughly controlled in the interest of the theme. The theme has, very properly, dictated the form, and the theme is an urgently felt personal one, an exploration of how a woman comes to maturity in the world of the writer's youth. Charlotte always insisted that Jane Eyre was framed 'as plain and as small' as herself to prove to her sisters that a heroine could be interesting without being beautiful – 'but', she added, 'she is not myself any further than that'. This is not correct, for Charlotte's experiences at the Evangelical school and as governess were transferred to Jane, and Jane's passionate desire for a wider life and richer and fuller experience was, we know, also her creator's.

I must protest also against a current idea that *Jane Eyre* belongs to the class of novels that Henry James called 'loose, baggy monsters' which, 'with their queer elements of the accidental and the arbitrary' are without 'composition...that principle of health and safety' and therefore, though they may contain 'life', are wasteful and meaningless. *Jane Eyre*, like *Wuthering Heights* and *Anna Karenina*, is quite as deliberately composed as any novel in existence, but like them is a unique organic structure and therefore does not qualify for (or invite the use of) James's term of praise for the art of his own novels – 'triumphantly scientific'. The nature of the success *Jane Eyre* represents was recognized by the intelligent Mary Taylor, who wrote to her friend after reading the copy of *Jane Eyre* sent her: 'Your novel surprises me by being so perfect a work of art', adding: 'It is impossible to squeeze a moral out of your production' – thus putting her finger on another element in the art of Emily and Charlotte which proves their break with the novel as they had known it. In this respect their art is more emancipated than George Eliot's, who was startled and repelled as well as fascinated by *Jane Eyre*, and by *Villette* ('even more wonderful', she wrote).

James's objection to George Eliot (whether true or not), that 'instead of feeling life itself, it is "views" on life that she tries to feel', could never be made against Charlotte or Emily Brontë, whose novels surely exemplify his claim that 'the perfect dependence of the "moral" sense of a work of art' is 'on the amount of felt life concerned in producing it' and that the question to ask of a novel is: 'Is it valid, is it genuine, is it sincere, the result of some direct impression or perception of life?' *Jane Eyre* because of its theme demanded a new kind of organization not based on 'narrative' and we are not put in possession of the theme by a logical exposition. Nor, though the novelist is examining the growth of moral fibre, has the book a moralistic framework. ('Nor can I write a book for its moral', Charlotte wrote in explanation to her publisher when frankly informing him of what he would consider her limitations.) Her object was to show how the embittered little charity-child finds the way to come to terms with life and society.[1]

Part of the undertaking involved examining the assumptions that the age made with regard to women, to the relations between the sexes and between the young and those in authority; in addition, conventions of social life and accepted religious attitudes come in for radical scrutiny. A 'good' man like the Rev. Mr Brocklehurst is revealed as a hateful object, and a 'noble' character like St John Rivers is shown to be a terrifying egotist in disguise. The scrutiny that Emily Brontë directed at the inhabitants of Thrushcross Grange and Wuthering Heights is often similar in its effects, and the two novels gain by comparative reading, Charlotte too having read *Wuthering Heights* first.

Jane Eyre, and its successor *Villette* (which while offering a different setting and different experiences from its predecessor is very similar in method and theme) seem to me perfectly clear and unmistakable in intention, though they have no continuity of plot and characters and do not answer the traditional requirement that a novel should entertain by telling a story. *Jane Eyre* moves from stage to stage of Jane's development, divided into four sharply distinct phases with their suggestive names: childhood at Gateshead; girlhood, which is schooling in both senses, at Lowood; adolescence at Thornfield; maturity at Marsh End, winding up with fulfilment in marriage at Ferndean. Each move leaves behind the phase and therefore the setting and characters which supplied that step in the demonstration – the novel is not an *éducation sentimentale* like *David Copperfield* but a moral-psychological investigation. A good deal of the effect of the book depends on the reader's making out associations, and the parts are not mechanically linked by a plot as in most previous fictions but organically united (as in Shakespeare) by imagery and symbolism which pervade the novel and are as much part of the narrative as the action.

One of the interesting and original features of the novel is the use made of literature – books are referred to for their symbolic meaning. No one can forget the striking opening of the book with its creation of cheerless November outdoors and a correspondingly wretched emotional climate for the unloved child within, taking refuge from a hostile world behind the curtain while consoling herself with Bewick's *British Birds*. The point of the detailed descriptions of some of Bewick's text and wood-cuts will be lost unless we realize that this book provides the child with images of storm, shipwreck and disaster, Arctic desolation and Alpine heights, death and mysterious evil – images which seem to express her own bewildered sense of what life is like, since they correspond with her condition in the home of the Reeds, cruelly oppressed both physically and morally and above all suffering in her isolation from a passionate sense of injustice. She cannot, of course, explain this, but concludes: 'With Bewick on my knees, I was then happy: happy at least in my way.' The other books she draws comfort from in Gateshead are *Gulliver's Travels* – which she believed, as children do, to be factual and which seemed to show her that there are other kinds of life in the world that she could perhaps escape to – and the *Arabian Nights*, which introduces her to the idea of magic, that magic powers can transform the conditions of life. These three books represent the particular aspects of the life of the imagination that she goes to books for, so that when, at Lowood, Helen Burns offers her Dr Johnson's *Rasselas*, she looks it over and finding as she says no magic or fantasy or poetic imagery in it, rejects it. But *Rasselas* is symbolic of the kind of wisdom, a disenchanted stoicism and the acceptance of reality, which Helen Burns has to teach her. Two years after *Jane Eyre* was published came *Copperfield*, with the child David taking refuge from the miseries brought into his home by a stepfather in picaresque novels, where he could play at being 'a child's Tom Jones' and assume the dignity of a Smollett naval captain: 'They kept alive my fancy, and my hope of something beyond that place and time – they, and the Arabian Nights, and the Tales of the Genii.' Dickens's method in his novels until his last period seems curiously old-fashioned, and his tempo slack, compared with *Jane Eyre* and *Wuthering Heights*, which provide a new standard of achievement in fiction.

Jane's mind at the opening is truly what Arnold wrongly thought the mind of the author of *Villette* must be, one 'containing nothing but hunger, rebellion and rage'. Arnold prophesied that this would be 'fatal to her in the long run'. That it is not so to Jane (as it was to be to Dickens's Miss Wade) is because the child is capable of judging her experiences by a fine instinct for what makes for her own psychic health and happiness, thus making her able to face life more successfully after each experience. Each, therefore, initiates a new phase of being for her, because she has learnt something new about the possibilities of living and so can make a further demand on life. Her first discovery is that moral courage can make a stand against moral oppression and gives one power. Her efforts conquer the nursery and win over Bessie the nursemaid, who alone at Gateshead stands, like Nelly Dean at Wuthering Heights, for the normal unrefined tradition of human kindliness,[2] expressed here chiefly in singing folk-songs and touching ballads and telling the children folk-lore – then 'the afternoon lapsed in peace and harmony'. Upon this Jane gains a psychological victory over the gorgon aunt; we notice the truth of the pathetic precariousness of the child's enjoyment of her triumph and sense of power – an insight new in English fiction. This first stage of emancipation from the thraldom of the family and custom ends with the introduction of Mr Brocklehurst, the 'black marble clergyman' who brings the bogy of hell-fire religion and a new oppression, the Evangelical attitude to life, into the child's world (a long while before Arthur Clennam bore his witness to it as the enemy). When Jane arrives at his school as an outlaw from Gateshead, 'Rain, wind and darkness filled the air', and as she enters, the door in the wall is locked behind her, for nine years more.

Jane has now to face the same conditions (the injustice and self-righteous callousness that characterized life in Charlotte Brontë's England) and start all over again in a larger unit, a working community, specifically religious in that it is governed by the doctrines of Mr Brocklehurst, whose creed she loathes and instinctively disbelieves. There are, however, two other representatives of religion whose influence is attractive to her because they are kind and morally impressive. The first is Helen Burns, who exemplifies an ideal of Christian practice (Mr Brocklehurst's practice is a mockery of the ideal): turning the other cheek, forgiving one's enemies (both are new and unacceptable ideas to Jane) and enduring meekly in this world in the confidence of a glorious rebirth in Heaven – which involves, Jane notes, despising the life here below. Helen is seen absorbed in *Rasselas* on the first two occasions Jane tries to get into touch with her; the argument of that impressive book is of course that only a resigned stoicism will enable us to bear up against the conditions of life. This Jane feels is inadequate to her expectations and she rejects *Rasselas* (the symbolism is plain) and Helen's example, for 'in the tranquillity she imparted there was an alloy of inexpressible sadness'. Helen is doomed to early death, and her religious philosophy is attuned to the recognition – we may deduce that the writer means to imply that such a religion is a death-willing one, for it turns away from and rejects life. Jane loves and admires Helen but she cannot be like her. She is too hungry for life. However, she is obliged to recognize the superiority of Helen's religion as strategy in the psychological warfare that, at Gateshead, she had found life must be.

The second influence is the significantly named Miss Temple, who embodies the best contemporary tradition of the lady. She is a pious and gentle soul in whom religion and love are restrained by training, custom, and social habit: she represents the ideal of the women novelists, the 'well-regulated mind'. Jane accepts Miss Temple's authority completely, for Miss Temple provides love and cherishing, food for body and mind. But when Miss Temple leaves the school her influence vanishes overnight, leaving Jane a prey to her dissatisfactions and her hunger. The account of how her repressed nature reasserts itself and how she seems to grow in stature and humanity as she throws off Miss Temple's yoke is striking psychologically and rendered in magnificent prose (chapter 9). Jane thirsts for 'real knowledge of life'; longing to 'surmount the blue peaks' on the horizon, she finds 'all within their boundary of rock and heath seemed prison-ground, exile limits'. Like Christian in Doubting Castle she suddenly realizes that it lies with herself to escape into freedom. That the tranquillity of Jane's second Lowood self was merely superficial is proved when we see the paintings she shows Mr Rochester, at which she had worked all through the vacations at Lowood – 'To paint them', she says, 'was to enjoy one of the keenest pleasures I have ever known.' These pictures of her inner life turn out to be versions of the old images from Bewick: the Polar regions, the cruel sea, shipwreck, isolation, death, and despair.[3]

Though as a governess at Thornfield Jane acquires at once a function, dignity, and affection, and something like a home, she is still dissatisfied. Looking through the gates and gazing from the roof of Thornfield she is restless for a fuller life than tending someone else's child: 'I believed in the existence of other and more vivid kinds of goodness.' Mr Rochester appears, in mid-winter, in thrilling circumstances to them both, to complete Jane's initiation into the existence of 'more vivid kinds of goodness', which are the experiences of love and marriage. The scene of the meeting (as strangers ignorant of each other's identity) is symbolic as well as dramatic; he cannot get home without leaning on her shoulder and it is through her that he has hurt himself slipping on the ice (in due course he is to try to persuade her into a bigamous marriage with disastrous results): his uncanny dog, which had presented itself to Jane in the dusk as the Gytrash of folk-lore, she finds domiciled on her hearth when she gets back to Thornfield – Mr Rochester is come, her Master.

Mr Rochester has been the object of a good deal of derision, and of course he represents a woman's man. The ideal of masculine tenderness combined with a massively masculine strength of character is familiar in the women novelists and is essentially the same in Mr Rochester as in Jane Austen's Mr Knightley. Unfortunately, unlike Jane Austen, who was immune to the vulgarization of the Romantic movement represented by Byronism, the Brontës' daydreams had clearly been formed on Byronic lines. Nevertheless, her 'Master', as Jane likes to call him, embodies a rejection of a falsehood that has some importance historically – it is a deliberate break with the conventional relation in courtship where the man had to kneel to the woman, and it rejects that convention in favour of the new reality founded on respect for individuality. Charlotte Brontë sees the relation as one of mutual need in which the woman is not idealized but is recognized as an active contributor – fearless, unashamed of passionate feeling, and, while needing to serve, still determined to have her rights acknowledged. At the end when, in his partial blindness, Rochester realizes the force of this having felt at their first pregnant encounter 'I must be aided, and by that hand', she loves him better than when he 'disdained every part but that of the giver and protector'. In the last chapter, when Jane summarizes the success of her married life by telling us: 'To be together is for us to be at once as free as in solitude, as gay as in company. To talk to each other is but a more animated and audible thinking', we have been shown that this *is* so. The courtship scenes are peculiarly un-Victorian and suggest a source for Lawrence's conflicts between male and female natures in love relations.

Mr Rochester is a value by which to place the Reeds when Jane returns to Gateshead and the scenes of her early sufferings. She is now able to understand the Reeds and so defeat them – the episode is remarkable for its integrity. No conventional theory or religious doctrine is allowed to soften the psychological facts; the history of a hostility which is basic in nature ends as it began – the aunt with 'her stony eye, opaque to tenderness, indissoluble to tears' retains her antipathy towards the child of the sister-in-law she was jealous of. Jane, recalling Helen Burns, attempts to practise her teaching, but without success. There is no reconciliation, as there would be in almost any other Victorian novel. Jane can 'forgive' her aunt because being now indifferent to her she can no longer be hurt or harmed. Mrs Reed cannot change her attitude to Jane because, as Jane shrewdly guesses, 'to believe me good would give her no generous pleasure: only a sense of mortification'. And so Jane automatically takes up their relation at the point she left it ten years before: 'I felt pain, and then I felt ire; and then I felt a determination to subdue her – to be her mistress in spite of both her nature and her will.' Jane succeeds in imposing herself again, as in childhood, by force of character, and the aunt dies without giving 'any sign of amity'. It is thus brought home to Jane that people do not have a change of heart as Mr

Brocklehurst's religion required. The Reed cousins are used to present effectively two types of women, extremes of possibilities that Charlotte despises. One is the fashionable beauty who lives only for admiration and marries for convenience, for a man to support her; the other is the spinster by nature who finds in the ritual of High Anglicanism a substitute for life and who ends logically in a convent. The naked distaste with which Eliza is presented is more striking when one remembers that the author, like her heroine, was a clergyman's daughter; and the satiric method is the more intense for its starkness:

Three times a day she studied a little book, which I found, on inspection, was a Common Prayer Book. I asked her once what was the great attraction of that volume, and she said, 'the Rubric'.

Perhaps this is the place to note that *all* the representatives or mouthpieces of religion in *Jane Eyre* (both the black and the white marble clerics, Eliza Reed, Helen Burns, and Miss Temple) are either 'placed', or destroyed by ironic analysis. It is relevant that Mr Brocklehurst's impassioned argument addressed to Miss Temple, demonstrating the necessity she is under of starving the children's bodies for the sake of their souls' salvation, is a use of Swift's method: a parody, involving what we are meant to feel is both intolerably inhuman and blasphemous, is produced to shock us into protest, simply by revealing the implications of a then current doctrine or practice. The techniques of satire (in its most serious, responsible sense) play a large part in *Jane Eyre*.

Jane had returned to Gateshead on the first of May (her life having entered its spring) and when she gets to Thornfield it is summer in lovely pastoral country, an appropriate setting for the courtship that follows. It is necessary to explain how Charlotte Brontë arrived at the whole conception of Thornfield, for without that one can't grasp the peculiar force of its symbolic function. It also gives one an insight into the process of literary creation and invention. Thornfield building, inside and out, was a combination of the country-house, 'Rydings', the home where she stayed with her closest friend, Ellen Nussey, in 1832, and a Yorkshire place, North Lees Hall Farm, which she probably visited as a sightseer when she stayed with Ellen at Hathersage in 1845. The latter contained a madwoman's chamber and a legend that the lunatic perished in a fire that burnt out the place in the seventeenth century, and it was moreover the property

of the Eyre family.⁴ Charlotte thus had as history the story of
the madwoman and the fire, and a deeply-felt episode in her
own life associated with another Yorkshire house, with Ellen
Nussey as the link. Miss Nussey wrote of Charlotte's first visit
to her at her brother's home Rydings (I quote the passage
because it is not easily accessible or well known):

Charlotte's first visit from Haworth was made about three months
after she left school (1832). Mr Brontë sent Branwell as an escort; he
was *then* a very dear brother, as dear to Charlotte as her own soul;
they were in perfect mutual accord of taste and feeling, and it was
mutual delight to be together. Branwell probably had never been far
from home before! He was in wild ecstasy with everything. He walked
about in unrestrained boyish enjoyment, taking views in every direction of the old turret-roofed house, the fine chestnut trees on the lawn
(one tree especially interested him because it was 'iron-garthed',
having been split by storms, but still flourishing in great majesty), and
a large rookery, which gave to the house a good background – all these
he noted and commented upon with perfect enthusiasm. He told his
sister he was leaving her in Paradise, and if she were not intensely
happy she never would be! Happy, indeed, she then was, *in himself*,
for she, with her own enthusiasms, looked forward to what her
brother's great promise and talent might effect...Charlotte liked to
pace the plantations or seek seclusion in these retreats...She felt
herself apart from others; they did not understand her.⁵

We have here the 'Eden-like orchard', 'the house I had found
a paradise' of *Jane Eyre*, where at Midsummer occurs the first
climax of the book; and above all the joyous, Wordsworthian
tone of life, a recreation of the Paradisal state of being at
Rydings with the then beloved brother, who, when *Jane Eyre*
was being written, was, Charlotte wrote, too sunk in degradation
to know of his sister's enterprise. The majestic 'iron-garthed'
chestnut-tree, split by storms, she not only registered but made
symbolic (as in the folk-tales she knew the tree is commonly a
life-symbol), for it is used, exactly as Ellen Nussey describes it
in *Jane Eyre*, as a symbol of the relation between Jane and Mr
Rochester. In the 'Eden-like orchard' by moonlight, free from
the restraints of everyday life and speaking a language
heightened above that of everyday intercourse, Jane finds a
lover, someone with whom, as she says, she can live 'a full and
delightful life'. But even as she contemplates 'the paradise of
union', darkness falls, the wind roars, the giant chestnut-tree
which is 'circled at the base by a seat' (lives united by marriage)

groans as the storm breaks and the newly declared lovers are drenched with rain. In the morning the tree is found to have been struck by lightning and half of it split away. So Mr Rochester's state is forecast when after the fire he is struck blind and maimed. When Jane meets him then he says: 'I am no better than the old lightning-struck chestnut-tree in Thornfield orchard.'

The chapter devoted to the day before the wedding recaptures the heightened tone of the scene in the orchard. Jane is full of foreboding of ill, owing to the night's dreams, explained by her natural feeling that 'her hopes were too bright to be realized'. Visiting the blasted tree she reflects on it in terms that prepare us for the coming disaster to her life. The whole chapter (25) is a wonderful poetic sequence of ominous and pregnant experiences, particularly the first dream of being burdened with a little wailing child she cannot put down (after the wedding has been stopped she likens the love Mr Rochester has created in her to a suffering child) and the second dream that Thornfield was a ruin that crumbled under her.

The handling of Jane's flight from Thornfield after the second, the symbolic, storm has broken over her at the altar, is again remarkable for its psychological truth. Condemnation of Charlotte Brontë for not making Jane take an emancipated line after the discovery that a mad wife exists, or praise for her nobly moral conduct in the face of temptation (which was the Victorian reaction[6]) are equally beside the point. If we give this part of the novel the attention it demands we can see that Jane's reaction is implicit in her previous history. She inevitably reverts to the condition of the insecure child deprived of love, so that in a 'trance-like dream' she imagines herself back at Gateshead in the red-room, where she suffered terror beyond bearing. There she sees the moon looking 'as though some word of doom were written on her disc' – and in obedience to the dream-vision she exiles herself from Thornfield. On the eve of her wedding she had seen a prophetic moon through a fissure in the cloven chestnut-tree, and to that tree she had said: 'You will never more see birds making nests and singing idylls in your boughs'; now, running away from her master, she tells herself: 'Birds began singing in brake and copse; birds were faithful to their mates; birds were emblems of love. What was I? In the midst of my pain of heart and frantic effort of principle, I

abhorred myself. I was hateful in my own eyes.' The torment
of self-reproach makes her action in abandoning Mr Rochester
less unacceptable, but actually that is compulsive and not
willed; she is outraging her nature by obeying her training. The
passage quoted continues: 'Still, I could not turn, nor retrace
one step.' She hopes to die. The collapse of will is perfectly
convincing. She has been thrown back on the early experiences
from which Lowood saved her and therefore the Lowood
training takes command again. Her artificially trained 'conscience' forces her to go, and the Lowood ideal of self-sacrifice
and obedience to convention reasserts itself. Mr Brocklehurst
had declared they were to be children of Grace ('we are not
to conform to nature'), so she goes off to starve on the moors – the
psychological compulsion is terrifyingly brought home to us –
obeying Mr Brocklehurst's ruling when he reproved Miss
Temple for giving the starving children an unauthorized meal
with the revolting argument that ends by quoting: 'If ye suffer
hunger or thirst for My sake, happy are ye.'

But Jane finds 'to die of want and cold is a fate to which
nature cannot submit passively'; she cannot be resigned like
Helen Burns, and her wanderings through the moorland, when
in the long nightmare sequence she tries to get food, shelter, and
sympathy and is everywhere repelled, are almost intolerably
poignant. The language throughout this section, though often
highly charged, is perfectly natural and stark. The wonderful
imaginative feat carries on without a false touch to when, in the
last stage of despair, stretched on the ground, she glimpses
through a tiny window another world – the deep peace of
warmth, study, and security, the image of family affection in
a cultivated home that has been her unconscious goal. Rejected
everywhere else she is taken in here and for three days lies in a
Lazarus-like suspension of living, after which she rises in a new
character. Presently the faces that she had gazed at longingly
through the window turn out to be her own kin and, unlike the
Reeds, peculiarly congenial. She has become possessed of all she
was without – status, a fortune, an enviable family of intellectual
cousins, an ancestral home. Moor House is the antithesis of
Gateshead as Diana, Mary and St John Rivers, the new cousins,
are the antithesis of the original cousins Eliza, Georgiana and
John (broken Reeds replaced by Rivers of life). It is a fairy-tale
which has come true (the Cinderella-story of the governess's

marriage to the Master of Thornfield had not); that this happens at Christmas-time underlines the fact that it is myth, deliberate art and not daydream.

When St John Rivers tries to argue Jane out of her pleasure in her new position on moral grounds, she retorts characteristically: 'I feel I have adequate cause to be happy, and I *will* be happy.' It is he who completes her education in spite of himself and sends her back to Mr Rochester; in him and her relation to him the theme of Nature and Grace is again examined. Just as Mr Brocklehurst with his doctrine was seen by the child Jane as 'a black pillar', so St John Rivers is 'a white stone', 'cold as an iceberg' to her. Both missionaries do their best to denature Jane. St John is *apparently* a high-minded cleric representing an ideal in Victorian literature, the man who prides himself on subduing his impulses for the service of God. But when Jane hears him preach, his exposition of Christianity sounds to her like 'a sentence pronounced for doom'. Actually he is only a more subtle moral bully than Mr Brocklehurst and his missionary vocation is an excuse for making others submit to *his* will and for forcing *them* to make sacrifices too. His refusal to follow nature by marrying a delightful girl who loves him but whom he despises himself for loving – because that represents self-indulgence and would conflict with his plan of going to India as a missionary – is a regular Victorian decision which in Charlotte Yonge's novels would be acclaimed as noble and right. 'So much has religion done for me', he tells Jane, 'pruning and restraining nature.' Jane sees through the surface appearance of the self-sacrificing missionary to the ambition, 'his hardness and despotism', the cruel desire to dominate and above all the inability to co-operate with a human being of the opposite sex in a relation that demands mutual love and tenderness. He can only *make use* of others (what Henry James thought the unpardonable sin). In his presence Jane loses all spontaneity and feels her nature is being racked, 'an iron shroud contract round' her, as his ascendancy grows. He is in effect the antithesis of Mr Rochester, who is now more thoroughly defined by contrast. The analysis of St John Rivers is really profound, anticipating the 'discoveries' of psychology (not a rare thing in the annals of the literary arts, of course).

The general assent to a convention of a sexless ideal produced one of the more unpleasant aspects of the Victorian novel – the idealization of the innocent brother–sister relation, under cover of which only was the married relation tolerable to the imagination. Leaving aside Dickens and Thackeray, the most instructive examples of this perversion are to be found in the very popular novels of the innocent, devout Charlotte Yonge, with her morbid preference for a relation between brother and sister that precludes marriage for either, with the implication that the kind of love that results in marriage is something inferior. To this unwholesome aspect of the Victorian conventions Charlotte Brontë is absolutely hostile, not only free from such a taint herself but also setting out to combat it with the spirit of D. H. Lawrence. In consequence she came in for a good deal of criticism which she never understood – she was always surprised and indignant when *Jane Eyre* was alleged to be 'coarse' (a word that covered a variety of shocked reactions). Even the hardy intellectual Harriet Martineau wrote of *Villette* and *Jane Eyre*: 'I do not like the love, either the kind or the degree of it' and complained of Miss Brontë's 'dominant idea, the need of being loved' – whereas, Miss Martineau stated, 'It is not thus in real life' for 'there is an absence of introspection, an unconsciousness, a repose in women's lives (unless under peculiarly unfortunate circumstances)'. With all the force of a healthy conviction that these things are vicious and that we should know the truth about ourselves, Charlotte Brontë created Jane Eyre, Lucy Snowe, Caroline Helstone, who know the difference between affection and love.

Jane finds the root of what is wrong with her cousin in his admission that 'Natural affection only, of all the sentiments, has permanent power over me' – he can feel only for his sisters. When he proposes to his cousin that she should marry him in order to help him in converting the heathen she bursts out: 'I scorn your idea of love', and then feels that having 'met resistance where his despotic nature expected submission', he now unconsciously hates her. As the psychological battle between them gathers force Jane tells him: 'If I were to marry you, you would kill me. You are killing me now.' He understands what she means, that he is destroying her true self, though of course he holds that that is what is necessary to be done. 'A very long silence succeeded. What struggle there was in him between Nature and Grace in this interval, I cannot tell: only singular gleams scintillated in his eyes, and strange shadows passed over

his face.' He has told Jane before he thought of marrying her
that he is 'a cold, hard, ambitious man', unable to feel
compassion, guided by 'reason, and not feeling'. It is clear that for
his creator he stands for a combination of elements in the history
of literature and ideas that she found repulsive – he is not
offered as a 'character' in a realistic novel but as a focus of
attitudes that she felt to be hostile to full life (though he is well
incarnated physically and given plenty of characteristic
behaviour: Charlotte Brontë is never *less* than a novelist). Thus,
in addition to the 'noble' ideal of self-denying asceticism that
is through him exposed, he represents the eighteenth-century
'Reason' founded on an education in the Classics – his 'Greek'
beauty of feature and his 'correct and classic pattern' of mind,
his cold opposition to intuition and to irrational apprehensions
of life are stressed: it is relevant, I think, to note that Charlotte
Brontë disliked the poetry of Pope. Jane says: 'To please him
I felt daily more and more that I must disown half my nature,
stifle half my faculties, wrest my tastes from their original bent',
in contrast to Mr Rochester who helped her to fulfil her nature
and to enjoy the sensation of living without mistrust of herself.
Charlotte was thus directing into the novel the discoveries of the
first generation of Romantic poets (there is also a strongly
Wordsworthian element in *Wuthering Heights* and in Emily's
poetry as in Charlotte's). Even the opposition between the
neo-classical and Romantic schools of poetry seems to be drawn
into Charlotte's thesis, too, for we are told in his disfavour that
Nature in the Wordsworthian sense meant nothing to St John
Rivers. Charlotte and Emily's genuine passion for the moors no
doubt helped to make them the enthusiastic heirs of the
Romantic movement in poetry.

Even when Jane has made the tremendous psychological
effort needed for escape from subservience to St John she
'shudders involuntarily' as she describes him to Mr Rochester.
Like Eliza Reed, too, he represents Religion without love
(though he bears the name of the Disciple no doubt to drive
home this point, that, with all his devotion to duty, he is lacking
in the essence of Christianity): as she substituted ritual for the
spirit of religion, he substitutes dogma and philosophy. The
novel ends not on the note of Jane's married happiness but with
the last phase of St John Rivers. He is shown us in India in his
characteristic attitude of inflexible spiritual pride and ambition,

to which religion is subservient: 'the ambition of the high master-spirit, which aims to fill a place in the front rank of those who are redeemed from the earth'. In contrast, Mr Rochester is shown to be truly contrite and capable of humility because he is capable of loving and accepting love. We are certainly meant to see the opposition here between dogmatic religion and instinctive goodness. Charlotte seems to have disliked about equally Catholicism, Evangelicalism, High Churchmen, and Non-conformists; Emily went further and said that what her religion was was nobody's business but her own. Charlotte's friend Mary Taylor wrote that Charlotte 'had a larger religious toleration than a person would have had who never questioned, and the manner of recommending religion was always that of offering comfort, not fiercely enforcing a duty'.

Jane's escape from St John to Mr Rochester is the reverse of her flight from Thornfield, and in leaving Moor House she has none of the doubts that she felt on leaving Mr Rochester formerly; to return to Mr Rochester is a mature decision now of her whole self and she is not to be dissuaded by conventional arguments. I think this answers Leslie Stephen's dissatisfied question: 'Suppose she had found the mad wife had not perished in the fire?' Inevitably she finds that, true to her dream, Thornfield is in ruins, and she must seek Mr Rochester out at Ferndean. This turns out to be a disenchanted place, unromantic and dismal, to which, performing an act of faith, she comes as a penitent – the episode reads like a pilgrimage and an ordeal (one wonders whether Dickens had it in mind when he composed the curiously similar opening to chapter 53 of *Great Expectations*):

The last mile I performed on foot...(in) small penetrating rain. Even when within a very short distance of the manor-house, you could see nothing of it, so thick and dark grew the timber of the gloomy wood about it. Iron gates between granite pillars showed me where to enter, and passing through them, I found myself at once in the twilight of close-ranked trees. There was a grass-grown track descending the forest aisle between hoar and knotty shafts and under branched arches. I followed it, expecting soon to reach the dwelling; but it stretched on and on, it wound far and farther: no sign of habitation or grounds was visible. I thought I had taken a wrong direction and lost my way. The darkness of natural as well as of sylvan dusk gathered over me. I looked round in search of another road. There was none: all was interwoven stem, columnar trunk, dense summer foliage...no opening anywhere. I proceeded: at last my way opened, the trees thinned a little; presently I beheld a railing, then the house – scarce, by this dim light, distinguished from the trees; so dark and green were its decaying walls...It was as still as a church on a week-day: the pattering rain on the forest leaves was the only sound audible in its vicinage. 'Can there be life here?' I asked.

The door opens and Mr Rochester steps blindly out. Jane has made her last journey. As she beautifully says to him after the reunion: 'The rain is over and gone, and there is a tender shining after it.'

The suggestive use of language and the magical quality of her writing, which distinguishes Charlotte Brontë equally from her predecessor Jane Austen and her successor George Eliot, is one of the characteristic aspects of her work, and gave her the right to demand that 'poetry' must be part of all great art. What we think of as peculiarly her creation is the thrilling suggestiveness she conveys through the simplest words, as in the passage just cited, in her description of the mad-woman's laugh that strikes Jane's ear, 'distinct, formal, mirthless', in the opening of *Jane Eyre*, in the first meeting with Mr Rochester, in the scenes in the garden at Thornfield...endless further instances spring to mind. Perhaps now something should be said about her methods of composition. She thought out exactly what she meant to write, choosing each word deliberately if she felt it necessary, writing her first draft in pencil on small sheets of notepaper in her minute hand, supporting the sheets on a piece of cardboard, before copying out the final version in ink for the printer. Her prose is apt to be a mosaic, noticeably Regency in its combination of eighteenth-century exactness and the new journalistic idiom which is frequently rhetorical and quite likely to contain vulgarisms (like 'optics' for 'eyes'). As regards her technical originality and the unique organization of her novels, the degree of consciousness involved is impossible to determine. Charlotte wrote to her publisher after sending him the manuscript of *Villette*, in which the heroine's name was Lucy *Frost*, to ask if it could be changed to *Snowe*, explaining:

As to the name of the heroine, I can hardly express what subtlety of thought made me decide upon giving her a cold name –

and saying that she had originally thought of Snowe, but then wrote Frost, for 'a cold name she must have' – the change was evidently from soft cold to hard cold and then felt to be more 'right' in the first form. Similarly, no doubt, when she thought of using the historic house with the madwoman's room, the knowledge that it belonged to the Eyre family (their memorials being in the village church) provided her with the kind of name *she must have* for her heroine – one free as *air* in herself, an *Ariel*-like spirit living, in her inaccessible world, the life of the imagination, to which the spelling with its suggestion of the eagle's *eyrie* is so appropriate. 'But I can hardly express what subtlety of thought made me decide' suggests the level at which her creative decisions were made. Even more so the larger organization of the novel must have half-offered itself from the depths of her own experiences and the only conscious decisions would have been whether something felt 'right' or not.

The amount of first-hand, as distinct from imaginative, experience on which *Jane Eyre* draws is noteworthy. In Jane's childhood at Gateshead, incidents that Charlotte suffered as governess (books thrown at her by hopeful pupils and even a painful stoning) are incorporated along with the feelings of humiliation inflicted by callous and class-conscious employers ('Love the *governess*, my dear!' protested one of them whose child had made an artless proffer of affection to Miss Brontë); these incidents and feelings are distributed between Gateshead Jane and Adèle's governess.[7] The second section reproduces the whole experience of Maria and Charlotte Brontë at Cowan Bridge School. The Thornfield section draws in, as I've shown, experiences and reminiscences of adolescence and very complex associations and emotional attachments. In the parsonage home at Moor House, Jane, Diana, and Mary are reflections of Charlotte, Emily, and Anne Brontë in their tastes, dispositions, and characters, pursuing their occupations as at Haworth; the old servant is the Brontës' old servant Tabby, and St John Rivers is based on a rejected suitor of Charlotte's (she received four offers of marriage and eventually accepted the Rev. Arthur Nicholls), though of course he is mainly schematic. The considerable element in the novel of folk-lore, fairy-tale, the supernatural, and the uncanny was deeply rooted in local beliefs, and supplied in the home by their devoted Tabby, who, born in the 1760s, had known the valley in pre-Industrial days and, besides superstitions, was a source of the dark family histories of those parts. Mr Rochester's partial blinding was I conclude the result of Charlotte's journey, taken with her father, who had cataracts, to see a surgeon and have him operated on – a very painful experience, as Mr Brontë insisted on her staying in the room throughout the operation. It seems to have been at Manchester during this that she started writing *Jane Eyre*, with characteristic courage, but the sadness and despondency of the writer at the time is evident in the novel's opening; however, it brightens eventually and Mr Rochester like Mr Brontë partially regained his sight.

Of course, no amount of pointing to sources affects the conclusion that Charlotte Brontë, no less than her sister Emily, was a splendidly original artist. The advantages of the new method are felt at once if we compare *Jane Eyre* with the later but comparatively old-fashioned novel *The Mill on the Floss*. Here a similar subject (the moral and emotional growth of a passionate, badly managed child into a woman) is treated in the naturalistic, episodic way, but even the best part, the study of the child and schoolgirl, is immensely inferior in power and achievement to the corresponding first two sections of *Jane Eyre*, nor are they, as in *Jane Eyre*, integrated with the rest of the novel. It is suggestive that George Eliot abandoned the method of *Adam Bede* and *The Mill* for something like the technique and stylization of *Jane Eyre*, particularly in *Silas Marner* and *Middlemarch*; Dickens followed a similar evolution and *Great Expectations* and *Little Dorrit* have likenesses of art as well as subject-matter to *Jane Eyre*. A critic not in the least given to easy enthusiasm, J. G. Lockhart, wrote to a friend when *Jane Eyre* appeared:

I have finished the adventures of Miss Jane Eyre and think her far the cleverest that has written since Austen and Edgeworth were in their prime, worth fifty Trollopes and Martineaus rolled into one counterpane, with fifty Dickenses and Bulwers to keep them company.

He could then have known no later Dickens than *Dombey* and the Trollope he refers to is of course the mother; still, it is a remarkable tribute from a professional literary man to an unknown novice. Another and more interesting tribute came from Thackeray to *Jane Eyre*'s publisher: 'It is a fine book, the man and woman capital, the style very generous and upright so to speak.' This surprising reference to the 'style', though not clearly defined, is quite understandable: it registers a sense of something personal and morally impressive which integrates the mixture of styles Charlotte Brontë uses.

# Villette

'I have only just returned to a sense of the real world about me, for I have been reading *Villette*, a still more wonderful book than *Jane Eyre*. There is something almost preternatural in its power', George Eliot wrote to a friend, and the opinion of the greatest of the Victorian novelists is surely worth something. Matthew Arnold, on the other hand, was repelled by *Villette* even more than by *Jane Eyre* – equally a tribute since he was a uniformly bad judge of novels (what he really seems to have enjoyed were Bulwer-Lytton's). Unlike George Eliot, the common reader has preferred *Jane Eyre* and, except by Brontë specialists, the rest of Charlotte's novels have been slighted in comparison; still more, they have slighted Charlotte's whole achievement in relation to her sister Emily's. Even though that consisted only in the one novel, *Wuthering Heights*, that looms so large now in its overwhelming effect of genius as almost to exclude Charlotte's whole achievement. Yet, for a real comprehension of what that astonishing novel of Emily's aimed at we need to know Charlotte's novels too, and most of all *The Professor, Shirley*, and *Villette* which, I should argue, are all closely related both to each other and to *Wuthering Heights*. To understand that we must be able first to place *Villette*, which embodies the final expression of the impulses that made her a novelist, in relation to Charlotte's previous writings which lead up to this novel, and, next, to see its connection with *Wuthering Heights* and how closely related the creative drive was that led to the writing of Emily's greater work.

One of the literary-critical discoveries of our own time has been that *Wuthering Heights* is not incoherent, lacking in construction and gratuitously unpleasant, as previously thought, but is a remarkably formal, schematic, and carefully controlled work of art whose complexity of meaning and impersonal intention required, and received, a new form, evolved by one of the most powerfully original of novelists.[1] Charlotte's search for and invention of techniques and forms of expression for her organized insights, however, have not been accredited to her by the modern reader. What we have in Charlotte's novels, as in Emily's novel, is a totally new conception of prose fiction, enriched and stimulated by the use of language and the sensibility that necessarily expressed itself thus in the Romantic poets, and in the Romantics' rediscovery of Shakespeare. For the Brontës, it seems to me, there was above all Scott, whose novels Mr Brontë owned and which they had avidly read and can be seen in *Wuthering Heights* and *Shirley* to have profited by. In contrast is Byron who had been an unfortunate source for directing their adolescent daydreams into their joint romancings. Until comparatively late in the Brontës' lives these immature fantasies filled the leisure of Emily, Anne, and Charlotte, even when they had become governesses. Yet, quite suddenly, we find them each making a bid for fame and fortune by producing, in addition to poems written over the years associated generally with their joint sagas about the imaginary countries of Angria and Gondal, a novel about real life and their own essential experience of it – *Wuthering Heights*, *The Professor*, and *Agnes Grey*. (Anne's, however, is insignificant; she was not gifted.) In *The Professor*, Charlotte began a chapter by writing: 'Novelists should never allow themselves to weary of the study of real life'; and this, her first true novel, shows indeed the strength of her reaction against the Angrian dissipations she wrote with her brother even more thoroughly than Emily's novel does against her similar preoccupations with her and Anne's Gondal romances, many traces of which are unfortunately visible in the portrayal of Heathcliff.

What had happened is that each of the two gifted sisters had found her own medium for the expression of the theme of 'real life' that they had shared and discussed and which mattered above all to them. They are the most striking manifestation of the truth of Henry James's statement, through the mouth of his novelist-character in 'The Figure in the Carpet', of a general principle: 'the particular thing I've written my books *most* for. Isn't there for every writer a particular thing of that sort, the thing that most makes him apply himself, the thing without the effort to achieve which he wouldn't write at all, the very passion of his passion, the part of the business in which, for him, the

flame of art burns most intensely?' The thing, it seems evident
to me, that precipitated them into true responsible creativity
was the shock they had had in 1842 when Emily and Charlotte,
in search of better education, foreign languages, and higher
qualifications for their profession of governess, had gone to
Brussels and entered the Pensionnat Héger, where they became
at the same time pupils and teachers, a difficult combination
of rôles in itself. The nine-month stay, supplemented by
Charlotte's subsequent year alone there throughout 1844, was
a social, moral, and spiritual earthquake for them; but though
it left them shaken and Charlotte permanently and deeply
disturbed, its consequences were not that they were essentially
altered or moved from their previous total position. What
resulted was that they arrived at a new awareness, as to the
nature of themselves and the relation of their own culture –
English, Yorkshire, Protestant, and poor-but-proud middle
class – to that of an alien world hitherto undreamt of. They had
to ask themselves questions about their own identity and find
a basis for their instinctive belief in the values of the society they
had come from, and in the superiority and truth, as they felt,
of their religion and its culture. They had even to examine what
they had been taught as right, proper, or natural in the relations
of man to woman. While the answers are fiercely, sometimes
painfully, personal in Charlotte's novels (which are always a
rewriting of this theme), Emily's are, equally characteristically,
expressed impersonally so that it is in general hard to locate her,
the author, at all. Charlotte is even obtrusively present as a voice
giving unmistakable opinions and forthright judgments.
Charlotte is as ardent as Emily is cool; Charlotte seems
passionate and prejudiced, Emily dispassionate and wise. This
may be because Charlotte was much longer exposed to the
experience of Brussels and, through her emotional involvement
with M. Héger (even if it was no more than a close friendship
born of congeniality and Charlotte's loneliness) she suffered
more, though Charlotte's account of Emily's sufferings in the
school (Emily never gives hers) is strong enough. Nevertheless
they both became through this experience what Melville has
described Shakespeare, the exemplar of creative literary genius,
as being: 'one of the masters of the Art of Telling the Truth'.
For there are both great art and exceptional truth-telling in
Emily's and Charlotte's novels.

Charlotte's account of Emily's homesickness at Brussels noted that it was 'heightened by the strong recoil of her upright, heretic, and English spirit from the gentle Jesuitry of the foreign and Romish system' – from the challenge represented by that system, foreign to them in every sense, making them aware of the virtues and value of their native culture as never before, when it had been something taken for granted. Charlotte wrote of Emily afterwards: 'She was never happy till she carried her hard-won knowledge back to the remote English village, the old parsonage house, and desolate Yorkshire hills'; there the provinciality, and the rural and the Protestant elements in their home culture, are associated also with the Yorkshire landscape beloved though ungenial, the whole seen defiantly in contrast to the richly European Brussels scene. These very English and Protestant sisters, Yorkshire-bred (and Yorkshire represented in many ways the essence of that kind of Englishness, with its boasted outspokenness, a deliberate rejection of politeness and civility) had to take the shock of encountering an unimaginable culture, that of a Catholic boarding-school for the wealthy bourgeois and the aristocratic young ladies of Brussels, a city which was a European capital complete with opera, theatre, royal court, university, and cathedral, with establishments for the Catholic religious orders and with impressive historical associations, institutions of government, and handsome buildings. It could not be despised and so dismissed. Indeed, Mrs Gaskell, a highly intelligent and shrewd as well as sensitive woman, and in Charlotte's confidence, wrote very acutely of this part of Charlotte's experiences in her indispensable biography:

And yet there was much in Brussels to strike a responsive chord in her powerful imagination...The great solemn Cathedral of St Gudule, the religious paintings, the striking forms and ceremonies of the Romish Church – all made a deep impression on the girls, fresh from the bare walls and simple worship of Haworth Church. And then they were indignant with themselves for having been susceptible of this impression, and their stout Protestant hearts arrayed themselves against the false Duessa that had thus imposed upon them.

This gives very well the outline of their case. Charlotte betrays a curious mixture of rejection of Catholicism for its theory and practice – giving rational if bigoted reasons – while unconsciously or reluctantly showing that it had for her a powerful fascination which she resented and feared. Its dramatic rites appealed to something starved in her nature as its command of authority did to her need to submit to a force superior even to her own strength. This ambivalence towards Catholicism is in fact a very Victorian phenomenon and is the only respect in which Charlotte can really be said to be Victorian. It is paralleled by many other of her contemporaries, particularly novelists (most notably Kingsley and Charlotte Yonge). Though not shared by the better-integrated George Eliot, it is diagnosed by her in *Middlemarch* as a characteristic result of a Puritan upbringing, focused in Dorothea Casaubon's alarm and helpless terror while on her honeymoon in Rome as she encounters and inevitably takes the impact of the historic, religious, and artistic culture evolved from the ancient world, the Renaissance and the 'degenerate' Catholic present which culminates for her in the festival in St Peter's, the memory of which she could never dispel. Dorothea also was 'a girl who had been brought up in English and Swiss Puritanism' and on whom 'the gigantic broken revelations of that Imperial and Papal city' were 'thrust abruptly' and who therefore had 'no defence against deep impression' at Rome and to whom the historic achievement of man's highest cultures was now seen to be 'set in the midst of a sordid present' and 'sunk in the deep degeneracy of a superstition'.[2]

The pull of Catholicism against all reason and Protestant habit was for Charlotte evidently great, and painful. She recognizes this in *Villette* in the words she puts into the mouth of Père Silas in chapter 15: 'You were made for our faith: depend upon it, our faith alone could heal and help you – Protestantism is altogether too dry, cold, prosaic for you' and in her reflections on this, that only by avoiding the priest could she resist the 'arms which could influence me'. Mrs Gaskell tells us also in this context that 'Wherever the Brontës could be national they were so, with the same tenacity of attachment which made them suffer as they did whenever they left Haworth. They were Protestants to the backbone in other ways beside their religion, but pre-eminently so in that.' While Emily had been with her, Charlotte had been contented at the Pensionnat Héger, but her second spell there, alone, was very different, and her sufferings from moral and social isolation, as described in chapter 15, made Charlotte in real fact seek the relief of the confessional that she very honestly shows Lucy Snowe succumbing to (but only the once – Protestant calibre triumphed). Emily was only briefly exposed to Brussels and she was not emotionally involved with the Hégers as her sister was; she suffered no such deep disturbances as Charlotte did. She seems to have easily shed the experience of 'abroad' and turned the ponderings it must have provoked on the clash of cultures into insights on the home ground only, where the debate is between the old life-style (in the farmhouse of *Wuthering Heights*) and the new gentility represented by the Lintons of Thrushcross Grange. Emily was much more firmly centred in Yorkshire than Charlotte, whose novels from first to last show her centre displaced; even in the home-based *Shirley*, the Belgian family, the Moores, are settled in Yorkshire but they are French-speaking and unassimilated. One of this family, Louis the tutor – a variant of M. Paul Emanuel and M. Héger – succeeds in subduing, in order to force marriage on, the Yorkshire heiress Shirley, while his brother carries off the other Yorkshire heroine. Mrs Gaskell notes Emily's very different nature from Charlotte's, an advantage for Emily in their Brussels phase, for Emily's 'reserve' was self-protective and her stronger character made her 'impervious to influences; she never came into contact with public opinion, and her own decision of what was right and fitting was a law for her conduct and appearance, with which she allowed no one to interfere'. But Charlotte's life there was one of constant clashes.

The first result for literature of Charlotte's Brussels experience was the short novel *The Professor*, a striking departure from the romances she had been fabricating till then (some of these have been edited by Miss Ratchford and others, and seem to me to show no promise whatever, whereas *The Professor* is splendidly original). The interesting thing about *The Professor* is that the Protestant reaction against the Catholic system of education (the system being used as at once the representative and the causes of the Gallic-Flemish culture) is divided between an Englishman who is the narrator, Crimsworth, and the Swiss girl, Frances Henri, he eventually marries. This first novel has, like its successor *Jane Eyre* and her last novel *Villette*, a decided formality of structure which arises from the object of writing: a critical estimate of the two cultures. The one in which Crimsworth has grown up, in Yorkshire, is given a very fair exposition, and the side that was odious to Charlotte Brontë – its industrial brutality – is not condoned, nor does she idealize the essential Yorkshire nature, whose characteristics were evolved historically and were conditioned by the hardships of climate and the struggle for existence in the West Riding (where both Emily and Charlotte had studied its extreme manifestations). These are represented here by Crimsworth's friend with the significant name of Yorke Hunsden, as in her later novel *Shirley* they are represented by a whole family of intensely individual variations on the type, the typical family called 'the Yorkes', who can only be described as bloody-minded Radicals. They pride themselves on telling painful home truths and pointing out everyone's mistakes and weaknesses, in fact rubbing them in. (This Yorkshire attitude contributes massively to the aggressive impression left on the reader by the inhabitants of Wuthering Heights.) Interestingly, and to the credit of Charlotte's honesty and the depth of her psychological penetration, Crimsworth is shown to be both admiring of Yorke Hunsden and resentful of his aggressiveness, of all his (deliberate and frequently only affected) spiritual loutishness, which makes him confer favours and do kindnesses in such a way as to make them 'irksome', 'poisoned', 'paying himself in taunts', as Crimsworth notes. Yorke Hunsden must dominate and domineer: an unlovely nature, but in the long run a rough diamond apparently and a trustworthy friend. In contrast to all this, Crimsworth is at first smitten by the charm of 'abroad', Charlotte's own unwilling reaction, of course, for Brussels was a revelation to the girl from the dismal Haworth home that Mrs Gaskell quotes a visitor describing as 'the dreary, blank-looking village of Haworth'. We are reminded of another English girl's similar enchantment at her first experience of Europe in James's *What Maisie Knew*. Crimsworth cannot but admit the superiority of the civilization represented visibly by Brussels and by the polished manners of his French employer. The excellent treatment accorded to Crimsworth as the new schoolmaster by the heads of both schools and his pupils' parents affects him as a revealing contrast to 'the atmosphere of brutality and insolence in which I had constantly lived at X' (his hometown), among the mill owners and his employers and acquaintances there. We know that this was a feeling of great depth for Charlotte by her constant admissions, in her novels and letters, of her delight in the spoken French language, in its elegance and its untranslatable shades of expression. This is revealed by her introduction in all her novels of French-speaking characters so that she may use the language herself. (There is a pathetic account in a letter, significantly at the time she was stoking herself up to write *Villette*, of meeting a Frenchman by chance in a railway carriage and her enjoyment of the rare opportunity of conversing with someone in her favourite language.) German, which she and Emily also studied and kept up, had no such hold on her, though, characteristically, in *Jane Eyre* she gives credit to Goethe as poet, whereas in both her novels and letters she exults in the superiority of English poetry compared with what she felt to be the poverty of French verse.

However, further experience shows that appearances were deceptive, of people at least. We meet for the first time the originals of Mme Beck and the snaky, vicious French school-mistress of *Villette*, combined in the head of the girls' school, Mlle Reuter; here also are the *allée défendue* of Villette and those deceptive 'angels', the young ladies of Brussels, who turn out to be morally corrupt, the victims of a system of education based on espionage and 'the discipline, if not the doctrines, of the Church of Rome'. Women and schoolgirls alike show the 'precocious impurity, so obvious, so general, in Popish countries', where all 'lie with audacity'. In the face of this evidence of moral and spiritual failure in the very roots of the society, Yorkshire defects are now seen to be virtues, for forthrightness however unpleasant is at least honest, so that when the insufferable Hunsden turns up again abroad, his character now seems tonic and his conversation bracing, a relief from 'the false glance and insinuating smile', the lack of 'straight integrity', which Crimsworth has had the shock of realizing are the characteristics of his polite employers of both sexes who are exposed at last as systematically treacherous. However, there is a resolution in *The Professor* as there is not in *Villette*: the Swiss Protestant girl – at once pupil and teacher (like the Brontë girls themselves at the Pensionnat Héger) who combines the Continental charms of *politesse* and the native possession of the French language and literature, without the taint of the Catholic education or religion – the exquisite Frances Henri, turns up: Crimsworth's ideal, in short. She is orderly, frugal, industrious, spotlessly clean and neat, and though extremely poor, preserving gentility, modest, and, with a fine understanding and a true love of poetry, she is also candid and morally fastidious. She suits Crimsworth's – that is, Charlotte Brontë's – taste; and we may note that all her other heroines, Caroline Helstone, Jane Eyre, Lucy Snowe, and even Shirley, share most or all of these qualities; and Paulina too is characterized as 'delicate, intelligent, sincere'. Charlotte Brontë's heroines may not be to everyone's taste, but they represent, both intentionally and instinctively, the Protestant ethos at its finest (even Yorke Hunsden is forced to admit admiration for Mrs Crimsworth). As regards the cold touch which Charlotte felt impelled to suggest in her heroines' names (Eyre, Snowe, Frost, Helstone), we note its first appearance in Frances's address: her home is in Rue Notre Dame aux Neiges. Of Lucy Snowe, Charlotte told her publisher, 'As to the name of the heroine, I can hardly express what subtlety of thought made me decide upon giving her a cold name...' and telling him that she first thought of Snowe but then changed it to Frost, now asked him to change it back before sending her manuscript to the printer for 'a cold name she must have'. Hence, we see that while she did not try to analyse her need for the suggestion of coldness for her heroine, though she had consistently felt it from her first venture into a novel, yet she could make a conscious choice between hard and soft cold, snow and frost. Her formula was in fact the piquant one of a cold, reserved surface and fire down below, which we recognize in all her heroines, not only in Lucy Snowe but also in Paulina in the same novel. I will return to this factor in *Villette* later. Before I continue with the subject of the courtship of Frances Henri by Crimsworth, I must note that the child of their marriage, Victor, is the first Brontë child; though we only make his acquaintance in the last chapter, he is immediately recognizable as *sui generis* – the Brontë fictitious children are quite different from the children of Dickens's novels, as both are from George Eliot's; and all these are different from either Lewis Carroll's or Mrs Ewing's – there was no stock Victorian child in creative Victorian fiction. Victor is very much a product of the sensibility of the Romantics: he is described as 'pale and spare', 'a glutton for books', proud, sensitive, and serious ('I never saw a child smile less than he does': 'But though still, he is not unhappy; he has a susceptibility to pleasurable sensations almost too keen'). These are the hallmarks by which we know also Jane Eyre and Paulina Home, and they answer to the account Mrs Gaskell gives in her *Life of Charlotte Brontë* of the five little Brontë girls, whose childhood was overshadowed by their mother's prolonged sufferings and death and by their father's adoption of them as premature companions in his reading and conversation. But just as George Eliot was forced to recognize under Miss Brontë's commonplace and unattractive surface 'what passion, what fire in her!' so there is 'a something in Victor's temper – a kind of electrical ardour and power – which emits, now and then, ominous sparks'. This is what makes Victor prefer, and be fascinated by, the dangerous, antisocial Yorke Hunsden, to the disquiet of Victor's parents, just as Paulina is drawn to the 'tawny lion' Graham Bretton in her childhood, and with whom she is ultimately to find happiness in marriage, like Jane Eyre with the violent Mr Rochester. Of this relation Lucy Snowe felt, on seeing the child Polly gather Graham in her little arms in a movement of intense affection: 'The action, I remember, struck me as strangely rash; exciting the feeling one might experience on seeing an animal dangerous by nature, and but half-tamed by art, too heedlessly fondled.'

No other Victorian novelist registers such insights into the undercurrents and anomalies of human feelings, the unpredictable and irrational human needs, until D. H. Lawrence. We notice also that all Charlotte Brontë's heroines can emit scorching fire when intolerably oppressed or provoked, in defence of their self-respect or of cherished views; however cold their names their nature is passionate, though normally under tremendous restraint. This gives them their highly-charged quality; even the delicate and gentle Caroline Helstone in *Shirley* fires up and 'tells off' that formidable Yorkshirewoman Mrs Yorke, while Shirley, the other heroine, actually turns the conceited curate out of her house (for expressing contempt for the Yorkshire way of life – 'How dare the lisping Cockney revile Yorkshire?' she demands).

Thus the relation between man and woman, in love and work, which is explored in the courtship and married life of the Crimsworths, is quite unconventional and seen as a special instance only of the complex and unpredictable relations of human beings in general: man to man and man to child and parent to child, as well as in sexual attraction between man and woman. Frances Henri is determined to maintain, and be recognized as having the right to, an equality with her husband in love and in work, though she also maintains the differentness between male and female, rendering to her husband a deference which her own self-respect as his wife requires and demanding from him a corresponding valuation of her personality. Her marriage gives Frances the opportunity to develop 'the vivacity, mirth and originality' of her nature, as Jane Eyre's does – Jane also tells her future husband that she will continue to earn her living after marriage as before, and Lucy Snowe is a worker to the end, too. The originality of Charlotte Brontë's position generally, so well thought out and based on deeply felt experience, is therefore evident in her first novel, and we meet everywhere in it the insights, the intuitive understanding of the problems of living in her time and place, the perceptiveness that is always translating its observations into value judgments, of the major practitioners of the novel. Thus while Crimsworth's relation with the clever self-confident Yorke Hunsden is through-out one of conflict and self-defence, he realizes that the good Belgian, M. Vandenhuten, who is sincere and benevolent though 'phlegmatic and of rather dense intelligence', is one whose character 'dovetailed' with his own because 'my mind having more fire and action than his, instinctively assumed and kept the predominance', and therefore Crimsworth 'became aware of a sense of ease in his presence'. This is Laurentian indeed, but the coda is, surprisingly, a revelation of spiritual humility in Crimsworth that shows why he must always resist Hunsden: 'As I exchanged a smile with him [Vandenhuten] I thought the benevolence of his truthful face was better than the intelligence of my own.' The insights of *Wuthering Heights* are similar, though for the most part not directly expressed; like Dickens's and George Eliot's, those of the two Brontë sisters are moral in effect without being moralistic because they arise naturally from an instinctive response to the actualities of a situation and the ability of a true artist to respond not only deeply but with a rare honesty.

We can now turn to *Villette* itself. Charlotte had further developed the interests, peculiar to herself, that I've noted in *The Professor*, in the course of writing *Jane Eyre* and *Shirley*, the former being a great advance in technical achievement, finding a form absolutely fitted to embody the themes. And though *Shirley* seems to us less of an achievement, she herself wrote: 'I took great pains with *Shirley*.' Thus the steady sequence of novel-writing (*The Professor* written presumably in 1845, *Jane Eyre* started in 1846, *Shirley* written in 1848–9, showing an almost continuous practice of the medium) meant that she knew her medium and her own capacities thoroughly by the time she started *Villette* (probably in 1851). She was however delayed constantly in the writing by ill health, and her vitality was sapped by her private troubles as well, but these were resolved happily by her father's at last consenting to her marrying his curate Arthur Nicholls in 1854, the year following the publication of the novel which had taken a couple of years to write. It is interesting to note what were the impelling elements that amalgamated at this date. In 1850 she had visited Scotland (of which Mr Home in *Villette* is a native) and wrote afterwards that it is 'the Scottish national character, that grand character which gives the land its true charm, its true greatness' – though no doubt she had been assisted in this insight by her enthusiastic frequentation of the novels of Scott from childhood onwards. In 1851, while spending a month in London she saw Rachel 'the great French actress' perform; the impression made on Charlotte who was as fascinated in spite of herself by the theatre as by the Roman Catholic religious rites, is introduced into *Villette* in the chapter 'Vashti': 'It was a spectacle low, horrible, immoral.' The next day she went to see another performance that affected her in the same way: Cardinal Wiseman holding a confirmation – 'impiously theatrical', she reported. This would recall her painful experiences of the Catholic world of Brussels, where she had written home to Emily of 'their idolatrous "messe"' and had become estranged from her employer Mme Héger. That lady (who in due course was indignantly recognized as a caricature by her family in Mme Beck) was, as Mrs Gaskell tells us, 'not merely a Roman Catholic, she was *dévote*...and her conscience was in the hands of her religious guides' and she was incensed therefore by Charlotte's uncompromising witnessing to the Protestant truths. The consciousness that M. Héger, the inspiration for M. Paul Emanuel, was, though not himself a bigot, also inalienably Catholic and under the dominion of his wife, had left her in social and moral isolation that produced the psychological condition she calls 'Hypochondria' (first described in *The Professor*). This condition leads Lucy Snowe to trying the resources of the confessional as well as to the painful dependence on the letters of Dr Bretton. Charlotte herself had depended for friendship and affection on a correspondence with M. Héger after her return home from Brussels but broke off the correspondence on finding that it was a cause of jealousy or resentment to his wife. The painfulness sustained throughout *Villette* must derive from such bitter memories. In the same visit to London Charlotte had attended Thackeray's lecture where incidents attributed in *Villette* to the lecture in Brussels had taken place. She had then made the acquaintance of her publisher and of his mother, Mrs Smith, and letters at this time to that lady show that she was in many respects the original of Mrs Bretton, Lucy's godmother, who stands in such a wholesome and protective relation to Lucy without any real understanding of what Lucy is at bottom. It must be borne in mind also that *Villette* was written slowly and at intervals broken by bouts of ill health, some of them mental anguish due to isolation and despair, in which, quite evidently, the most painful experiences of her past life thrust themselves on her (though she herself wrote characteristically of her use of real life in her fictions: 'We only suffer reality to *suggest*, never to *dictate*', and 'I hold that a work of fiction ought to be a work of creation'). Mrs Gaskell saw her recourse to writing novels now, in her loneliness, as self-therapy: 'The interests of the persons in her novels supplied the lack of interest in her life; and Memory and Imagination found their appropriate work, and ceased to prey upon her vitals.' She missed while writing *Villette* the discussions about their work that the sisters had always held at nights – fault-finding as well as sympathizing – until only the one was left and the faithful servant told Mrs Gaskell on her first visit to the parsonage: 'now my heart aches to hear Miss Brontë walking, walking, on alone', every night. Charlotte's most intelligent friend, the 'Rose Yorke' of *Shirley*, told Mrs Gaskell that Charlotte, the ambitious and energizing member of the family, had organized the publication first of the sisters' volume of verse and then of a novel each, because she thought of literary fame as 'a passport to the society of clever people' but that 'When at last she got it, she lamented that it was of no use. Her solitary life had disqualified her for society. Her fame, when it came, seemed to make no difference to her. She was just as solitary, and her life as deficient in interest as before.' Yet it was at this dreariest of all times in Charlotte's life, left alone with her father and thinking her preferred suitor would never be allowed to marry her, that a visitor gained the impression which she subsequently described thus in a letter to Mrs Gaskell:

Miss Brontë put me so in mind of her own Jane Eyre. She looked smaller than ever and moved about the house so quietly and noiselessly just like a little bird, barring that all birds are joyous, and that joy can never have entered that house since it was first built. Now there is something touching in the sight of that little creature entombed in such a place, and moving about herself like a spirit, especially when you think that the slight still frame encloses a force of strong fiery life, which nothing has been able to freeze or extinguish.

The Professor had ended in success for both tutor and governess – a happy and financially prosperous marriage based on mutual respect and the united purpose of a working professional partnership culminating in a leisured retirement together with an interesting son to rear (Charlotte did not then look forward to a life passed in teaching schoolgirls or tending a demanding father). *Villette* replaces this pleasant daydream by a tragic withdrawal of all happiness, for not only is the death by shipwreck of Lucy's betrothed envisaged (veiled, to please her father, but uncompromisingly forecast) but there is also, it seems to me, the recognition that no marriage could take place and work between the Protestant English Lucy Snowe and the Jesuit-trained and -dominated foreigner.

The radical difference between *The Professor* and *Villette* is a technical one – not merely technical of course – the change of narrator from a man to a woman. This everyone sees as a gain. It may be asked why Charlotte originally used a male persona at all. There are two reasons: the obvious one, which led Mary Ann Evans to write under the name 'George Eliot' and the Brontë girls to choose to add to their pen name of Bell three Christian names (Acton, Ellis, and Currer) which suggested masculine authors. The other reason is more likely to have been secondary to this, as giving extra protection against being slighted or accused of impropriety as a woman: writing from the point of view of a William Crimsworth gave the authoress more freedom to treat the relations between the sexes with the frankness and fire of unconventional arguments, it also gave more imaginative scope, a proof of genius demanded by Coleridge in his statement of the principle that a creative artist should initially be seen to choose a situation as far as possible from his own to write about. In *Villette*, as in *Jane Eyre*, Charlotte succumbed to the temptations of the more directly personal autobiography, though she claimed that Jane Eyre was not herself 'any further than being plain and small', and she took pains to make Lucy Snowe even less attractive than Jane, concentrating on those aspects of herself which she evidently wished to examine. In this matter we have the evidence of a remarkable letter to her publisher in which she answers his criticism that Lucy will 'be thought morbid and weak' by replying:

I consider she *is* both morbid and weak at times... and anybody living her life would necessarily become morbid. It was no impetus of healthy feeling which urged her to the confessional, for instance; it was the semi-delirium of solitary grief and sickness. If, however, the book does not express all this, there must be a great fault somewhere.

All the episodes on which the charge of morbidity and what is here classed as 'weakness' could be made were in the identical or similar forms experienced by the author herself, which she recognizes in the last sentence I have quoted as the reason for writing the novel. But Charlotte was not weak except physically since she never gave in to her misfortunes save on the occasion of once succumbing to the use of the confessional, no sooner done than repented.

And yet the novel is not a document for the psychiatrist but a deliberate work of art. There is self-criticism and a holding aloof of her grief and sickness, and this has produced the schematic form that *Villette*, like *Jane Eyre* and *Wuthering Heights*, has taken. All these novels are equally the products of thought and planning, and *Villette* bears an interesting technical relation to both *The Professor* and *Jane Eyre*, for each novel shows successively a development of idea and a greater richness and profundity of treating it.

Here we must make an exception of the episodes devoted to the Nun, which may be seen as an unfortunate inheritance from Mrs Radcliffe and the Gothic novels of horror that the Brontë children had read with evident *empressement*. But why, we naturally ask, should it have survived in Charlotte's last novel, having been suppressed after the early manuscript fictions of her youthful scribblings? There is nothing of the sort in *The Professor* or *Shirley* and, except for the concealed mad woman in *Jane Eyre* and her inexplicable appearances at night, there is no source of terror. It seems to me due to her unhappy experience in failing to get *The Professor* published. Though she had tried six publishers before giving it up and starting *Jane Eyre*, it was rejected by all, and she was never able to get it published in her lifetime in spite of her attempts to persuade Smith, Elder & Co., who had done so well out of her, to add it to their list of her successful novels. The reasons they had all given for rejecting this first novel, evidently peculiarly dear to its author, were, she told the critic G. H. Lewes, that though 'original and faithful to nature such a work would not sell' because 'it was deficient in "startling interest" and "thrilling excitement", so that it would never suit the circulating libraries'. Hence, we may conclude, the importation, to satisfy publisher and circulating libraries, of 'startling interest' and 'thrilling excitement' into her later novels – the mystery of the mad wife secreted in the heart of Thornfield with her 'goblin laugh, distinct, formal, mirthless', the more legitimate excitement provided by the Luddite riots in *Shirley*, and the detective-story element in *Villette* in both the deception about Dr John's identity (which readers rightly resent as unfair) and the bogus supernatural theme of the Nun: *Villette*, a rewriting and rethinking of *The Professor*, was *not* to be refused publication if Charlotte could help it. (Correspondence with her publisher about the manuscript as she sent it to him in instalments shows her insecurity and her doubts as to its success.) Her use of the pseudo-supernatural to play on the reader's nerves follows Mrs Radcliffe and her school of Gothic fiction in the determination to have it both ways: there is the thrill of the terror of the supernatural; but, eventually, a rational explanation of what had apparently been miraculous satisfies the eighteenth century's rationalism and the Protestant's common sense. Charlotte Brontë was no true Romantic, for Romantic writers really believed in the supernatural (or tried to pretend that they did) and did not explain it away when they had made use of it. Byron in the last episode of *Don Juan* ends with the very similar anti-Romantic revelation that the supernatural friar haunting Juan is actually an amorous lady using the friar's garb as cover, and it seems probable to me that Charlotte, who at eighteen recommended Byron's poetry to a friend as 'first-rate' (along with Shakespeare, Milton, and Wordsworth) had borrowed the

idea and merely reversed the sexes to produce de Hamal
disguised as a nun to further his pursuit of Ginevra.

A genuine source of excitement in *Villette*, not present in *The
Professor*, is the battle of wits and wills and temperaments
between Lucy and Paul Emanuel. Complementary in his
irritability and egotism to Lucy's self-restraint and humble
desire to learn, and an intellectual she can respect, he also has
the necessary warmth to thaw her coldness and give her the love
she craves as well as psychic support. The relation of Lucy to
her 'master', if curious, is psychologically convincing and
founded in a truth of experience recognized by Charlotte in
these passages from a letter home from Brussels, during her first
spell there when she had Emily as companion, where I see the
very germ of *Villette*.

I was 26 years old a week or two since; and at this ripe time of life
I am a schoolgirl, and, on the whole, very happy in that capacity. It
felt very strange at first to submit to authority instead of exercising
it – to obey orders instead of giving them; but I like that state of
things...It is natural to me to submit, and very unnatural to
command.

The difference in country and religion makes a broad line of
demarcation between us and all the rest. We are completely isolated
in the midst of numbers. Yet I think I am never unhappy; my present
life is so delightful, so congenial to my own nature, compared to that
of a governess.

In *Villette* the opposed cultures sketched in *The Professor* are
located in two symbolic centres which, with their inhabitants,
are played off against each other as moral-sociological concepts.
There is Bretton in England, and there is Villette across the sea,
and then Bretton establishes itself in Villette-land but is not
assimilated, any more than Lucy can be united with M. Paul
Emanuel. *Bretton* is of course Britain, and our heroine Lucy
Snowe is godchild of the Brettons of Bretton, a thorough
Englishwoman. The other people there are called *Home*[3] – Mr
Home is half Lowland Scotch, Charlotte admiring the Lowland
Scotch character and having a theory that the combination of
English and Scotch produces one of the best types; and his
kinsman, red-haired Graham Bretton, is described as a Celtic
type. The symbolic intention is rather too obvious perhaps – the
whole constituting Great Britain. Britain is exquisitely typified

by the minster town, peaceful, clean (the cleanliness is associated with the quiet and the order and the sense of a perpetual Sunday atmosphere in the place to suggest a spiritual quality), and Lucy's visits to Bretton remind her of a beatific episode in *Pilgrim's Progress*. Britain and Home – the British Protestant culture: the intention is plain. (Practically all the names in *Villette* are symbolic, and Bunyan must have been closer to her here than to any other novelist, often as he stands in the background of English novelists.)

A real and remarkable subtlety, however, is to be found in the use of little Polly in the early chapters. She is, we see, only a variation on the child Jane Eyre and the child Victor Crimsworth and the first three chapters are given up to an exposition of her equally exquisite sensibility for suffering and her need of affection, but in a totally different relation. Lucy Snowe is in the limited scenes at Bretton as a mere spectator, presented as a neutral and even adversely critical one, for example when the child's father leaves her at Mrs Bretton's:

During an ensuing space of some minutes, I perceived she endured agony. She went through, in that brief interval of her infant life, emotions such as some never feel; it was in her constitution; she would have more of such instants if she lived. Nobody spoke. Mrs Bretton, being a mother, shed a tear or two. Graham, who was writing, lifted up his eyes and gazed at her. I, Lucy Snowe, was calm.

That is, Lucy characteristically conceals her real feelings, which are much more sympathetic than those of the others, in an affectation, almost – to avoid revealing that she is one of the same nature as Polly. It is not until the child's little history is finished and she is about to disappear in this character from the book, when Lucy, taking the 'elfish' creature in her arms, gives her true reaction, reflecting:

How will she get through this world, or battle with this life? How will she bear the shocks and repulses, the humiliations and desolations, which books, and my own reason, tell me are prepared for all flesh?

that we realize that this *is* Lucy Snowe and that the questions relate to herself. Polly, she says, 'departed the next day; trembling like a leaf when she took leave, but exercising self-command'. The child represents Lucy's sensibility externalized, suffering for its delicacy and proud refinement as ordinary souls do not. Her history is to be Lucy's history, not least in the relation to Graham Bretton we have witnessed. Lucy Snowe is what the world sees, to all appearance calm, cold as her name implies, self-disciplined; little Polly is an externalization of her inner self (always characterized as 'elfin' or 'faery-like' throughout the book, suggesting something supernatural and spiritual in essence).

The forecast in the first three chapters of Lucy's relation to Graham Bretton, the forecast enacted by Polly, is followed immediately by the history of Miss Marchmont, the intention being to prepare the reader emotionally for a tragic outcome. This prefigures Lucy's later history which ends with her lover drowned at sea on his way home to marry her. Miss Marchmont when young was robbed by violent death of *her* bridegroom and lives on 'stern and morose', treasuring in her memory the year when there was 'a living spring – a warm glad summer – strength of hope under the ice-bound waters'. The formal, stilted language of this episode is intended to mark it, like the play within *Hamlet*, by its stylization as an epitome framed off from the text. Lucy, whose fate has thus been sketched for us (she lets drop that *she*, Lucy, is now an old white-haired woman telling *her* story) crosses the sea on a ship called the *Vivid* – other ships called the *Consort*, the *Phoenix*, and so on, are not hers, she notes – reminding us of Jane Eyre's desire for 'other and more vivid kinds of goodness' than a woman's conventional allowance (a child's or a good woman's – Adèle's and Mrs Fairfax's). Painfully Lucy arrives at Villette. Here instead of an English home is a foreign girls' school, instead of forthright Mrs Bretton is Mme Beck ('her name was Modeste; it ought to have been Ignacia'). English probity is contrasted with Catholic intrigue, the English system of trust with the French system of '*surveillance*', English delicacy of feeling with Latin coarseness and 'realism', Lucy's external coldness but inner intense sensibility with Mme Beck's appearance of '*bonté*' that covers only callous self-interest; and the moral obliquity or absence of any sense of conscience among the pupils is registered by the contrast with the self-respect of the English girls (only partially undermined in the case of the frivolous Ginevra Fanshawe, who marries a foreign count). This is all rendered with the most convincing concreteness. The unfeeling and unprincipled upbringing by Mme Beck of her daughters contrasts significantly with Polly's by her loving

Scotch father. Only in M. Paul does Lucy find that fineness of nature, warmth of feelings, and disinterestedness can exist in the atmosphere of Villette. But neither Lucy nor M. Paul can conceivably be converted by the other, and the closing shipwreck is, as Charlotte rightly felt, inevitable. The comparison with Julien Sorel's sojourn in the seminary (in *Le Rouge et le Noir*) is interesting because whereas Stendhal's morally superior hero conquers his environment by strategy and cunning, by assimilating himself to it in externals, the Englishwoman manifests her moral superiority by inflexibility and undisguised aversion. In consequence, she suffers such an extremity of isolation that, like Jane Eyre, she is driven beyond her own control and has a break in consciousness. This happens on her leaving the church where she has gone to obey an irresistible impulse to make use of the confessional: this is the point where she touches bottom, when she is driven to behave *as if she were a Catholic* and belonged to the community of Villette. At this, the tension of the Protestant-Catholic conflict breaks and the dark waters close over her, she drops lifeless in the street. No doubt it was from *Villette* that Hawthorne took the idea of making Hilda, the New England girl in *The Marble Faun* (1859), enter the confessional at a crisis, he having been struck by the dramatic situation it presents. But in Hawthorne the incident is not related to the rest of the novel and is preposterous; indeed it is morally offensive. We can see how, in contrast, the incident is led up to in *Villette* and is an integral part of the structure, the turning point in both the plot and the moral scheme.

Lucy recovers herself in a new place which turns out, as in *Jane Eyre*, to be the home of her kindred; she is thus provided with affection, social status, and a congenial environment (Bretton transported abroad). The pattern is similar in *Jane Eyre*, where Jane in extremity of isolation is rescued by her kindred the Rivers household, but this is not a mere repetition of that, and the treatment of it all is even more astonishingly original than in the earlier book. The night-wandering ending in a psycho-physical collapse is in both books a symbolic account of the experience of acute isolation followed by the opposite experience, of being taken into a family, of *belonging*. Lucy says: 'I seemed to pitch headlong down an abyss', and thereupon begins the next chapter ('Auld Lang Syne') with an account of the sensations she had when recovering. There is a terrifying momentary time lag before the memory functions again. 'The divorced mates, Spirit and Substance, were hard to reunite: they greeted each other, not in an embrace, but a racking sort of struggle.' This experience Charlotte Brontë daringly extends to give it symbolic dimensions. 'The life-machine presently resumed its wonted and regular working', Lucy says, but she cannot recall her surroundings; though familiar she cannot place them except as belonging to another time and country, a different phase of existence from her recent life in Villette. Even when she recollects that the contents of the blue room were those of her godmother's drawing-room at Bretton, she knows the room itself is not that but one unknown to her. Dropping off again she finds on regaining consciousness that she has left lamp-lit night and blueness for 'leaden gloom' and sea-green surroundings, where she thrillingly recognized 'Bretton! Bretton! and ten years shone reflected in that mirror.'

The author means to show Lucy recognizing a past phase of her life without being able to connect it with the present, owing to the split in her life between Bretton and Villette. 'Where my soul went during that swoon I cannot tell', the chapter begins, and what we are shown is the soul rising from the 'abyss' out of the blue and up from the depths of the sea (the blue chamber and the sea-green). Is this fanciful? No, for in the next chapter we find they had this significance for the writer:

My calm little room seemed somehow like a cave in the sea. There was no colour about it, except that white and pale green, suggestive of foam and deep water: the blanched cornice was adorned with shell-shaped ornaments, and there were white mouldings like dolphins in the ceiling angles. Even that one touch of colour visible in the red satin pincushion bore affinity to coral; even that dark, shining glass might have mirrored a mermaid. When I closed my eyes, I heard a gale, subsiding at last, bearing upon the house-front like a settling swell upon a rock-base. I heard it drawn and withdrawn far, far off, like a tide retiring from a shore of the upper world – a world so high above that the rush of its largest waves, the dash of its fiercest breakers, could sound down in this submarine home, only like murmurs and a lullaby.

The movement of the prose endorses the meaning. There is plainly no danger in attributing to the details of these novels the maximum meaning, the greatest significance, the widest-ranging interpretation that we may be able to find for them, for we can be sure the author strove to put it there herself. We must not overlook either the simile just before this passage which likens her godmother to a 'stately ship crossing safe on smooth seas' and herself to a lifeboat manned by 'the half-drowned lifeboat man', 'only putting to sea when cloud encounters water, when danger and death divide between them the rule of the great deep'. Half-drowned, she has risen through the sea that separates Villette from Bretton, to safety and a fresh start in a regained Bretton which sustains her against Villette. The recognition scene is completed by the reappearance of Paulina, now a woman. She also has suddenly acquired status, riches, a title, and a new name in the foreign land. She and Lucy rediscover each other in a magical scene of recognition in the sea-green chamber, where she says to Lucy who fails to recognize her as little Polly, though knowing her as Countess de Bassompierre: 'No, not Miss de Bassompierre for *you*. Go back to Bretton. Remember Mr Home.' Again she shares Lucy's life with the peculiar sympathy of another self, for she is a parallel self – what Lucy might have been in favourable circumstances – and she acts out the destiny that Lucy had formerly desired for *her*self, becoming Graham Bretton's wife. It is when Lucy has seen that Paulina and Graham are drawn to each other by their complementary natures, as in the opening of the novel, that she makes the decision to stand alone, burying his letters that had sustained her in her isolation. This is yet another break in her life, but it represents a healthy movement towards independence, as she recognizes when sealing up the letters:

The impulse under which I acted, the mood controlling me, were similar to the impulse and mood which had induced me to visit the confessional...I was not only going to hide a treasure – I meant also to bury a grief...This done, I rested...I felt, not happy, far otherwise, but strong with reinforced strength.

Therefore when, in the second remarkable night scene, she wanders through Villette *en fête* under the influence of Mme Beck's narcotic, she remains equally aloof from both the Home–Bretton party and the Beck–Emanuel clan as she encounters each in turn. When recognized by Graham, who wishes her to join them, she insists on being 'let alone'.

The passages I have quoted above substantiate my opening contention that the structure we find here is different from that of a rigidly controlled novel like *The Magic Mountain*, *Jude the Obscure*, or *The Custom of the Country* (which I specify because they are recognized as novels which *have* structure). It is not, like theirs, a structure just sufficiently covered by its materials, like a kite, and like a kite tethered by a line; it is like a living bird winging away free but on a flight with an object. One explanation of this live quality, I think, is that Charlotte needed to write these novels: they are a form of self-expression, not confessions (like Constant's *Adolphe* or Tolstoy's *The Kreutzer Sonata*), but communications. The frequent reference to the reader is oppressive to us, but it was the sense of a reader there to impart them to that made her write down and evaluate those highly-charged experiences, for it was only by arranging them so that they convey a meaning for someone else that she could be eased.[4] Yet, it would be quite unjust to suggest that she was (as Lord David Cecil for instance, alleges in his standard work *Early Victorian Novelists*) 'extremely simple' and 'naïve'. What she did for the novel she did consciously, as is proved by her criticism of Jane Austen. She wished to write, unlike Miss Austen, as 'a complete woman', and part of that undertaking was to draw on the submerged levels of being to convey her sense of the nature and quality of living. No novelist before would have described a character in the terms she uses for Diana Rivers in *Jane Eyre*: 'In her there was an affluence of life and certainty of flow, such as excited my wonder, while it baffled my comprehension'; or for Lucy Snowe: 'I still felt life at life's sources.'

Her awareness of what had hitherto been overlooked by the English novelist was undoubtedly due to her own physical and psychic peculiarities. Always sickly, ailing, and often desperately unhappy, she was sometimes morbid from physical under-nourishment and psychic starvation; novels had hitherto been written by the vigorous and the healthy-minded, and if by women, then women who subscribed to the theory of propriety. Charlotte showed what 'proper feeling' and 'a well-regulated mind' were worth because she had a fine understanding and a free courageous spirit of her own, but the notation of states of deprivation and the awareness of the extra-rational elements of experience come from one who suffered from what she called 'the tyranny of Hypochondria, a most dreadful doom'. 'I can never forget', she wrote, 'the concentrated anguish of certain insufferable moments, and the heavy gloom of many long hours, besides the preternatural horrors which seemed to clothe existence and nature, and which made life a continual waking nightmare' (*Letters*, 1846). 'Hypochondria' is attributed to the hero of *The Professor* as well as to Lucy and Jane. Her life was very like Lucy's, as she struggled to write *Villette* alone at Haworth after the death of all her sisters. She had also, undoubtedly, a nervous susceptibility to the idea of the supernatural and death; the dream of carrying the little wailing child she gives to Jane Eyre was a dream she had repeatedly had herself and which, she said, preceded a misfortune. She had an intensity of reaction that fixed her experiences for her to an exceptional degree – 'Lowood' and the originals of Mr Brocklehurst and Helen Burns were registered in her memory forever at the age of eight, and there is every reason to believe her assertion that she was 'an observer of character at five'.

A less unquestionable advantage was that it was in Yorkshire that her father happened to get a parish. Jane Austen certainly shows how much better off was the novelist who, though also a poor parson's daughter, was surrounded by gentlefolk. One of the striking things about Charlotte's heroines is their shrinking from, their confident expectation of, being jeered at for any unconscious manifestation of fine feelings or for any kind of sensitiveness. Hence Lucy's assumption of 'a cooler temperament' than little Polly's, and Caroline Helstone's stern self-repression. One of the attractions of Thornfield, and one of the privileges of knowing Mr Rochester listed by Jane Eyre, it may be remembered, was that here 'I have not been trampled on.' We note that the *Yorke* family in *Shirley* exert themselves to flay poor Caroline alive, *Yorke* Hunsden does his best to perform the same service for the hero of *The Professor* and to hector the heroine, and the family doctor in *Wuthering Heights* who tells Hindley Earnshaw that his wife is dying adds gratuitously: 'It can't be helped. And besides, you should have known better than to choose such a rush of a lass!' This suggests what the spirit of the shire meant to Charlotte and her sisters. No wonder that she makes her first heroine, the charming Frances of *The Professor*, feel: 'I must cultivate fortitude and cling to poetry; one is to be my support and the other my solace through life.' So felt all her heroines.

Charlotte was born in 1816 (Emily two years later), and with tastes and character formed early in life the sisters were decidedly not Victorian, but, like most of those we think of as the great Victorians (Dickens, Thackeray, Trollope, George Eliot, for instance), were essentially pre-Victorian, critics of the Victorian scene and characteristics that they saw visibly and potently threatening or superseding the culture of an older and healthier England, which they felt to be in some important respects preferable. (The real Victorians were those formed entirely in the Victorian era and who reacted against it by exaggerated unconventionality, like Swinburne, Oscar Wilde, William Morris, Samuel Butler, and Shaw.) For Emily, it was the totality of the debate between Wuthering Heights and Thrushcross Grange that typified the social loss; for Charlotte, the change centred in the rôle newly imposed on woman in courtship and the marriage relation, which seemed to her false and insulting to the woman. Her heroines cling to the right to love passionately, not to be adored as angels but accepted as equal but different and to be allowed to enter a working partnership. They are too proud to be supported by a husband and, moreover, have a need to work. It is a pity she could not recognize that in *Emma* Jane Austen had cast a similar disapproving look at the newly-emerging image of the Victorian bourgeois ideal of married life, creating to illustrate it the home life of the John Knightleys. 'Poor Isabella' is entirely confined by domesticity and is absorbed in fussing over her husband and children; her irritated husband is shown as worshipped and his rudeness never noticed by his adoring wife. Her sister, the more intelligent Emma, resents the whole set-up and conducts *her* relations in courtship with the other Mr Knightley on the basis of witty provocation, in feminine resistance to his claims to necessarily better judgment as being a man; Emma's prospect of marriage is to continue on this equal-but-different basis, which is also Charlotte Brontë's idea. But Charlotte added to it a recognition of the passionate basis of love between the sexes and this is neither Regency nor Victorian but what we think of as modern. Hence the shocked reaction of her reviewers and readers to *Jane Eyre* as 'coarse' and improper; though Jane's conduct is impeccably moral by conventional standards, she offers her love to Mr Rochester and refuses to be set on a pedestal. Harriet Martineau, that dragon of enlightenment and rationality, primly disapproved of this feature of her friend's novels, and Charlotte, who felt such an attitude to be insulting, broke off the friendship. Miss Martineau's objections to *Jane Eyre* and *Villette* were expressed in this interesting form: 'I do not like the love, either the kind or the degree of it', complaining of Miss Brontë's 'dominant idea, the need of being loved'; whereas, Miss Martineau said, 'It is not thus in real life', for 'there is an absence of introspection, an unconsciousness, a repose in women's lives – unless under peculiarly unfortunate circumstances – of which we find no admission' in these novels. Charlotte could not accept this nor Mrs Gaskell's explanations of it, and continued to find 'puzzling' the reviews which described her work as coarse or improper.

Another disadvantage she suffered was that of being formed as a writer in a bad period when a new vulgarity had, through journalism, begun to undermine the language and destroy the elegance of the eighteenth-century prose style. The early Victorians show this in their novels, but Lamb and other journalists of the Regency period had succumbed to some extent even earlier. That a master of such fastidious prose as Charlotte Brontë should sometimes refer to eyes as 'optics' and misuse 'transpire' habitually in the journalistic sense, is one of the kinds of vulgarity I mean. In addition, a new 'elevated' style of prose was born in the early nineteenth century whose ups and downs are both represented in De Quincey's essays. De Quincey published in *Blackwood's*, which was read at Haworth Parsonage; *Levana and Our Ladies of Sorrow* appeared there in 1845, and parts of *Villette*, such as the apostrophe to Hypochondria, seem to me curiously like it and quite unlike anything in *Jane Eyre*. Moreover, she suffered very noticeably from having been taught rhetoric on the French schoolmaster's principle in Brussels, the results of which pervade *Shirley* and to a lesser extent *Villette*.

When Charlotte wrote home from Brussels mentioning for the first time 'M. Héger, the husband of Madame', she described him as the 'professor of rhetoric, a man of power as to mind, but very choleric and irritable in temperament', adding, 'Emily and he don't draw well at all together.' Mrs Gaskell has an anecdote which serves as a useful illustration to this comment, highlighting a difference between the sisters. M. Héger proposed to initiate them into the beauties and individuality of the major French stylists by the 'sedulous ape' method later recommended by Robert Louis Stevenson:

After explaining his plan to them he awaited their reply. Emily spoke first; and said that she saw no good to be derived from it; and that by adopting it, they should lose all originality of thought and expression. She would have entered into an argument on the subject, but for this M. Héger had no time. Charlotte then spoke; she also doubted the success of the plan; but she would follow out M. Héger's advice, because she was bound to obey him while she was his pupil.

We have little knowledge of Emily other than what can be deduced from her novel and poems, and this anecdote is therefore the more precious. It proves her independent, full of character at twenty-four, and concerned above all, as we'd expect from the author of *Wuthering Heights*, to preserve 'originality of thought and expression', which she rightly saw as threatened by the method of imitation of the styles of other writers, in this case of masters of French rhetoric, a mode of oratory which is fatal in English. Charlotte however, to whom it was 'natural to submit to authority' – and M. Héger had for her as well as the authority of a superior intellect a fascinating temperament – fell in with the plan, and the unfortunate consequences are to be seen in the rhetorical passages in *Shirley* (from the pen of the heroine who writes just such 'devoirs' for her French-speaking tutor, Louis Moore, as well as from the author herself) and in some parts of *Villette*. The credit side of this concentration on the Pensionnat and its society is that it is used successfully in both the novels as a suitable symbol for life in general: we are all teacher and student, and the tension and affection between pupil and teacher is only a special version of the human relation; the classroom is a miniature world, and battles are equally fought and won here, we are shown. In *Jane Eyre*, the faults are not those of journalese or of schoolgirl rhetoric but are only what is visible in the society scenes at Thornfield, stilted melodramatic dialogue, which go with similar scenes at the beginning of *The Professor*. These are the last traces of the Brontës' addiction to fantasy writing throughout their childhood. Why it should recur in the mature works is interesting and, I think, easily explicable. Charlotte had, from the days when she entered Miss Wooler's boarding-school at fifteen with a strong Irish accent caught from her father and old-fashioned clothes, a painful sense of social inferiority (witness her remarkable dream about her two dead much-admired elder sisters Maria and Elizabeth, who had died in her early schooldays; in the dream, they came home again but 'were changed; they had forgotten what they used to care for; they were very fashionably dressed, and began criticising the room...'). This was accentuated later by the treatment she received as governess in the homes of wealthy Yorkshire snobs, such as the Sidgwicks (cousins of Archbishop Benson); it was Mrs Sidgwick who perpetrated the snub to Charlotte and Charlotte's affectionate little pupil by exclaiming: 'Love the *governess*, my dear!' Hence the exaggerated tone in her castigation of the snobbish and the creation of the insufferable Ingrams in *Jane Eyre*, the Sympsons in *Shirley*, and Ginevra and her circle in *Villette*, in order to load them with contumely, passages which read at times rather like Marie Corelli.

Nevertheless, in spite of the occasional lapses, her prose in general demands recognition as a fine specimen of what Henry James called 'the sacred fluid of fiction'. Her ear for the sounds and meanings of wind and water, as well as for speech which records character and impulse, her eye for landscapes and interiors that convey emotional associations, her perception of personality and character and certain states which no other novelist had ever before noted, and for the agonies of moral and emotional isolation which no one, not even Conrad, has since investigated more impressively, all these characteristics are of the first order. And when we say that, we are admitting that she is a great prose-writer, for of course our only knowledge of one is through the language in which her ideas are communicated to us. Her best work – most of *Jane Eyre* and a great deal of *Villette* – is written in an economical and incisive prose which somehow has power to suggest to the imagination what only poets had before attempted, writing which is not purple or 'fine', not even Romantic prose, and yet is essentially poetic. The long chapter in *Jane Eyre* when Jane wanders over the moors and follows the light into the Rivers' home is an example of sustained power of this kind. The force of details comes, it seems to me, from the total method of the novel as I have tried to analyse it. The passages which earlier critics complained of as obscure and irrelevant are just those to which I should point as the source of the peculiar suggestive power of the novel as a whole, as being essential to the narrative and giving emphasis to the intention of the novel. I would point in *Jane Eyre* to the Bewick passage in the first chapter with its recurrences later in the book, the fire-and-ice passages and references, the storm and the chestnut tree, the dream of the child and the ruin, the paradisal orchard before and after the storm. When G. H. Lewes wrote to her, after reading *Jane Eyre*, urging her to exercise restraint and advising her to respect convention as a novelist and to emulate the classic qualities of Jane Austen's novels, she retorted by rejecting altogether the novel of the Georgians and the Age of Reason, explaining her own method and artistic beliefs thus:

When authors write best, or, at least, when they write most fluently an influence seems to waken in them, which becomes their master – which will have its own way – putting out of view all behests but its own, dictating certain words, and insisting on their being used, whether vehement or measured in their nature; new-moulding charac-ters, giving unthought-of turns to incidents, rejecting carefully elaborated old ideas, and suddenly creating and adopting new ones. Is it not so? And should we try to counteract this influence? Can we indeed counteract it?

Here we see her testimony to the strength and importance of an overmastering influence, a theme which seizes the author and impels the writing of a novel in a form uniquely suited to embody that theme and which distinguishes the truly original creative writer of novels from what Lawrence described (in referring to Arnold Bennett) as 'an old imitator'. The ideas and the expression here are characteristically Laurentian, and one sees that D. H. Lawrence owed a good deal to Charlotte and Emily Brontë, his insights and the technical aspects of his novels being evidently developments of theirs. Still more like him is Charlotte's expression of what to her seemed the limitations and deficiencies of Jane Austen as novelist:

She does the business of delineating the surface of the lives of genteel English people curiously well...What sees keenly, speaks aptly, moves flexibly, it suits her to study; but what throbs fast and full, though hidden, what the blood rushes through, what is the unseen seat of life and the sentient target of death – this Miss Austen ignores. She no more, with her mind's eye, beholds the heart of her race than each man, with bodily vision, sees the heart in his heaving breast. Jane Austen was a complete and most sensible lady, but a very incomplete and rather insensible (*not senseless*) woman. If this be heresy, I cannot help it.

Here we see her rejection of the idea of the lady as distinct from the woman, of the social man in favour of the unique individual,

and of the world of polite manners and custom which she
demands should be replaced by the realities of passion, impulse,
and 'new ideas'. What she was concerned with, felt to be of
paramount importance, was the source of life, its springs and
undercurrents. Her spirited rebuttal of Lewes's claim for Jane
Austen as 'one of the greatest artists and one of the greatest
painters of human character', took the form of a question: 'Can
there be a great artist without poetry?' and she goes on to argue
that 'Miss Austen being without *poetry*, maybe is sensible, real
(more real than true), but she cannot be great.' Her own idea
of a great novelist is evidently associated with the achievement
of Shakespeare and the Romantic poets (she disliked Pope); and
the contrast between the realism of Jane Austen and a
profounder reality, truth to the whole of experience as rendered
by the great poets, is made with critical acumen. As always, an
original critical insight has preceded true creativeness. We have
therefore a good idea of what the sisters discussed as they paced
('like wild animals') round the table in the parsonage sitting-
room every night from nine to eleven o'clock. They were
bringing into being a new conception of the novel and of the
novelist's function.

   That she has 'power' and 'genius' has always been admitted,
but the academics who admit it have shown what they think
of these qualities in a novelist by relegating Charlotte Brontë
to a group of 'writers like Melville and D. H. Lawrence',
novelists who are somehow embarrassing because unsound (so
different from Scott and Thackeray and Meredith); that the
former group were also innovators who extended the scope and
depth of the novel, a feat implying great intelligence, was not
noticed. A typical Bloomsbury critic referred on the same
principle to 'writers like Ouida and Charlotte Brontë who are
at the mercy of a white-hot imagination'. I have tried to show
that her two greatest novels, at any rate, were not thrown off
like that, that they show an even exceptional power of analysing
experience and ordering the products of the imagination so as
to impose a meaning on them and serve an artistic intention.
Not to recognize that Charlotte Brontë has done so is to show
great obtuseness, I think. I have quoted her criticism of Jane
Austen. Charlotte meant *her* novels to be the expression of *a
complete woman*, and not only of what in a woman 'throbs fast
and full, what the blood rushes through', but also of 'what is

the unseen seat of life' and, she might have added, of the mind and the will. What an extraordinary ambition this represents for a novelist in the 1840s in England, still more for one who was a young spinster and a clergyman's daughter! The intention was conscious and produced a theme, the theme determining the conscious structure, and there is a morally impressive quality in the honesty of exposition in spite of the lapses into rhetoric. This quality is what Thackeray must have been responding to when he expressed his admiration for *Jane Eyre* by writing to its publisher: 'It is a fine book, the man and woman capital, the style very generous and upright so to speak.'

There is no question, as we have seen, of her being 'at the mercy of her imagination'. Her novels are really not equivalents to the drawings made by Jung's patients. She was in control throughout: *Jane Eyre*, after all, bears a recognizable likeness in method and other respects to *Anna Karenina*, the supreme instance of the novelist in perfect command of his material at *all* levels and directing the whole experience of his life to one purpose. Like Tolstoy, Charlotte Brontë is outside as well as inside her novels. Perhaps she is not so indisputably one of the great wise novelists like Tolstoy, George Eliot, and Conrad. Yet, she is not merely one of the sufferers like Kafka. She is one of the novelists we could not do without. If it is argued that Jane Austen (for instance) was better balanced, we must ask what kind of balance is in question and whether one kind can be compared with another – there is the balance of a canoe on the surface of the water and the balance of an iceberg of which four-fifths is out of sight. The former is more economical and direct in movement, but the latter has irresistible strength, force and appeal to the imagination, and incomparable beauty.

There is a more subtle and much more interesting comparison to make instead, it seems to me. There is a distinction to be made between a novel written deliberately, like *Adam Bede* or *Daniel Deronda*, and a novel by the same author, *Silas Marner*, which (as we know from George Eliot's journal and letters) came to her involuntarily and was written under a kind of compulsion, making her shelve the novel *Romola* which she had been intending to write. The source of the compulsion is plainly in her state at that time, as I have argued in my introduction to the Penguin edition of *Silas Marner*. The point I want to make is that *Silas Marner* is not less well constructed, less an artistic feat, than George Eliot's other novels; though apparently simpler, this is deceptive for it is more tightly and closely constructed than the other, deliberated novels and deals with at least an equal delicacy with the moral and psychological aspects of social life. The underlying theme, however, is really a primitive one – *Silas Marner* treats isolation, exclusion from the community and its effects, ultimate acceptance into the community, and the achievement of happiness – very much what *Jane Eyre* treats in its so different detail. *Jane Eyre* resembles *Silas Marner* more than it does *Middlemarch* in the nature of its theme and subject-matter, and like *Silas Marner* it shows a high degree of organization of minute particulars. At what stage, at what level, these details were created is another interesting point.

Still another relevant point in comparing the conditions that produced *Silas Marner*, *Jane Eyre*, and *Villette* is that in George Eliot's novel too, the theme is adumbrated by passages and incidents which do not contribute to the plot in the ordinary sense but which take stress nevertheless; they are what no sensitive reader can fail to accept as significant. Such an instance is the story of the haunted stables and the London tailor, which comes towards the beginning of *Silas Marner*. Whether George Eliot could have explained why she wrote the episode is another interesting question; as it is vital to an understanding of the theme of *Silas Marner*, one must assume she could. The general technique was invented by Hawthorne and Melville independently rather earlier. I think some conclusions might be profitably drawn by a psychologist who should be intelligently interested in literature.

There is another point in which Charlotte's novels (and *Wuthering Heights*) raise the question of the relation of literature to psychology. The early work, the 'little books' which chronicle Angria, Charlotte's and Branwell's joint enterprise, a daydream paralleled by Emily and Anne's lost Gondal saga, was not merely a resource of childhood but was continued by the girls into adult life. If the Brontës were the most precocious of children, they were as certainly very retarded adolescents. We do not know what the Gondal books were like, but the Angrian romances show a concentration on immorality, vice, and sadism which is odd in a clergyman's daughter brought up in seclusion. But the most unpleasant and melodramatic of these we see was written by Charlotte at eighteen. None of them (in spite of Miss Ratchford's claims) show the slightest literary promise and none of them deal with the real world of Charlotte's everyday life and interests. Somehow, between the last of these productions and *The Professor* (we don't know how short the interval may have been), Charlotte discovered another basis for constructing fiction and another kind of prose and dialogue. No doubt the Brussels expedition made for Charlotte, as for Lucy Snowe, a decisive and in some ways wounding break with her previous life. For so long the Brontës, especially Charlotte, would seem to have been incurable daydreamers of a particularly uncontrolled and vulgarly uninteresting kind. But at some point, both Charlotte and Emily forced themselves, or perhaps found themselves able, to turn their daydreaming from self-indulgence to the service of life and health and art.

A fresh approach to *Wuthering Heights*

Prefatory note

I took to Adams House, Harvard, and to Cornell in 1966 a
mass of material on and about *Wuthering Heights*, some of it
written out in full for lecturing and some in note form for
seminars and for the discussions that I hoped would arise out
of the lectures, of which I delivered one at Adams House,
Harvard, and one at Cornell. These two lectures were made
out of various parts of my material with a good deal of
overlapping; but there remained much that was unused, even
in conversation, which I had been using in working with
Cambridge undergraduates in England for some years. When
the lectures – inseparable Siamese twins – were to be written
out for publication, it was necessary to include all I had taken,
in order to make my case out convincingly, as well as in order
to satisfy my purpose, which was to put into circulation
grounds for a responsible and sensitive approach to *Wuthering
Heights* in its context (both literary and historical) as well as
to provide a fresh assessment, which should also be corrective,
of its merits absolutely as a literary creation. Where my
material fell outside the direct line of my argument, I have
relegated it to appendices, but since the conclusions drawn
therefrom are necessary to enforce my case, I hope the
appendices will be read as part of the whole.

Q.D.L.

After its initial adverse reception ('too odiously and abominably
pagan to be palatable to the most vitiated class of English
reader' – *The Quarterly Review*) and its subsequent installation as
a major English classic (of such mystic significance that while
its meaning transcends criticism adverse comment on any
concrete features would be in the worst taste), *Wuthering Heights*,
to my knowledge as a university teacher of English Literature,

seems to be coming under attack from a new generation. To those who find the novel mainly melodrama, complain that the violence is factitious or sadistic, or object (with justice) to the style as often stilted and uneven, and to those who can see no coherent intention but find incompatible fragments and disjointed intentions at different levels of seriousness, an answer that the novel's greatness is unquestionable is useless. Some of these charges cannot be altogether refuted, though they can be generally accounted for as inevitable features of the kind of undertaking by such a writer at such a date, and some agreement reached about the nature of the success of the book on the whole: for that *Wuthering Heights* is a striking achievement of some kind, candid readers can and do feel. The difficulty of establishing that a literary work is a classic is nothing compared to the difficulty of establishing *what kind* of a classic it is – what is in fact the nature of its success, what kind of creation it represents. One has only to read the admiring critics of *Wuthering Heights*, even more the others, to see that there is no agreed reading of this novel at all. Desperate attempts to report a flawless work of art lead to a dishonest ignoring of recalcitrant elements or an interpretation of them which is sophistical; other and more sustained sophistry has resulted from such academic bright ideas as the one confidently asserted to me in an American university by a professor of English Literature who had discovered that 'The clue to *Wuthering Heights* is that Nelly Dean is Evil.'

Of course, in general one attempts to achieve a reading of a text which includes all its elements, but here I believe we must be satisfied with being able to account for some of them and concentrate on what remains. It is better to admit that some of the difficulties of grasping what is truly creative in *Wuthering Heights* are due to the other parts – to the author in her inexperience having made false starts, changing her mind (as tone and style suggest) probably because of rewriting from earlier stories with themes she had lost interest in and which have become submerged, though not assimilated, in the final work.[1] Another source of confusion to the reader is that she tried to do too much, too many different things (a common trouble in first novels and in most Victorian novels) and that some of these interfere with her deeper intentions – though of course this is also one source of the richness of this novel and we wouldn't care to sacrifice many of these, I think. The novel has all the signs of having been written at different times (because in different styles) and with varying intentions; we must sort these out in order to decide what *is* the novel. In spite of the brilliantly successful time-shifts and what has been called, not very happily, the 'Chinese box' ingenuity of construction, it certainly isn't a seamless 'work of art', and candour obliges us to admit ultimately that some things in the novel are incompatible with the rest, so much so that one seems at times to find oneself in really different novels.

Even criticism that is felt to be very helpful because unusually honest and sensitive may end by leaving the stress in the wrong place. I will instance a pioneer critique, Mr Klingopulos's revaluation of *Wuthering Heights* in *Scrutiny* under our collaborative heading 'The Novel as Dramatic Poem'. In 1947, when we published it, it was very salutary that *Wuthering Heights* should thus be rescued from the woolly treatment that was then current (e.g., in Lord David Cecil's *Early Victorian Novelists*). But in order to make the case and points he felt needed making, Mr Klingopulos ignores or slights elements and scenes which impinge on me, at least, as of fundamental importance. For instance, though he starts by saying, very properly, that 'the main problems in any account of the book are these: to decide on the status of Catherine and her relationship with Edgar and Heathcliff: to decide on the status of the Cathy–Hareton relationship and the appropriateness of reading it as a comment on what happened earlier' – nothing could be better than this clearing of the ground – yet he makes Catherine as a matter of course the splendid and valuable creature of conventional esteem (without noting Nelly's, Edgar's and at times Heathcliff's 'placing' of her, as well as more subtle insights of the novelist's own), and he goes so far as to assert as a general truth of *Wuthering Heights* that 'the author's preferences are not shown' and therefore, he deduces, it is not 'a moral tale'. Actually, I shall argue, the author's preferences *are* shown, Catherine is judged by the author in the parallel but notably different history of the daughter who, inheriting her mother's name, and likenesses both physical and psychological, is shown by deliberate choice, and trial and error, developing the maturity and therefore achieving the happiness, that the mother failed in, whereas we have seen the mother hardening into a fatal

immaturity which destroys herself and those (Heathcliff and
Edgar principally) involved with her. Nor is the author's
impersonality (deliberately maintained by the device of a
narrator who records other narrators and all of whom are much
less like their creator than Conrad's Marlow his) – nor is that
impersonality inconsistent with a moral intention. That is, the
reader is obliged to draw moral conclusions, from the very
nature of the scenes and actors in whose lives he is involved by
sympathy and compassion or horror and repulsion.

I would first like to clear out of the way the *confusions* of the
plot and note the different levels on which the novel operates
at different times. It seems clear to me that Emily Brontë had
some trouble in getting free of a false start – a start which
suggests that we are going to have a regional version of the
sub-plot of *Lear* (Shakespeare being generally the inspiration for
those early nineteenth-century novelists who rejected the
eighteenth-century idea of the novel). In fact, the Lear-world
of violence, cruelty, unnatural crimes, family disruption and
physical horrors remains the world of the household at Wuthering
Heights, a characteristic due not to sadism or perversion in the
novelist (some of the physical violence is quite unrealized)[2] but
to the Shakespearian intention. The troubles of the Earnshaws
started when the father brought home the boy Heathcliff (of
which he gives an unconvincing explanation and for whom he
shows an unaccountable weakness) and forced him on the
protesting family; Heathcliff 'the cuckoo' by intrigue soon
ousts the legitimate son Hindley and, like Edmund, Gloucester's
natural son in *Lear*, his malice brings about the ruin of two
families (the Earnshaws and the Lintons, his rival getting the
name Edgar by attraction from *Lear*). Clearly, Heathcliff was
originally the illegitimate son and Catherine's half-brother,
which would explain why, though so attached to him by early
associations and natural sympathies, Catherine never really
thinks of him as a possible lover either before or after marriage,[3]
it also explains why all the children slept in one bed at the
Heights till adolescence, we gather (we learn later from Catherine
(chapter 12) that being removed at puberty from this bed
became a turning point in her inner life, and this is only one
of the remarkable insights which *Wuthering Heights* adds to the
Romantic poets' exploration of childhood experience). The
favourite Romantic theme of incest therefore must have been

the impulsion behind the earliest conception of *Wuthering Heights*. Rejecting this story for a more mature intention, Emily Brontë was left with hopeless inconsistencies on her hands, for while Catherine's feelings about Heathcliff are never sexual (though she feels the bond of sympathy with a brother to be more important to her than her feelings for her young husband), Heathcliff's feelings for her are always those of a lover. As Heathcliff has been written out as a half-brother, Catherine's innocent refusal to see that there is anything in her relation to him incompatible with her position as a wife, becomes preposterous and the impropriety which she refuses to recognize is translated into social terms – Edgar thinks the kitchen the suitable place for Heathcliff's reception by Mrs Linton while she insists on the parlour. Another trace of the immature draft of the novel is the fairy-tale opening of the Earnshaw story, where the father, like the merchant in *Beauty and the Beast*, goes off to the city promising to bring his children back the presents each has commanded: but the fiddle was smashed and the whip lost so the only present he brings for them is the Beast himself, really a 'prince in disguise' (as Nelly tells the boy he should consider himself rightly); Catherine's tragedy then was that she forgot her prince and he was forced to remain the monster, destroying her; invoking this pattern brought in much more from the fairy-tale world of magic folk-lore and ballads, the oral tradition of the folk, that the Brontë children learnt principally from their nurses and their servant Tabby.[4] This element surges up in chapter 12, the important scene of Catherine's illness, where the dark superstitions about premonitions of death, about ghosts and primitive beliefs about the soul, come into play so significantly;[5] and again in the excessive attention given to Heathcliff's goblin-characteristics and especially to the prolonged account of his uncanny obsession and death. That this last should have an air of being infected by Hoffmann too is not surprising in a contemporary of Poe's; Emily is likely to have read Hoffmann when studying German at the Brussels boarding-school and certainly read the ghastly supernatural stories by James Hogg and others in the magazines at home. It is a proof of her immaturity at the time of the original conception of *Wuthering Heights* that she should express real psychological insights in such inappropriate forms.

In the novel as we read it Heathcliff's part either as Edmund in *Lear* or as the Prince doomed to Beast's form, is now suspended in boyhood while another influence, very much of the period, is developed, the Romantic image of childhood,[6] with a corresponding change of tone. Heathcliff and Catherine are idyllically and innocently happy together (and see also the end of chapter 5) roaming the countryside as hardy, primitive Wordsworthian children, 'half savage and hardy and free'. Catherine recalls it longingly when she feels she is dying trapped in Thrushcross Grange. (This boy Heathcliff is of course not assimilable with the vicious, scheming and morally heartless – 'simply insensible' – boy of chapter 4 who plays Edmund to old Earnshaw's Gloucester.) Catherine's dramatic introduction to the genteel world of Thrushcross Grange – narrated with contempt by Heathcliff who is rejected by it as a plough-boy unfit to associate with Catherine – is the turning point in her life in *this* form of the novel; her return, got up as a young lady in absurdly unsuitable clothes for a farmhouse life, and 'displaying fingers wonderfully whitened with doing nothing and staying indoors'[7] etc. visibly separates her from the 'natural' life, as her inward succumbing to the temptations of social superiority and riches parts her from Heathcliff. Heathcliff's animus against his social degradation by his new master Hindley is barbed by his being made to suffer (like Pip at the hands of Estella in *Great Expectations*)[8] taunts and insults – mainly from Edgar Linton – based on class and externals alone. They are suffered again (thus making Emily Brontë's point inescapable) in the second half of the novel by Hindley's son Hareton at the hands of Catherine's and Edgar's daughter Cathy as well as from his other cousin Linton Heathcliff, Isabella's son. And this makes us sympathetic to Heathcliff as later to Hareton; we identify here with Nelly who with her wholesome classlessness and her spontaneous maternal impulses supports Heathcliff morally while he is ill-used (and even tries to persuade Catherine not to let Edgar supplant him in her life) – she retains this generous sympathy for him until she transfers it to her foster-child Hareton when in turn he becomes a victim (of Heathcliff's schemes). Her sympathy for Heathcliff's hard luck, even when she sees that his return is a threat to the Lintons' happiness, is at odds with her loyalty to her new master Edgar, and leads her to consent to some ill-advised interviews between Catherine and the desperate Heathcliff –

though she also feels that to consent to help him there is the lesser of two evils (as it probably was), and she has no doubts about her duty to protect Isabella from becoming Heathcliff's victim.

Nelly Dean is most carefully, consistently and convincingly created for us as the normal woman, whose truly feminine nature satisfies itself in nurturing all the children in the book in turn.[9] To give this salience we have the beginning of chapter 8 when the farm-girl runs out to the hayfield where Nelly is busy to announce the birth of 'a grand bairn' and to give her artless (normal feminine) congratulations to Nelly for being chosen to nurse it since it will soon be motherless: 'I wish I were you, because it will be all yours when there is no missus.' Nelly's greater sensibility in realizing that from the bairn's point of view this is not altogether a matter for rejoicing is shown in the next chapter when she says 'I went into the kitchen, and sat down to lull my little lamb to sleep... I was rocking Hareton on my knee, and humming a song that began

> 'It was far in the night, and the bairnies grat,
> The mither beneath the mools heard that'...

The ballad is evidently one expressing the widespread belief, in folk-song and folk-tale, that a prematurely dead mother cannot rest in the grave but returns to suckle the babe or help her child in the hour of need,[10] an indication of what is going on in Nelly's compassionate mind. But the whole episode of Hareton's birth and childhood exposes Catherine's insensibility, that her self-centred nature is essentially loveless. (Her only reference to her own pregnancy later is the hope that a son's birth will 'erase Isabella's title' to be Edgar's heir.) Yet Nelly's limitations are made clear and the novelist's distinct position of true insight, where necessary. Like Dolly in *Anna Karenina* who is also the normal maternal woman, Nelly is inevitably too *terre-à-terre* (Vronsky's complaint about Dolly), therefore unable to sympathize with difficulties that seem to her the result only of will, and a perverse will at that ('"I should not have spoken so, if I had known her true condition, but I could not get rid of the notion that she acted a part of her disorder"'). These limitations and not ill-will are of course the reason why Nelly makes some mistakes in trying to act for the best in situations where no easy or right solution offered itself. But in doing Catherine full justice ('"she was not artful, never played the coquette"') and giving her sound advice in her 'perplexities and untold troubles', Nelly convinces us of her right to take a thoroughly disenchanted view of Catherine's disposition. In fact, both Heathcliff and Edgar know the truth about Catherine and Hindley is under no illusions – '"You lie, Cathy, no doubt"' he remarks (correctly) of her explanation of Edgar Linton's visit in his absence. One of the most successful indications of the passage of time is Nelly Dean's change, from the quick-moving and quick-witted girl who for little Hareton's sake copes with the drunken murderous Hindley, to the stout, breathless, middle-aged woman who, though still spirited, cannot save Cathy from a forced marriage.

To hark back to Heathcliff: it follows from this 'social' development of the theme that Heathcliff should go out into the world to make his fortune and come back to avenge himself, 'a cruel hard landlord', 'near, close-handed' and given over to 'avarice, meanness and greed', plotting to secure the property of both Earnshaws and Lintons and also to claim equality with them socially – we are now in the Victorian world of *Great Expectations* where money, as Magwitch the convict learnt, makes a gentleman. Emily Brontë took no trouble to explain the hiatus in Heathcliff's life – irrelevant to her purposes – and in fact it is enough for us to gather that he comes back a professional gambler at cards; a real flaw however is wholly inadequate illustration of the shared life and interests of himself and Catherine that makes it plausible that on his return she should be so absorbed in conversing with him as to cut out immediately and altogether her young husband. After all, we reflect, they couldn't always have been talking about their childhood escapades – that is to say, we recognize a failure in creative interest here in the novelist; nor do we ever hear what they talk about till Catherine attacks him over Isabella and they quarrel, when it becomes clear even to Catherine that he can be only the monster he has been made by his history. This aspect of him is kept before us from now till the end and accounts for his brutalities and violent outbreaks. For various reasons, therefore, after envisaging several alternative conceptions of Heathcliff, Emily Brontë ended by keeping and making use of them all, so that like Dostoievski's Stavrogin he is an enigmatic figure only by reason of his creator's indecision, like Stavrogin in being an unsatisfactory composite with empty places in his history and no continuity of character. And like Iago and

Stavrogin, Heathcliff has been made the object of much misdirected critical industry on the assumption that he is not merely a convenience. There is nothing enigmatic about either Catherine, we note, and this points to the novelist's distribution of her interest.

There are various signs that the novelist intended to stress the aspect of her theme represented by the corruption of the child's native goodness by Society and to make this part of the explanation of Catherine's failure in life. She evidently had in mind the difficulties and dangers inevitable in civilizing children to enter the artificial world of class, organized religion, social intercourse and authoritarian family life. This is the point of Catherine's childhood journal that Lockwood reads, which gives a caricature of the torments suffered by children in the enforcement of the Puritan Sabbath, and another caricature is the account given by the boy Heathcliff of the parlour life of the broken-in Linton children as seen from the other side of the window by a Noble Savage whose natural good instincts have not been destroyed like theirs. More impressive is the beautifully rendered exemplary relation between the child Catherine and the adults as reported by Nelly in chapter 5. Her father's attempts to improve her, or tame her to an approved pattern,[11] resulted only in 'a naughty delight to provoke him: she was never so happy as when we were all scolding her at once, and she defying us with her bold, saucy look, and her ready words; turning Joseph's religious curses into ridicule, baiting me, and doing just what her father hated most' – 'Mr. Earnshaw did not understand jokes from his children', Nelly notes, 'he had always been strict and grave with them'.

After behaving as badly as possible all day, she sometimes came fondling to make it up at night. 'Nay, Cathy' the old man would say, 'I cannot love thee; go, say thy prayers, child, and ask God's pardon. I doubt thy mother and I must rue that we ever reared thee!' That made her cry, at first; and then, being repulsed continually hardened her, and she laughed if I told her to say she was sorry for her faults, and beg to be forgiven...It pleased the master rarely to see her gentle – saying 'Why canst thou not always be a good lass, Cathy?' And she turned up her face to his, and laughed, and answered, 'Why cannot you always be a good man, father?'

We note that the child is allowed the last word – and a very telling rejoinder it is. Emily Brontë, the girl in the family most sympathetic to the black-sheep brother, was the most recalcitrant to the domestic training of her rigid aunt, to schooling, and to orthodox religion; she had plainly thought about the psychological effects of conventional disciplines and taken this opportunity to report adversely in the strongest terms a novelist can use – by showing their part in destroying the possibilities of a happy childhood and maturity.

But this originally naïve and commonplace subject – the Romantics' image of childhood in conflict with society – becomes something that in this novel is neither superficial nor theoretic because the interests of the responsible novelist gave it, as we have seen above, a new insight, and also a specific and informed sociological content. The theme is here very firmly rooted in time and place and richly documented: we cannot forget that Gimmerton and the neighbourhood are so bleak that the oats are always green there three weeks later than anywhere else, and that old Joseph's Puritan preachings accompany his 'overlaying his large Bible with dirty bank-notes, the produce of the day's transactions' at market; and we have a thoroughly realistic account of the life indoors and outdoors at Wuthering Heights as well as at the gentleman's residence at the Grange. In fact, there would be some excuse for taking this, the pervasive and carefully maintained sociological theme which fleshes the skeleton, for the real novel. This novel, which could be extracted by cutting away the rest, was deliberately built, to advance a thesis, on the opposition between Wuthering Heights and Thrushcross Grange, two different cultures of which the latter inevitably supersedes the former. The point about dating this novel as ending in 1801 (instead of its being contemporary with the Brontës' own lives) – and much trouble was taken to keep the dates, time-scheme and externals such as legal data, accurate[12] – is to fix its happenings at a time when the old rough farming culture based on a naturally patriarchal family life, was to be challenged, tamed and routed by social and cultural changes that were to produce the Victorian class consciousness and 'unnatural' ideal of gentility.[13]

The inspiration for this structure, based on a conflict between, roughly speaking, a wholesome primitive and natural unit of a healthy society and its very opposite, felt to be an unwholesome refinement of the parasitic 'educated', comes from observation – in the Brontës' youth and county the old order visibly survived (see Appendix A). But the clue to making such perceptions and sympathies into a novel was found, I suspect, in Scott, whose novels and poetry were immensely admired by Charlotte and Emily. His own sympathies were with the wild rough Border farmers, not only because they represented a romantic past of balladry. He felt that civilization introduced there entailed losses more than gains, and a novel where – before, with characteristic lack of staying power, he divagated from a serious theme into tushery – he made some effort to express this, *The Black Dwarf*, has long been known as the source for surnames used in *Wuthering Heights*. Scott's Earnscliffe (= Eaglescliff) and Ellieslaw suggested Heathcliff[14] and Earnshaw no doubt, but more important is their suggesting, it seems to me, that Emily Brontë found part of her theme in that novel's contrast between a weak, corrupt, refined upper-class, and the old-style Border farmers' 'natural' or socially primitive way of life in which feuds and violence were a recognized part of the code (though transacted for the most part strictly according to rule and tradition and quite compatible with good-humour and a generous humanity); there, the rich and great live in their castles, are treacherous, and come to grief, the rough Borderers, eking out subsistence farming by hunting, suffer drastic ups and downs with hardihood and survive; the setting is on the moors and hills, and an essential element in establishing the primitive social condition of the Borderers is the superstition and folk-lore believed in by them all. Now the Yorkshire moors with the hardy yeomen farmers of pre-Victorian times who had lived thereabouts and whose histories Tabby used to tell the Brontë children[15] in her broad dialect, must have seemed to them not essentially different from Scott's Border farmers. Emily and Charlotte were genuinely attached to their moorland country but Scott's example was what made it usable for them as literature and gave it rich associations, so it is natural that in her first attempt at a novel Emily should draw on even a poor fiction like *The Black Dwarf* to give meaning and purpose to her feelings about what was happening or had happened recently to the world she lived in. It is proof of her development out of her daydream world of the Gondals that she was thus interested in the real world and roused to the need to enquire into the true nature of the change, perhaps as a way to alert her own (Early Victorian) generation to what this was. From being a self-indulgent storytelling, *Wuthering Heights* thus became a responsible piece of work, and the writer thought herself into the positions, outlooks, sufferings and tragedies of the actors in these typical events as an *artist*.

But if we were to take the sociological novel as the real novel and relegate the Heathcliff–Catherine–Edgar relationship and the corresponding Cathy–Linton–Hareton one, as exciting but ex-centric dramatic episodes, we should be misconceiving the novel and slighting it, for it is surely these relationships and their working out that give all the meaning to the rest. For instance, though Cathy has in the second half to unlearn, very painfully, the assumptions of superiority on which she has been brought up at the Grange, this is only part of her schooling; it is only incidental to the process by which we see her transcend the psychological temptations and the impulses which would have made her repeat her mother's history; and this is not a question of sociology or social history but is timeless.

Another misconception for which the novelist gives little excuse is to attribute a mystique to the moor; the moor is not meaningful like Hawthorne's forests that surround the Puritan settlements in the wild, it is not even powerful over man's destiny like Egdon Heath. The moor is a way of pointing a distinction: to the child Cathy brought up in the gentleman's park at the Grange, the moor means freedom from restraint, and romantic Nature to which she longs to escape, and in which she delights, but to the people who live there of necessity it is something they have to wrest a living out of: in the long run man lives by farming, and the farmhouse at the Heights is braced against the challenge the extreme conditions there represent (for instance, on our first sight of it we see that the architecture is determined by the violence of the winds). Lockwood (characteristically) demands that the farm should provide him with a guide home when, though snow threatened, he foolishly paid a call, and he thinks, as we at first do, that the refusal is brutal and wanton; but there is no guide to spare – the hands are needed to get in the sheep before the animals are snowed under and to see to the horses. Similarly, when Cathy in her thoughtlessness uses her new power over Hareton to get him to pull up the fruit-bushes to make her a flower-garden, old Joseph, who has worked all his life at the Heights and meant to die there, is so outraged that he gives notice rather than stay to witness such a sinful proceeding as to sacrifice food to flowers. Unattractive as Joseph usually is, his disinterested identification with the family's well-being is impressive and as so often he is the vehicle for expressing a truth to which we need to have our attention called: here, that where fertile soil is precious, flower-gardens are an unjustified self-indulgence. Another example (there are plenty) is Linton Heathcliff's selfishness, due like Cathy's to ignorance of the facts of life on such a farm: Zillah complains 'he must always have sweets and dainties, and always milk, milk for ever – heeding naught how the rest of us are pinched in winter'. The novelist knows that thrift as well as austerity is a necessary virtue in such a context, so that old Joseph's indignation when the feckless Isabella flings down the tray of porridge is wholly respectable: '"yah desarve pining froo this tuh Churstmas, flinging t'precious gifts uh God under fooit i' yer flaysome rages!"'

The clearest light is thrown on the moor by Catherine's likening Heathcliff to 'an arid wilderness of furze and whinstone' when trying to make the romantic Isabella understand the basic irreducibility of the nature of the man Isabella fancies she is in love with. But Catherine has also said to Nelly, in trying to explain her own 'love' for Heathcliff, that it is like 'the eternal rocks: a source of little visible delight, but necessary', in fact it is not love but a need of some fundamental kind that is quite separate from her normal love for Edgar Linton, a love which leads to a happily consummated marriage and the expectation of providing an heir.

The focus of the first half of the novel is most certainly Catherine, and it is her case that is the real moral centre of the book. This case is examined with wonderful subtlety and conveyed in a succession of brilliantly managed dramatic scenes with complete impersonality. Charlotte Brontë rightly defended her sister against allegations of abnormality by pointing out that, as well as what Charlotte justly describes as 'the perverted passion and passionate perversity' of the first Catherine, and Heathcliff's 'warped nature', Emily had created the wholesome maternal Nelly Dean, Edgar Linton's touching devotion and tenderness, and the 'grace and gaiety' of the younger Cathy – she might have instanced much more. And what precisely is this case, in which – and not in the sociological novel, which is more a matter of course in its age – lies the real originality of

Wuthering Heights? Here I think we can draw very usefully on a remarkable modern novel, *Jules et Jim* by Henri-Pierre Roché. The film is more widely known that François Truffaut made from it – so intelligently that the film can serve the purpose for those who haven't read the book.[16] I should have thought the resemblance of the plot and theme of the film to the core of the first half of *Wuthering Heights* was very striking, but the novel is still more like, while providing, in its challenging modernity and absence of all that makes it possible to describe *Wuthering Heights* as a regional novel, a means of showing critically why the older novel is more important and interesting. I must therefore use not the film but Roché's novel (pub. Gallimard, 1953). After a diffuse start it becomes the record of relations developing between two men and a woman (Kate, though confusingly – for *Wuthering Heights* purposes – named Catherine in the film). Kate answers exactly to Charlotte Brontë's description above of Catherine Earnshaw as well as in nearly all other essentials – it seems not to matter that, living in a sexually permissive society (twentieth-century Germany and France) she takes full licence, for she ends in Catherine's situation, and endures and causes similar suffering. Jules whom she marries is gentle, with bookish and philosophic leanings, like Edgar Linton, while Jim, a writer, is passionate, hard and violent, providing for Kate something that she needs to keep her alive and whole that her husband lacks – though she can't do without what Jules stands for either. Acquiescent as Jules inevitably is, considering the sophisticated society in which they live, and even by choice since his deep friendship with Jim antedates their meeting with Kate, and also because he hopes that, Jim being for Kate a lover who supplements himself in temperament, his marriage will be saved (he has two little girls) – yet the situation is inherently disastrous and ends with Kate's destroying herself and dragging the not unwilling Jim with her, while Jules survives, like Edgar Linton, only to foster his little daughters.

Except for the bond between the two men, the likeness to the first part of the English novel is obvious – and enlightening as to Emily Brontë's intentions in developing out of a simple sociological conflict an original psychological exploration. One would assume that the later (French) novel might have been based on the earlier (English) one, and that Lawrence's *Women in Love* also provided a model for Roché (one sees that Lawrence's respect for *Wuthering Heights* must have owed something to its usefulness for him). To check this I wrote to M. Roché (in 1964) only to find that he had died a few years before at the age of eighty, and that the events in his apparently very contemporary novel which are there placed in the years 1911–30 did actually take place then. Mme Roché kindly assured me that the novel was in fact written up from the daily journal her husband kept, during those years, of his personal history (before she knew him), written up long after, when they were refugees during the last war and without the journal at hand, but still closely following the journal, as she can testify. He did rewrite the novel three times at intervals (no doubt to achieve greater impersonality, though at the start of the novel particularly the shapelessness of life confuses the reader). Mme Roché informed me also that though he had read *Wuthering Heights*, and probably *Women in Love*, she thinks it would have been *after* the events recorded in his diary and which are reproduced in *Jules et Jim*, nor does she think he was influenced by *any* literary work in this composition.

There are no distractions in *Jules et Jim* to prevent us seeing that it is a psychological drama written with an almost clinical detachment; both it and the film (in which Kate is fairly adequately embodied by Jeanne Moreau) achieved notoriety as an astonishing case-history. No mystical explanation is needed for Kate, and we can therefore see that none is needed for Catherine Earnshaw – though it is natural that at that date Emily Brontë should feel obliged to provide something of the kind, and inevitable that it should take the form of not very impressive rhetoric (in chapter 9, ' " If all else perished and *he* remained " ' etc., and elsewhere). Natural too that Emily Brontë should have had difficulty in explaining even to herself her genuine insights and that she should be driven to attach, to the delicately truthful notation of them in action and dialogue, explanations of them as ' poetry ', a prose rhetoric of declamation which is in resonance with much that is unsatisfactory in the rhetorical verse of the Gondal cycle.[17] It is very unfortunate that the brief, and on the whole misleading, ' metaphysical ' parts of *Wuthering Heights* should have been not only overrated but universally seized on as a short cut to the meaning, the significance of the novel (to the virtual exclusion of the real novel enacted so richly for us to grasp in all its complexity). We might consider as a related weakness Heathcliff's mainly melodramatic explanations of himself, Heathcliff being made up of so many inconsistent parts that the novelist evidently was in some perplexity to make him cohere enough to make an impressive final appearance and exit. (In contrast to her carelessness about Heathcliff we must note the care she took to make plausible Lockwood's burying himself at Thrushcross Grange, being kept there by illness to hear Nelly's long narration, and returning for the conclusion of the Linton–Earnshaw history, as also her providing an explanation of Nelly's being more sensitive and better educated than an ordinary house-keeper, as she needs to be.) A weakness arising out of this is the disproportionate space allotted to Heathcliff's final lapse into the desire to die in order to join Catherine and the disintegration of his will; and another is the occasional flirtation with the juvenile conception of him as possessed by the Devil. (There are, however, two places where this idea is given temporary justification: one is the momentary appearance of Heathcliff 'on the door stones' which makes Nelly, who has come to fight for the interests of little Hareton, lose her nerve and rush away 'as if I had raised a goblin', the other is Joseph's account, of how Heathcliff is deliberately ruining Catherine's brother, in what might be a passage from the *Pilgrim's Progress*: '"I' course, he tells Dame Catherine hah hor father's son gallops dahn t'Broad road, while he flees afore tuh oppen t'pikes?"')

To return to the argument from *Jules et Jim*: as Kate's history was taken from an actuality there is no reason why an observer of genius should not have deduced and composed Catherine Earnshaw from reported or observed real life, for her behaviour is essentially that of Roché's Kate, though whereas M. Roché was personally an actor in his drama it is certain that Emily Brontë had no such first-hand facilities. There is less felt anguish in her novel than in his in consequence, but more useful insight. This is proved by her adding the second half to her novel instead of leaving us with a case on our hands – though one which M. Roché's diary shows to have been a human possibility and in fact a not unrepresentative one once one recognizes that the kind of woman of which Catherine Earnshaw and Kate are specimens is not uncommon.[18] Inevitably, since the Romantics had made love between man and woman the focus of values, succeeding novelists were led to ask what in terms of daily life does love become. Roché's novel, though consummations of love frequently occur in it, is not about sex, any more than *Women in Love* is: it is entirely an examination, in Jim's words, of 'what people call love'. Emily Brontë seems to have been equally occupied with this problem though as a much finer artist she saw it in all its complexity. Kate is a woman who uses her exceptional attractions to dominate men, humiliate them, punish them, or reward them if they obey her, and is jealously possessive of their persons and their inner selves too while demanding the right to retain complete liberty herself. Like a child, she assumes she is the centre of the world and has no sense of responsibility. Her power lies not in crude sex but in being, like Catherine Earnshaw, a dazzling original character whose personality enchants because she is able to make sunshine and happiness for everyone around her if she can only be kept contented.[19] Though there are in the background of Roché's novel other women, they are all neutralized by or summarized in her (Jules and Jim call her 'the queen bee'), so that we conclude that Kate is not offered as a perverse or dangerous woman but as WOMAN in essence, a menace to masculine stability and man's achievement of a civilized code, and yet indispensable to any life worth living – I take it this is the point of that 'archaic smile' which gets such a lot of stress in the novel and symbolizes the archaic characteristics which in spite of the dangers they imply are what Roché thinks men seek in a woman and which are seen to be stronger than men's civilized selves. Kate is shown as absolutely hostile to man-made rules: she cheats, steals without any reason, tells lies shamelessly, rejoices in violent scenes, acts on intuition always, refuses to admit any moral law except a childish tit-for-tat which always has to work in her own interest, and has no patience with the masculine world of logic, reason and impersonal justice (though she is no fool and has literary and artistic ability). When she is ill, generally through her wilful bouts of passion, she demands devotion from men, but is unfeeling and irritated when they fall ill. What she cannot and will not bear is that men should escape from her into their world of intellectual interests. It is the first meeting between the friends after her marriage when they insist on discussing their work, ignoring her, that makes her take the desperate step of jumping into the Seine and swimming underwater to alarm her husband into submission (tough-minded Jim is unmoved except by admiration) – this is also a forecast of her last desperate bid for power when seeing Jim about to escape from her by marriage she deliberately drives their car into the Seine to drown him with her.

Now, not only does Catherine Earnshaw behave similarly and often identically, she has even the same disgust for her husband's bookishness, which she identifies as the source of his weakness or inadequacy. It is true the Lintons seem to shrink from healthy outdoor life and prefer to get their ideas about life from literature (in Isabella's case leading to her disastrous infatuation with Heathcliff conceived as a sensitive, noble Byronic soul – Catherine knows better); and that Wordsworth's mistrust of books and meddling intellect apparently gives respectable support to Catherine's attitude. But it is also apparent that Catherine feels her husband's intellectual tastes to be rivals – when intolerably provoked by her he retires to his studies, and it is this she thinks of when, on what she feels to be her death-bed, she envisages him with great bitterness as '"offering prayers of thanks to God for restoring peace to his house, and going back to his *books*!"'. The Emily Brontë who kneaded the dough with a German book propped before her cannot be supposed to endorse Catherine's hostility to learning; and though we must beware of identifying the novelist's attitude to Catherine with Nelly's, yet in general she endorses Nelly's shrewd analysis of Catherine's behaviour. Unlike Nelly however the novelist, though concerned to diagnose, does not blame Catherine, because she understands, as Nelly cannot, why a Catherine can hardly help behaving as she does. But she is as far as possible from admiring Catherine; being a woman, Emily Brontë has none of Roché's fascinated respect for his Kate as a force of nature. The woman novelist does not believe that all women share these characteristics more or less and are unfeminine without them, in fact, she takes pains to show that these characteristics are incompatible with what is required of a wife and mother. On the other hand, Roché's strength lies in being able to evoke a civilization made by the efforts of men which is indestructible by Woman. The friendship between the two men who have been students together and have in common a devotion to literature and the arts, though they are of different nationalities, a friendship which, to make the point clear, is shown as surviving even their fighting on opposite sides in the first World War as well as their being in love with the same woman – this is the point in which *Jules et Jim* is more subtle than *Wuthering Heights*, where the ill-will between Edgar and Heathcliff is dramatically commonplace. (Of course their hostility was necessary also in the sociological context of the novel where Edgar's assurance of class superiority and the unfeeling social contempt Heathcliff is exposed to in adolescence condition Heathcliff to become the Frankenstein monster we are introduced to by Mr Lockwood at the opening of the novel. Even so, Emily Brontë struggles to suggest some deeper truths than the situation seems to hold: for instance, Heathcliff's protestation to Nelly that he is superior to mere rivalry for Catherine's love – ' "had he been in my place and I in his, though I hated him with a hatred that turned my life to gall, I never would have raised a hand against him. I never would have banished him from her society as long as she desired his... I would have died by inches before I touched a single hair of his head!" ')

Over and above their hostility, Catherine deliberately foments trouble between them as part of her need for violence and domination; and the scene where she locks the three of them in and then throws the key on the fire, putting her delicate (though by no means cowardly) husband at the mercy of the brutal Heathcliff, and humiliating him by her insults, disloyalty and indifference to what happens to him, is extremely painful reading. She has no moral sensibility to comprehend that he is stricken not by cowardice but by her attitude to him. In these ways she behaves quite as insufferably as Kate but unlike her she is offset in the context of the novel by many other and very different feminine natures and dispositions,[20] this point being driven home in the second half where the younger Catherine, with similar drives and temptations to her mother's, is able to profit by experience and get a moral education from her sufferings because she is also her father's daughter. It is the men who strike one as making a consistently poor showing in *Wuthering Heights* – not only Heathcliff and his odious son Linton but the generally callous Joseph, the misguided older Earnshaw, his drunken son Hindley, the crude youth Hareton, the conceited narrator Lockwood, and even Edgar Linton who is imprisoned in class and for all his civilized virtues ineffective. But in spite of these inevitable differences in prejudice by a male and a female novelist, there is a wide agreement in Roché's and Emily Brontë's investigations into 'what people call love'. Both isolate the striking irrationality that impels the heroine of each to destroy her own possibility of happiness, both note that the only kind of love a woman like Catherine or Kate can feel is death-centred. A surprising insight of Emily Brontë's is that apportioning moral blame is impossible. Nelly Dean after describing the precarious nature of the Lintons' married happiness says:

'It ended. Well, we *must* be for ourselves in the long run; the mild and the generous are only more justly selfish than the domineering; and it ended when circumstances caused each to feel that one's interest was not the chief consideration in the other's thoughts.'

This is a basic truth, that the identification of interests in marriage is the only way of getting over the conflict of egos. Heathcliff's return is the spark that set off the train of gun-powder, but something else would have done so otherwise. Later on, in Edgar's tender devotion to Catherine in her final illness and even mental decay, we get another answer to the enquiry, 'What is it that people call Love?'; this answer is not cynical. But Catherine, like Kate, is shown to be incapable of love in this sense – '"I care nothing for your sufferings. Why shouldn't you suffer? I do,"' she says to Heathcliff in their last interview – and Heathcliff justly says of her haunting spirit, as her husband might equally have done: '"She showed herself, as she often was in life, a devil to me."' Even when Heathcliff is taking farewell of the dying Catherine he upbraids her with her 'infernal selfishness'. In fact, the scenes between Catherine and Heathcliff after his return are the climax of the novel as regards establishing this theme; so thoroughly is the author determined to develop them that she hardly troubles to bring them about naturally, thus exposing Nelly to charges of connivance or worse.

But though *Jules et Jim* is an unforgettable novel, it belongs for me in the *Adolphe* class – something I hardly want to read again because with all its genuineness it gives so much more discomfort than satisfaction. And compared with *Wuthering Heights* it is a novel of so much less interest, in spite of its freedom from a Victorian novelist's limitations in dealing with sex (which nevertheless, in *Wuthering Heights*, are not a handicap). Why does one feel that in spite of its intensely painful scenes –

painful in a great variety of ways – *Wuthering Heights* always
repays rereading? It is easy to lay a finger on a passage that
shows why what only disturbs in *Jules et Jim* moves us profoundly
in the other novel, because instead of a clinical presentation we
get a delicate annotation of behaviour that convinces us that
it is not perverse but natural, human and inevitable. Take the
sequence (chapter 8) when Catherine at fifteen is transferring
her interest (unintentionally) from the now degraded Heathcliff
to Edgar Linton, who besides being a desirable match does
genuinely represent standards she must admire, even though it
is a strain for her to have to appear to share them. We are
actually shown her suffering from this strain and what the
consequences are. Expecting Edgar, she has ungraciously to get
rid of Heathcliff who hangs about her, and so she is already out
of temper because uneasy about her treatment of her childhood
friend. Consequently she is spitefully cross with Nelly who (on
orders from the master) thwarts her desire to be alone with
Edgar, is driven to defend herself to Edgar by a patent fib, then
to laying hands in temper on her little nephew who naturally
supports his foster-mother, and then when Edgar interferes to
rescue the child she instinctively boxes *his* ear, in an irresistible
progress of passion. Edgar, 'greatly shocked at the double fault
of falsehood and violence which his idol has committed', reasons
with her, but to reason she has no answer.

Catherine was mute.
'And you told a deliberate untruth!', he said. 'I didn't!' she cried,
recovering her speech; 'I did nothing deliberately.'

To him, telling a lie and striking him in a most unladylike way
are serious offences, as well as quarrelling with a servant
(Nelly – to him always 'Ellen') and ill-treating a child. To her
(as to Roché's Kate) that her behaviour was spontaneous
justified it ('I did nothing deliberately'). She is not ashamed
of being herself, having no such standards and no image of
correct behaviour as he has which he feels obliged to sustain.
She continues: '"Well, go if you please – get away. And now
I'll cry – I'll cry myself sick"', and she proceeds to do so. If he
is unjust enough to blame her for what she can't help she will
punish him by making herself ill, a child's revenge and self-
protective technique – '"She set to weeping in serious earnest,"'
Nelly reports then. What is pardonable at fifteen becomes,

however, the pattern of her mode of domination ('falsehood and violence'), leading her when married to starve herself into delirium, threaten suicide, and look forward to death as a release[21] from an intolerable self as well as from an intolerable situation, destroying also in effect both the men who love her. And this self is not archaic Woman like Roché's Kate but is shown in growth as the product of strains in social and emotional life in childhood and adolescence. Jules placates Kate because he 'considers her as a natural force expressing itself through cataclysms' – this seems too pompous and to explain nothing; the superior sophistication of the French intellectual, the artists' world in which Roché's novel is set, and the complete lack of any moral code (except that of 'enlightenment') in any of the characters, are seen to be disadvantages because there is really no moral interest, only a series of shocks and surprises. Even the surprises in *Wuthering Heights* though not showy are much more rewarding ultimately. The scene I've just summarized between the young people ends by Nelly's noting that though she urged Edgar to 'take warning and be gone' (both for his own sake and in Heathcliff's interests), he couldn't:

The soft thing looked askance through the window. He possessed the power to depart, as much as a cat possesses the power to leave a mouse half killed, or a bird half eaten.

The surprise is that 'the soft thing' (soft applying to his nature and not to the cat's – with which he is surprisingly identified – but only to the cat's furry exterior, which is a shock in itself) Edgar, is not compared as one would expect with the mouse or bird, but with the cat that kills and eats them, a double shock. (Later on this is underlined by Joseph's referring to 'yon cat uh Linton'.) This surprise when we register it makes us realize a new truth, that a cat is really a victim of drives it can't resist too[22] (just as, later, we learn that 'the mild and generous' are just as selfish as 'the domineering' because they too '*must* be for themselves in the long run' – a law of nature). Moreover it obliges us to compassionate Catherine who is, justly, identified with the mouse or bird that Edgar the cat will catch and consume; she is pathetic because she is helpless before Edgar's fascination for her as someone who represents a finer social life and moral type than she has been used to, even though marrying him will be, as Heathcliff points out too late, like planting an oak in a flower-pot. A final surprise and another psychological truth is Nelly's observation that this scene had an opposite effect to what might have been expected: 'the quarrel had merely effected a closer intimacy – had broken the outworks and enabled them to confess themselves lovers'.

And this episode (chap. 8, that is) not only leads inevitably to Catherine's self-destruction; it is recalled by contrast when we read the scene in chapter 11 where Nelly goes up to the Heights to see how her foster-child Hareton is getting on and to warn his father, her old playmate Hindley, against Heathcliff. Full of tender reminiscences of their joint childhood, she comes on the child Hareton, whom she at first takes for his father a generation ago, to find, to her horror and ours, that he has forgotten his foster-mother completely and, schooled by Heathcliff, greets her with curses and stones. With the most admirable restraint she suppresses her natural reactions, even grief, to try to do something for the child's welfare. Recalling Catherine's behaviour ('wicked aunt Cathy') to the same child, we realise that Catherine's kind of femininity is neither exhaustive of the possibilities of Woman nor really typical. And Nelly's adult and selflessly maternal behaviour prepares us for her foster-child's, the younger Catherine's, evolution away from the possibilities of repeating her mother's disaster, though Cathy is shown to have similar impulses and in some ways nearly as unfortunate an upbringing (she is everyone's idol at the Grange). Cathy achieves the self-knowledge and wisdom that bring her to a successful coming of age as a woman with which the novel ends. Roché's novel and Truffaud's film with equal and unnecessary pessimism show Kate's daughter committed in childhood to an instinctive repetition of the mother's attitudes. Their message seems to be '*Così fan tutte*'.

It is quite otherwise in *Wuthering Heights*, where a careful integrity of observation and a finer, more informed insight, are apparent. We may note the care taken to make conventional moral judgments impossible (its original readers would have been only too inclined to make them) by showing always the psychological reasons for certain kinds of behaviour, so that there is nothing mysterious or incredible about Catherine or even, in essentials, about Heathcliff. And it is important to realize that the principal events are made to take place in the early adolescence of all the main actors, when they are so young

as to be at the mercy of their impulses. Also (as we should have
realized even if the actors and actions were not transmitted to
us through the critical medium of Mr Lockwood who is so
conscious of being stuck in a half-savage country) the time is
the eighteenth century and the place remote and northern. The
unconscious brutality of the family doctor who, telling Hindley
that his wife is dying, adds: 'It can't be helped. And besides,
you should have known better than to choose such a rush of a
lass!' is an early index of the northern plain-speaking that is
proud of putting sense in place of feeling.[23] (Zillah fills this post
in the second half of the novel.) But after the shock this gives
us, we realize it is truth and an important truth in the world
of the Heights. A farmer's wife, especially in such testing
conditions, needed to be robust to do what was required and
provide healthy children. By choosing a delicate lass Hindley
was flouting traditional wisdom (as the doctor points out) –
fatally. He had gone to college (we now see why he was made
to) and acquired an unsuitable taste in women, for which he
must now pay; Nature is ruthless too. And in such ways the
sociological element or setting of the book is indispensable, in
reinforcing these radical truths on which life has to be built. It
is what gives Emily Brontë an immeasurable advantage over
Roché. For when it is finally borne in on Jim that any sustained
relation between Kate and Jules or between Kate and himself
is hopeless, he reflects that this breakdown 'might have been
avoided if Kate and he had belonged to the same race and
religion, or if Kate and Jules had, but as things were they could
only speak to each other ultimately in translation. Words hadn't
exactly the same sense for them both, nor even gestures; their
notions of order, authority, the part played by man and woman.
were all different.' This is because Jim was French and
Catholic, Kate German and Protestant, and Jules a German
Jew. We are *told* so, but we have never had these differences,
so basic, acted out or decisively indicated. The corresponding
differences between the farm-house culture of Wuthering
Heights and the polite world of Thrushcross Grange in social
attitudes, instinctive behaviour, physical appearance and
health, style of speech, way of living, dress, deportment,
emotional habits – the whole idiom of life – are perpetually kept
before us and are given their due importance in determining
action, plot and characterization. Even the difference between

both these orders and the fashionable society of city and watering-place from which Lockwood takes his tone, is never forgotten (brought out afresh at the opening of chapter 32 when Lockwood pays his final visit to the Heights). Isabella's illusions which lead to her wretched marriage are as characteristic of the over-sheltered life at the Grange as the lung-disease from which all the Lintons die except Catherine's daughter (who is half an Earnshaw). The importance of the sociological content of the novel to the novelist is proved by her pains to show Heathcliff's eventual regrets about his enemies' son Hareton, only because Hareton's wounded feelings (due to the position Heathcliff has deliberately placed him in) remind him of his own embittered youth as the uncouth ploughboy; he never softens to Cathy, the child of his other enemy, though she is also the daughter of his beloved Catherine and has suffered more at his hands than Hareton.

Yet though *Wuthering Heights* is concerned to replace moralistic judgment by compassionate understanding, it has a very firm moral effect. The technical means invented by Emily Brontë for implying moral criticism without stating it, for making the reader do this work himself, is the technique of contrast and parallelism. I have indicated some of these passages already which we are intended to take note of in this way, though of course the whole novel is really constructed on this principle, in its two complementary halves. In the second half, to which I've hitherto given little attention, there is a very striking example, in Zillah's narrative (chapter 30) reported by Nelly. After the forced marriage Cathy has been shut up at the Heights to take care of her diseased young husband. She having asked 'all in a quiver' for a doctor as 'her cousin was very ill':

'We know that!' answered Heathcliff; 'but his life is not worth a farthing, and I won't spend a farthing on him.'
  'But I cannot tell how to do,' she said; 'and if nobody will help me, he'll die!'
  'Walk out of the room,' cried the master, 'and let me never hear a word more about him! None here care what becomes of him; if you do, act the nurse; if you do not, lock him up and leave him.'

There is no mistake here about the response we must make: Heathcliff's brutal callousness is as unpardonable as possible since the dying lad is his own son. But immediately on this follows Zillah's own reaction to an identical plea for help from Cathy:

'Then she began to bother me, and I said I'd had enough plague with the tiresome thing; we each had our tasks, and hers was to wait on Linton, Mr Heathcliff bid me leave that labour to her.'

This is only a softened version of Heathcliff's reply. But Zillah is no monster and she has an uneasy sense that she must justify herself to Nelly, as is evident in the worried but self-protective narrative that follows:

'How they managed together I can't tell. I fancy he fretted a great deal, and moaned hisseln, night and day; and she had precious little rest, one could guess by her white face, and heavy eyes – she sometimes came into the kitchen all wildered like, and looked as if she would fain beg assistance; but I was not going to disobey the master: I never dare disobey him, Mrs Dean, and though I thought it wrong that Kenneth [the doctor] should not be sent for, it was no concern of mine, either to advise or complain; and I always refused to meddle. Once or twice, after we had gone to bed, I've happened to open my door again, and seen her sitting crying, on the stairs' top; and then I've shut myself in quick, for fear of being moved to interfere. I did pity her then, I'm sure: still I didn't want to lose my place, you know!'

This, while pointing out of the book at the reader, more immediately acts as a check on an easily righteous condemnation of Heathcliff, who is now seen as being not so much worse than the self-respecting, chapel-going Zillah (her godly upbringing indicated by the Biblical name chosen by pious parents); Heathcliff differs only in being brutally honest instead of, like Zillah, complaisant in callousness owing to selfishness and ill-will. The corollary, that we must recognize in Zillah's self-adjustments a likeness to everyone's excuses for failing to behave in accordance with standards we are uneasily aware we subscribe to, is subsidiary though inescapable. And if we think about it we realize that this technique has been used from the start of the novel. At the opening, setting the pattern, Mr Lockwood's horror (ours too) at the brutal attitudes prevailing at the farmhouse – the point of opening the novel with his report of his two visits there – at their shocking refusal to adopt the ordinary code of civility and even a minimal consideration for a visitor, is underlined by Lockwood's dismay at finding that what he had first put down to a refined misanthropy in

Heathcliff, such as he affects himself, is a genuine savagery and malevolence, so that he feels he has strayed into a nightmare world. And Lockwood's horror of the household at Wuthering Heights is immediately offset by *our* horror at *him* when he then, in a real nightmare, brutally fights off the child begging (as he had just done himself) to be let in after losing the way on the moor:

'...my fingers closed on the fingers of a little, ice-cold hand! The intense horror of nightmare came over me: I tried to draw back my arm, but the hand clung to it, and a most melancholy voice sobbed, "Let me in – let me in" "Who are you?" I asked, struggling, meanwhile, to disengage myself. "Catherine Linton", it replied shiveringly. "I'm come home: I'd lost my way on the moor!" As it spoke I discerned, obscurely, a child's face looking through the window. Terror made me cruel; and finding it useless to attempt shaking the creature off, I pulled its wrist on to the broken pane, and rubbed it to and fro till the blood ran down and soaked the bedclothes: still it wailed, "Let me in" and maintained its tenacious grip, almost maddening me with fear...I hurriedly piled the books up in a pyramid against it, and stopped my ears to exclude the lamentable prayer..."Begone!" I shouted, "I'll never let you in, not if you beg for twenty years."'

Of course we don't suppose that his waking self would have gone to such lengths (he knows it was cruel) but, we must feel, his savage response in the dream to the ghost-child's plea for compassion is instinctive; so that under the civilized surface there is a Wuthering Heights self buried, and not made more attractive by his explanation 'Terror made me cruel'. This alerts us, right at the beginning, to a general theme in the novel, that concealing or denying the realities of human nature, shrinking from facing the facts, is to court disaster – the gently-bred Linton children show up badly at Wuthering Heights, with their own mean and cowardly brand of ill-feelings; only when Isabella is plunged into the realities of life at the farm does she become capable of courage, aware of her true self and her eyes opened to Heathcliff's, and able to take the initiative. Thus Catherine's famous speech to Nelly beginning 'I *am* Heathcliff' has no need of a mystical interpretation in so far as meaning can be extracted from it; Catherine is testifying that the qualities Heathcliff has and which Edgar's code has tried to suppress (because though they are necessary to maintain life at Wuthering Heights they seem shocking at the Grange) – that these qualities are essential parts of herself now, and that trying to outlaw them and tame herself will prove disastrous. The idyll of her early married life could never have lasted, for her suppressed irritation with and contempt for Edgar is there to be touched off by Heathcliff's reappearance. He releases the now repressed part of her nature (the 'half savage'), which has no relation to the fact that she is happy with Edgar as a lover – we had heard in chapter 9 that she had accepted Edgar on the assumption that she would never have to be separated from Heathcliff so that she would be able both to have her cake and eat it – a childish fallacy. (Nelly had told her that would not do and tried to show her the dangers of marrying Edgar in such circumstances.) It is Edgar's genuine inability to understand why she rejoices in Heathcliff's return that shocks Catherine into awareness of a gulf between her husband and herself and which undercuts their happily consummated physical love. Edgar in fact is guilty in failing her at this crisis – like Jules he is imaginatively inadequate as well as too civilized to master his wife by the only means she could understand, a display of moral and physical strength. Tenderness, and any fine appeal to the civilized code, are despised or resented by her as by Roché's Kate.

In each novel the wife therefore never becomes integrated or truly mature. Both Roché's Kate and Emily Brontë's Catherine behave like spoiled children who vent their dissatisfactions by destroying the men they need to dominate. Emily Brontë's genius has shown Catherine to be literally a spoiled child (the 'marred child' of Nelly's observation) by giving us her early history; and Catherine *Linton* who is nevertheless only a lost child trying to find her way home is the ghost who is our first knowledge of her, just as in her transported state in chapter 12 she recognizes what has brought her to her deathbed. When her self-torments begin to tell on her, then she reveals the child's egocentric delusion: '"Oh, I've been haunted, Nelly! I begin to fancy you don't like me. How strange! I thought, though everybody hated and despised each other, they could not avoid loving me. And they have all turned to enemies in a few hours."'

I've been trying to show that the complexity, subtlety and richness of texture of *Wuthering Heights* point to a far greater achievement in insight and wisdom than a comparable novel of apparently greater sophistication and emancipation where sexual relations are concerned, and that *Jules et Jim* though in part treating the same theme, and with the advantage of first-hand experience, is actually less instructive about the human problems both novels are concerned with. It is true that Roché offers no more than a record of two men's experience of Woman, a record that, while avoiding any moral conclusion, indeed suggesting that any is impossible, sets up a moral vacuum in which the characters merely exhibit themselves, so that the characteristic reaction of reviewers was to admire and endorse the heroine. While Roché seems to share the view that his Kate is a splendid creature, there is no doubt that Emily Brontë's attitude to Catherine is not indulgent. She provides no general-izations either about Woman or Life; the impression her novel leaves, of responsibility and impersonality, is endorsed by an insufficiently known report on her by Charlotte's lifelong friend Ellen Nussey who had known the Brontë family since they were schoolgirls together: 'Emily's extreme reserve seemed impene-trable, yet she was intensely lovable; she invited confidence in her moral power.' Her sister Charlotte stresses Emily's intel-lectual superiority: 'In some points I consider Emily somewhat of a theorist: now and then she broaches ideas which strike my sense as much more daring and original than practical; her reason may be in advance of mine, but certainly it often travels a different road', and she felt the presence of something disquieting of which she was clearly in awe: 'The tie of sister is near and dear indeed, and I think a certain harshness in her powerful and peculiar character only makes me cling to her more' (when Emily was dying).

Wuthering Heights is highly (though never obtrusively) schematic and the demonstration of the corrective case-history of the second part is not just a matter of winding up the story and restoring the land to the legitimate heirs. If it had stopped with the death of Catherine and the virtual withdrawal from life of Heathcliff and Edgar (the point at which *Jules et Jim* ends) it would have been unsatisfactory. *Jules et Jim*, we can see in comparison, doesn't tell us enough about women to show that Kate does not represent a general truth, as its author seems to imply, or one to which there is no alternative. The second half of Emily Brontë's novel however contains much that is indispensable to the true reading of the first half. The young

Cathy's first visit to the farmhouse where her innocent ideas about her status are seen to be ridiculous, as well as offensive to the workers there who serve only their chosen master and are not servile, is characteristically conveyed through spirited dialogue: '"What's the matter? Get my horse, I say." "I'll see thee damned before I be *thy* servant!" growled the lad (Hareton)..."How dare he speak so to me? Mustn't he be made to do as I ask him? You bring the pony," she exclaimed, turning to the woman. "Softly, Miss, you'll lose nothing by being civil...I was never hired to serve you."' Cathy has had that Linton education which is seen to be finally purged when, having recognized Hareton's merits and her own needs, she freely chooses him as her husband, to become Catherine Earnshaw like her mother: but she has moved in the opposite direction from her mother who, born Catherine Earnshaw, became Catherine Linton of Thrushcross Grange – even though, with the progress of social history, they have to abandon Wuthering Heights to be farmed by old Joseph and settle at the Grange as gentry. Cathy's mother had abandoned the degraded Heathcliff but her daughter generously takes the lad he has formed on that very pattern for revenge, thus righting the wrong. Another stage in her development is seen in chapter 24 where accepting Linton Heathcliff's apologia (that he cannot help being what he is) she says: 'I felt I must forgive him.' But the forgiveness carries with it the recognition that she is committed to him and has 'learnt to endure his selfishness and spite with nearly as little resentment as his sufferings'. The hard road begun when she refused to enter into competition with Linton in unkindness is completed when she has tended him till his death, and gone through the pangs of rebirth. Our attention is focused on this in one of the most memorable passages in the book. Cathy has roused the unwilling Zillah to bid her tell Heathcliff his son is dying at last.

I delivered Catherine's message. He cursed to himself and in a few minutes came out with a lighted candle, and proceeded to their room. I followed. Mrs Heathcliff was seated by the bedside, with her hands folded on her knees. Her father-in-law went up, held the light to Linton's face, looked at him, and touched him; afterwards he turned to her.

 '"Now – Catherine", he said, "how do you feel?"

'She was dumb.

'"How do you feel, Catherine?" he repeated.

'"He's safe, and I'm free," she answered: "I should feel well – but," she continued with a bitterness she couldn't conceal, "you have left me so long to struggle against death, alone, that I feel and see only death! I feel like death!"

'And she looked like it, too.'

Cathy has still a long spell to serve before she is really free, however. The admirable resistance the thoroughly masculine Hareton puts up to her inherited impulses (she also is a Catherine) to torment and manipulate him as soon as she sees he loves her, helps her on the way to maturity. The last sign of the old Eve in her is the attempt to provoke a battle between Hareton and Heathcliff – '"If you strike me, Hareton will strike you" she said' – (just as her mother had deliberately provoked the fight between Heathcliff and Edgar). Her first instinct after securing Hareton's friendship and affection is to prove and show her power by making a violent scene to break the attachment between Hareton and Heathcliff (which exists in spite of all that has gone before, is completely convincing, and not the least of the proofs of Emily Brontë's genius). But on finding that Hareton has loyal feelings towards Heathcliff that are filial and make a tie beyond reasoning with, 'which it would be cruel to attempt to loosen', Nelly notes that 'She showed a good heart thenceforth, in avoiding both complaints and expressions of antipathy concerning Heathcliff; and confessed to me her sorrow that she had endeavoured to raise a bad spirit between him and Hareton.' She shows herself, unlike her mother, capable of self-education and not least in such remarkable restraint where her enemy was concerned; even more perhaps in tolerating a relation between men that excludes herself, but which it seems to be implied, is essential to their being men (Roché and D. H. Lawrence both make this point more clearly). Cathy brings gaiety into Hareton's life, 'sticking primroses into his plate of porridge' and planning a garden with him by importing plants from the Grange, effective symbolic gestures, like the present of books she has made Hareton to express her repentance and change of heart towards him. She even accepts the necessity for replanting the fruit-bushes and relegating her flower-garden to an unwanted corner (chapter 34).

Cathy's selfless devotion to her tormenting husband Linton

reminds us of Edgar's tenderness to his broken wife in *her* decline: this combination of inheritances from both sides in Cathy is clearly offered as something ponderable about the nature of the human family in general and an assertion of the novelist's belief in free will as well as in psychological and sociological determinism.[24] The chosen ground is intended to be representative. '"Oh, here we are the same as anywhere else, when you get to know us"' says Nelly to Lockwood, rebutting his idea that 'in these regions' people are different from elsewhere. This theme gets other illustrations, notably, and very appropriately since his ideas on the subject are theological, from old Joseph. We recall his sardonic delight on witnessing Linton Heathcliff's murderous outburst against his cousin Hareton: '"Thear that's t'father!" he cried. "That's father! We've allus summut uh orther side in us."' Joseph had earlier identified the mother in Linton when the boy refused to eat the family meal of porridge. Nelly noted the 'perverse will' Cathy showed in childhood, like her mother's. And so on.

And these elements which give depth to the novel are enclosed in a sociological whole which serves as the framework of a parable or moral fable of extended interest. Think of what the household at the Heights comprised, with old Joseph, who refuses his portion of Christmas fare on principle and deplores even the hymns Nelly sings because they sound like 'songs', raising the voice of the traditional Puritanism (though wise as well as harsh); while Nelly offsets him with her equally traditional pagan enjoyment of life, of folk-song and ballad as well as of rearing babies and sympathizing with love-affairs. '"This is 'Faery Annie's Wedding' – a bonny tune – it goes to a dance"' is Nelly's mischievous reply to Joseph's groans that '"Aw cannut open t'Blessed Book, bud yah set up them glories tuh Sattan."' Yet they are equally indispensable, Joseph as devoted farmer and Nelly as nurse and housemother. And in another respect Joseph is indispensable too: one of his functions is to offer his own, a rigid religious, interpretation of all events as they happen, so that he sees Heathcliff's life, for example, as a drama of the wicked man whose soul the Devil in due course inevitably collects – for which judgment he falls on his knees beside the corpse to thank God. This is not of course the novelist's view, but it registers her understanding of an important moral vein in the English tradition, one which has fed both folk and 'literary' literature. The novelist is careful to show that Isabella's and the two Catherines' contemptuous attitudes to Joseph are not justified, though their dislike of him is understandable. His piety, for instance, is not hypocrisy as they assume, but a true natural piety expressed in the only idiom he commands other than his everyday dialect – it is the traditional language of Puritanism, of course, as when he calls food 't' precious gifts uh God' – and his sour disapproval of both Isabella and Cathy on the grounds that they are idle inmates where everyone else works, is as reasonable and sound as his anger at Catherine's effect on young Heathcliff which has caused the lad to carelessly leave the gate open so that the pony gets into the cornfield. His duty to the farm, to his master, and to God's laws, are not separate duties in his mind but form together a rule of life. In fact, a Shakespearian character.[25] The whole social pattern provided for us by the farmhouse at the Heights, with its house-place shared by master and man, is created for us as something to be respected, and regretted when it is superseded, whatever its limitations. There all were united in their efforts to make farming possible – the heroic human enterprise of struggling with nature for a living and being formed by that struggle, in this hard country where, as Lock-wood notes for us in the very opening, the north wind slants the stunted firs and 'the gaunt thorns all stretch their limbs one way as if craving alms of the sun', a struggle which does not permit mellow memories such as give charm to *Adam Bede* and *Silas Marner*. The ethos of the household evokes the England of Squire Western (who would have been quite at home there – a fact that suggests that a historical eighteenth-century rural society is the author's aim) at a time when this was being superseded by the new gentility of Thrushcross Grange – where servants live in their own quarters and know their place (unlike old Joseph whose scolding voice can never be avoided) and where the children are kept from the realities of life in an Early Victorian world (it seems, though prophetically) of papas and mammas, parlours and picture-books. We remember that Nelly and others have said that it is healthier at the Heights than at the Grange.

The plight of Catherine Earnshaw is thus presented as at once a unique personal history, a method of discussing what being a woman means, and a tragedy of being caught between socially incompatible cultures, for each of which there is much to be said for and against. Perhaps what *Jules et Jim* chiefly shows, without intending to, is the worse danger of existence in a world that gives no guidance, imposes no restraints and in which conscience and obligations are unknown. That Emily Brontë intended to create a coherent, deeply responsible novel whose wisdom should be recognized as useful we can have no doubt, and this is supported by what Mrs Gaskell reported Charlotte as telling her that her sister suffered from the uncomprehending reception of her novel:

But Emily – poor Emily – the pangs of disappointment as review after review came out about *Wuthering Heights* were terrible. Miss Brontë said she had no recollections of pleasure or gladness about *Jane Eyre*, every such feeling was lost in seeing Emily's resolute endurance yet knowing what she felt.

When Charlotte and Emily were at the school in Brussels, in 1842, M. Héger proposed to teach the sisters to improve their French by setting them to imitate the style of some of the best French authors. While Charlotte acquiesced Emily refused, saying 'she saw no good to be derived from it; and that, by adopting it, they should lose all originality of thought and expression'. 'Originality of thought and expression': yes, one sees that this was prized by the author of *Wuthering Heights* and that it made some sacrifices seem negligible to her – sacrifices of plausibility, of consecutiveness, of proportion, even of consistency – which could often have been saved if the novelist had cared about such things. Besides the unexplained hiatus in Heathcliff's life and his disparate selves, the most careless gesture is the history of the little savage Hareton, whom we have glimpsed in childhood stoning and cursing visitors and 'hanging a litter of puppies from a chair-back', Heathcliff's promising pupil; the unlikelihood of *this* Hareton's turning up as a generous-minded and warm-hearted youth not unfit to marry Cathy, seems clear. But we need hardly notice the anomaly for Hareton is seen fragmentarily and not in chronological order at that, he is only there to serve different purposes and doesn't matter in himself till the final drama with Cathy. We notice also that the novelist has attempted to correct the disparity between the child and the youth Hareton by bridge episodes reported by Zillah, where Hareton shows to advantage compared with Linton ("'and if Hareton, for pity, comes to amuse him –

Hareton is not bad-natured, though he's rough – they're sure to part, one swearing and the other crying"'") and in chapter 30 where he is seen to have tried to get Heathcliff to let them sit up with the dying Linton to relieve Cathy. In fact, throughout *Wuthering Heights*, we may see, unless we refuse to do so, that a true novelist is at work, whose material was real life and whose concern was to promote a fine awareness of the nature of human relations and the problem of maturity.

And we may reflect on the care taken with an even less important character (apparently) – Frances Earnshaw, the 'rush of a lass' whom Hindley brings home after his father's death. We see her first through Catherine's girlish diary, read by the uncomprehending Lockwood, where Frances figures as ridiculous because unashamedly in love with her husband, and disagreeable because disapproving of the 'gypsy' Heathcliff as a playmate for her young sister-in-law Catherine. Then follows Nelly's account of her coming to the Heights as a bride, the kind of 'foreigner' whom the natives 'don't take to', in spite of her delight at 'the white floor and huge glowing fire-place, at the pewter dishes and delf-case, and dog-kennel and the wide space there was to move about in where they usually sat' – at, that is, the 'house-place', often called simply and significantly 'the house', which was used as a common living-room by the domestic- and farm-workers as well as by the family, and even by the dogs (essential members of a farming household and for whom built-in provision was made, as Lockwood noted, in 'an arch under the dresser'). But the result of her coming is that Joseph and Nelly are turned out into the back-kitchen. Frances's appreciation, that of a 'foreigner', was of the picturesque appearance only. She could not comprehend the reality of the purpose served by 'the house', so essential to the proper functioning of the small farm, and this underlines her unsuitability as wife to the master. Her folly is shown in another way, by her helping to orient her young sister-in-law towards the Lintons' idea of gentility and encouraging Catherine's vanity and egotism. Frances thus belongs to the sociological meaning of the novel. But, as with everyone else in the novel, she is also something more. The final impression we are (deliberately) left with is not that of a silly woman; we can't write her off and she is not predictable. Her courage and spirit in refusing to admit that she is suffering and doomed, her raptures at the birth of

her boy, her 'gay heart that never failed her' as Nelly reports
with a mixture of admiration and compassion that we must
share and that culminates in the touching account of her actual
dying, as well as the fact that her loss leaves her husband so
desolate that he begins to drink himself to death – prove that
the novelist has something more profoundly human to convey
through Frances. For one thing, before we are shown what
Catherine makes of marriage we are given a norm to compare
that with. And then there is the moving history itself of a
domestic tragedy. Frances has no 'metaphysical' meaning and
is not indispensable to the plot, but she makes an important
contribution to the truly human novel which *Wuthering Heights*
is. How can we not feel that Frances's poignant death, the
husband's life left empty and the fatal loss to her child of a
mother, did not spring from the novelist's need to register the
memories of the comparable Brontë tragedy? Like Hindley,
Patrick Brontë had been reared on a small farm, managed to
get to the university, and brought a delicate bride (from warm
Cornwall) to a bleak northern home where, after great suffering
cheerfully borne, she died prematurely, leaving six little children
(when Emily was two), a disaster for the family that affected
their whole lives. As for the horrors of a home containing a
desperate drunkard, she had no need to draw them from
anywhere but their own household: even the gentle Anne
Brontë felt obliged to make a novel to record that.

I would make a plea, then, for criticism of *Wuthering Heights*
to turn its attention to the human core of the novel, to recognize
its truly human centrality. How can we fail to see that the novel
is based on an interest in, concern for, and knowledge of, real
life? We cannot do it justice, establish what the experience of
reading it really is, by making analyses of its lock and window
imagery, or by explaining it as being concerned with children
of calm and children of storm, or by putting forward such bright
ideas as that '*Wuthering Heights* might be viewed at long range
as a variant of the demon-lover motif' (*The Gates of Horn*,
H. Levin) or that 'Nelly Dean is Evil' – these are the products
of an age which conceives literary criticism as either a game or
an industry, not as a humane study. To learn anything of this
novel's true nature we must put it into the category of novels
it belongs to – I have specified *Women in Love* and *Jules et Jim*
and might add *Anna Karenina* and *Great Expectations* – and

recognize its relation to the social and literary history of its own time. The human truths *Wuthering Heights* is intended to establish are, it is necessary to admit, obscured in places and to varying degrees by discordant trimmings or leftovers from earlier writings or stages of its conception; for these, stylistic and other evidence exists in the text. Nor could we expect such complexity and such technical skill to have been achieved in a first novel otherwise; it is necessary to distinguish what is genuine complexity from what is merely confusion. That there is the complexity of accomplished art we must feel in the ending, ambiguous, impersonal, disquieting but final. And when we compare the genius devoted to creating Nelly Dean, Joseph, Zillah, Frances, Lockwood, the two Catherines, and to setting them in significant action, with the very perfunctory attention given to Heathcliff and Hareton as wholes (attention directed only when these two are wheeled out to perform necessary parts at certain points in the exposition of the theme to which – like Isabella and Edgar Linton – they are subsidiary) then we can surely not misinterpret the intention and the nature of the achievement of *Wuthering Heights*.

Appendixes to
'A fresh approach to
Wuthering Heights'

The northern farmer, old style

To give some grounding to what the novelist was trying to convey to us as the traditional culture of the Yorkshire moorlands and its characteristic human product, contrasting so radically with the conventional norm of the English gentry (represented by the Lintons of Thrushcross Grange), I have selected the following as coming closest to the description of the farmhouse at the Heights. I found it in the Introduction to a collection, published in 1881, of anecdotes and tales serially published 1853–57, J. H. Dixon's *Chronicles and Stories of the Craven Dales*. This introduction, by the Rev. Robert Collyer, a native of those parts, recalls his boyhood there in the 1830s – this takes us back to Emily Brontë's girlhood, as she was born in 1818. It is the more interesting for not being written with *Wuthering Heights* at all in mind, and for being by a minister. The Craven Dales, though also in the West Riding of Yorkshire, are in a different part of it from the Brontës' Haworth; this bears out the representativeness of the home, people and life at the Heights as witness to an originally pagan, Scandinavian farming culture, once common to much of northern England, with all its rugged qualities that made for survival, and in particular its great antiquity and its almost unchanged character in Emily Brontë's youth. Even the 'wuthering' wind features in Collyer's reminiscences as formative; we note too the panelled bed which has a memorable part in the novel, and we get a juster idea of what Nelly meant (in chapter 17) by saying that she 'insisted on the funeral [of Hindley Earnshaw] being respectable'.

I find myself wishing also that Dr Dixon had written one more chapter for us – a chapter containing a picture of a genuine old Craven homestead and its inmates, because no man could have done it so well. I have such a picture in my mind. It is almost half a century old. It is a picture of a sturdy, low thatched house, in which the first thing that attracted my child's eyes was a wonderful bedstead of black oak, built up all round with oaken boards for curtains, panelled and carven, with a door through which you went to find the piled-up feathers, shutting and bolting it after you, so that, if the burglars came, you could get ready for a fight. Then there was a settle of black oak, with a very old date on it, and a chair to match, of a discomfort equal to

Calvin's chair in Geneva. A quaint old clock in the corner, with a face of brass on which there was a picture of the sun of such a rotund jollity that it ha touched the original with lines of laughter to my mind through all the years The great 'fleak' for the oatbread comes out next, and the flitches of beef anc bacon hanging from the black beams. Then the flagged floor with fine sanc for a carpet, and the great peat fire with its aromatic pungency; the rack against the wall with its splendid store of pewter plates, the great oaken dresser under it, and a carven 'kist' where it was whispered the old man kept his 'brass'. He was a man of the real old Craven breed. I used to think he could not speak in level tones, but must needs address you as if you stood at some distance, a habit caught, I suppose, from talking in the teeth of the wind which blows for ever across the Craven uplands. His dress was but slightly altered from that of the peasants in Chaucer's time. He cut his grass with a scythe, and his grain with a sickle, and hated the French, though he could not tell you why. It was the smouldering hate, no doubt, of 800 years, kept alive ever since the Conqueror laid Craven waste... His good wife saved a bit of the old yule-log, wrapped in white linen, to kindle the new withal, and would let no fire go out of the house during the days between 'owd and new Kersmas'. The old man believed fervently in witches and t'gy-trash.[26] He was, in truth, as I think of him now and remember his queer ways, one third pagan, one third catholic, and the rest was little better than veneer – I imagine, dating from the Reformation. So he lived as his fathers had lived time out of all mind. They were there on the moor side – the warm side dipping well toward the meadows and woods – in Earl Edwin's time; saw the Percies and Romillies and Cliffords come and go, while they still held on eating their brown- and oaten-bread and bacon, and drinking their milk and 'honey-drink' and beer. They will last to the crack of doom. When the old man's time came to die, it comes back to me how 'he gave commandment concerning his bones' and would have everything done 'i t'owd way'. I think indeed, he had a dim idea that he would be there as a sort of silent spectator, and might be troubled if things went wrong. So he would have no wine and biscuit served at the funeral – 'nễa nut he'. They must brew plenty o' drink and bake plenty o' spice cễak and cut it thick, and hand it round at least three times, and everybody must eat and drink their fill. How one hungry growing lad did enjoy that funeral, to be sure; but he wist not, any more than the old man in his coffin, that it was the last long-lingering echo and refrain of the funeral feasts of his pagan ancestors a thousand years ago. And I can remember how they decked his shroud very much as if Ophelia had been there to direct them. There were violets and pansies, columbines and daisies, sweet thyme, rosemary, and rue, for that was the ancient way; and he must be laid away as he had lived, with all the old rites and observances about his dust. Then as they bore him to his burial along the green shadowy lanes to Bolton they sang old funeral chants Job might have written, and Jeremiah set to music, they were so shorn of all that sheds a new radiance on death and the grave.

'*Violence*'

Though we are now less inclined than earlier critics to think violence of feeling and action so improbable as to imply something abnormal in a novelist who depicts it, yet criticism still boggles, it seems, at the violence in *Wuthering Heights*. This, about which so much has been written, certainly needs distinguishing as to kinds. In general, the intention at the outset to create a tragedy on a Shakespearian pattern, specifically, as I've suggested, by drawing on the sub-plot of *Lear* (there are also references to *Lear* in the text), has brought with it a sense of being in the *Lear* universe, though it is Heathcliff who (understandably, if my account of his conception is admitted) seems to belong there most consistently – that is, who, for the novelist, is a reminder to put in such features whenever he is operative. Sometimes the horrors of the *Lear* world are almost dutifully inserted, as the knife under Isabella's ear, the fight between Heathcliff and Hindley and the account of Hindley's death – all in chapter 17; though none of these seems to me to achieve the horror of the plucking out of Gloucester's eyes, which no doubt inspired them. The worst and almost the only genuine wounds received in *Wuthering Heights* are given by the tongue, as we can prove by reading the extremely painful scene of violence between Catherine, Heathcliff and Edgar in chapter 11 where the only physical violence is the blow Edgar is forced to give Heathcliff and which does no more than 'take his breath for a moment'. Much of the violence is the result of women's characteristic provocation to which the men can react only by blows – this is equally true of *Jules et Jim* where there is also a good deal of violence – by blows or, as in the final parting between Heathcliff and the dying Catherine, when he is goaded by her 'wild vindictiveness' and her tearing out his hair, into bruising her by holding fast her arms. The most horrible cruelty, like Lockwood's rubbing the child-ghost's wrist against the broken window to free himself from its grasp, is a nightmare only, and is kept as such before us (as unreal) by his having first broken the window by thrusting his own arm through without suffering; while other happenings of gratuitous cruelty such as Heathcliff's hanging the pet dog Fanny, and Heathcliff's allegedly setting a trap over the lapwings' nest which starved the nestlings, are symbolic (Fanny represents her mistress Isabella who is eloping with Heathcliff to her doom, and the dog's life is actually saved by Nelly; while we have only the delirious Catherine's word for the lapwing exploit in a speech in the tradition of Ophelia's and Lucy Ashton's mad utterances). Another class of horrors are juvenile and seem to be left over from the Gondal game (which Emily and Anne were still playing together as late as 30 June

1845 – *Wuthering Heights* being written, it seems, in its present form in the autumn and winter 1845–46): for instance, Isabella's account of Heathcliff's looking in at the window when 'his black countenance looked blightingly through . . . his sharp cannibal teeth gleamed through the dark' etc. – such horrendous passages contrast with the perfectly simple, sincere and delicately poetic or forcefully colloquial language of the maturer parts. Little Hareton's hanging a whole litter of puppies from the chair-back as Isabella departs (it is quite out of character with everything subsequent in his history) seems to be thrown in as a last proof that she has supped full of horrors and is, as she says, 'escaped from purgatory'.

Besides the need to emulate what seemed essential to an Elizabethan tragedy, Emily Brontë, I have no doubt, was also deliberately trying to realize a historical past (the novel takes place in the eighteenth century) when manners were generally supposed to have been brutal and, in out-of-the-way places, lawless. We may note here the indication provided as to lawlessness by Heathcliff's having been able to bribe Linton's lawyer from making a new will before Edgar's death which would have kept the daughter's property out of Heathcliff's hands. Certainly there is an impression of effort to achieve the effect of a past age but one historically accurate.[27] Charlotte seems to endorse this when, in her preface to the 1850 edition of the novel, she describes the 'harshly manifested passions' of the 'rugged moorland squires' of local history as authentic models for the book, telling how her sister steeped herself in 'those tragic and terrible traits of which, in listening to the secret annals of every rude vicinage, the memory is sometimes compelled to receive the impress' as the reason for the 'sombre' materials of the novel. I don't know why subsequent critics should be convinced they can write this off, discrediting both Charlotte and Mrs Gaskell as evidence in this respect; Mrs Gaskell gathered supporting data from many oral sources. Mrs Gaskell wrote from Haworth during her first visit to Charlotte: 'They are a queer people up there. Small landed proprietors – dwelling on one spot since Q. Elizabeth – & lately adding marvellously to their incomes by using the water power of the becks in the woollen manufacture which had sprung up during the last 50 years: – uneducated – unrestrained by public opinion – for their equals in position are as bad as themselves and the poor, besides being densely ignorant, are all dependent on their employers.'

So all things considered, it does seem preposterous to feed such utterly disparate features of *Wuthering Heights* as can be thrust into the one category of 'Violence' into an academic computer in order to produce a cover-all interpretative thesis which confidently classifies the novelist as a case.

APPENDIX C

Superstitions and folk-lore

The first half of chapter 12, in which Catherine explains herself, partly in delirium and partly conscious, and which is crucial to her history, depends in places on the reader's understanding Yorkshire superstitions and folk-lore. But there is nothing esoteric about them, they were once general in northern England and also in various other parts of the country.

Ripping open the pillow in her fever Catherine says: 'Ah, they put pigeons' feathers in the pillows – no wonder I couldn't die. Let me take care to throw it on the floor when I lie down.' This is because it was widely believed that dying persons could not be released from their sufferings and die a peaceful death if there were any game-birds' feathers, particularly pigeons', in either the pillow or feather-mattress on which they lay,[28] so it was important to see that only domestic poultry feathers went into the home-made bedding. There were therefore unlikely to be either wild duck's or pigeons' or moor-cock's or lapwing's feathers in Catherine's pillow at Thrushcross Grange, as she alleges, and the soliloquy is to be understood as an expression of her longing to be released from the Grange and to fly free across the moor, and her sense of being prevented; she identifies herself with the lapwing: 'Bonny bird; wheeling over our heads in the middle of the moor. It wanted to get to its nest, for the clouds had touched the swells and it felt rain coming.' Then follows the obscure but unforgettable image of the lapwings' nest that Heathcliff set a trap over for the old birds, so starving the nestlings, which she and Heathcliff saw in the winter as skeletons trapped in the nest. While the general intention of the distressing simile is clear, it seems to me unwise to try and nail it down by an interpretation. It is the point where she approaches Shakespeare most nearly in a chapter that is as Shakespearian in dramatic and poetic effect as a novel in prose can be, one feels.

Nelly takes the pillow away from her and her attention is next caught by the mirror; she thinks it the black clothes-press of her childhood bedroom at the Heights and that her face reflected in the mirror is due to candle-light on the piece of furniture. To soothe her, Nelly covers the mirror with a shawl so she will not see her reflection. The sense is not perfectly clear but it seems to me that Nelly's covering it makes her realize that it was a mirror, since mirrors were always covered or turned face to the wall immediately after death had taken place in the house, in order that the reflection of the dead spirit might not, as superstition feared, be seen in the glass, with dire consequences to the viewer. Nelly cannot persuade her that it was her own face she saw reflected: '"Who is it? I hope it will not come out when you are gone! Oh! Nelly, the room is haunted!"' Then Nelly again reassures her: '"There's nobody there! It was *yourself*, Mrs Linton." "Myself!"' she gasped, "and the clock is striking twelve! It's true, then! That's dreadful!"' Her fear of a ghost is replaced by a worse fear, that it *was* her own reflection she saw. Sick people, it was held, should not see themselves in a mirror because the soul (thought of as a separate entity like a bird) might easily take flight from the weak body by being projected into the mirror and so bring about the sick person's death. So Catherine, having seen herself in the mirror and hearing the clock strike midnight too, the ghostly hour when spirits walk and death comes, thinks she is about to die. Of course she does want to die and presently dwells on her imminent death as a way of getting out on the moor and recovering Heathcliff, instead of being 'Mrs Linton, the lady of Thrushcross Grange'. The dream in which she thought herself back in the oak-panelled bed, alone for the first time after her father's burial (death is running through her mind continually) was broken, she says, by her waking to find herself stretched on the carpet (where she had fallen in her fit or swoon). But this gave her a dreadful shock – presumably because she thought it meant she was dying since those absolutely on the point of death were removed from the bed and placed on the floor (out of kindness) to die 'naturally'. The premonitions of death in this scene prepare Catherine to accept it with relief so that she thinks she sees a candle in her window on the Heights to guide her home (we now recall Lockwood's dream of the pathetic child-ghost calling itself Catherine Linton trying to get back into its oak-panelled bed), though she knows that 'we must pass Gimmerton Kirk, to go that journey!' Her wrestling to hang out of the window and her commands to Nelly to 'Open the window: throw it wide open!' is not only that she may breathe the air from the hills but would be readily understood as another anticipation of death, since when the moment of death was unmistakably at hand, it was the custom to throw open all doors and windows, that nothing should hinder the flight of the spirit.[29]

Her boast next that as children she and Heathcliff had often stood in the churchyard defying the ghosts of the dead (like Don Giovanni) by inviting them to come, establishes their impious pride which will bring about Heathcliff's death, obsessed by Catherine's ghostly presence – 'intolerable torture' – until he can no longer remember to eat or even breathe. She is one ghost that accepts the invitation. Like Don Giovanni he rejects the opportunity to repent Nelly offers him (chapter 34) and maintains his 'godless indifference' to the last, dying with a sneer on his face, 'girnning at death', as Joseph says of his corpse. In many respects Heathcliff follows the pattern of the original tradition of Don Juan, who, before he became merely a womanizer, was the typical wicked man who broke all the Ten

Commandments. There is a suggestion that Heathcliff too has been dragged away to hell (in Joseph's words, 'The divil's harried off his soul'), and at the end of the novel we hear that the country folks believe 'he *walks*', an unquiet spirit. The little boy herding sheep actually sees the ghosts of 'Heathcliff and a woman', and though Nelly dismisses it as imagination fed on gossip (she is not one to see spirits) she also notes that the sheep won't pass the spot. This impartial treatment of belief in the supernatural and of its concomitants, the evocation of a whole pagan mode of thought about life and death, then and there still current, which gave dignity and meaning to a hard and narrow existence, has nothing to do with such Romantic or 'Gothic' aberrations as cannibal teeth and the reopening of coffins to look at beloved corpses. It is, rather, a mark of the creative artist's respect for an essential element in the culture she values but sees disappearing, worsted by something less healthy and, in its moral triteness, altogether inferior – Nelly never voices Christian piety or moralisms without their seeming either inadequate or irrelevant. It also implies recognition of the poetry and wisdom inherent in the old beliefs – as in the ballad Nelly sings in her tenderness for her 'little lamb' which was based on a mysterious fact of experience, the profound tie between mother and child.

Another parallel mark of respect for that culture is the novelist's concern to do justice to the local country speech. The dialect, whether in its undiluted form as spoken by old Joseph or in modified forms such as Zillah's, Hareton's and others', is full of life, not only in idiom but in intonation and vocabulary, above all notable for the independent and sensible attitudes it expresses so forcefully. The common people's speech here is so much more lively in general than that of the educated (just as in Scott) that it makes one feel there is some justice in Max Müller's dictum that 'The real natural life of language is in its dialects.' It is odd that Emily Brontë's ear should be so much better for uneducated than for educated speech, where she is liable to use stilted or literary phrases whenever her imagination had no pressure behind it. It was difficult for her, it seems, to find a staple style (Dickens and other Early Victorian writers betray the same difficulty). This is a specimen of her writing on her twenty-third birthday (three years before writing *Wuthering Heights*): 'It will be a fine warm summer evening, very different from this bleak look-out, and Anne and I will perchance slip out into the garden for a few minutes to peruse our papers.' Literary words like 'peruse' and 'perchance' incongruously mixed with the idiomatic 'slip out' and 'look-out' betray an uncertain taste, and similarly uneasy oscillations can be noticed in the novel – but not often where they matter. This is, however, the literary style used by Catherine in the journal Lockwood reads while trying to get to sleep in the panelled bed at the Heights, a very improbable style for a

country child and which, along with some puerilities and long-winded
episodes such as the sermon part of Lockwood's nightmare, bear out
the supposition that the first three chapters contain some unregenerate
writing from an earlier attempt at a novel or this novel.

APPENDIX D

Wuthering Heights and The Bride of Lammermoor

Mrs Gaskell tells us that Sir Walter Scott's writings were among the
standard literature owned by Mr Brontë, and in 1834 we find
Charlotte writing to a friend who has asked for a reading-list: 'For
fiction, read Scott alone; all novels after his are worthless' – proof
enough that the Brontë girls read them, and with enthusiasm. My very
strong impression is of a considerable carry-over from *The Bride of
Lammermoor* to *Wuthering Heights* (and *Lammermoor* and *The Black Dwarf*
have enough common elements to coalesce as one united source for
inspiration and memory). To start with, *Wuthering Heights* is, in the
Scott tradition, a historical and not a contemporary novel. Then the
tone of *Wuthering Heights* is at times that of Scott, and the doomed
Ravenswood is laid under contribution not only for the pattern of
Heathcliff's name but for his nature and circumstances. Ravenswood
early in life gives himself up to the passion for vengeance on those
who have wronged him; he is characterized by his 'dark and sullen
brow' and, in the words of the heroine's young brother, Henry,
'looked like a Spanish grandee come to cut our throats and trample
our bodies underfoot', and he does indeed perform acts of desperate
violence. But he is also named *Edgar* in his character of tender lover
to Lucy Ashton, whose family have ruined him and turned him out
of his home and then used him cruelly in respect to Lucy. He is driven
to raging violence when Lucy is induced to give him up for a more
suitable husband, bringing about first her violent death and then his
own. Moreover, violent passions, violent actions and revenge, omens
and dreams, dementia of the heroine, bloody and supernatural deaths,
are common to both novels; Catherine follows Lucy in being driven
out of her senses by the conflicting claims of lover and bridegroom;
Alice the nourice's part is taken by Nelly Dean and old Caleb's by
old Joseph. That Scott founded his tale and in some detail on the
real-life historical case of a Lord Rutherford and the daughter of the
first Lord Stair, must have given it a desirable authority for a novelist
who, as I hold, was not romancing but concerned to examine the real
basis and effects of love and the relations between the sexes as well
as the relations between child and parent, and who sees all these as
inseparable from their social context in time and place. Here Scott,
with his acute interest in the unique nature of Scottish society and its

historical development was again, as in *The Black Dwarf*, a highly educational influence and an influence visible directly in *Wuthering Heights*. Ravenswood is the last of a noble line, cheated out of his inheritance and prospects alike by the rising lawyer of humble Puritan origin who is representative of the new dominant type and class – inevitably, just as the supersession of the Wuthering Heights life-form by the world of Thrushcross Grange was inevitable. No doubt Scott's insights sharpened Emily Brontë's, but it is proof of her genius that she could recognize such larger forces operating behind the domestic and personal drama of a love-story, as her sister Charlotte, for instance, could not.

Scott's serious use of broad Scots in *Lammermoor* must also have decided our novelist to draw on the West Riding dialect for similar effects. An important contribution to the thrilling atmosphere of *Lammermoor* comes from the mouths of village characters who supply the superstitions, second sight, knowledge of the leading characters' histories and dooms; and who provide a chorus-commentary on the progress of the tragedy of the two families involved, as Nelly Dean and old Joseph do. Scott not only suggests dark forces at work through the irrational and traditional beliefs of the countryfolk, but he frequently works through a suggestive symbolism which I imagine is a direct result of his sympathy with the mode of Scottish folk-song and ballad, though compared with folk-literature he shows up as clumsy and self-conscious in these efforts. Some comparisons with very similar passages in *Wuthering Heights* will show what a great genius does when it makes them its own. I will cite a diffused and a specific instance.

The chapter that introduces us to Ravenswood ends by suggesting that, like Heathcliff, he was thought to have been under diabolic influence (his death too is uncanny): 'The peasant who shows the ruins of the tower, which still crown the beetling cliff and behold the war of the waves, though no more tenanted save by the seamew and cormorant, even yet affirms, that on this fatal night the Master of Ravenswood, by the bitter exclamations of his despair, evoked some evil fiend, under whose malignant influence the future tissue of incident was woven. Alas! what fiend can suggest more desperate counsels than those adopted under the guidance of our own violent and unresisted passions?' The scene described here, after the tragedy is ended and the participants long dead, provides, with its suggestive imagery of sea eternally at war with cliff and the ruins of the Ravenswood home inhabited now only by symbolic sea-birds, a similar pregnant and melancholy after-picture for the reader to the ending of *Wuthering Heights* (in the last three paragraphs), but how stilted and creaking Scott's prose is and how conventional the moralizing! In his chapter 29 we have a more instructive parallel. The painful images the delirious Catherine evokes in chapter 12 as a metaphor to express her sense of her position – the images of the lapwing unable to take shelter in its nest and of Heathcliff starving the nestlings to skeletons by setting a trap over the nest for the parent birds – this metaphor and its context has an obvious origin in Scott's set piece when Lucy Ashton, like Catherine in beginning to lose her reason under stress, is roused by Henry's telling her innocently about his falcon which '"just wets her singles in the blood of the partridge, and then breaks away, and lets her fly; and what good can the poor bird do after that, you know, except to pine and die in the first heather cow or whin-bush she can crawl into?"' "Right, Henry – right, very right", said Lucy mournfully, holding the boy fast by the hand; "but there are more riflers in the world than your falcon, and more wounded birds that seek but to die in quiet, that can find neither brake nor whin-bush to hide their heads in."' Lucy is pathetic, but our sympathy and interest are quite cooled by noting how rationally and logically she makes the case for a parallel between her own situation and the victim's of Henry's anecdote. Emily Brontë is not, like Scott, constrained by rationality, but nevertheless Scott's artificial rhetoric has left its impress in a corresponding vein in some places (the weakest) in her novel, though not here, where what is only skilful rhetoric in Scott has been transformed with Shakespearian power into the rhythmically convincing expression of deep disturbance. But then Catherine Earnshaw is an infinitely more interesting character than Lucy Ashton, and that Emily Brontë should replace Scott's conventional passive heroine by the study of a challenging type of feminine nature is significant of where her interest and talent lay.

We conclude then that Emily Brontë shows herself to have had far greater imaginative power than Scott as well as much greater complexity of feeling and construction, that hers is altogether a finer art than Scott's; but there seems to me no doubt that novels of Scott and tragedies of Shakespeare were equally present in her mind as it organized the insights on which *Wuthering Heights* is based. The sense in which one writer is indebted to others is always interesting, and more particularly in the case of a work which has so generally been claimed to have been as wholly original and unaccountable as *Wuthering Heights*. It may also help us to see exactly in what the true distinction of the work consists.

Silas Marner

I

It is in *Silas Marner* that we come closest to a George Eliot who is everywhere present in her letters and Journal and in other people's reminiscences of her, but who has been buried by the legend of the masculine blue-stocking, the editor of the Benthamite review, the admirer of Comte, the student of all the ancient and modern languages, the friend of Herbert Spencer and the consort of G. H. Lewes, that middleman of all the arts and sciences. This other George Eliot reread the *Pilgrim's Progress* while reading the newly-published *Origin of Species* and having reported of the Darwin that 'it is not impressive, from want of luminous and orderly presentation', went on to note that she was 'profoundly struck with the true genius manifested in the simple, vigorous, rhythmic style' of Bunyan. This was the George Eliot who wrote to Lady Ponsonby to beg her to 'Consider what the human mind *en masse* would have been if there had been no such combination of elements in it as has produced poets. All the philosophers and *savants* would not have sufficed to supply that deficiency. And how can the life of nations be understood without the inward life of poetry – that is, of emotion blending with thought?'

Acquaintance with her life is still best made through the volume called *George Eliot's Life* published by her widower J. W. Cross, which he made out of selections from her Journal and letters and the reminiscences he collected from her relatives and friends. The Letters can now be read complete in the edition by Professor G. Haight, who has now published a biography too. Cross himself gives all the necessary details of her appearance and qualities. He tells of 'the organlike tones of her voice', of

275

her fine brows and musician's hands,[1] and while mentioning her 'impressive speech which claimed something like an awed attention from strangers',[2] he tries to stress her hearty laughter and humour and her pride in being a skilful housekeeper, concluding: 'She had the instinctively feminine qualities which lend a rhythm to the movement of life.' All this is borne out by Henry James's letter to his father after first meeting George Eliot: 'a delightful expression, a voice soft and rich as that of a counselling angel – a mingled sagacity and sweetness – a broad hint of a great underlying world of reserve, knowledge, pride and power – a great feminine dignity and character in these massively plain features'. Cross's account of his first meeting with his future wife satisfies one's notions of her personality but he gives a very unexpected insight into the Lewes home in 1878, when G. H. Lewes was near his end:

between bouts of pain he sang through, with great *brio*, though not much voice, the greater portion of the tenor part in the *Barber of Seville* – George Eliot playing his accompaniment, and both of them thoroughly enjoying the fun.

George Eliot was nearly sixty at this time so the anecdote should correct any false idea that she was a solemn prig.

II

It is evident that by the time George Eliot came to write *Silas Marner* her ideas about the Novel had matured. She confesses that while 'there are portraits in the "Clerical Scenes"', 'that was my first bit of art, and my hand was not well in'. In *Adam Bede* she claimed there were no actual portraits from life, and rose to some theorizing about the art of fiction, offering in the text a well-known defence of Dutch pictures of 'homely existence' which is generally taken to be a defence of 'realism'. But it is in fact a quite different argument; the intention is to plead for humble life to be treated in art on theoretic grounds of moral obligation, not aesthetic ones: 'In this world there are so many of these common coarse people, who have no picturesque sentimental wretchedness! Therefore let Art always remind us of them...your common labourer, who *gets his own bread*, and eats it vulgarly but *creditably* with his own pocket-knife.' These are the people, she says, who have '*done the rough work of the*

world'. (All my italics.) This is more Radical than even
Wordsworth's grounds for choosing humble life as the subject-
matter for true poetry. And this Radicalism is an important
constituent of *Silas Marner*.

By 1859 George Eliot could write to a friend: 'I have turned
out to be an artist – with words.' And after *Adam Bede* and *The
Mill on the Floss* the remarks she makes in her letters and Journal
about her own books and the books she reads show more
sophistication and more understanding of the problems a
novelist has to solve. Whereas in 1857 she was saying: 'my
stories always grow out of my psychological conception of the
dramatis personae', by 1866 she has completely changed her
position. There are some sign-posts on the way: her report that
'I went to hear *Faust* at Covent Garden; I was much thrilled
by the great symbolical situations – more, I think, than I had
ever been before', and her numerous accounts of hearing
orchestral concerts or herself playing the piano in chamber-music
concerts at home, and her unexpected dictum 'The Opera is
a great, great product'. In 1866 in a letter to her friend Frederic
Harrison she makes an important revelation of the way in which
she now (soon after finishing *Felix Holt*) recognized that she
composed:

That is a tremendously difficult problem; its difficulties...press upon
me, who have gone through again and again the severe effort of trying
to make certain ideas thoroughly incarnate, as if they had revealed
themselves to me first in the flesh and not in the spirit. I think aesthetic
teaching is the highest of all teaching because it deals with life in its
highest complexity. But if it ceases to be purely aesthetic – if it lapses
anywhere from the picture to the diagram – it becomes the most
offensive of all teaching...Well, then, consider the sort of agonizing
labour to an English-fed imagination to make out a sufficiently real
background for the desired picture, – to get breathing individual
forms, and group them in the needful relations, so that the presentation
will lay hold on the emotions as human experience – will, as you say,
'flash' conviction on the world by means of aroused sympathy.

Far from the 'portrait' being the foundation of a novel or the
'story' being dictated by her 'psychological conception of the
dramatis personae', she now feels the danger of being too
schematic and of failing to create convincingly and to 'group'
naturally enough the lives needed to incarnate her 'ideas' '*as
if they had revealed themselves to me first in the flesh*'. That is, she now

starts with the ideas, and stresses what she also calls 'symbolic situations', and 'the myth' – because she is preoccupied with her *theme*. *Silas Marner* is the first novel in which she is seen to have worked like this but, as I hope to show, she did not have to do this consciously: the theme forced itself on her. *Felix Holt, the Radical* followed in theme out of *Silas Marner* and as a complement to *Adam Bede*, but the 'idea' in *Felix Holt* was a subject outside herself, it had to be read up for like *Romola* (as we see from her Journal) and though this subject embodied some of her most cherished beliefs these could not be 'incarnated' so naturally in felt life as in *Silas Marner*. In 1868 she makes an observation about Greek tragedy which repeats the theory of creative composition she had explained to Frederic Harrison earlier:

The Greeks were not taking an artificial, entirely erroneous standpoint in their art – a standpoint which disappeared altogether with their religion and their art. They had the same essential elements of life presented to them as we have, and their art symbolized these in grand schematic forms.

So it was not only the concept of Nemesis that George Eliot gained from reading Greek. Her youthful enthusiasm for Scott had yielded at the *Silas Marner* period to a critical view of his inadequate ideas of composition in spite of his fertile imagination, his ability to tell a story and 'create' characters: 'But somehow experience and finished faculty rarely go together. Dearly beloved Scott had the greatest combination of experience and faculty – yet even he never made the most of his treasures, at least in his *mode* of presentation' (1861). Shakespeare, Molière ('I think the *Misanthrope* the finest, most complete production *of its kind* in the world', she wrote in 1859), Bunyan, Greek tragedy, opera, orchestral and chamber-music, we see, helped her to extend the scope and richness of the novel and make a more intelligent use of her 'experience and faculty'.

III

In his reminiscences *The Middle Years*, written in his old age, Henry James, when starting on his memories of George Eliot, refers to her as 'the author of *Silas Marner* and *Middlemarch*', a selection from her novels intended either to represent her at her best or as covering two distinct kinds in her creative art, or both. He goes on to describe her work in general as 'a great treasure of beauty and humanity, of applied and achieved art, a testimony, historic as well as aesthetic, to the deeper interest of the intricate English aspects'. Of none of her novels is this more true than *Silas Marner*; one could only have wished that he had been specific. What deeper interest of the aspects of England, what aesthetic and historic testimony, does *Marner* represent? That it is not to be dismissed as the mere moral 'faery-tale' or '*divertissement*' of many critics we might have guessed from the quite exceptional nature of its origin, of which we luckily have an account. Our first knowledge of this book is a note in George Eliot's Journal (28 November 1860): 'I am now engaged in writing a story – the idea of which came to me after our arrival in this house [a depressing furnished London house] and which has thrust itself between me and the other book [*Romola*] I was meditating. It is *Silas Marner, the Weaver of Raveloe*.' Thus at the outset Silas was identified by his trade. And we note also that this same day's entry in her Journal opens:

Since I last wrote in this Journal, I have suffered much from physical weakness, accompanied with mental depression. The loss of the country has seemed very bitter to me, and my want of health and strength has prevented me from working much – still worse, has made me despair of ever working well again.

Six weeks later, in writing to tell her publisher of her new book she again stresses the involuntary nature of this new undertaking: 'a story which came *across* my other plans by a sudden inspiration'. She adds: 'It is a story of old-fashioned village life, which has unfolded itself from the merest millet-seed of thought.' On 10 March 1861 she notes: 'Finished *Silas Marner*.' Previously she had replied to Blackwood's comment, that so far as he had read he found it 'sombre', that she was not surprised and doubted if it would interest anybody 'since Wordsworth is dead', but assured him that it was not sad on the whole, 'since it sets in a strong light the remedial influences of pure, natural human relations'. Thus the Weaver's story belonged to the village life of the past and exemplified a theory congenial to Wordsworth (and Coleridge); and the impulse to write it sprang from a deep depression of health and spirits due to living in conditions which were the very negation of 'old-fashioned village life', a depression that, as we see, was morbid, since it involved irrational despair of succeeding again as a novelist, in spite of the great success of *Adam Bede* and *The Mill on the Floss*. The letter to Blackwood ends: 'It came to me first of all quite suddenly, as a sort of legendary tale, suggested by my recollections of having once, in early childhood, seen a linen weaver with a bag on his back; but as my mind dwelt on the subject, I became inclined to a more realistic treatment' – that is, she dropped the association with a faery-tale figure. And this is borne out by her saying that she felt 'as if the story would have lent itself best to metrical rather than prose fiction' 'except that, under that treatment, there could not be an equal play of humour'. The humour is not only quite as much a characteristic of the book she finally wrote as the 'poetry', but is itself no simple matter; it contains much irony of various kinds and a great deal of pointed social criticism which no light-weight legendary tale could support, not even those art-versions of the faery-tale so characteristic of nineteenth-century literature with which *Marner* might be associated if superficially read. Even the author's own account here is misleading; that something essential has been left out is proved by the truer, fuller version contained in a letter from Major Blackwood to his wife in 1861: '*Silas Marner* sprang from her childish recollection of a man with a stoop and expression of face that led her to think that he was an alien from his fellows.' Physical deformity and the stamp of alienation are the important factors; the bag then ceases to be sinister, suggestive of a figure in Grimms' Tales, and connects the man with the one in another vision that we often feel to be behind George Eliot's in *Marner*, the Man bowed under 'a great Burden upon his back' crying lamentably, '*What shall I do?*' and setting out from the City of Destruction to another country to seek salvation.[3] It is in keeping with this serious intention that the author insisted that in the title and in advertising the book the word *story* should be avoided, undoubtedly because she felt this was a misleading description, tending to make the book appear something slight and fanciful. And rightly, for in *Marner* she had found a framework within which she could present the problems that pressed on her, that life had shown her must be solved or managed, and which were more than merely personal. Though *Marner* prepares us for its successors *Middlemarch* and *Felix Holt* it is superior to these in an art of concentration that

uses always the minimum – the loaded word and the uniquely
representative act – an art which puts *Marner* with Shakespeare
and Bunyan rather than with other Victorian novels. It is very
evidently the source of Hardy's novel-writing, but he never anywhere equalled the characterization of Raveloe and the talk in
the Rainbow in his efforts at the same kind of thing, nor did
he ever manage to invent a plot where coincidence, as in
Marner, is felt as part of a natural and just order of things, or
a plot which, like *Marner*'s, perfectly exemplifies its theme.

Leaving aside for the moment why this book insisted on being
written when its author was struggling to write a quite different
novel, we ask first: Why was this stooping man alien? what
country did he not belong to and why?

The book begins by deliberately establishing in 'anthropological' terms the conditions of a poor nineteenth-century
Christian whose burden is not Original Sin but loss of faith and
of a community – in fact what the City had given him in the
way of a religion and a community was not recognizable as such
by the traditions of the countryside, the village life in which the
English civilized themselves. To this, the original state, the man
makes his way by instinct with his only skill, his loom, and all
that is left of his religion, his Bible.[4] In Raveloe the Industrial
Revolution has not yet been felt and it is the countryside of the
timeless past of packhorse and spinning-wheel, of the organic
community and the unified society. To the people of Raveloe
professional weaving, though necessary, is an alien way of
working; it produces 'pallid, undersized men who, by the side
of the brawny country-folk, looked like the remnants of a
disinherited race', objects therefore of a superstitious repug-
nance; we are first shown the weaver through the eyes of a
peasantry. The machinery *they* know is their servant; the
country-bred novelist understood the real distinction between
mechanical aids and a mechanized industry, and her feeling for
music provided the natural human reaction: she expresses it in
the countryfolk's perception of a difference in rhythm – 'the
cheerful trotting of the winnowing-machine and the simple
rhythm of the flail' – human or animal rhythms, contrasted
with the mechanical rhythm which is *imposed* on the worker by
his loom; significantly Marner is described as working *in* his
loom, which eventually turns him into a machine component,
so that he had the same sort of impression as a handle or a

crooked tube, which has no meaning standing apart'. The signs of his enslavement are 'the bent treadmill attitude' and the short sight, produced by his work, that cuts him off from seeing his fellow-men both actually and metaphorically. He is the opposite of the country craftsman like Adam Bede whose healthy livelihood made him a superior type of manhood.

Silas's solitary working round could find compensation only in an inward spiritual life and 'incorporation in a narrow religious sect'. But the religious life available to him was not beneficial, taking as guidance a pathetically ignorant inner light ('Lantern Yard') which has proved delusive when tested. Moreover, it has deprived him of his cultural inheritance (represented, by a stroke of genius, by the medicinal herbs) without providing anything in the way of education in living instead. George Eliot presents more of the truth about Dissent in *Marner* than in the earlier and very partial account of Methodism in *Adam Bede* – *Marner* is more truthful in many ways. Besides the problem of the machine toil which is dehumanizing, she has brought in another major problem of her age, the threat to the traditional heritage by the now dominant Evangelical outlook.[5] 'The little store of wisdom which his mother had imparted to him as a solemn bequest' (the knowledge and preparation of medicinal wild herbs) Calvinism had taught him to mistrust, 'so that the inherited delight he had in wandering in the fields in search of foxglove and dandelion and coltsfoot began to wear to him the character of a temptation'. This symbol is finely chosen, for it conveys that help for others, contact with Nature, and a kind of education, as well as the satisfaction of knowing he is maintaining the wise lore of his ancestors, are all denied him. There is thus a multiple typicality about the case of Silas Marner. In him the dire effects of the Industrial Revolution are examined; the current form of religion, a Christian fundamentalism, has finished the effects of denaturing him by disinheriting him. How can such losses to the race be made good? – it is George Eliot who describes Marner's kind as 'a disinherited race'.

Driven by 'something not unlike the feeling of primitive men, when they fled from an unpropitious deity', Silas leaves the alleys for the immemorial countryside. (It is not an accident that Raveloe lies in the 'rich central plain of what we are pleased to call Merry England', the countryside of George

Eliot's infancy, which was still in essentials Shakespeare's.) To Silas, fresh from Lantern Yard, the lives of the people there seem merely unspiritual and misdirected ('women laying up a stock of linen for the life to come' is not only humorous but has a scriptural phrasing hinting their blindness to their eternal welfare, or what seems blindness to Silas); but as we presently see, their materialism is an art of living. The clue to the basis of their lives is in a word we keep meeting: 'neighbourly'. Silas, with his refusal to mix by attending church or dropping in to gossip at the Rainbow or courting a girl, is suspect.

This is why his spontaneous attempt to help the woman, whose suffering recalls his mother's, with the herbal medicine he knows will relieve her, only projects him into the vacant office of Wise Woman, and when his honesty rejects it, consigns him to an even more undesirable one.[6] The irony is poignant, and the incident a proof that George Eliot is not sentimental about the people of Raveloe. But their superstition is more than offset by their shrewdness: they realize as soon as Silas has been robbed that this proves that far from being 'a deep 'un' he is only 'a poor mushed creature'. The contrast with the stupid behaviour of the Lantern Yard brethren when they too had to find out whether Silas was telling the truth is to Raveloe's credit – the villagers' superstition does not prevent them from being wiser in the end than the town artisans who have a 'purer' form of Christianity. The Raveloe people chiefly appreciate the pagan survivals (carols, and keeping 'a jolly Christmas, Whitsun and Easter tide') but they practise the true religion of neighbourliness. The village way of life is shown to foster some virtues that the city does nothing to promote: Jem the poacher, unlike William Dane, is really an honest man barring 'the matter of a hare or so' (nobody in an English village ever believed that game was not rightly common property), the villagers don't steal money or goods if only because these couldn't be used without discovery, and cheating of any sort is despised (the dishonesty of Dunsey is covered by his birth, but to the cottagers he is 'that offal Dunsey'). Morality is also ensured because there is no privacy, and wisdom because everyone through gossip has the communal assessment of everyone's character, even the gentry's to draw on. Above all, mutual helpfulness is as necessarily practised in the village as competition in the city.

George Eliot's presentment in *Marner* of the peasant code as the justification of what she calls 'the old-fashioned village life' is so minimal an account of the civilization of the English folk that it is barely adequate even for her special purpose, so that now, when first-hand knowledge of that culture has gone for ever, and its very existence is denied by the intellectuals of our phase of civilization, the reader must educate himself into that knowledge in order to understand what *Silas Marner* is about – George Eliot could assume her readers did not need instruction of that kind. Now, something like the chapter on 'The Peasant System' in George Sturt's *Change in the Village* is essential reading for our understanding of this novel. Though the character of his village had been destroyed by the enclosure of its commons and an invasion from the town, Sturt could still at the beginning of this century recover from the older cottagers the traces of the independent life of fifty years before and his intelligent observations really illuminate *Silas Marner* for us. Here are a few of his relevant generalizations from his data:

The 'peasant' tradition in its vigour amounted to nothing less than a form of civilization – the home-made civilization of the rural English. To the exigent problems of life it furnished solutions of its own...Best of all, those customs provided a rough guide as to conduct – an unwritten code to which, though we forget it, England owes much...The cheerfulness of the cottager rests largely upon a survival of the outlook and habits of the peasant days. It is not a negative quality...In the main the force that bears them on is a traditional outlook. In the little cottages the people, from the earliest infancy, were accustomed to hear all things – persons and manners, houses and gardens, and the day's work – appraised by an ancient standard of the countryside...The people stood for something more than merely themselves.

These are confirmations and explanations of what George Eliot says in *Silas Marner* or sometimes only shows in action. But that civilization had impressive material forms too in the crafts and arts of country work and leisure, most of which have been or are being destroyed or lost, though enough evidence exists to put the case beyond dispute.[7]

George Eliot probably felt that she had already shown in *Adam Bede* the material beauty and achievement of the old order of the countryside and that she would do most by limiting her case in *Marner*. It is the moral feeling in the village, Sturt's 'ancient standard of the countryside', that she presents so appreciatively, as when Raveloe felt 'it was *nothing but right* a man should be looked on and helped by those who could afford it, when he had brought up an orphan child, and been father and mother to her'. And in a different way, she registers their acceptance of the hard realities, the risks which must be taken of things turning out ill, as well as the certainty of old age and failing strength, which can never be forgotten: even when admiring little Eppie, 'Elderly masters and mistresses told Silas that, if she turned out well (which, however, there was no telling), it would be a fine thing for him to have a steady lass to do for him when he got helpless.' In comparison, the attention given to the gardener, the fiddler, the wheelwright and other representative figures of the community is slight indeed; even the dairy-farming is done by Priscilla Lammeter off-stage. We have to accept these sketches as being deliberately outlines only of the full world George Eliot registered in her childhood (G. H. Lewes said: 'She forgets nothing that has come within the curl of her eyelash') and draws on so impressively for *Adam Bede* and *Middlemarch*. The point that is kept to in this book is, how can Marner achieve reintegration into this community? Marner's private case is now merged into a general one, an illustration of how and how not to set about this. This is the purpose of that narrative in the Rainbow which is high-lighted by being placed just before Silas bursts in with his tale of being robbed, the turning point of his relations with Raveloe.

The tale told in the Rainbow is recognized as Mr Macey's peculiar property and is one which Raveloe never tires of hearing and discussing. As tailor, parish-clerk and brother to the foremost fiddler Mr Macey has a status and qualities that fit him for the part of Chorus; and that his narrative is important is shown by its having become a local legend to which ghosts and other folk-lore characteristics have accrued with time. The first part, old Mr Lammeter's story, is a contrast to Silas's experience so far. Like Silas this worthy came from 'a bit north'ard', but in contrast to Silas he was a countryman, for 'he brought a fine breed o' sheep with him' and 'it was soon seen as we'd got a new parish'ner as know'd the rights and customs o' things, and kep' a good house, and was well looked on by everybody'. So his son was able to marry into one of the best Raveloe families and 'for prosperity and everything respectable, there's no family more looked on'; in fact, their daughter Nancy is being courted by Squire Cass's heir, to everyone's satisfaction. So old Mr Lammeter's story ends happily ever after. The apparent link with the other half of the narrative is that Mr Lammeter settled at The Warrens, the estate and house left to charity by one Cliff – who is never given the respectful handle to *his* name. There is also a real link, for Cliff's story is the opposite of the other's and an awful warning of what Silas's might be: Cliff dies crazy and childless. *He* was no acquisition but 'a Lunnon tailor, some folks said, as had gone mad wi' cheating'. His madness consisted at first simply in wanting to pass as a gentleman, a kind of cheating which ended by driving him mad, for having been a tailor – that is, one who had to work sitting cross-legged – he was inevitably unfitted for the part of a gentleman, which implied, demanded, good riding.[8] Thus Mr Macey says of Cliff: 'For he couldn't ride; lor bless you! they said he'd got no more grip o' the hoss than if his legs had been cross-sticks...But ride he would.' Cliff is the type of man who won't recognize that, however rich, he can be nothing but what he is. Mr Macey, a tailor himself, has better sense and greater self-respect. He despises Cliff for being 'ashamed o' being called a tailor' – 'not but what I'm a tailor myself, but in respect as God made me such, I'm proud on it, for "Macey, tailor"'s been wrote up over our door since afore the Queen's heads went out on the shillings'. He has his own honourable pedigree, tailors are essential, and besides he is proud of his craft.[9] So Eppie's final refusal to be raised out of the class she was reared in is shown as being consistent with this folk tradition, 'a little store of inherited wisdom', and not improbable or sentimental. We are given an insight into a theory of class which has nothing to do with snobbery and which rules out the passion to rise in the world socially.

Cliff's story has moreover a thematic relation to Godfrey Cass's, for Cliff, since he couldn't get accepted as a gentleman himself, determined to 'ride the tailor' out of his son against the boy's nature, bringing about his death, so that Cliff died childless. This prefigures Godfrey's fate when his cheating shall have produced its own Nemesis, as he recognizes in the end when he tells his wife: 'I wanted to pass for childless once – I shall pass for childless now against my wish.' And Cliff's story stands also as contrast to Silas's, for the latter, by eventually

assimilating himself like old Mr Lammeter, ends up by accepting 'the rights and customs o' things', being 'well looked on',
and leaving (adopted) heirs. True, Silas has to learn as a foreign
language, which he never really masters and whose principles
he certainly doesn't understand, what was native for Mr
Lammeter; but he is saved from Cliff's fate by his humility. So
this parable within a parable is the clue to the whole, and Mr
Macey justly sums up in what might be an epigraph for the
novel: 'there's reasons in things as nobody knows on – that's
pretty much what I've made out'. There *are* laws of life, George
Eliot shows, and they were 'made out' in village life although
they can't be stated.[10] In Mr Macey's narrative and its
affiliations with the rest of the book we have one example of the
wonderfully complex organization and the unobtrusive structure
of symbol and theme which make the text of *Silas Marner* so
dense and rich in meanings and yet so economical in words.

The laws of life are shown in operation in what follows
immediately after Silas has made known his misfortune to the
village. His relations with the villagers follow the same impartial
logic as before, but his impulse to turn to them for help in his
trouble, and his compunction at accusing Jem of robbing him
without evidence, which has stirred up memories of being falsely
accused himself, have made a bridge between them. They see
he is an innocent soul and in need of help. First 'contemptuous
pity' replaces distrust, then the traditional neighbourly attempts
to help him follow. The sympathetic ears, the good advice, the
welcome presents and soothing attentions culminate in Dolly
Winthrop's well-judged efforts to reach him by all the different
channels she feels likely to work on him. She brings the cakes,
with their religious sanction in the traditionally pricked 'good
letters'; the child, as certain to touch his heart if he has one and
moreover to sing a carol to move his Christmas sentiments; and
a gentle remonstrance about his not going to church. All these
good means fail to reach him, and we cannot but sense that
something is being conveyed, in the cross-purposes and mis-
understandings of their conversation, sometimes comical and
sometimes full of pathos, about the difficulty of achieving any
real communication between people who don't belong to the
same culture. Silas doesn't even recognize the religion of Church
as the same Christian religion that he subscribed to in the first
half of his life, for all his knowledge of the theory of salvation;

here no doubt something more ironical is intended. Dolly's religion is about as far from Calvinism as possible; it is seen to be a matter of custom, traditional pieties and pagan practices, and she makes no distinction between christening and inoculation.

But George Eliot makes her point, that the ignorant village wheelwright's wife has the advantage over the city weaver who could talk knowingly about Assurance of Salvation in his youth. The difference between their two cultures is illustrated by the episode of the 'I.H.S.' on the lard-cakes. Dolly pricks them, without knowing what the letters are, because tradition has assured her that they have a good meaning (even though she has noticed that sometimes the letters won't hold and also that the cakes don't always turn out so well); the proof that she can trust the inherited wisdom is that these same letters are on the pulpit-cloth at church.[11] But Silas, who *can* read them, is yet seen to be really worse off than the illiterate Dolly, for, like her, he doesn't know what the letters stand for and unlike her he has no pious associations with them. Even if he had known what they stood for, we reflect, his chapel-formed prejudices would have prevented him from venerating them as it had deprived him of the medicinal herbs.

Silas never does acquire the pieties inborn with the villagers. He gets along eventually by adopting all the village customs without questioning them, but never, of course, has the traditional associations which make people benefit by them. We are given an undoubtedly humorous illustration in the daily pipe-smoking which Silas takes up because it is the done thing and because he is told, against the evidence of his senses, that it is good for him. Eppie believes it does do him good and that he enjoys it, and though he would rather not smoke he does not like to set himself up against received opinion or to pain Eppie by undeceiving her. George Eliot does not press the general point here illustrated, which would have forced on us an awkward scepticism, but once again it expresses her freedom from sentimentality and her refusal to simplify, to make a 'story' by suppressing discordant facts.

All the attempts to bring Silas back to a place in the community fail because except for the case of Sally Oates they have no purchase on him and in that one case he has bad luck (as he has good luck in being sent Eppie – chance is impartial).

Dolly believed the sight of her child Aaron was bound to do him good, yet this fails because Silas is too short-sighted to see Aaron's features at all. But (again the impartial laws of life operate) this very short sight is just what leads him to accept another child later as his gold come back. Then all the right conditions are seen to have been met at last. The process of being restored to life,[12] which actually began with the loss of his gold, has accelerated. The aspect it seems to have of coincidence is ruled out when we consider that Eppie's appearance follows upon many attempts against Silas's isolation that occur in the natural course of events. The only faery-tale element lies in the fact that Eppie appears on New Year's Eve, when the luck is liable to turn with the New Year, but again this is seen to be one of the essential conditions for the chance to take effect since the excitement brings on Silas's trance. What *is* unsatisfactory is the device of the catalepsy, since it is not, like Dr Manette's psychological losses of memory and reversions to another personality, a product of his misfortunes but the cause of them, posited for the plotting – after which Silas ceases to have any fits onstage. The fits were needed to make William's treachery and theft possible and to give the villagers an excuse for their superstitious horror of a man whose 'soul was loose from his body and going out and in like a bird out of its nest' (though this last is a true piece of folk-lore and helps to show us how primitive was the mentality of the countryman). And lastly, the catalepsy is necessary to get Eppie into the cottage without Silas knowing, so that she *seems* to him initially to be of supernatural origin. But even so the fits are worked into the pattern of an impartial operation of the laws of life: twice chance introduces a thief into Silas's home, the third time – there is a popular belief: 'The third time, lucky' – the same chance lets in Eppie, who makes good the previous losses.

Leslie Stephen's (and others') amused scepticism about an old bachelor's reception of a baby and his return to the bosom of society in consequence, seems to me superficial. George Eliot has been careful to explain that Silas, like many children of the poor, had been used to look after his baby sister and cherished that memory; he is domesticated by habit and handy by virtue of his trade, and he has Dolly's assistance. As for the Wordsworthian part of the enterprise, what follows seems to me a more plausible and particularized demonstration of Wordsworth's tenets than anything the poet ever wrote himself. The 'remedial influences of pure, natural human relations' and a revived ability to enjoy the natural world are conveyed persuasively in exquisite detail and poetic imagery. But it is characteristic of the economical and pregnant construction of *Marner* that these Wordsworthian passages are something more than lovely episodes; besides their inherent poetical quality they are precipitations and enactments of the deeper meanings of the novel. Take only one of these and that the slightest: the influence of little Eppie in making Silas share her delight in everything outdoors or in nature 'even to the old winter flies that come crawling forth in the early spring sunshine, and warming him into joy because *she* had joy'. We perceive that Silas is vividly imaged as being himself an old winter fly crawling out under the reviving spring sunshine which Eppie is to him. And this passage builds up with what follows to convey Silas's gradual return to a life of feeling, ending by bringing into play again the herbs that not merely recall his mother but represent something like the traditions of the race.

Sitting on the banks in this way, Silas began to look for the once familiar herbs again; and as the leaves, with their unchanged outlines and markings, lay on his palm, there was a sense of crowding remembrances from which he turned away timidly, taking refuge in Eppie's little world, that lay lightly on his enfeebled spirit.

As the child's mind was growing into knowledge, his mind was growing into memory: as her life unfolded, his soul, long stupified in a cold narrow prison, was unfolding too, and trembling gradually into full consciousness.

We are shown also that besides reviving Silas's consciousness of the world around him and its associations with his past, Eppie makes him aware of a future happiness, so that he can deduce from the present 'in the ties and charities that bound together the families of his neighbours' 'images of that time' to come, another application of the Wordsworthian doctrine. In the spirit of Wordsworth's poetry too is the description of how Eppie forges a bond between Silas and all animate and even inanimate life: 'there was love between the child and the world – from men and women with parental looks and tones to the red ladybirds and the round pebbles'.

Wordsworthian, we say, but the imagery drawn from Nature is so apt[13] and so freshly observed that we recollect that 'George Eliot' was Mary Ann Evans, a country child, before she became a learned woman, and that on reading Wordsworth's poems for the first time on her twentieth birthday she wrote of them: 'I have never before met with so many of my feelings expressed just as I could wish them.' So Nancy's person is described as giving 'the same idea of unvarying neatness as the body of a little bird', Dolly 'pastures her mind' on the sadder elements of life, Godfrey sees himself becoming as 'helpless as an uprooted tree', the patched and darned baby-clothes are 'clean and neat as fresh-sprung herbs', Silas's 'sap of affection was not all gone' and the imagery that describes his shrunken life as 'the rivulet that has sunk far down from the grassy fringe of its old breadth into a little shivering thread, that cuts a groove for itself in the barren sand' recurs in various forms. But far more memorable than anything of the kind in Wordsworth is the episode of Silas's broken water-jug whose homely earthenware shape had become dear to him by association:

It had been his companion for twelve years, always standing in the same spot, always lending its handle to him in the early morning, so that its form had an expression for him of willing helpfulness, and the impress of its handle on his palm gave a satisfaction mingled with that of having the fresh clear water.

When he stumbled and broke it, he 'picked up the pieces and carried them home with grief in his heart. The brown pot could never be of use to him any more, but he stuck the bits together and propped the ruin in its old place for a memorial.' But this also has a function, to show that Silas retained even in his extreme isolation that 'natural piety' which is a proof of being fully human[14] and without which he could not have been rescued by Eppie. It is part of the sequence of evidence proving that, though he had lost his faith, still compunction, compassion, gratitude and honourable feelings were alive in him; but it comes also from the George Eliot who wrote in a letter, during the very period when she was composing *Marner*: 'In proportion as I love every form of piety – which is venerating love – I hate hard curiosity'; who when reading the newly-published *Origin of Species* the year before wrote to her friends that though 'it makes an epoch' yet 'To me the Development Theory and all other explanations of processes by which things came to be, produce a feeble impression compared with the mystery that lies under the processes'.

But it is not the Wordsworthian 'message' in any simple form

that George Eliot is endorsing. 'Love had he found in huts
where poor men lie, / His daily teachers had been woods and
rills' would not have been true in any way of Silas if he had not
been shown these truths by Eppie. And Eppie's influence would
have been inadequate without the village there to take them both
into its neighbourly care and teach them how to live, with what
Sturt calls 'the home-made civilization of the rural English'.[15]
We meet one of its impressive aspects at the Red House's New
Year dance where the villagers, admitted to watch by custom,
discuss the characters, conduct, appearance and history of the
gentry, drawing on their own experiences and showing their
good sense and decent feeling while making shrewd criticisms;
and earlier at the Rainbow we have seen their understanding
of the 'reasons in things', of the nature of social life.

Another aspect of the character of this peasant tradition is
embodied in Dolly Winthrop herself. The dual strain in the
English folk tradition is represented by the marriage (happy
enough) of tipsy, jovial Ben Winthrop and the grave, scrupulous
Dolly, a good woman who performs Dinah Morris's function
without being given a halo. We are introduced to her as one
'having her lips always slightly screwed; as if she felt herself in
a sickroom with the doctor or the clergyman present' and
'inclined to shake her head and sigh, almost imperceptibly, like
a funereal mourner who is not a relation'. Yet she is not to be
ridiculed. What Dolly represents is the strength of the village
code that makes it religious in character but as remote as
possible from dogma, theology or ritual practice. How exactly
she corresponds to George Sturt's account of the cottager's
character familiar to him in life!

To some extent doubtless it rests on Christian teaching, although
perhaps not much on the Christian teaching of the present day...from
distant generations there seems to have come down, in many a cottage
family, a rather lofty religious sentiment which fosters honesty,
patience, resignation, courage. Much of the gravity, much of the
tranquillity of soul of the more sedate villagers must be ascribed to this
traditional influence, whose effects are attractive enough, in the
character and outlook of many an old cottage man and woman.[16]

One of Dolly's many functions is to incite us to decide in what
ways the code she lives by differs from Nancy Lammeter's, for
Nancy's is seen to be as inferior to Dolly's as the Lantern Yard's

is to Raveloe's. Nancy actually reminds us of the Lantern Yard in the narrowness of her outlook and her arbitrary moral laws.

IV

In chapter 3, with the introduction of the Cass family, the assumption that in this novel we are in the timeless world of 'Once upon a time' is finally destroyed. It specifies the England of the Napoleonic Wars and even the facts of economic history which were to ruin the landowning classes and their helpless labourers. Radicalism, the product of this age, comes out strongly in *Marner*, to produce later *Felix Holt, the Radical*. It is George Eliot's Radical sympathies that account for her distaste for the squirearchy and her compassion for the poor. It is no accident that makes the Nemesis in *Marner* the gentleman's fate and the happy outcome of luck the cottager's, for Godfrey's history is in large and in detail an inversion of Silas's, and when their dramatic confrontation at last takes place, all the elements in the novel come into play and we are left in no doubt about the conclusions we are to draw. The Nemesis that overtakes Godfrey is inextricably mixed up with his position in society and his conditioning by that; slight as his chances were of getting Eppie to live with him as his daughter, it is not until he makes clear, inadvertently, how he thinks of the working-class that he alienates Eppie and Silas for ever. The Casses retire helpless and humiliated, and we feel impelled to cheer.

Mary Ann Evans was peculiarly qualified by her background and upbringing to appreciate the fine distinctions of the English class system of her day and their consequences. Her father, born and bred a carpenter like Adam Bede, 'raised himself', in his daughter's proud words, to being notable in the ways that Caleb Garth is shown to be in *Middlemarch*, but to an even better position. He had some of Adam Bede's qualities of bodily strength and character combined with Mr Garth's social submissiveness to his wife, who was 'superior' – a Dodson in family though a Mrs Poyser in nature and activities. Their daughter must therefore have been socially sensitive even without any knowledge of her father's aristocratic employers, and in due course this class of beings complicated her ideas of the social system even further, as J. W. Cross was well aware, no doubt from her own mouth. He stresses the effect of 'being

constantly driven by her father' to the 'fine places' of these
gentry as 'accentuating the social differences – differences
which had a profound significance and which left their mark
on such a sensitive character'. Coming home from her excellent
education at a boarding-school at Coventry a convert to the
'ultra-Evangelical tendencies' of the teachers, she was in
conflict for years with her brother, whose private tutor's
establishment had imbued *him* with strong High Church views.
The future George Eliot was thus thoroughly equipped to feel
in person all the strains and anomalies of the contemporary
social and religious system, and being born in 1819 (a time of
political and economic trouble) to know the distresses of the
workers too.

Her escape from the blight of Evangelicalism was, by her own
account, and as one would expect, through literature, Scott first
unsettling her orthodoxy and Shakespeare becoming the book
of books for her by 1842. The Evangelical fervour was, as so
often, replaced by a desire to serve humanity which soon led
her to a concern for social reform, and we find her rejoicing in
the earlier Carlyle and even in the French Revolution of 1848:
at this date we have her denunciation of England ('I feel that
society is training men and women for hell') and her admiration
for Louis Blanc. In 1851 she launched herself into the London
of the congenial *Westminster Review* set; three years later she
bravely united her life with G. H. Lewes's, and since marriage
was legally impossible for him she found herself in a new position
of complete detachment from the social system. (The effect was
peculiar. While she shows in her novels complete emancipation
from restrictive ideas of class, and while her criticisms of its
causes, manifestations and effects are always penetrating, sensitive and unbiased, she is surprisingly conventional about *moral*
conduct in the narrow Victorian sense.) *Silas Marner* is the only
novel in which she makes Class a major cause of the different
treatment she gives human beings; even in *Adam Bede* both
Arthur *and* Adam incur a Nemesis – Adam's 'hardness' is
rebuked by seeing the harshness with which Hetty's 'fall' is
treated by his world (though it is true he gets a plaster by being
allowed to marry Dinah). The experiment no doubt helped to
equip George Eliot for the more systematic, and unprejudiced
examination of society in *Felix Holt, the Radical* and for the
wider-ranging impartial treatment of the whole subject in

Middlemarch.[17] Class is dominant even in church at Raveloe (see chapter 16) and in the last few pages we learn that Godfrey couldn't bear to stay in Raveloe on the day his daughter marries a 'low working-man' – whom *we* know to be the admirable Aaron Winthrop.

The effect of staying for the first part of the book with the peasantry and Silas is that we identify with them, so that when Squire Cass is brought before us at last he figures very large indeed, though only a very small squire. It is at once explained that these things are relative and that in his ambience he is 'quite as if he had been a lord' – this is the Lilliputian treatment which implies that a lord is only an enlarged Squire Cass. He is then shown as typical of a class whose 'extravagant habits and bad husbandry' are preparing them for ruin when the 'glorious wartime' ends. The sarcasm at their expense is different from any irony in the previous chapters, it tends to take on a savage tone and to become caricature. The fatuous selfishness of believing wartime 'to be a peculiar favour of Providence to the landed interest' is succeeded by this speech of the Squire's, by which we cannot but be disgusted and in which we catch the selfish indignation in the querulous rhythm:

And that fool Kimble says the newspaper's talking about peace. Why, the country wouldn't have a leg to stand on. Prices 'ud run down like a jack, and I should never get my arrears, not if I sold all the fellows up.'

His class wants to keep the country at war for its own interest, a traditional Radical charge. His callous lack of concern for his tenants so long as he can get his rent shows he is a bad landlord too. The interior of the Red House is squalid and the sons degraded by dissipation. The villagers have already passed judgment: 'Raveloe was not a place where moral censure was severe, but it was thought a weakness in the Squire that he had kept all his sons at home in idleness', 'though some licence was to be allowed to young men whose fathers could afford it'. The villagers know that the same standard can't be expected of the gentry as of their own sons. Godfrey is 'equally disinclined to dig and to beg'. When we find that Dolly and Silas and worthy Mr Macey think of these people as their 'betters', it makes us think (along Radical lines of course).

Along with this concept of 'betters' we learn not only that

the Casses are not better but that the Squire differs from the farmers of the parish only by 'that self-possession and authoritativeness of voice and carriage which belonged to a man' who has never met anyone superior to himself. As the villagers are characterized by 'neighbourly' attitudes he is distinguished by *patronizing* ones, he even feels his position obliges him 'to fulfil the hereditary duty of being noisily jovial and patronizing' and he speaks 'in a ponderous and coughing fashion, which was felt in Raveloe to be a sort of privilege of his rank'. This is amusing and intelligent observation, but it ceases to be amusing when we find that this has imposed itself as an acceptable image of gentility on the villagers; Ben Winthrop even describes Godfrey with admiration as 'one as 'ud knock you down easier' than anyone – knocking you down being the symbolic function of one's betters. All this is meant to be subversive and expresses George Eliot's reaction to a class that must in her childhood and youth have appeared a blot on the landscape.[18] But active political feeling is needed to account for other manifestations of the same situation: a very stock piece of Radical propaganda is the picture of the Squire cutting beef off his joint for his deer-hound as he breakfasts – 'enough bits of beef to make a poor man's holiday dinner' – reminding us that working-men could afford 'butcher's meat' at best on only a few occasions a year.

So when we are returned to the company of the poor we feel relief. Here is charity and fellowship and we can enter into their difficulties and pleasures with sympathy without meeting their 'betters' again till Eppie is at the critical stage of courtship. Then we are taken back to the Red House (chapter 17). True the old Squire and the vicious Dunsey are gone and the Lammeters' 'liberal orderliness' is in charge, while the refinement compared with what went before suggests that Nancy may really be a 'better'. Her attitude to adoption compared to the villagers' is one test, and others follow. She is seen to be made up of 'rigid principles', a conventional good woman, loving and dutiful to her own relations but fatally limited, as is proved when she goes with her husband to claim Eppie. 'Used all her life to plenteous circumstances and the privileges of "respectability"' we are told, she cannot understand that Eppie's life can have its own attractions and compensations. This is exactly in keeping with Godfrey's conviction that Eppie would readily fall in with his wish to adopt her, he having formed 'the idea that deep affections can hardly go along with callous palms and scant means'.

The ensuing drama is really instructive, no longer easily satiric. Godfrey loses any sympathy we may have felt for him by his selfishness, his obtuseness to the feelings of the Marners, and his dishonesty in persuading himself that he is doing for Eppie's good what now suits himself. This analysis of 'moral stupidity', one of George Eliot's favourite subjects, proceeds magnificently as Godfrey finally accuses the weaver of selfishness and reproaches him that without her real father's (his) protection 'she may marry some low working-man'.[19] Godfrey's brutality here is the more dreadful for not being conscious; it is a class reaction only, not personal. We look to see Nancy's reaction to this test. But she notices no insult, and this comes as a shock to us because Nancy has been shown as superior to the rest of her world in delicacy of feeling. We are forced to realize that insulation by class destroys the power of imaginative sympathy in everyone. Nancy presses Godfrey's rights on Eppie, who answers the spirit of the insult with a passionate affirmation of class solidarity as well as of loyalty to the only father she has ever known. It is characteristic that the first thing Nancy then thinks of is relief that her family and the world now need never know about Godfrey's past and the relation with Eppie. What is uppermost in her mind is respectability; she is a variety of Dodson[20] and this is the real gulf between her and the village folk who have not yet been tainted with the religion of 'respectability' (a word which George Eliot herself puts into inverted commas here). Eppie's reaction is quite plausible if we remember what social and literary history abundantly confirm, what Sturt summarizes in this sentence: 'It seems singular to think of it now, but the very labourer might reasonably hope for some satisfaction in life, nor trouble about "raising" himself into some other class, so long as he could live on peasant lines.'

Now this constant play of ironical social criticism, and the general reflections about human nature, are what prevent the artifices (such as the elaborate parallels between Silas's and Godfrey's histories and the providential arrangements of the fits, little golden-haired girls, and so on) from being felt as artificial

by the reader, for they never obtrude as such: far from being
incited to work out the pattern, our attention is always being
directed elsewhere. Yet without dwelling on these things we do
get as we read a sense that these complexities of reference are
further illustrations of those laws of life that, as the novel is
concerned to demonstrate, so mysteriously exist.

They are not laws that can be stated, but as we've seen they
cover parts of human experience investigated by Wordsworth
and Bunyan, Cobbett and George Sturt, among others, and
embody the truths of parables in the New Testament as well
as the traditional wisdom expressed in folk-tales. The central
thesis in Mr Macey's narrative at the Rainbow is the contrast
between the rich man's folly and the meek man's success in
living, a theme often present in folk-tales of course. Godfrey
with his uneasy conscience and his childless hearth gets no
benefit from his riches and the wife he has gained by deception
while the humble Marner household have the last word: '
think nobody could be happier than we are.' Eppie has brought
into the home, to complete it with a garden, Aaron the
gardener. That his occupation is, like the tailor's, deliberately
chosen[21] is made quite explicit in his criticism of the mal
distribution of goods – a return to the Radical vein:

there's never a garden in all the parish but what there's endless waste
in it for want o' somebody as could use everything up. It's what I think
to myself sometimes, as there need nobody run short o' victuals if the
land was made the most on, and there was never a morsel but what
could find its way to a mouth. It sets one thinking o' that – gardening
does.

And we are presently told that Aaron does all the gardening
for the Raveloe gentry: his kind do the world's work and have
a better idea than the property-owners of the right use o
property, this tells us. Again we are led to ask: Who are the
'betters'?

Yet, it must be emphasized once again, the cottagers are not
idealized. The coarse repartee and the illiterate arguments in
the Rainbow, drink and stupid jokes and superstitions are there
and coexist with great good sense and kindliness and love o
children, and with the hospitality and co-operation that are
obligatory in the Raveloe code. And as regards their weaknesses
the reader is always being nudged into realizing that the world

in general is no better, that behaviour in polite circles can be worse.[22] Rarely is any incongruity felt when the cool voice of the anthropologizing critic modulates into the sympathetic tone which conveys all the pathos of the lives of the humble. Silas's helplessness and even the comical effects of his simplicity never prevent us from seeing that his inner life is to be respected. This is great art, and throws up scenes that remain in the memory as strangely impressive, such as that where Godfrey and his young child exchange looks without the child's giving him any recognition, turning instead to pull lovingly at the weaver's face – impressive in itself, but still more so when, having read to the end, we realize that it has forecast Eppie's eventual rejection of Godfrey in the final scene which is the result of Godfrey's refusal in this earlier scene to recognize the natural bond between them. The novel is full of dramatic ironies both of scene and speech (such as Silas's assurance to Godfrey Cass that he will keep the baby Eppie 'till anybody shows they've a right to take her away from me'). These ironies tie the book together firmly.

V

After the Radical vein has been worked out there still remains to determine the theme of Silas's past suffering in the city. Seen through Eppie's country-bred eyes the city is 'a dark ugly place' and 'worse than the Workhouse', and Silas notices for the first time that it 'smells bad'. A factory has swept away Lantern Yard (is it a relief?) and Silas can say, 'The old home's gone; I've no home but this now.' The irony latent in the name 'Lantern Yard' is brought out by Dolly's innocent encouragement to him to go back to the city to find out the truth: 'And if there's any light to be got up the yard as you talk on, we've need of it i' this world.' Actually, the Lantern Yard community could only darken counsel (there is scriptural reference of this kind implied in the constant play upon the words 'dark' and 'light' and we cannot avoid the suggestion of 'Lighten our darkness' in the offing). The social criticism in *Marner* therefore is inseparable from spiritual values. This is consonant with the early tradition of English Radicalism, which is why *Marner* had to be both a realistic novel and a symbolic spiritual history and why Bunyan, as I've shown, offered a suitable source for reference. *Silas Marner* really asks: What was it that characterized the way of life of the English village in its heyday, so that its passing has meant a heavy loss? One of the most memorable points made in the last part is that Silas's return to his birthplace is partly to enlighten the minister: 'I should like to talk to him about the religion o' this country-side, for I partly think he doesn't know on it.'

So we come back to the factors in George Eliot's personal life which forced her to undertake this book. Hating the conditions of life in London, she remembered her childhood not only for its green fields and her mother's dairy but for the whole agricultural way of life which, she saw, enhanced the aesthetic aspects of Nature as well as shaped the lives of a people whose human achievement in creating a community she deeply respected; a people whose speech, an art of expression manifested in a dialect notable for its force, rhythm, and subtlety, had a flavour quite absent from educated English. She felt her loss of these things the more for having pined for them for ten years in London among the claustrophobic streets, the choking smoke and the anonymous crowd – these facts are liberally documented in her letters and Journal. An intellectual circle she had, but this was no substitute for the neighbourliness of 'old-fashioned village life'. With this sense of her own loss went her realization of what it must mean for the utterly disinherited masses, no longer a folk, deprived of a community by the forces we sum up as the Industrial Revolution, the city poor whom all the serious Victorian novelists had on their minds, inheritors as all these novelists were, whatever their formal political allegiances, of that earlier ethos of Cobbett's humane Radicalism and Carlyle's appeals to conscience.[23]

She had also the impulse at this date to give her generation the benefit of her own discovery of a point of rest – which *Marner* in its positive final serenity proves she had achieved. The authoritative account of George Eliot's spiritual history is given by herself in a letter written a year before starting *Silas Marner* (6 December 1859). She writes of her early bigoted Evangelical phase, followed by her 'attitude of antagonism which belongs to the renunciation of *any* religious belief', and that she can now say that she has a sympathy with any faith that has been the expression of human sorrow and longing for righteousness: 'I have a sympathy with it that predominates over all argumentative tendencies.' Silas goes through a similar process, ending by accepting not dogmatic religion but a place in a community whose religious system has passed the pragmatic test – it visibly works as right and wise practice, and this brings personal happiness. Only Dolly appears to feel that faith must somewhere rest on, or imply, divine powers, but owing to her humility, or a sense of the remoteness of these powers, she refers to them only as 'Them above', suggesting those pagan deities ('the beliefs of primitive men') constantly invoked in the first two chapters. What the others describe as Providence seems to associate more naturally with their belief in Luck than with the Christian hope. The Raveloe poeple's attitude to church is that it provides social cohesion with some good magic attached (as in their belief in the necessity of taking the sacrament annually). Dolly's (and her creator's) conclusion that 'We must trusten' is really no more than Axel Heyst's discovery in Conrad's *Victory*: 'Woe to the heart that has not learnt while young to put its trust in life.' Unlike Hardy's burden: 'Life offers – to deny', George Eliot says that, in the long run, Life gives a fair deal, or at any rate it did in the village world.

Silas 'had come to appropriate the forms of custom and belief which were the mould of Raveloe life', and by blending these with 'the elements of his old faith', 'recovered a consciousness of unity between his past and his present'. Personal happiness has made this possible and adequate for him, as for George Eliot herself, who had found objects to live for in Lewes and his three motherless boys, and in the creative work which Lewes had launched her on and sustained her in – and which, she wrote, 'gives value to my life'. She felt justified in sustaining a faith in the possibilities of social life, however discouraging some of the manifestations of human nature may be, and she shows in *Adam Bede* and *Silas Marner* that the old culture, of village units centring on the market town, manifested such a possibility.

There are so many meanings in *Silas Marner* that it is surprising there was room in such a short space for them all; it is a feat to have wrapped them up with such neatness, charm, poetry and wit. The remarkable stylization of *Marner*, which is really due to its being an extension of the parable form, is something quite unprecedented in George Eliot's fiction hitherto; it has no anticipation in any of the short stories that make up

Scenes of Clerical Life; while the lax association of different centres of interest that constitutes *Adam Bede* and *The Mill on the Floss* is as different from *Marner* as is *Romola*, its successor. But we can see that in the symbolic confrontation scenes in *Felix Holt* and in the use of poetic symbolism in *Middlemarch*, the discoveries made in *Marner* have been consolidated.

A note on the text

There is no difficulty about the text of *Silas Marner* for George Eliot was a careful proof reader and had made up her mind in the first edition of 1861. The present edition is based on the one which appeared in 1868 in the complete edition of her works issued from 1867 onwards.

The only textual interest lies in the changes in the manuscript itself which I have given in the notes here (except those which are trivial), and in the change from the manuscript, where William's surname is throughout 'Waif', to the surname 'Dane' in the first edition. The manuscript George Eliot actually sent to the printer, now in the British Museum, contains really very few alterations, and those slight but always improvements. If she did not copy this manuscript from an earlier one, it *does* seem as if she must have written from a fully charged memory under something like inspiration; very long stretches have no alterations except those due to mistakes of a kind natural when writing fast, or to a desire to have a more concrete verb (e.g. 'set' instead of 'place') or to concentrate by expunging words. One would like to know how Ben Winthrop was described before a long phrase was crossed out and 'an excellent wheelwright' written above instead. On the title-page the book was called 'Silas Marner, the Weaver of Raveloe, A Story by George Eliot'. But as I have already explained, George Eliot subsequently told her publisher she must have the description 'story' removed from the title and from any advertising.

George Eliot was too preoccupied with each current composition to tamper with the texts of her previous novels, as we could deduce from what she writes in a letter in November 1872:

When a subject has begun to grow in me, I suffer terribly until it has wrought itself out – become a complete organism; and then it seems to take wing and go away from me. *That* thing is not to be done again – that life has been lived. I could not rest with a number of unfinished works on my mind.

And a little later she writes to another friend about how, when 'a book has quite gone away from [her] and become entirely of the *non-ego* – gone thoroughly from the wine-press into the casks' she can then think of it quite impersonally, and, as one gathers from what she implies elsewhere, leave it behind.

The Englishness of the English novel

We of course take the English novel for granted. We think of it, with its long-established tradition – if we think of it at all – as the inevitable product of some literary law of Nature. But if we look at the novel as it has been established in other countries, as well as look at other countries which have failed to produce a national tradition of the novel at all (even one which, like Italy, has an old civilization and early achievement in poetry) we must realize that our English novel is a unique product. This is because it is the largely accidental result of our luck at having had in the last two and a half centuries a succession of gifted creative writers, born in different times and places and stations, who saw prose fiction as a suitable medium for expressing their human concerns; as well as the less accidental fact that their concerns were directed by our changing social, political and economic history, and even more by our emerging religious traditions and spiritual needs which had different aspects in different ages. Therefore, the novel is the art most influenced by national life in all its minute particulars. It has also been the art most influential upon English national life, until the emergence of radio, television and the cinema, institutions which seem to have some connection with, though by no means all the responsibility for, what is generally recognized to be the decay and approaching death of the English novel as a major art (though not of course of English fiction as commercial entertainment).

A live tradition must, obviously, contain both continuity and innovation – a novelist learns from congenial predecessors, as in every other art, and contributes his own extensions and alterations to his models; and we recognize a difference between the popular novelist, or mere purveyor of entertainment, and the major novelist – the latter being a writer peculiarly sensitive to national tensions and conflicts and one who, by the accidents of his personal history, is specially qualified to feel and register the characteristic and deeper movements of the life of his time, has a true sense of values, and has the wisdom and insights which make him a warning voice for his generation. This is why such very different novelists as George Eliot, D. H. Lawrence and our contemporary Solzhenitsyn have all claimed for the novel a special status among the arts, and for the novelist a unique dedication and function as necessary critic of society. Such an artist must be an original mind and so inevitably an innovator, as distinct from what Lawrence called 'an old imitator', by which he meant the novelist who does not extend, revise or reinterpret the tradition he has received but merely exploits a form created by others. I'm interested here in the innovator, the true major novelist on whom the maintenance of the tradition depends, who is never an irresponsible intellectual playing technical games, or one who puts together a fiction to illustrate an arbitrary literary theory: we can see how such misguided preoccupations have been fatal to a novelist's development in the different cases of Flaubert and Sterne, for instance, and in our own era, Calvino and Iris Murdoch. While in contrast a truly creative novelist like Camus passed from *L'Etranger* to *La Peste* – passed, that is, from the examination of an 'idea' to a committed consideration of what civilization entails and what is indeed the nature of man: Camus had seen that his former position was untenable as he grew from irresponsible solipsism to full humanity. A different but corresponding process of growth is to be found in Jane Austen's novels: starting, in *Sense and Sensibility*, with an attempt to endorse the moral conventions of her youth regarding the duties of the individual to society but concerned also to find what rights the individual is entitled to compared with the claims of family, parents and civility, she is seen to move gradually through each succeeding novel by dramatic argument, actions and overt discussion, till she reaches in *Persuasion* an almost opposite position from her starting-point. Dickens, as a wholly professional novelist with a long career that had started in his youth, is the most striking case of such true growth as an artist, from the light-hearted improvizations of *Pickwick* and the piecemeal picaresque novels, to the later great novels where in each he is wholly possessed by a theme that is so cogent for him that it is realized integrally in a series of unique works of art, from *Dombey* onwards.

England is the country that pioneered the novel and long held the supremacy in this form of literature, so that our novels were in the eighteenth century extremely admired and imitated by the Western European countries, and in the nineteenth century were decisively formative for the classical Russian novelists. How the English novel came into existence, and so rapidly reached its full stature, is a process of real interest, and should be a concern for all of us here who, I hope, believe in the function of literature. We know that some novel traditions – the Irish, the American and the Russian – had their origins in a deliberate effort to achieve a national identity, while the French novel owed its birth, and developed, as an aristocratic society's preoccupations with the art of love and of refined social intercourse, in the specially conditioned world of the French Court; and we see it retained these characteristics – so strong is an established tradition – even after the French Revolution, as Stendhal's novels show, and Proust's, and has not essentially altered even though from the mid-nineteenth century onwards it fell into the hands first of literary theorists and then of barren Marxist intellectuals. But our English novel has a very different character and no simple account of its evolution, Marxist or otherwise, will cover the facts of its origin and development. Not only did innumerable accidents of our history combine to nourish it, but in a peculiarly English way its art was achieved pragmatically, the result of a scarcely conscious process in the novelist of trial and error in building something newly appropriate on the work inherited from *all* our forms of literature. The English novel grew by adapting literary models to new purposes, by selection and accretion, and translation from another medium – such as drama and pictorial art – in the search for forms suited for exploring the pressing problems of living. But 'search' is misleading, suggesting a deliberate procedure, whereas in fact our novelists, being peculiarly open to the influences of creativeness, were naturally drawn to what they felt to be cogent for themselves.

A tradition of major novelists implies a body of less gifted but equally serious practitioners who support the form, and looking back we see that our tradition of the novel is so rich and diversified because it includes the work of, among others, one-novel novelists like Emily Brontë and Samuel Butler, novelists who didn't even know they were writing novels or proto-novels like Bunyan and Swift, or who tried to disguise that they were, like Defoe, novelists who were amateurs like Peacock and Emily Eden and the author of *The Semi-Attached Couple* and Howard Sturgis the author of *Belchamber*, or who wrote novels as a by-product such as a professional politician like Disraeli or men of other professions like Trollope, or clergymen like Kingsley, playwrights like Fielding and Goldsmith, journalists like Dickens and Thackeray; and it has even been enriched by drawing in gifted foreigners like Henry James and Conrad. Not to mention an unbroken sequence of lady novelists, major and minor, from the eighteenth century onwards, whose work would alone be enough to set up any other country with a considerable novel tradition. And in fact, no other country can show anything so variously splendid as ours, and it was a sad day for English novelists when they began to lose their nerve and listen to the Francophile snobs who preached the inferiority of England in The Art of the Novel, even before the Bloomsbury criticasters adopted that attitude too. We can see how Arnold Bennett's best novel, *Anna of the Five Towns*, essentially a fine regional novel which in the English way is more than regional too, being a rendering and analysis of a special local variety of Victorian culture – breaks the tension, and distracts the reader's interest from the theme, at the point where the author felt obliged to insert a detailed account of the workings of a pottery in order to obey the theory of Balzac and Zola. The same misguided theory ruined George Moore as a novelist when it stopped him writing about the Anglo-Irish society he really understood and felt strongly about, and turned him into a barren aesthete and 'old imitator', a maker of dead Naturalist fictions like *Esther Waters*. Our exemplary novel tradition should be a source of pride to English people as much as is the tradition and achievement of English poetry or the Elizabethan drama. Of course, in the hour at my disposal I can only indicate some points which characterize this tradition, not give its history or even adequate attention to any one novel.

We all know that the English novel as we understand it started, apparently quite suddenly, in the middle of the eighteenth century, with Richardson and Fielding under mutual provocation, and that it somehow at once achieved distinctive form. But of course this was only possible because English literature, through poetry, drama, satire, periodical essays and the writings of English historians, and the English cultural characteristics, and qualities of the English character, had provided materials for it, in critical attitudes and moral and social preoccupations to feed such novels. Most notably, the English fully human, sympathetic and yet critical interest in *people*, already present in Chaucer and developed in our seventeenth century by the English character-writers, was adapted thence for examining real-life individuals as something more complex than types, by the historians of the Civil War and after, like Clarendon and Bishop Burnet. This tradition was extended and deepened for creative literature, and made contemporary, by Dryden, Pope and the other Augustan poets, in whose hands presentation of character was by no means merely satiric, as we see in Crabbe's poetic Tales, which are really condensed novels, recognized as such by Jane Austen as akin to her own art. What wouldn't we give to have the prose novels Crabbe wrote but which, his son tells us, he later destroyed because he felt that to publish novels was not compatible with the clerical profession! Bunyan fortunately had not thought so, though he didn't of course think of *The Pilgrim's Progress* as a novel although it is, if remotely, indebted to the language and method of the romances and the medieval quests. To his theological arguments Bunyan was impelled to add very human individual characters to discuss the problems of their pilgrimage in spirited colloquial language. Thus both the religious and the political battles of the seventeenth century were in the outcome highly profitable for the coming novelists.

But before them was the great fact of Shakespeare. His incomparable usefulness to novelists is obvious. How lucky we were! – Racine and Corneille were of no use to French novelists, and the heartless Italian comedy tradition was a positive disservice to Italian novelists. For the eighteenth-century English writer, Shakespeare offered a model for combining action, plot, dialogue and characterization in tragedy, comedy and that in-between ground that is especially the province of the English novelist. And his lesson was that these elements of a fiction must be employed in the service of a theme, a theme which is exemplified in the action. For eighteenth-century, and many subsequent, English novelists Shakespeare was inescapable as a directing force. Richardson and Fielding prove it, and Jane Austen explicitly tells us why in *Mansfield Park*, where two young men agree that

> Shakespeare one gets acquainted with without knowing how. It is part of an Englishman's constitution. One is intimate with him by instinct, and we all talk Shakespeare, use his similes, and describe with his descriptions.

Richardson shows how he was helped by this national possession of Shakespeare to make prose realism significant when he makes his anti-hero Lovelace conscious of playing the part of archetypes – of enacting the destructive duplicity of Iago as well as Satan's temptation of Eve in Milton's epic (also then a national possession like Bunyan). After the revaluation of Shakespeare initiated by the Romantic movement, Shakespeare became for our novelists the standard of the highest art, an art of dramatic poetry to which novelists also could and should aspire, so that we notice the novelist then considers himself as being in the category of 'poet'. This implied that prose fictions aspiring to greatness had somehow to find means of achieving a poetic as well as a realistic truth to life; English novelists were not going to be content merely to hold a mirror up to the life of the streets, which Stendhal considered the function of the novelist.

   We see this striving for something more than a prose realism in the language and techniques created for *Jane Eyre* and *Wuthering Heights* and *Silas Marner* and *Great Expectations*. And George Eliot, urging on her French translator the importance of preserving all the shades of her diction in *The Mill on the Floss*, from dialect to educated English speech, cites the example of Shakespeare 'and indeed of every other writer of fiction of the first class' as being 'intensely colloquial even in his loftiest tragedies'; here we see how Shakespeare is unconsciously merged with the novelists and has become *the* model for them. Again, Shakespeare's girl heroines, with their lively minds and forthright tongues, judging and acting for themselves in noble innocence but open to passion, appealed so strongly to the national taste that the type was recreated in each succeeding generation of novelists. We see it in Richardson's Charlotte Grandison and Clarissa Harlowe (interesting psychological studies in different ways), then Mrs Inchbald's Miss Milner, and from her directly to Jane Austen's Elizabeth Bennet, through the Brontë heroines and the provincial Margaret Hales and Maggie Tullivers of earlier Victorian novels to Meredith's heroines, and we see this conception of the impressively intransigent maiden continued notably in Arnold Bennett's Anna Tellwright and Mrs Humphry Ward's Laura Fountain. I'll return later to this significant factor in the English novel.

The general debt of the English novel to the English drama includes much more than that to Shakespeare. Eighteenth-century comedies, particularly *The School for Scandal* (Jane Austen delighted in the character of its Mrs Candour) overlap with eighteenth-century novels, just as Gay's *The Beggar's Opera* does with Fielding's satiric proto-novel *Jonathan Wild*, while the earlier Victorian novelists were considerably under the influence of the popular theatre of the time and found a use for some of the melodrama's conventions and techniques – they appear very obtrusively in *Mary Barton, Adam Bede, Oliver Twist*, for instance, mixing incongruously with the truly creative elements of the new novel that is struggling to free itself from such stock features of a cruder popular dramatic form; and in *Nicholas Nickleby*, Dickens can actually be seen in the process of trying to expose the ridiculous aspects of this melodrama (through the Crummles family) while at other places in the novel still under their influence enough to employ them for tragic expression. Richardson had shown, in another very English way, that a truly creative use was possible for outworn conventions when he rethought the nature of the hero of Restoration Comedy (a product of the Restoration Court). Richardson was the heir of a society that had discarded with contempt the assumptions on which Restoration Comedy depended, as *The Spectator* had noted, and with the insight of genius Richardson took the heartless, triumphant seducer who had figured as its hero and showed him as Lovelace to be a psychological case – 'loveless' – but yet as one having claims on our interest and pity since with all his talents and charm he becomes the victim of the idea on which he had formed himself and so destroys himself as well as all those involved with him.

Hogarth was another lucky accident for the rising English novelists, giving them yet another congenial model for criticizing their society, a model at once pictorial, moral and satiric, and which though realistic revealed the forces of disruption and

corruption that were at work in human nature. Hogarth's serie
were pictorial novels lacking only dialogue, a stimulus to the
imagination of many Victorian novelists as well as of the leading
eighteenth-century novelists. Hogarth's techniques for conveying
moral content indirectly, through subordinate relevant symbol
bearing on the tableaux, was a valuable addition to their ar
and their ideas about social life. We see how Dickens brilliantly
translated Hogarth's pictorial techniques into truly literary
equivalents in *Dombey and Son*, but Hogarth's world was already
reflected in *Oliver Twist* in association with a related world, that
of *The Beggar's Opera*: Gay's undermining cynicism, where
satire is directed at the overworld as much as at the underworld
that is its reflection, suggested to Dickens a vision of his own
early Victorian society as one of moral horror, both in the
daylight world of law and the lawless night-world of organized
vice and crime, a society in which innocent children are born
to be victimized or corrupted and in which the well-meaning
adult is ineffective. Thus in the various influences literary,
poetic, dramatic and pictorial, that its novelists responded to,
the English novel had from its start an essentially and profoundly
moral (I don't mean moralistic) framework and intention, and
these influences, seizing on the imagination of the novelist, did
in fact contribute to the super-realism that the English novelist
characteristically felt to be necessary.

But it was the work of the periodicals of Addison and Steele
early in the eighteenth century that were the immediate
preliminary to the launching of the novel. *The Tatler* starts
uncertainly as a mixture of political news, risqué stories and
coterie gossip for a select upper-class circle, but it quite soon
found for itself a serious function and an increasingly wider
audience, and only partly from a desire to promote the Whig
cause, whose policy was to democratize its basis. Addison and
Steele saw a corresponding extra-political function for their
paper, 'to extend the circumference of wit' – and 'wit' by now
meant civility and culture – by which they not only spread
enlightenment but also systematically extended their readership
to women, tradesmen and servants in order to raise these to the
reading-level of educated men. They thus brought into being
a national reading-public for the future novelists. Their essays
often became like chapters from the as yet unwritten novels –
dramatic scenes from domestic life, carrying out Steele and

Addison's declared ambition 'to bring the stage into the drawing-room'. The whole, very English, process is illustrated in the delightful *Tatler No. 165* which, starting off with a Theophrastian 'character' of 'the dogmatical Critick', then moves into an embodiment of a scene of drawing-room comedy with lively dialogue, where an over-bearing advocate of the neo-classical laws of drama is ridiculed, refuted and dismissed by the sprightly and intelligent young lady he is courting, a girl who in the true English spirit, and before Dr Johnson, appeals against theory to experience. This is the kind of discussion of ideas dramatically that we find characteristic of Jane Austen's novels, among many others of the eighteenth century and the Regency period, but in these novels the discussions are also functional.

We should also note a characteristic translation into acceptably English terms of Cervantes' old lunatic, Don Quixote, so that he becomes an eccentric but essentially sane upholder of true values that expose the false values of the unthinking. The 'Quixotic' character developed by the English was a man of feeling and integrity whose unworldliness may expose him in a ludicrous light to the vulgar but who shames the sinner and rebukes the proud and great: Fielding created him as Parson Adams, who was the father of Goldsmith's Vicar of Wakefield, and he appears later as a layman in the innocent philanthropical Mr Pickwick and Thackeray's Colonel Newcome. The once general English sympathy with the under-dog no doubt made for the popularity with readers of this recreation of Don Quixote, but we can see in Fielding's first real novel, *Joseph Andrews*, how such a figure emerged almost of necessity. The ex-playwright started very naturally with a comedy situation which might have come from a Restoration play, but it led nowhere, so Fielding moved into the popular picaresque mode. Evidently dissatisfied with random satire, he found he could give point to his improvizations by creating a central character who embodied his own real sense of values, thus establishing in Parson Adams a serious positive such as satire requires or must imply if it is to be more than merely destructive or frivolous. Thus Fielding set one line of the English novel – for he was admired by Thackeray, Trollope, Dickens and Henry James – on a more profitable line than any coarsely satiric goal could have done or a cynical view of human nature produced. As Boswell said of him, Fielding 'cherishes the generous affections'; but this is less a characteristic of the English novelist nowadays than it has been hitherto. Nor was the English Quixote unrealistic: the poet and parson Crabbe was a living embodiment, as his patron Lord Thurlow noticed, for after Crabbe had dined with him, the 'rough old Chancellor', Crabbe's son tells us, declared 'By God!, he was as like Parson Adams as twelve to the dozen' and promptly gave Crabbe two livings in appreciation – both of the likeness and the original.

We know that two such powerful critics as Dr Johnson and Coleridge, as well as many women novelists like Jane Austen and Mrs Oliphant, agreed in finding Richardson to be a much finer novelist than Fielding. And obviously *Clarissa*, as a highly integrated and thoughtfully-constructed work of art, on a large scale in order to convey the author's insights into the family relations of his age and the position of the individual in its social system and the sexual conflicts between man and woman, was an important advance towards the great Victorian novel. Richardson saw a rich middle class hell-bent on the social and material advancement of the family towards aristocratic status and acquisition of estates, sacrificing the happiness of its children to this ambition. To expose and indict such harmful attitudes Richardson with complete originality devised a novel that consists of three stages of increasingly disastrous but logically consecutive consequences; from a vivid picture of the Harlowe family it moves from surface realism to uncover the inner life of characters who embody the psychological drives, and the actual, not theoretic morality they variously live by. The stages consist of the three successive choices Clarissa has to make: the first is to defy the accepted duty of a daughter to submit to an arranged marriage, the second is in consequence a psychological battle between Clarissa and her lover, and the third is a choice between conventional and a higher morality. She is shown to be the victim not only of her elders' ambitions and the jealousy of her elder sister and brother, but also of her own proud self-confidence, lack of self-knowledge and innocence of the evil in human nature. In spite of the disadvantages of the epistolary form, Richardson thus provided his successors with the model of a major novel. Jane Austen carried on his work on the smaller scale and with the quieter action suited to the society she belonged to, when public opinion had considerably civilized family relations, but the massive novel which probed the assumptions behind family life and explored the difficulties for the individual members was so valuable that it was adapted for every succeeding generation, as we can see in *Mansfield Park*, *David Copperfield*, *Little Dorrit*, *Middlemarch*, *Clayhanger*, *The Rainbow* and *Women in Love*, while a novel like *The Forsyte Saga* is a desiccated, do-it-yourself version of this model, and Conrad's *Nostromo* a magnificent extension of it for examining the social and moral and psychological complexities of a multi-national country.

This abandoning of the Continental picaresque form for a sociological unit of some kind was a great gain artistically. The new English model allowed a concentration of purpose, consistency of tone, and increasing tension. Already in the opening of *Our Village*, Miss Mitford writes of the choice of such a microcosm – 'a little world of our own, close-packed and insulated like ants in an ant-hill, or bees in a hive, or sheep in a fold, or nuns in a convent, or sailors in a ship', and goes on to specify her contemporary Jane Austen's success with such a community, 'a country village'.

It seems to me much more satisfactory, in its truth to life and its scope, than the novel of ideas which is so popular on the Continent and is now admired and imitated over here. For the ideas in *our* best novels arise naturally from a sensitive open-minded exploration of the fully human world and from a sustained creative effort in which the important parts of the novelist's experience of life are drawn on, so that he arrives at his conclusions without, as Lawrence would say, putting his finger on one side of the scales. A rare English novel like *Jude the Obscure* we find unsatisfactory, and perhaps feel to be 'unEnglish', because of its obtrusive skeleton, barely fleshed over, and its distortion of life in the interests of an arbitrary philosophy. It is rigidity, not openness; whereas the tradition exemplified by the major English practitioners is more in the nature of a spiritual exercise for both novelist and reader. This is why Dickens, his friend Forster tells us, 'believed himself to be entitled to a higher tribute than he was always in the habit of receiving'. One could not say of our classical novels what Henry James said with justice of Balzac's *oeuvre*, that however many heroes and heroines there are in the novels that constitute his *Comédie Humaine* 'the great general protagonist is the twenty-franc piece'. Even in our Victorian novels, which are concerned with a society in which money and property were of great importance, the novelists show that man does not live by bread alone, as Trollope registers in chapter 8 of *The Warden* where we visit the Archdeacon's rectory with its opulent comfort but where, the novelist says, something is lacking that matters. Trollope said later: 'My Archdeacon was the simple result of my moral consciousness'. And very much in this English novel's tradition is the mill-owner hero of Charlotte Brontë's *Shirley* who finally arrives at self-knowledge and admits that:

Something there is to look to beyond a man's personal interest, beyond the advancement of well-laid schemes. To respect himself, a man must believe he renders justice to his fellow-men.

He does not mean only what is now called social justice.

Thus oriented, English novelists didn't reduce life in the interests of an aesthetic concept of the novel either. Lawrence was really voicing an instinctive national preference when he wrote of the Continental worship of Flaubert and Mann as being a craving for logic in its aesthetic form, and drew a distinction between such writers and 'the more human artists like Shakespeare who must give themselves to life as well as to art'. Whereas the other kind suffer, Lawrence says, from the disease of Flaubert 'who stood away from life as from a leprosy'. It is this English preference that made Charlotte Brontë reject G. H. Lewes's claim for Jane Austen to be 'a *great* artist', describing *Pride and Prejudice* and *Emma* as 'more real than true', meaning that though they are realistic they do not convey the whole experience of living. They ignore, she complained, in a formula Lawrence might have supplied, 'what throbs fast and full, though hidden, what the blood rushes through, what is the unseen seat of life and the sentient target of death'. Jane Austen does not, she says, 'with her mind's eye behold the heart of her race'. We probably feel that Jane Austen in *Mansfield Park* (which Charlotte Brontë had not read) *does* behold the heart of her race in that generation, the Regency world, and that it was really her pre-Romantic style that the heirs of Byron and Wordsworth found deficient. The mind's eye with X-ray powers, and a profound sense of obligation to humanity, was present in the English novel from Richardson onwards. Dr Johnson said he preferred Richardson to Fielding because the former understands how a watch is made, while the latter can only look at the dial-plate and tell you the time. And this demand on creative writers for inwardness, understanding, and the Shakespearian 'fullness of life', accounts for the English novel-reader's suspicion of the doctrinaire in politics and religion. It has fortunately made English literature immune in the long run to seminarism and political dogmatisms, as witness the failure of either Marxism or Fascism to take root here or father novels of any merit and the fact that the novels of Graham Greene and Evelyn Waugh are not taken as seriously here as they and their like are on the Continent.

But the surviving eighteenth- and nineteenth-century English novels of religious experience are different. They do not proceed from religious absolutists but show the virtues of a candid testing of the value, the strength and the weaknesses, of a religious culture as it actually existed. Thus Mrs Inchbald's pioneer novel of this kind, *A Simple Story* (1791), which was widely known and admired for a century at least, though written by a good Catholic from an Old Catholic family is notably different from the novels of our Catholic converts of recent times. Mrs Inchbald set herself to enquire, by means proper to the novel, what were the differences between the character typically produced by a Protestant and a Catholic education, what the qualities of mind and feeling, what attitudes that promote or threaten happiness. This was clearly a matter of concern to herself, as a Catholic living in a Protestant society. Through dramatic action and dialogue, with very little authorial comment and that impartial, she shows these differences as they were expressed in actions, conversation, and reactions to the difficulties of living, especially in the crucial tests of love and marriage. Even Charlotte Brontë, from an Evangelical parsonage, with an Ulster Protestant father, and brought up with the anti-Catholic suspicions of her time, prejudices moreover that were exacerbated by her experience of a Belgian school for the daughters of the rich, shows herself in *Villette* (1853) holding a similar balance between the Puritanical Lucy Snowe and her Jesuit-trained Continental teacher and lover, these antagonists chosen of course as the extreme examples of the Protestant and Catholic product respectively. At the end of the century Mrs Humphry Ward's one fine novel, *Helbeck of Bannisdale*, was founded in her experience of a home bitterly divided between an unstable father (brother of Matthew Arnold) who was converted to Catholicism some years after his marriage, and a mother with Huguenot traditions and thus an hereditary horror of the Catholic Church. Nevertheless, *Helbeck* is an exploratory novel which ends inevitably in tragedy for both the leading characters, a profound and moving work of art. And it is not autobiographical: the heroine is not Mary Ward nor in her position, though Laura's situation is founded, as the novelist said, on her own mother's, that of one who while passionately loving a devout Catholic, abhors Romanism with an inherited moral repulsion. The hero and heroine are firmly placed in the conflicting traditions that had shaped them, as were Mrs Inchbald's and Charlotte Brontë's characters, and Mrs Ward managed to achieve such imaginative impartiality that, as her husband had predicted, some readers thought the novel pro-Catholic.

And thanks to this English tradition of distaste for bigotry, the successive waves of religious conflicts registered abundantly in nineteenth-century fiction, though often initially acrimonious by partisans or opponents of, in turn, Evangelicals, Tractarians, Roman Catholics, Anglican ritualists, Neologists and subsequently the scientist rationalists, soon settled down into a controlled and objective treatment that contributed a most valuable extension to the seriousness and scope of the English novel, an extension comparable to that effected by early Victorian novelists who had to find forms in which the new industrial society could be examined and which had already enriched English literature with *Sybil*, *Shirley*, *Hard Times*, *Mary Barton* and *North and South*, *Alton Locke*, and subsequently with novels like Gissing's *The Nether World* and Arnold Bennett's novels based on the Five Towns. Without having behind her these novels of religious controversy, George Eliot would hardly have opened *Middlemarch* with a symbolic first chapter in which she shows how an Evangelical education had caused Dorothea Brooke (as in youth George Eliot herself) to mistake her own needs and nature, with disastrous results. But the novelist also gives full credit to Evangelicalism for the social conscience it very generally stimulated and which makes Miss Brooke's life useful beyond the conventional young lady's, and fortifies her in enduring her misguided first marriage. *Tess of the D'Urbervilles* seems a most unlikely setting for a similar exploration of an

Evangelical upbringing, but we see that Angel Clare's conditioning by, in spite of his reaction against, his parsonage home
is the prime cause of the tragedy, though in the English tradition
Hardy credits Angel Clare's parents with their virtues of sincerity
and consistency and shows them to advantage compared with the
next religious phase represented by their unattractive High
Church parson sons and Ritualist daughter-in-law, Mercy
Chant. Butler's *The Way of All Flesh* is a cynical, and in its
conclusion advocating an irresponsible hedonism, a superficial
novel of the same type; but a more interesting development from
the novels of religious controversy is Gissing's *Born in Exile*,
where the social criticism is inseparable from criticism of the
Victorian Established Church. The dead conventions of this
religion are exposed as a snobbery of class attitudes buttressed
by a religious conservatism from which any real religious beliefs
have evaporated and so inevitably challenged by the new
religion of scientific scepticism. While the latter is the only
alternative open to Godwin Peak, a gifted scientist and intellectual whom poverty has condemned to drudgery in a chemical
works and his low birth to loneliness and frustration, the creed
of the scientific circle of 'advanced' thinkers he frequents is
inadequate to his human needs, in spite of his attempts to
suppress these needs in obedience to the rationalism he wishes
to endorse. Here the traditional function of our major novelists
is seen in operation, just as in a later novel, *Helbeck of Bannisdale*,
the conflict in Laura Fountain between passion and integrity
is pursued to its inevitably tragic conclusion because of the
impossibility of resolving, in the novelist's words,

the sharp clash between the reviving strength of passion...and those
facts of character and individuality which held them [the lovers]
separated – facts which are always, and in all cases, the true facts of
this world.

This is the wisdom that all our best novelists have manifested
in the long tradition back to *Clarissa* – they first explore to find
'the true facts of this world' and then face them to enable the
reader to draw the necessary conclusions.

And this tradition of radical and responsible enquiry into the
human condition, its problems being recognized to be both
moral and psychological, has focused on what one can only
think of as the Protestant heroine – even if, like Laura Fountain,

she represents the extreme of Protestantism as a duty to question and doubt in the interests of Truth and rejects Religion itself as the enemy. These heroines or protagonists are high-minded young women who with dauntless courage act upon the findings of the individual conscience. Thus Anna Tellwright braves her terrifying father and destroys the cheque he intends to use to ruin a wretched debtor, who has been driven to forge it as a temporary measure to stave off disaster, because she feels herself indirectly responsible and that it is therefore right to do so and necessary. And Fanny Price, Margaret Hale, Little Dorrit, Clarissa, Jane Eyre, Dorothea Brooke, Laura Fountain and innumerable other such girls (perhaps Scott's Jeanie Deans is the best of all such examples) though modest, sensitive and domesticated, are in any crisis prepared to act in defiance of the conventions of their society if their sense of what is just prompts them to do so. This is a very different conception of virtue from what we find in Continental girl heroines of esteemed novels of the same periods, for instance *I Promessi Sposi* or *Eugénie Grandet*, and suggests that the English novel owes more than anything else to the fact that it has traditionally been the product of an essentially Protestant culture. Whereas the Latin heroines were characteristically required to be morally docile and blindly obedient to authority, the English heroines were expected to examine and test, not merely keep to, the rules – they are bravely heretical. The only exceptions I know are in the novels of Catholic propagandists such as Josephine Ward, whose career as a novelist exactly coincided with the part of Mrs Humphry Ward's that produced *Helbeck*. Josephine Ward, wife of Wilfrid Ward the Catholic publicist, wrote independently a novel, *One Poor Scruple*, published the year after *Helbeck* and hailed by the *Dublin Review* as a counterblast, which it is a critical exercise to compare with *Helbeck*, of which it is unconsciously a mirror-image; in fact it unwittingly makes the points advanced in *Helbeck*, and confirms the argument of Dean Milman when he reviewed Newman's *Essay on Development*, that the glories of English literature are innately Protestant in character. Mauriac in *Le Baiser au Lépreux* attributes to the religious conditioning of the heroine her resigned acceptance of the disgusting marriage arranged for her by her curé and her parents, which condemns her to a life of martyrdom. Surely it is the positive moral life and sense of personal responsibility that gives the significance and interest to the histories of the heroines of the English novels and is something we miss in classical French novels and in all Italian novels, where we feel that the absence of a sense of true moral responsibility is a disability. But Stendhal noted this favourably, directing his irony at the Protestant conscience in his brilliantly witty novel *La Chartreuse de Parme* whose heroine, the charming Duchess of San Severina, having inspired the murder by poison of the reigning monarch because he had imprisoned her beloved nephew, learns that her nephew is in prison again and about to be poisoned by the prison governor. Stendhal comments:

She didn't make this moral reflection, which could not have escaped any woman brought up in one of those Northern religions, which require self-scrutiny, the thought 'I employed poison first, and I shall perish by it'. In Italy [Stendhal continues] this sort of reflection, in moments of passionate feeling, would seem very poor-spirited.

But not to be subject to self-scrutiny in such circumstances is surely to be sub-human, and the fact that such a situation would have been impossible for an English novelist (in the past) to record admiringly is one proof that our novelists had a more mature and civilized tradition to work in. Or once had, for the decay of the traditional culture that we have witnessed has meant the withdrawal from moral responsibility of novelists – we see a parody of it in the novels of Graham Greene or *Brideshead Revisited* – and a consequent lapse of the novel into triviality or, in the cases of novelists like Greene and Waugh, spiritual pedantry.

If we look at Greene's novels and compare them with Conrad's – and, apart from showing the influence of Somerset Maugham, Greene owes everything to the Conrad of *The Secret Agent*, *Heart of Darkness*, *Nostromo* and the related tales and novels – we can't help seeing that the relation is parasitic: Greene, whether he thinks he is writing a serious novel or only an 'entertainment', merely writes an undistinguished thriller with detective or shocker interest (as in *The Human Factor*), very often using an exotic background, evidently from his notebooks, which has no integral relation with the novelistic substance, nor that with the alleged moral interest which remains invariably a matter of interspersed doctrinal points and is never convincing as spiritual experience. A fair example of his method is *A Burnt-Out Case*, where the extensive account of a leper centre has nothing to do with the trivial magazine-story of the French couple and the protagonist's farcical involvement with them; it is intended to be justified by a parallel suggested between the physical 'burnt-out' condition in leprosy and the spiritual state of the leading character, but remains only a bright idea. Where there is no exotic setting to distract the reader's attention, as in *The End of the Affair*, the triviality of the intrigue and the arbitrary nature of the theological mix-in is inescapable. Greene's novels are of course 'popular' in a sense Conrad's never were or could be, and are easier to read than Conrad because there is neither subtlety or real thought nor the complexity that integration demands. This difference between a major creative writer and 'an old imitator' shamelessly exploiting sleight-of-hand illustrates the kind of decay of the English novel that I mean. And the difference between a journalist's travel-notebook account of a country and the response to it of a true creative mind, sensitive and concerned to understand and profoundly moved by the whole culture of a country is evident if one compares Greene's use of an African (or any other) setting with a genuine first-hand document like Karen Blixen's *Out of Africa* or Carlo Levi's *Christ Stopped at Eboli*. Conrad was for a very short time in South America, but his great novel *Nostromo* is remarkable, I was told, for the understanding of the history and peoples of those countries, an imaginative feat. Cunninghame Graham, an authority, wrote that this novel 'forms an epic of S. America, written by one who saw it to the core by intuition'.

The consistency of English traditions must be due to another English asset, the early unification of the country without this meaning a tyranny of capital and Court as in France and yet escaping the disadvantages of late unification which was the fate of Germany and Italy – if indeed Italy can be considered to have been unified at all culturally, since the hostility of the regions to the capital Rome has meant that all good Italian novels are regional novels. England enjoyed an early development of a truly national literature – Chaucer is already recognizably an Englishman – of which regional cultures were variations, but they were not mutually incomprehensible nor, as in many European countries, divided by hostile traditions of religion, government or language. And the mobility of English classes from the end of the Middle Ages has meant a more open and interpenetrated society here than the stratified class structure of the Continent, and thus a more fertile scene socially for the English novelist. The traditional English life of the countryside, one of great house, parsonage, chapel, schoolhouse, farm and cottage united in a local culture and centring economically on the market-town and spiritually on the cathedral close, made for mutual knowledge and accommodation. George Sand, Balzac and Tolstoy all admitted that they really had no knowledge of what went on in the mind of the French or Russian peasant about whom they nevertheless undertook to write novels; but in novels like *Wuthering Heights* and *Adam Bede* and *Silas Marner* and Hardy's Wessex novels and Adrian Bell's Suffolk ones, we see that English authors were not cut off by education or class from the life of farmhouse and cottage, and that they were able to appreciate the special quality of such lives without idealizing them.

Closely bearing on the emergence of such novels, or such elements in a great many English novels, is the fact of our having an equally rich related literature in the form of autobiography. Not the egocentric literary kind like Goethe's and Rousseau's, but the personal histories that are records of a local life that shaped their writers. These sometimes merge into fiction as autobiographical novels, but even without plot or romance they show the English gift for recapturing the formative experiences of childhood – something that has been an important element in the English novel – and the English attachment to and understanding of a locality. I am thinking of such examples as Bewick's recording of his eighteenth-century Northumberland in his *Memoirs*, Cobbett's and Richard Jefferies' and George Sturt's books on their Southern England, Miss Mitford's Berkshire in *Our Village*, Alison Uttley's Derbyshire farmhouse childhood recorded in *The Country Child*, Cecil Torr's Devonshire squire's family memoirs, *Small Talk at Wreyland*, Percy Lubbock's tribute, *Earlham*, to a blissful childhood centring on a Norfolk great house and its Evangelical family, Gordon Russell on what it meant to a boy to grow up in a Cotswold village full of craftsmen in *Designer's Trade*, Flora Thompson's cottage childhood in an Oxfordshire village recorded in *Lark Rise*, Adrian Bell's essays and books about Suffolk life and character as he had known them as farmer and neighbour. Additionally, there are the innumerable eighteenth-century, Regency, Victorian and Edwardian autobiographies and memoirs from people of all classes, a positive personal literature of social history of town and country, when every town had its own character. These writings I've mentioned and the vast number of the kind I haven't, which reveal the hinterland of the English novel, show how naturally it came to the English to write from their roots, and with that 'fullness of life' that Lawrence thought the mark of a great novelist. Both Henry James and Hawthorne complained of the deprivations from which American novelists suffered in not having any comparable culture to draw on, and indeed one sees this in the pitiful thinness of *The House with the Seven Gables*, for instance, if compared with even the least of Hardy's Wessex novels.

What strikes me with apprehension for the future of the English novel is how diminished the tradition has become in the hands of the most well-known practitioners of this age, who have uncritically been accepted as classics – as well as how commercialized: novelists like (and there are many like) C. P. Snow, Kingsley Amis, Anthony Powell, Iris Murdoch, etc. One first noticed this shrinking in the acclaimed novels of the preceding period, in the novels of Norman Douglas and David Garnett and Aldous Huxley and in the pre-War novels of E. M. Forster, even in Virginia Woolf's, from all of which the novels of D. H. Lawrence, T. F. Powys, and Conrad, for instance, stood apart. I can't believe any of Virginia Woolf's even will survive except as literary curiosities, apart from *To the Lighthouse* – this is the only one she wrote from her roots, and with sympathetic understanding of the relationships that con- stitute living, because she was expressing the experience of living in her special variety of Victorian family and its basic relations of mother and child, husband and wife, father and son, and between friends – man and man and woman and woman. Even so, these things were better done in the Garth family and their circle in *Middlemarch* and the Grantleys in Trollope's Barsetshire novels, where these relations are more intimately known and better presented as critical appreciations of Victorian marriage and family life. The attenuation was the price the Bloomsbury novelists had to pay for belonging to a mutual admiration clique and for their cult of moral and sexual irresponsibility. The world of Lytton Strachey round whom it circulated and whose ethos they shared was in essence a very inferior, self-indulgent caste society, as the many biographies, autobiographies, journals, letters and memoirs, that have long been appearing for an avidly voyeuristic public, prove. The pervasive irony, common to the literary members of the group, was merely self-protective and an assertion of superiority: it is a give-away, even in Forster's best novel *A Passage to India*. There is all the difference in the world between their petty irony and the irony of eighteenth- and nineteenth-century English literature, or the genuinely intellectual irony, a responsible irony, that characterises Randall Jarrell's witty, but essentially serious and feeling novel *Pictures from an Institution*, where irony is a means of exploring the American cultural scene of his time (mid-twentieth century), of exposing the assumptions in education and the practice of the arts (especially literature) of the progressive American university, by examining the representative campus culture it foisted on the nation. This has now spread to England, of course, but compare Jarrell's novel with *our* 'university novels', which are irresponsible and advance no argument, such as Kingsley Amis's *Lucky Jim* (which astonishingly made him an immediate reputation but is surely only a puerile scenario for a cinema-type farce) which has had many imitators in our younger novelists. Though he has gone from bad to worse, Eng. Lit. academics write respectful articles on Amis's novels and Amis has become, significantly, an Establishment figure.

Jarrell's concern was that of a true novelist – to understand and discriminate; he feels a genuine sympathy for his characters, who are shown to be naïve victims of the misguided theories accepted by the educated American class and who are placed by him by being seen also through the eyes of a distinguished European couple, refugee musicians, whose firmly held values are proofs that there existed in Europe a traditional, creatively fruitful, culture and intellectual discipline, that had supported them. For Jarrell was really anxious to answer the question that most concerned him as a frustrated poet and a literary critic – one in which, considering the present state of the English novel, *we* should be interested too. He wanted to know what conditions sustain the arts, and why his rich, powerful, democratic country was so inferior in this respect to even small and poor European monarchies which had in the past abundantly produced creative masters and still did, and publics to support their artists. The conclusion that Jarrell comes to is that there is no real critical American public and so in the cultural conditions shown in his novel, the creative talents are forced into destructive forms. Of his typical American woman novelist (an amalgam of three contemporary such) he notes:

She did not know – or rather, did not believe – what it was like to be a human being...and her worse self distrusted her better too thoroughly to give it much share, ever, in what she wrote.

'So because of this', he explains, 'even the best of Gertrude's novels were habitat groups in a Museum of Natural History... inside them were old newspapers, papier-mâché, clockwork.' Yet, Jarrell notes, 'it was a fairly popular' version of the world. We now have such novelists in England too, and they also are popular. Worse, they are accepted as major novelists by the intelligentsia – novelists for instance like Angus Wilson and Anthony Burgess.

For this is how our most acclaimed novels affect one now, even when their content is, like that of Gertrude's novels, scandalous. They deal with artificial worlds, inhabited by cardboard characters whose behaviour is arbitrary, so one forgets each novel immediately after reading it. But one doesn't forget Solzhenitsyn's novels, or *Dr Zhivago*, perhaps because the hinterland of *The First Circle* and *Cancer Ward* is in writings like *The Gulag Archipelago*, Marchenko's *My Testimony*, Shostakovich's *Testimony*, Nadezhda Mandelstam's *Hope Against Hope* and *Hope Abandoned*, and all the other first-hand Russian records of their terrible experiences since 1917 – moral and emotional ordeals even more than physical sufferings, and which show that, having survived them, these men and women have emerged not less but more fully human beings than the comfortably placed beneficiaries of a Welfare State with 'a rising standard of living'. These Russians writers, in spite of all their suffering, give us hope for the indomitable human spirit's survival. Perhaps this is a general definition of a great novelist, in whom moral courage is a necessary constituent. Our novelists seem to have abdicated from moral responsibility, to have become sub-human. I notice this particularly, and with sadness, in the output of women novelists of our present and recent past. They seem to be universally determined, forgoing their heritage as English novelists, to belong to an international women writer's movement, a movement characterized by a jargon that is the opposite of wisdom or maturity. Judging from a current publisher's catalogue, women novelists are now invariably committed to 'the search for identity', 'sexual fulfilment', a 'need for connection and commitment' and 'a search for her primitive self', with demonstrating 'love–hate relationships' and 'the varieties of sexuality' open to women. It's true that many of the women novelists in this catalogue appear to be either American or what used to be called colonials, but the English women's novels seem to be written to the same formulae.

This seems to mark the end of our great tradition of women novelists, unique formerly, whether major or minor. Women's Lib. and Progressive education and popular psychology, with their brave new slogans, seem to have produced simply an up-to-date variety of women's magazine fiction, which is where I should place the novels of Margaret Drabble, Pamela Hansford Johnson, Olivia Manning, to take a few outstanding examples, though they are at least superior to the railway-bookstall fictions of novelists like John Fowles which now command an educated public. It seems odd that the dreadful problems that face our run-down Britain have not inspired novelists, particularly women novelists, to rise above this preoccupation with their egos. In contrast, the great depression of half a century ago did. It produced, for instance, a minor novel by a woman (Ruth Adam) I admire very much, called *I'm Not Complaining*, which I reviewed in *Scrutiny* when it came out and have found memorable for, among other things, its abnegation. Its title is an index to its writer's attitude, as a supply teacher of considerable experience in slum schools.

The England that bore the classical English novel has gone forever, and we can't expect a country of high-rise flat-dwellers, office workers and factory robots and unassimilated multi-racial minorities, with a suburbanized countryside, factory farming, sexual emancipation without responsibility, rising crime and violence, and the Trade Union mentality, to give rise to a literature comparable with its novel tradition of a so different past. Rescuing the individual from the family is no longer a concern, the problem is to find any stable family life for the individual to develop full humanity in. But though this may account for, it does not excuse, the stream of novels with pretensions to being more than commercial enterprises which admire the brutally selfish, and anti-social man or, like the new women novelists, glorify the untrammelled female egotist, or, like Kingsley Amis's, inculcate 'militant philistinism'. These represent a complete rejection of the English tradition. A once representative Englishman as well as eminent literary figure, the robust and unsentimental Dr Johnson, declared that 'want of tenderness is want of parts, and no less a proof of stupidity than depravity'. A century later George Eliot described in her novels something she indicted there as 'moral stupidity'. And Dr Johnson passed another judgment which has implications for the novelist when he said: 'The French writers are superficial because they proceed upon the mere power of their own minds.'

George Eliot was the antithesis of Jarrell's Gertrude Johnson in being a mature and fertile creative writer, each of whose novels is unique and memorable. Her view of the novelist's function is therefore worth considering. Fortunately for us she was more introspective and articulate about her work than most English novelists. She wrote:

My books are deeply serious things to me, and come out of all the painful discipline, all the most hardly-learnt lessons of my past life,

and she wrote of 'the high responsibilities of literature that undertakes to represent life'. She perceived that though a novel must start from within, rooted in experience, it must find exposition in the form uniquely suited to its theme, and so becomes an impersonal creation.

When a subject has begun to grow in me, I suffer terribly until it has wrought itself out – become a complete organism; and then it seems to take wing and go away from me. *That* thing is not to be done again, that life has been lived.

She said she believed that 'aesthetic teaching is the highest of all teaching, because it deals with life in its highest complexity'. 'But', she added, 'if it ceases to be purely aesthetic – if it lapses anywhere from the picture to the diagram – it becomes the most offensive of all teaching.' She is here bearing testimony to the fact that a novel must be a responsible work of art and engage the real and whole human experience of its author, focused in a 'representation of life', not a diagram that, in Dr Johnson's words, 'proceeds upon the mere power of the mind'.

These views of George Eliot's on the art of the novel really do represent the best English practice of the past. They may now seem impractically high-minded. It should therefore be

remembered that George Eliot also wrote for money, which she
badly needed, and in a period when there were a great number
of competing novelists; and that in spite of her high ideals she
was able to make a considerable fortune from her novels, which
are demanding reading even now, and made it without in the
slightest respect compromising her integrity by yielding to
pressures or criticism from her publishers, and that her most
difficult novel, *Middlemarch*, sold the most, with large sales in its
cheapest edition for the masses. This is greatly to her credit, and
surely tells us also a good deal about the England and its
reading-public that enriched her, that is to *their* credit. On this
note from a happier state of the English novel I will end.

Appendix: Dating *Jane Eyre*

When Jane Eyre tells us at the end of her book that she has now been married for ten years and, knowing she married in her twentieth year, we therefore deduce that she is writing her autobiography at more or less the same age as Charlotte Brontë was when starting to write her novel about Jane Eyre in 1846 – we naturally tend to identify the two young women; at least to the extent of assuming that Charlotte and Jane were coeval, contemporary. But in spite of appearances, and some supporting evidence, this cannot be so. For we have one firm date. In chapter 32 St John Rivers kindly brings a copy of *Marmion* to divert the new schoolmistress of his parish. She describes it as a *new* publication: 'he laid on the table a new publication – a poem: one of those genuine productions so often vouchsafed to the fortunate public of those days – the golden age of modern literature. Alas! the readers of our era are less favoured.' It is significant that Miss Brontë should consider the age of Scott's poetry, the first Romantic period, to be the Golden Age of literature; and natural, for the Brontës were the heirs of the first generation of the Romantics even more than of Byron, and particularly delighted in Scott, whose hills and moors lent theirs rich associations.

But *Marmion* was published in 1808, and this date surely makes us pause. One had naturally assumed that *Jane Eyre* ended in time when it was published (1847), or at least when it started being written, the year before. But in that case Jane Eyre would have arrived at Morton schoolhouse in 1835 or 1836, whereas no, that was in 1808 it appears. Yet the year before Jane was at Thornfield, where Miss Ingram expressed her admiration for Corsairs and other Byronic heroes of that order, whom she could not have known of in 1807 since *The Corsair* was not published till seven years later. And there are other things wrong with the dating too. The year Jane was first at Thornfield (1807 if we date the Morton episode by *Marmion*) Mr Rochester had told Jane the story of his life ending: 'Ten years since, I flew through Europe half mad; with disgust, hate and rage as my companions', etc. This tour then was started in 1797. But Mr Rochester was plagiarizing Childe Harold, who did not leave our shores to tour Europe in this spirit till 1816. Again, if we accept *Marmion* as just out when Jane opened it, her autobiography ends in 1819. Charlotte Brontë herself was not born till 1816 and the Lowood episode in the novel at least is historic, that is, the events described in it are factually what happened to Charlotte and her eldest sister, the unfortunate Maria (the 'Helen Burns' of the novel), in 1825, whereas Jane Eyre apparently left Gateshead for Lowood school in 1799.

This therefore leads us to the interesting, the baffling question: When is the novel *Jane Eyre* supposed to have taken place? One needs to know because of having to decide who are the 'less favoured readers of our era'. Which era? The readers of 1819 or the readers of 1847? (We are unlikely now to think of the readers of either era as in need of sympathy but it would be nice to know which Charlotte Brontë thought were.) And why did she attempt to back-date the novel? In order to dissociate herself from it? One reason may suggest itself at once to those familiar with Mrs Gaskell's *Life of Charlotte Brontë*. If Jane Eyre went to Lowood at the end of the eighteenth century, as she must have done if she was at Morton in 1808 aged nearly nineteen, obviously Lowood could not be Cowan Bridge school, which was not founded till 1823, and Jane Eyre's (or Currer Bell's) account of Lowood and its founder, the Reverend Mr Brockle-hurst, might be (and indeed, to Mrs Gaskell's embarrassment, was indignantly said to be when the *Life* appeared) libellous. But in fact Charlotte Brontë had no reason to cover her tracks by back-dating, for she never expected anyone would identify Lowood and its founder with Cowan Bridge school and the Reverend Carus Wilson; she told Mrs Gaskell that she would never have so written if she had thought such a thing likely. Alternatively, Charlotte was delighted when Lowood *was* identified, writing to her publisher at the beginning of 1848 that she had seen a clergyman reading *Jane Eyre* and 'I wondered whether he would recognize the portraits, and was gratified to find that he did, and that, moreover, he pronounced them faithful and just. He said, too, that Mr (Brocklehurst) "deserved the chastisement he had got".' These two reactions to the identification of 'Lowood' may be conflicting (how curious human nature is, even in a scrupulously truthful woman like Charlotte Brontë!), but neither is a reason for her fixing her experiences at Cowan Bridge school a generation before they occurred.

If it were merely back-dating, Charlotte Brontë might be said to be illustrating the general tendency of Victorian novelists to set their work in the past. Thus Emily Brontë tells us that *Wuthering Heights* ends at the beginning of the nineteenth century, though it feels Early Victorian to me at Thrushcross Grange; and *Shirley*, which was intended by Charlotte to incarnate her sister Emily, is placed historically during Luddite riots before the end of the Napoleonic Wars (though even so Charlotte's intelligent friend Mary Taylor complained that the actual riot used occurred not during the wars but in 1820). But the back-dating of *Jane Eyre*, as I have shown, is not consistent and seems purposeless. The female Brocklehursts are a striking anachronism, whether they irrupted into the Lowood school-room in 1825 (when Charlotte was at school) or, even worse, in 1799 (when Jane Eyre was). In their shameless discrepancy between theory and practice – all right for them to have their hair elaborately curled, but the orphans' naturally curly hair must be cropped as sinful – they clearly belonged to the Victorian phase of Evangelicalism when, as G. M. Young notes in *Victorian England*, the Evangelicals' work was done in so far as they had had something worth doing and they had 'grown complacent, fashionable, superior'. In the earlier period, when *Middlemarch* takes place, we are quite correctly informed by Mrs Plymdale that her friend Mrs Bulstrode, the wealthy banker's wife who is the leading Evangelical in the town, 'wears very neat patterns always. And that feather I know she got dyed a pale lavender on purpose to be consistent.' (Lavender being a shade of conventional mourning and therefore not a 'colour'.) This is a different generation of Evangelicals from the Brocklehurst ladies who wear 'shot orange and purple silk pelisses'; and they are justly dated by their fashionable dress, for shot silk, so far as I can make out, was an invention of the late 1830s and not in use till after Victoria came to the throne. Consistency, so essential in the eyes of all Evangelicals of the pre-Victorian era,

is in Mr Brocklehurst's mouth a parody of the original ideal and
practice. It had evaporated with the earlier fervency by Victorian
times, but professedly Evangelical ladies could not have flouted
the strong feeling for consistency in dress a generation earlier.
Mrs Brocklehurst seems contemporary with Mrs Proudie's type,
for whom 'Dissipation and low dresses during the week are,
under her control, atoned for by three services, an evening
sermon read by herself, and a perfect abstinence from any
cheering employment on the Sunday' (*Barchester Towers*). In
fact, Charlotte Brontë did not play fair as regards the family
of the Reverend Carus Wilson – if he had one at all, for though
we are repeatedly told how widely Yorkshire readers of *Jane Eyre*
recognized the originals of Mr Brocklehurst and all the Lowood
teachers, we never hear of anyone specifying Mrs and the Misses
Brocklehurst as drawn from life.

   The general confusion of dates, eras, fashions and facts in *Jane
Eyre* is even more irrational than anything Dickens allowed
himself, suggesting the timeless world of the myth and the
daydream. And it is, very strangely, the opposite of her sister's
practice in *Wuthering Heights*, where every date and fact coheres
perfectly and stands up to the strictest scrutiny of the legal mind
(as witness *The Structure of Wuthering Heights*, by C. P. Sanger,
a Hogarth Press pamphlet). I say strangely because, though no
one seems to notice it, the two sisters used the same myth to
launch their first published novels. At both Wuthering Heights
and Gateshead the trouble is caused by the master bringing
home an orphan whom he insists on cherishing in spite of the
resentment of his wife and children, fostering their jealousy by
preferring the cuckoo in the nest to his own children, so that
after his death the child (Jane, Heathcliff) is ill-used by them
and driven out into a hostile world. Yet the novel that is full
of real-life experiences of its author is not realized in time,
whereas the other, which so far as one can tell contains no
personal experiences, is carefully actualized. This seems to tell
us something about a radical difference between the two sisters.

   A mistake, or refusal to recognize the facts of life in *Jane Eyre*,
which certainly would not have occurred in Emily's novel is
Jane's division of her inheritance between herself and her three
Rivers cousins. She inherited their uncle's property in her
nineteenth year, it seems, and after sharing out the fortune she
goes off the following year to find and marry Mr Rochester, still

well under twenty-one. Of course she could not legally have done anything so serious and irrevocable as signing away three-quarters of her property till she was of age. This does not matter unless one thinks one is reading realism and not fairy-story at this point.

It remains to be said that probably no reader of *Jane Eyre* ever notices these anomalies until after repeated readings, if then, such are the charm and power of the novel and the imparted belief in her creation of the novelist.

Notes

A glance backward, 1965

1 In fact the book was re-issued as a hardback by Chatto in 1965 (reprinted in 1968 and 1978) and appeared as a Peregrine paperback with Penguin Books in 1979.
2 Raymond Williams, *Culture and Society 1780–1850* (1958); Richard Hoggart, *The Uses of Literacy* (1957).
3 'Professor Chadwick and English Studies', *Scrutiny*, XIV (1947).
4 *Scrutiny*, VII (1939).
5 Both introductions are now included in the Penguin English Library *Jane Eyre* and *Silas Marner*, edited by Q. D. Leavis in 1966 and 1967 respectively.

Jane Austen: novelist of a changing society

1 See *Belinda* (1801) where the leader of fashion, Lady Delacour, had been persuaded to this because 'it was the fashion for fine mothers to suckle their own children: so much the worse for the poor brats. Fine nurses never made fine children.' Her son died at three months old – 'If I had put it out to nurse, I should have been thought an unnatural mother, but I should have saved its life... I determined that if I ever had another child, I would not have the barbarity to nurse it myself... when my girl was born, I sent if off immediately to the country, to a stout, healthy, broad-faced nurse, under whose care it flourished... at three years old it was brought back to me.' This is the theory on which the Austen children were reared, but, unlike Maria Edgeworth, Jane Austen welcomed its passing, another sign of her sympathy with the movements in her lifetime regarding family life. By 1858, when *Dr Thorne* was published, though some great ladies were still persistently not nursing their own babies, Trollope felt he had public opinion with him enough to castigate this unnatural conduct. In an unusually outspoken passage he wrote: 'They are gifted with the powers of being mothers, but not nursing-mothers. Nature gives them bosoms for show, but not for use. So Lady Arabella had a wet-nurse' – one brought from her brother Lord de Courcey's estate, 'a supply being kept up on

the lord's demesne for the family use'. But owing to the wet nurse's being addicted to brandy, the Gresham heir nearly died. The opposite theory to the eighteenth century's in this respect had become morally obligatory; Jane Austen lived through and endorsed the changeover.

2 By 'new-built boxes' she meant the small villas that the Regency had invented. Conservative minds in social habits like Maria Edgeworth and Cobbett despised the Regency small houses, the 'villas', as trashy modern inventions which were neither honest farmhouses or cottages, nor dignified mansions; and 'boxes' was quite unjustly the dismissive term used for them.

3 George Eliot shows she was aware of this principle when she makes Mrs Cadwallader, of noble origin and a flourishing matron before the Reform Act, express disgust at Miss Brooke's preferring to marry Mr Casaubon instead of Sir James Chettam: 'Young people should think of their families in marrying.'

4 An exaggeration in the interest of argument, perhaps, but there was a 'parlour' for the eighteenth-century family for everyday use.

5 I imagine there is an implied reference to the famous cedar parlour of Sir Charles Grandison's stately home, Richardson's novel being so well known; and by now the model eighteenth-century nobleman that Sir Charles was designed to embody had become so out of keeping with the new ideas as to be a symbol of the past. Jane Austen however had been born when Richardson's novel was in vogue, and her nephew (J. E. Austen-Leigh, *A Memoir of Jane Austen*) tells us that 'Every circumstance narrated in *Sir Charles Grandison*, all that was ever said or done in the cedar parlour, was familiar to her.'

6 In the memoir of Jane Austen written by her nephew he feels it necessary (rightly) to give the reader a description of the difference between the home of his aunt's youth and that of his time of writing, saying he must 'note some of those changes in social habits which give a colour to history, but which the historian has the greatest difficulty in recovering'. He continues with such details as 'a general deficiency of carpeting', the absence of piano, spinet or harpsichord except in great houses, and 'There would often be but one sofa in the house, and that a stiff, angular, uncomfortable article. There were no deep easy-chairs, nor other appliances for lounging; for to lie down, or even to lean back, was a luxury permitted only to old persons or invalids.' He mentions also that 'the furniture of the rooms would appear to us lamentably scanty'. This bears out the actuality of Repton's contrast.

7 A drawing showing a family doing this in *c.* 1825 was made by Henrietta Thornton, where the ladies are reading, 'working' and apparently also studying with their brothers, and with plenty of sofas and armchairs. See *Marianne Thornton 1797–1887: A Domestic Biography* by E. M. Forster.

8 Particularly true of Ireland, where the building fever which seized the Irish landed gentry in the eighteenth century was brought to an end after the Regency period, principally owing to the potato famine which ruined

Notes 335

many landlords and impoverished the country (see *Irish Houses and Castles* by Desmond Guinness and William Ryan for illustrations of Regency interiors, and which explains that the effects of the impoverishment were good for the architecture, since it was not spoiled, as so often in England, by subsequent alterations, additions or pulling down altogether to be replaced by something Victorian).

Northanger Abbey is an eighteenth-century skit in inception and still immature in parts, but was evidently much added to to make it publishable – more substantial and *contemporary*. Chapman suggests a revision was made in 1800 and the presentation of General Tilney as the Regency Man of Taste, must be one of the later additions.

9 Modelled on the circle customary at Court, presumably: every great house and its social neighbourhood being in theory a Court in its function.

10 *Villas and Country Houses (Adapted with economy to the Comforts and Elegancies of Modern Life)*, 1808, a characteristic and revealing title.

11 Exactly like Lady Russell with regard to Anne Elliot, Maria Edgeworth had stopped a favourite younger sister from accepting the hand of a worthy man who loved her and whom she loved, simply because Maria felt a lovely young Miss Edgeworth could expect a better match. And it was only after many years, when she had seen the effects of her sister's unhappiness, and that she would remain faithful to her lover, that Maria gave in to the marriage. She lived to admit, like Lady Russell, that she had been wrong, and that her sister's marriage, though only to a doctor, had turned out very happy, and that such a husband could be worthy of sister Fanny.

12 The part played by Anne's friend Mrs Smith in making Anne's decision should be noted. She also is common – 'a poor widow, a mere Mrs Smith' says Sir Walter – and has lost her social position and money and is crippled by illness; but Anne finds pleasure and sympathy in her society and conversation because of her 'elasticity of mind' and warm open nature, helping Anne to see further the real poverty of mind and spirit in the Elliot world. This is Mrs Smith's rôle in the *theme*. She also plays an essential part in the *plot*, as the only person who can enlighten Anne as to Mr Elliot's character and intrigues. The economy of this double-barrelled use of Mrs Smith is characteristic of Jane Austen's art – 'elegant' in the mathematician's sense of a neat solution to a problem .

13 Anne is of course specially created to be able to feel and express such a radical judgment on her own family, by implication her own class. The products of a titled family, they would probably be incapable of such a revolutionary conclusion. George Eliot (born 1819), whose father served such families as land agent and who took her about with him to these neighbouring great houses in her childhood, represents the type in *Felix Holt, Adam Bede, Middlemarch* and *Deronda*, and in *Felix Holt* shows their reaction to a Parliamentary Radical in their midst (a younger son who had made a fortune as a merchant in the Levant). In contrast to Anne, Mrs Cadwallader in *Middlemarch* (an earl's grand-daughter) 'believed as

unquestioningly in birth and no-birth as she did in game and vermin...a De Bracy reduced to take his dinner in a basin would have seemed to her an example of pathos worth exaggerating, and I fear his aristocratic vices would not have horrified her'. Mrs Cadwallader must have been born at the end of the eighteenth century, and the acute note made by George Eliot on an aristocratic lady's tolerance of vices in the well-bred is supported by Maria Edgeworth's witness to herself after deprecating the Ricardos: 'You know my aunt Ruxton said "Maria dislikes vulgarity more than vice."'

A critical theory of Jane Austen's writings

1 A. C. Bradley, address to the English Association.
2 *The Times Literary Supplement*, 9 February 1922.
3 All now published (1967).
4 Edited by R. W. Chapman.
5 The only instance of a character being repeated in a final rewrite is Lady Bertram, who in her functional character and consequent characteristics, and even in some of her remarks, is of course the anti-chaperone Mrs Allen. But this use was justified since the author believed that *Susan* (or *Catherine*) would never be publishable when she was taking *Mansfield Park* through its last revision.
6 *Scrutiny*, March 1940.
7 Harriet fancying herself in love (but twice over) was taken in some detail from Fanny's account of her own mistaken affair, down to stimulating her imaginary feelings. See *Letters*, Nov. 18, 1814: 'Your trying to excite your own feelings by a visit to his room amused me excessively. – The dirty Shaving Rag was exquisite! – Such a circumstance ought to be in print. Much too good to be lost.' It was not lost. It appeared in print as Harriet's piece of court-plaster and pencil-stub. Emma's fancying herself in love with Frank Churchill and then him with herself is also adapted from Fanny's confidences. That the dilemma, the heart-searchings and the self-deception should be divided in the novel between two characters is Jane Austen's characteristic process of making life fit for art.
8 E.g., the account of her work in vol. III, edited by Professor Dobrée, of *Introductions to English Literature* (1940): 'Unlike Scott she cared more for her art than its subject...She would change nothing and is content to enjoy...She knows more than her characters do but not so much as to make us feel that their shortcomings are not exhibited rather for our delight than for our edification.'
9 If not the favourite, like Charles, he was certainly the most congenial of her brothers, later managing her literary business. The *Life and Letters* states that there was 'a special link' between Jane and Henry from infancy.
10 As James Austen was only sixteen when Eliza married the Comte de

Feuillide, there is evidently some confusion here. The period when James was possibly Henry's rival for Eliza's hand was during her widowhood and when James was a widower, at which period James had long been in holy orders. But she may have been prejudiced against James on that account; he re-married earlier in the same year that saw Henry's long courtship rewarded, and his wife, Mary Lloyd, Anna's step-mother, seems to have borne Eliza an otherwise unaccountable ill will.

11 'I have never yet found that the advice of a Sister could prevent a young Man's being in love if he chose it' – *Lady Susan*.

12 Here is one of many in language. The Miss Manwaring who has designs on Sir James Martin is said to be 'absolutely on the catch for a husband'. Mrs Norris uses the same term, of which there is no other instance, I believe, in any of her novels, in connection with Mr Rushworth, who replaces Sir James – 'there were girls enough on the catch for him'.

13 Price is the same order of name as Williams, and names meant a great deal to Jane Austen. She appears to have had a sort of private catalogue and dictionary of them, shared with her family, and most of those used in the MS volumes reappear in the novels, generally with similar associations.

14 Lady Susan as a mother is sometimes held, with great likelihood, to have come from a neighbour's family history. Jane's friends the Lloyds (two of whom married her brothers later) had had a grandmother, Mrs Craven, notorious for her unnatural behaviour to her daughters, who were forced to elope from their home. The cruel Mrs Craven was a beauty and moved in Society. Her story would be well known to the Austens, and could be amalgamated with Eliza's in the manner congenial to Jane when adapting from life. It is significant that Mrs Craven was thrown out again when in *Mansfield Park* she returned to the story of her brother and cousin as it had affected herself.

15 For instance, Mary had originally intended to marry the eligible Tom, as Lady Susan had thought of marrying Sir James before turning him over to her daughter, and Lady Susan's explanation of her change of views – 'but I must own myself rather romantic in that respect, and that Riches only will not satisfy me' – is what Mary's failure to satisfy herself with Tom Bertram amounts to. Again, Lady Susan's attention to Reginald, like Mary's flirtation with Edmund, is not at first meant by either lady to lead anywhere. The contest of wills, expressed in conflicting moral attitudes, remains the fundamental feature in the situation between hero and siren in both stories. It is Mary who says, referring to Edmund's change of attitude about the play-acting: 'His sturdy spirit to bend as it did! Oh, it was sweet beyond expression,' but Lady Susan who had aimed explicitly at subjugating Reginald's will and who says: 'There is exquisite pleasure in subduing an insolent spirit,' etc. The clash between incompatible moral values is in both books the rock on which the relation between the two people founders. In life matters seem to have worked out happily enough,

but a sister may be pardoned for having felt, like Fanny, 'He will marry her, and be poor and miserable. God grant that her influence do not make him cease to be respectable!'

16 This idea was not wasted. Out of keeping with Mary's part, it was worked into Henry's in the last rewriting of the book. We actually have a scene (after dinner at Mansfield in vol. III, ch. 3) where we hear Henry endeavouring to subdue Fanny in the same way, and almost the same description is given as above: 'This would be the way to win Fanny. She was not to be won by all that gallantry and wit, and good nature together, could do...without the assistance of sentiment and feeling, and seriousness on serious subjects.' As this scene is connected with the ordination subject, and is dramatic, it must have been written into the final version.

17 With these last two quotations compare ch. 7 of *Mansfield Park*: 'and to the credit of the lady it may be added that without his being a man of the world or an elder brother, without any of the arts of flattery or small talk, he began to be agreeable to her...he was not pleasant by any common rule, he talked no nonsense, he paid no compliments, his opinions were unbending, his attentions tranquil and simple. There was a charm, perhaps, in his sincerity, his steadiness, his integrity, which Miss Crawford might be equal to feel.' The hero, we observe, remains the same, but the lady's attitude to his qualities has been changed from contempt to unwilling respect. This is one of the many changes in the rewriting of *Lady Susan* away from melodrama to real insight.

18 We may note that the qualities Henry Crawford shares with Henry Tilney are those Henry Austen possessed, to judge by references in the *Letters*, where there are also significant allusions to the name Henry, which seems to denote for Jane and Cassandra a lively, talented man with brilliant conversational powers.

19 These terms are repeatedly used in describing Henry Crawford; cf. 'It was a love which, operating on an active sanguine spirit, of more warmth than delicacy, made her affection appear of greater consequence because it was withheld' (vol. III, ch. 2).

20 That the theory was a current belief is proved by the 'Opinions on *Mansfield Park*' collected by our author, where her niece Fanny Knight is reported to object that she 'could not think it natural that Edmund should be so much attached to a woman without Principle like Mary C.'.

21 Mrs Inchbald, too, was already connected with *Mansfield Park* as the translator of *Lovers' Vows*.

22 *Letters*, Dec. 18, 1798.

23 *Review of English Studies*, October 1933, '*Mansfield Park* and *Lovers' Vows*'.

24 As far as the hedgerow goes, it may be objected that she intended only a lightning alteration of a dull narrative piece into a dramatic scene, as she rewrote overnight the flat re-engagement of Captain Wentworth and Anne into the brilliant White Hart chapter. But the ordination idea is in another class from a local change of form.

25 cf. 'I am proud to say that I have a very good eye at an Adultress...I
fixed upon the right one from the first...she was highly rouged, and looked
rather quietedly and contentedly silly than anything else'. *Letters*, May
1801. Elinor had had no tremors in discussing Willoughby's relations with
Eliza Williams, a few years before *Mansfield Park*, and shortly after
Mansfield Park Emma Woodhouse concludes, as a matter of course, that
Mrs Churchill's death may have brought to light the existence of half a
dozen natural children of Mr Churchill's.

26 A letter from Eliza to another cousin is quoted in the *Life and Letters*
begging her (Philadelphia Walter) to come and stay at the rectory
'provided she could bring herself to act, "for my Aunt Austen declares
'she has not room for any *idle young people*'"'. Philadelphia seems to have
been unable to bring herself to act on any terms – a hint for Fanny's
situation in the casting of *Lovers' Vows* at Mansfield.

27 The stress is always on the acting and not on the play itself. Hence I cannot
agree with Miss E. M. Butler's case (*Modern Language Review*, July 1933,
'*Mansfield Park* and Kotzebue's *Lovers' Vows*') that a moral protest against
Kotzebue's lax moral standard is the source of *Mansfield Park* and that Jane
Austen 'condemned it mercilessly and punished it savagely' in her novel.
Miss Butler's article does at least confirm my account of the novel as giving
the reader a sense of something strained in the moralizing and unnatural
in the condemnation, for this, I imagine, is what she felt impelled to
explain by contending that the plot of the novel is an inversion of the play.
One agrees with Miss Husbands in her reply in the same journal (April
1934) that 'likenesses there certainly are, but they are by no means fitted
to bear the weight which Miss Butler attaches to them'. The play, so useful
in the first volume, probably influenced the novelist to a certain extent
in adapting all her diverse materials to the revision of *Lady Susan*, without
her being quite aware of the extent of its influence. And some deliberate
reference was no doubt intended as well, as reference to *Cecilia* is, I believe,
intended in *Pride and Prejudice*.

28 E.g. the necklace episode. Edmund is charmed by Mary's kind, thoughtful
attention to Fanny in offering her a necklace so that she may wear
William's cross on it at the ball. He falls into a 'reverie of fond reflection,
uttering only now and then a few half-sentences of praise'. A hundred
pages later Mary lets out that the idea of lending Fanny the necklace, a
present from Henry to his sister, was entirely Henry's; we know then it
was part of his scheme for insinuating himself into Fanny's affections at
the time before his intentions became honourable: 'It was his own doing
entirely, his own thought. I am ashamed to say, that it had never entered
my head.' Mary had actually been helping her brother in his efforts to
destroy Fanny's peace of mind, we realize.

29 Lord David Cecil, *Jane Austen*.

30 E.g. 'Sir Thomas, poor Sir Thomas, a parent, and conscious of errors in
his own conduct as a parent, was the longest to suffer. He felt that he ought

not to have allowed the marriage, that his daughter's sentiments had been sufficiently known to him to render him culpable in authorizing it, that in doing so he had sacrificed the right to the expedient, and been governed by motives of selfishness and worldly wisdom. These were reflections that required some time to soften; *but time will do almost every thing.*' (My italics.)

There is contempt here, not only for Sir Thomas but for the tendency of human nature generally to forgive itself too easily.

31 This is not really true, but we are encouraged by the author's own attitude to feel that there may be something in it. The novelist's next step was to say: Suppose it were true...She then had at her disposal the identical relation described as that existing between Emma and Harriet Smith. Frederica is thus actually described by her mother in the same letter, in the same spirit of irritation: 'I never saw a girl of her age bid fairer to be the sport of mankind. Her feelings are tolerably lively and she is so charmingly artless in their display, as to afford the most reasonable hope of her being ridiculed and despised by every Man who sees her' and as 'a born simpleton'. This was enough foundation for Harriet's disposition. Poor Frederica had only fallen in love with Reginald at first sight; Harriet was easily produced on this basis by multiplying her susceptibility; and artlessness combined with a propensity for falling in love without encouragement is more suitable for the heroine of a burlesque than for a sentimental heroine as Frederica was meant to be. This very limited kind of artistic imagination is exactly what is described by her nieces (quoted in J. E. Austen-Leigh's *Memoir*) as occasioning the endless stories she made up for them.

32 In letters, I imagine, for she says of the final book: 'I have lop't and crop't so successfully, that I imagine it must be rather shorter than *Sense and Sensibility*' – letters are a spacious way of narrating, and *Pride and Prejudice* has, like *Mansfield Park*, many signs of a previous epistolary form.

33 A good recent instance of this refusal to accept Jane Austen as anything but the creator of comic parts is Mr George Sampson's account of her work in *The Concise Cambridge History of English Literature* (1941) which ends: 'It is absurd to claim too much for a writer who claimed so little for herself [did she?]...The true lovers of Jane Austen are those who do not advertise their devotion, but are content to whisper "Dear Jane" as they pause at the grave in the ancient aisle of Winchester Cathedral.'

34 Though there are some falsifications in the Biographical Notice, I see no reason why he should have invented the above. Henry was an Evangelical clergyman by this time, and we can see in his notice that doctoring of his sister's personality to suit a Victorian taste which is so evident in their nephew Edward's *Memoir* later, a tradition which has never been broken.

35 [This had been written before the discussion of *Measure for Measure* contained in the same number of *Scrutiny* (vol. x, 1942) proposed itself. – Ed.]

36 Their nephew complained: 'Her nearest relatives, far from making provision for such a purpose (a biography), had actually destroyed many

of the letters and papers by which it might have been facilitated. They were influenced, I believe, partly by an extreme distaste to publishing any private details' – *A Memoir of Jane Austen* by J. E. Austen-Leigh.

37 *Jane Austen and her Art*, by Mary M. Lascelles (1939).

38 *Jane Austen: A Biography*, by Elizabeth Jenkins (1938).

39 Of the five Austen brothers we know about (the sixth was 'weak in intellect' and nothing else is known of him but his name), four married twice, while the fifth remained a widower after the death of his wife – whom Jane deeply admired and loved – from bearing her eleventh child, when Jane was thirty-two.

40 See *Northanger Abbey*, chapter 5.

41 On the strength of a family tradition based on a circumstantial story of Cassandra's and recorded by their niece.

42 Eliza de Feuillide, a sophisticated person, after eleven years of marriage and residence abroad, reported on visiting them that 'Henry is certainly endowed with uncommon abilities, which indeed seem to have been bestowed, though in a different way, upon each member of this family'.

43 Their nephew wrote: 'There was so much that was agreeable and attractive in this family party that its members may be excused if they were inclined to live somewhat too exclusively within it.'

44 Mrs Austen is described as 'shrewd and acute, high-minded and determined, with a strong sense of humour' and great energy. Her correspondence illustrates these qualities, and some of Jane's tastes and prejudices too, e.g. after a visit to London: 'I was not so happy as to see my nephew Weaver – suppose he was hurried in time, as I think everyone is in town; 'tis a sad place, I would not live in it on any account, one has not time to do one's duty either to God or man.'

45 Their niece Anna wrote of them: 'They seemed to lead a life to themselves within the general family life which was shared only by each other. I will not say their true, but their *full* feelings and opinions were known only to themselves. They alone fully understood what each had suffered and felt and thought.'

46 Cf. 'I am glad you liked my lace, and so are you, and so is Martha, and we are all glad together. I have got your cloak home, which is quite delightful – as delightful at least as half the circumstances which are called so' (1799);

'...in short, has a great many more than all the cardinal virtues (for the cardinal virtues in themselves have been so often possessed that they are no longer worth having)...' (1804);

and her dislike of the Evangelical Movement. This extreme sensitiveness ranges from jokes like 'Miss X. and I are very thick, but I am the thinnest of the two' to the perfectly serious epitaph on a friend: 'Many a girl on early death has been praised into an Angel I believe, on slighter pretensions to Beauty, Sense and Merit than Marianne.'

Mansfield Park

1 See above, pp. 111–30.

Jane Eyre

1 Though *Jane Eyre* seems to have been on the stocks before *Dombey and Son* could have reached her, it would be interesting to know if she had read of Oliver Twist, and of Smike and Nicholas at the Yorkshire school, which she would have found congenial, and even helpful, in creating Jane Eyre and her sufferings. Where Charlotte Brontë is so superior to Dickens is in her creation of positives – the demonstration of the conditions for Jane's growth into full life and the possession of lasting happiness are entirely original and entirely convincing.

2 Bessie's name 'Leaven' is clearly to convey that she is the 'little leaven that leaveneth the whole'.

3 We know that originally Charlotte thought of Art as her likely career, until she ruined her eyes by copying engravings and had to confine herself to writing.

4 There is a Yorkshire rival to North Lees Hall for inspiring 'Thornfield', also with a legend of a madwoman (said to go back to the eighteenth century) but the connexion with the Eyre family seems to me to favour this one. These legendary madwomen may seem suspect (especially to those who may have read the third chapter of Lord Raglan's *The Hero: A Study in Tradition, Myth and Drama*), but no doubt before the days of asylums decent families housed their own lunatics and often suffered such consequences.

5 *Reminiscences of Charlotte Brontë*, by Miss Ellen Nussey, 1871, reprinted in the Brontë Society Publications, vol. II, 1899.

6 Except for George Eliot, who herself acted otherwise, and wrote of it: 'All self-sacrifice is good, but one would like it to be in a somewhat nobler cause than a diabolical law which chains a man body and soul to a putrefying carcase.' We note that the enlightened George Eliot acquiesces in a Victorian assumption – 'All self-sacrifice is good' – which Charlotte Brontë would never have done, since it is exactly such unrealities, dangerous and damaging, that it is Emily and Charlotte's distinction to be always alert to expose in the concrete human actualities.

7 Everything necessary to say about the treatment of governesses had already been said in *Emma* via Mrs Elton and her friends who wanted to employ Jane Fairfax and in *Martin Chuzzlewit* where we visited Ruth Pinch in the brass-and-copper-founder's family, but the governess herself had never spoken out with such bitterness before.

Villette

1 I have argued this case in an extensive essay on *Wuthering Heights*, F. R. and Q. D. Leavis, *Lectures in America* (Chatto and Windus, 1969).

2 George Eliot read the *Life of Charlotte Brontë* when it came out in 1857 and found it 'deeply affecting throughout: in the early part romantic, poetic as one of her own novels; in the later years tragic... Mrs. Gaskell has done her work admirably, both in the industry and care with which she has gathered and selected her material, and in the feeling with which she has presented it.' She may well have borne Charlotte's case in mind as typical, and thus suitable for the heroine of her long-pondered novel *Miss Brooke*, which was finally published in 1871 when absorbed into a more comprehensive work, *Middlemarch*. This is, like Charlotte's novels, a comparison and criticism of cultures, where 'Rome' and the values of the arts and artists are deployed in a critical examination of English provincial life in the early nineteenth century.

3 Even if Charlotte had known that this Scotch name is pronounced 'Hume' she would not have been deterred since the pun is visually there.

4 Her most intelligent friend said: 'She never criticized her books to me farther than to express utter weariness of them, and the labour they had given her.'

A fresh approach to *Wuthering Heights*

1 Mr Justice Vaisey, giving a legal opinion on the text ('The Authorship of *Wuthering Heights*', Brontë Society Publications, 1946), notes such a distinction in 'diction, style and taste' between 'the introductory portion' and the rest of the book, that he believed it to indicate two authors; which would give ground to an old theory or tradition that Emily worked from a manuscript of Branwell's at the start (joint composition being probably a practice of the Brontë children, and Emily and Patrick are said to have written practically indistinguishable minute hands). Writing at two different periods by Emily alone, and at the earlier under the influence of Branwell or in deliberate imitation of his style (as Lockwood) would, however, account for such a disparity.

2 Appendix B.

3 The speech (chap. 9) in which Catherine explains to Nelly why she couldn't marry Heathcliff – on social grounds – belongs to the sociological *Wuthering Heights*. But even then she intends, she declares, to keep up her old (sisterly) relations with him, to help him get on in the world – 'to *rise*' as she significantly puts it in purely social terms.

4 Tabby had, Mrs Gaskell reports, 'known the "bottom" or valley in those primitive days when the faeries frequented the margin of the "beck" on moonlight nights, and had known folk who had seen them. But that was

when there were no mills in the valleys, and when all the wool-spinning was done by hand in the farm-houses round. "It wur the factories as had driven 'em away", she said.'

5 Appendix C.

6 I am referring to the invaluable book, *The Image of Childhood*, by P. Coveney, though this does not in fact deal with *Wuthering Heights*.

7 This very evident judgment of Nelly's on the gentility with which Catherine has been infected by her stay at Thrushcross Grange (lavishly annotated in the whole scene of her return home in chap. 7) is clearly endorsed by the author, since it is based on values that are fundamental to the novel and in consonance with Emily's Wordsworthian sympathies. It is supplemented by another similar but even more radical judgment, put into old Joseph's mouth, the indispensable Joseph who survives the whole action to go on farming the Heights and who is made the vehicle of several central judgments, as well as of many disagreeable Calvinistic attitudes. Resenting the boy Linton Heathcliff's contempt for the staple food, porridge, made, like the oat-cake, from the home-grown oats, Joseph remembers the boy's fine-lady mother: 'His mother were just soa – we wer a'most too mucky tuh sow t'corn fur makking her breead.' There are many related judgments in the novel. We may note here the near-caricature of Lockwood in the first three chapters as the town visitor continually exposing his ignorance of country life and farming.

8 A regular Victorian theme, springing from the consciousness and resentment by creative artists of a new class snobbery and expressed in such widely different novels as *Alton Locke*, *North and South*, *Felix Holt*, *Dombey and Son*, *Great Expectations*, as well as *Wuthering Heights* which is earlier than all these.

9 David Copperfield's Peggotty is the same type, registered through the nursling's eyes (she is supplemented, as he grows out of her, by his great-aunt Betsy Trotwood) and Dickens's testimony to such truths is important. It will be noticed that Peggotty has to mother not only David but also his permanently immature mother. Our nineteenth-century fiction and memoirs are full of such nurses (sometimes they are spinster aunts), bearing witness to the living reality (see, e.g., Lord Shaftesbury's nurse, the Strachey nurse, and the Darwin nurse in Gwen Raverat's autobiography *Period Piece*). Nelly Dean seems to have incurred a good deal of unjustified ill-will, and perverse misrepresentation in consequence, from Catherine's defenders. That Peggotty and Miss Trotwood haven't (so far – or so far as I know) must be due less to Dickens's fairly unambiguous presentation of David's Dora and (but to a lesser degree) of David's mother, than to the fact that Doras are not now in esteem.

10 Hence Nelly's indignant rebuke to Hareton's father in chap. 9 takes the form of telling him: '"Oh! I wonder his mother does not rise from her grave to see how you use him".'

11 Significantly, because old Joseph 'was relentless in worrying him about ruling his children rigidly', as religion required.

12 C. P. Sanger's *The Structure of 'Wuthering Heights'* (a Hogarth Press pamphlet).

13 Other pre-Victorian novelists noted and resented the effects on children too. In the original preface to her children's classic *Holiday House* (1839), Catherine Sinclair wrote: 'In these pages the author has endeavoured to paint that species of noisy, frolicsome, mischievous children, now almost extinct, wishing to preserve a sort of fabulous remembrance of days long past, when young people were like wild horses on the prairies, rather than like well-broken hacks on the road.'

14 With the added force of Scott's dark and violent *Ravenswood* who both in name-pattern and type of hero suggests Heathcliff. See Appendix D, '*Wuthering Heights* and *The Bride of Lammermoor*'.

15 Mrs Gaskell says she told 'of bygone days of the countryside; old ways of living, former inhabitants, decayed gentry who had melted away, and whose places knew them no more; family tragedies, and dark superstitious dooms; and in telling these things, without the least consciousness that there might ever be anything requiring to be softened down, would give at full length the bare and simple details.' This is evidence of external, real life, sources for *Wuthering Heights* which cannot be dismissed.

16 In general, the film wipes out inessentials and makes the theme inescapable; it telescopes with advantage, translates intellectual elements successfully into dramatic forms while wherever possible exactly reproducing the original, and interpolates very little. It is a faithful rendition which shirks almost nothing – unlike the usually over-praised 'film of the novel', or dramatized version (contrast the film of the novel *Saturday Night and Sunday Morning*, which both softens and shirks, or the dreadful play *The Heiress* which misinterprets and denatures *Washington Square*). Nevertheless, this film omits the physical violence of the novel and is thus more suave and less disturbing than Roché's work.

17 For the nature of the rhetoric, see *Scrutiny*, vol. XIX, no. 2, F. R. Leavis: 'Reality and Sincerity', where the poem 'Cold in the earth' is analysed in a comparison with a poem by Thomas Hardy. (Reprinted in *A Selection From Scrutiny*, vol. II.) Systematic attempts to argue that the Gondal poems are the basis of *Wuthering Heights* provide a harmless academic pastime, but we have only to ask whether, the novel being lost, we could have deduced anything even remotely resembling it from the poems, to see how preposterous the claim is.

18 What might be called the Catherine complex did not go unnoticed by other Victorian novelists. Mrs Gaskell, who had a sound knowledge of the dialects and culture of her own parts of England, had thought of introducing into her novel *North and South* a young girl from 'humble, retired country life on the borders of Lancashire' to be angry, jealous and passionately in love with the hero – 'I know', she wrote in this connexion, *Letter No. 191*, 'the kind of wild, wayward character that grows up in lonesome places, which has a sort of Southern capacity of hating and loving.' Dickens's Rosa Dartle, perhaps his most interesting female,

registers his recognition of the woman with whom something has gone wrong so that her passionate nature must vent itself in destructive rages against those necessary to her. The only outlet Rosa's restricted life allows is a practice of undermining everyone by ironical questioning (the hint from real life on which Dickens built the character); her face is scarred from a hammer thrown at her by the young Steerforth (whom she has always loved passionately) owing to her having goaded him to such exasperation – symbolic of their relation to each other. But Miss Dartle is only a minor character in *David Copperfield*, and Dickens seems unable to do anything with it beyond a few impressive sketches of her in action. Further thinking on those lines presumably produced Miss Wade in *Little Dorrit*. She has been impelled to break off her approaching marriage (an excellent love-match), and later also a *liaison* with a cynical pseudo-artist who supplemented the worthy fiancé, because she can maintain no relation requiring love and self-discipline; she is actually shown most convincingly creating around herself finally a *Huis Clos* life of destructive passion and self-torment quite equal to the vortex set up by Catherine. Both Rosa Dartle and Miss Wade are clever, handsome and highly-sexed, but have been put into disadvantageous positions by life – the one is a poor relation, the other illegitimate, and both are resentful, so that like Catherine (but unlike Roché's Kate) they are accounted for by circumstances in their early conditioning.

19 Catherine Earnshaw is well in line here, e.g. 'Mr Linton ventured no objection to her taking Isabella with her to Wuthering Heights in the afternoon; and she rewarded him with such a summer of sweetness and affection in return, as made the house a paradise for several days; both master and servants profiting from the perpetual sunshine.' And even in the first phase of the marriage: 'It was not the thorn bending to the honeysuckles but the honeysuckles embracing the thorn. There were no mutual concessions: one stood erect, and the others yielded...I observed that Mr Edgar had a deep-rooted fear of ruffling her humour. He concealed it from her...and for the space of half a year, the gunpowder lay as harmless as sand, because no fire came near to explode it...It ended...'

20 In *Wuthering Heights* there is a much greater range of feminine types than in either *Jules et Jim* or *Women in Love*, for example.

21 Not merely as a release, but, characteristically, she must represent it as a triumph: '"Nelly, you think you are better and more fortunate than I; in full health and strength: you are sorry for me – very soon that will be altered. I shall be sorry for *you*. I shall be incomparably beyond and above you all."'

22 Other insights of the same kind are that Heathcliff's worst potentialities are roused by what Nelly describes as Cathy's 'accustomed look of nervousness, and yet defiance, which he abhorred', and also by Isabella's combination of the hated Linton looks with her fatuous delusions about

himself (which reminds one of Byron's reactions to poor Annabella both before and after marriage).

23 The economy and impersonality with which this point is made, and the complexity of apprehension – so that what seems gratuitously wounding is seen to be also natural (i.e. necessary) in the context of such a way of life – contrasts, greatly to Emily's advantage, with Charlotte's raw reaction to the same Yorkshire plain-speaking, as seen in *Shirley*. There Emily's sister presents a whole family (drawn from life), given the typical name of 'the Yorkes', to show the hurtful effect of this much-vaunted 'outspokenness'; Charlotte has the father and mother 'told off' by both heroines, making an obtrusively personal episode which is not integral to the novel. Charlotte, that is, could see only the disagreeable effects of this northern characteristic, whereas Emily understood and made clear the reasons why it came about and prevailed, since, as she shows, it made for survival originally, though of course unnecessary to the Linton class now.

24 In this, as in the combination of convincing realism and symbolic action in which the belief finds expression, *Wuthering Heights* is remarkably similar to *Great Expectations*. The latter too is a work of art which also contains a sociological novel on the surface.

25 It is characteristic of *Wuthering Heights* that though Emily Brontë sees how old Joseph affects her Catherines and Isabellas, she makes it clear that she is perfectly aware that there are other points of view from which he makes a better showing – he has dignity, utility and even higher virtues, and an unprejudiced examination of all he says and does himself (ignoring what others say of him) proves this. But concentration on the 'metaphysical' account of *Wuthering Heights* has lost sight of the realistic novel it really is. And when I say 'Shakespearian' I mean also that Joseph is an indication of his creator's indebtedness to Shakespeare for novelistic method and technique that she could have learnt nowhere else.

26 The guytrash was a supernatural northern animal generally taking the form of a large shaggy dog with saucer-eyes which was to be met on field-paths and in churchyards after dusk, appearing to warn of sudden death in the family – if it looked you in the face you were the one doomed; 'trash' being a verb signifying to walk wearily through mire. It may be remembered that Jane Eyre, meeting Mr Rochester's dog Pilot in such circumstances, took it for 'the Gytrash'; Charlotte used what Mrs Gaskell describes as 'the grim superstitions of the North', 'implanted in her by the servants who believed in them' with very good effect in *Jane Eyre*, and so did Emily, as can be seen throughout *Wuthering Heights*, particularly in chapter 12 (see Appendix C).

27 She would have got the tone of the period from their old servant, nurse and faithful friend Tabby who died in their service at above eighty and whom I deduce was born in 1769 – in the same decade, that is, as Catherine Earnshaw is supposed to have been born; Tabby of course

would have inherited and passed on the traditions of the generation before her own birth also, the period of Fielding's and Smollett's novels with their evidence of an age in which a good deal of violence, brutality and domestic harshness was manifest.

28 Cf. Mrs Gaskell's novel *Mary Barton* (1848) where the characters though also northern are Lancashire folk: '"Did he die easy?" "He was restless all night long." "And in course thou plucked the pillow away? Thou didst not! Well! with thy bringing up and thy learning, thou mightst have known that were the only help in such a case. There were pigeons' feathers in the pillow, depend on't. To think of two grown-up folk like you and Mary, not knowing death could never come easy to a person lying on a pillow with pigeons' feathers in!"' (chap. 36).

29 See E. M. Wright, *Rustic Speech and Folklore* (Oxford, 1914). Mrs Wright (who collaborated with her husband on the English Dialect Dictionary), added that 'In Yorkshire there exists an idea that the door must not be locked for seven years after a death in the house.' All the above death-superstitions can be found documented in her chapter on 'Birth, Marriage and Death Customs' as belonging to Yorkshire (as well as various other parts of England, of course), though some are better explained in Frazer.

Silas Marner

1 She was an accomplished pianist, performed with professional musicians in her own home, and was an ardent concert-goer and opera-addict, even accepting Wagnerian opera with sympathetic intelligence.

2 Not all: Henry James notes with some amusement mixed with his respect her 'tendency to *aborder* only the highest themes' when he attended her *salon*. But she did not find it easy to talk to a number of people, or to strangers at all.

3 There are many overtones from *Pilgrim's Progress*, e.g. Silas has to live away from the village at the Stone-pits by the Waste; a consequence of his adopting Eppie is that the waste is drained and a flower-garden and fertile fields replace it; in his youth Silas has worshipped in Lantern Yard, 'a turning out of Prison Street, where the jail is'; he comes from a 'region called "North'ard"' which, while suggesting the Industrial North to us, seems in the mouths of the peasants who are quoted to be in the same parts as Mr Honest's 'Town of Stupidity' where '"we lie more off from the Sun, and so are more cold and senseless"' than even the City of Destruction itself – Bunyan consistently uses descriptions of places for allegorical purposes. It is his Giant Despair who has disabling fits, which may have suggested Silas's equally convenient 'fits'. But unlike Christian and the rest, Silas finds his reward and the end of his pilgrimage in Raveloe on earth.

4 'The Bible as you brought wi' you from that country', says Dolly, confirming that in spite of having lost his faith he had kept his Bible. This is precisely what George Eliot did, valuing it, says Cross, who was in a

position to know, 'not only from early association, but also from the profound conviction of its importance in the development of the religious life of man'. In 1862 we find her writing of G. H. Lewes: 'He is not fond of reading the Bible himself, but "sees no harm" in my reading it.'

5 Compare an earlier novel, *Alton Locke* (1850), and we find Kingsley trying through the technique of fictional autobiography to register the deprivation suffered by the poor London boy, cut off from green fields, and – by his mother's religion – from poetry. Bewick's *Memoir* is a useful contrast to both *Alton Locke* and *Silas Marner*.

6 Again, we have in this novel as opposed to *Adam Bede* an admission of the dark side of cottage mentality. We were not shown any fear of witchcraft in the illiterate and superstitious Lisbeth Bede, only the attractive side of her supernatural beliefs, though the latter was hardly likely to exist without the former. Another aspect of this new concern for unglamorous truth lies in the poor figures chosen to represent the gentry – the rector is commonplace, the doctor tiresome, their wives are ludicrous, the squire's family all worse than unattractive, the worthy Lammeters uncharacterized yeomen farmers with daughters respectively narrow and rough; and the whole social life of the gentry is either insipid or gross. There is no figure like *Adam Bede*'s Mr Irwine to embody the highest values of the scholar, the gentleman and the Christian.

7 One recent piece of rescue-work that might be adduced as peculiarly relevant is *English Churchyard Memorials* by Frederick Burgess, both for its abundant illustrations, and for its scholarly understanding of how complex this culture of the countryside was and how completely its structure was destroyed by outside forces in the nineteenth century, however much against the wishes and interests of those who lived and worked there.

8 The symbolism is brilliantly chosen and is consistently used of the gentry. For example, we remember that to Silas his 'betters' were 'tall, powerful, florid men, seen chiefly on horseback', and that, to 'a young gentleman like Dunsey', to be 'reduced to so exceptional a mode of locomotion as walking' implied 'a too bewildering sense of unwontedness in his position'. So the horsewhip identifies Dunsey's skeleton very appropriately. Mr Lammeter recalls his prime by saying 'I always *would* have a good horse, you know' and Godfrey's self-reproach at letting himself be tricked into marrying a barmaid takes the form of visualizing himself as a horse sinking in the mire because he had lost 'the strong silken rope, by which Nancy would have drawn him safe to the green banks'. My list is not exhaustive. I doubt whether the imagery was deliberately fixed on; it is more likely that for George Eliot the gentry in her childhood were inseparably associated by her with horse-riding powers.

9 Cf. his brother Solomon who bowed to the company while he fiddled without pausing 'as much as to say that he respected the company, though he respected the keynote more'. This seems to me one of those wonderful strokes in which George Eliot shows herself fully equal to Tolstoy. And Mr Macey himself, the parish clerk who led the singing in church, says

complacently: 'our family's been known for musicianers as far back as anybody can tell'. Here skill and talent are above money and rank, and, generally recognized as this truth is, it gives those who have them something better to pride themselves on than class superiority. Note Ben Winthrop's testimony that the Squire 'used to invite him [Mr Macey] to take a glass, only to hear him sing the Red Rovier. It's a natural gift.' The village is rich in natural gifts even in music alone: Ben is leader of the church choir and his gift is inherited by his boy Aaron ('he can sing a tune off straight, like a throstle'), the butcher 'has music in his soul', and two of the Rainbow gossips are known as 'the bassoon' and 'the key-bugle'.

The pride in a craft was general – hence the unforgivable sin of the London tailor. Richard Jefferies in *Amaryllis at the Fair*, based on family reminiscences, tells how old Iden the baker, who started to bake in the Waterloo era, had his favourite peel ('The peel is the long wooden rod, broad at one end, with which loaves are placed in the baker's oven') 'ornamented with silver' in his old age, 'being proud of his trade'. There is an immense amount of other evidence of the kind.

10 Cf. Turgenev in *A Lear of the Steppes*: 'Everything in the world, good and bad, comes to man, not through his deserts, but in consequence of some as yet unknown but logical laws which I will not take upon myself to indicate, though I sometimes fancy I have a dim perception of them.'

11 We should be wrong, I think, to assume that George Eliot, who is inevitably amused by some aspects of this culture, does not intend a slightly Erewhonian satire on the Catholic nature of Dolly's belief.

12 In Dickens's *A Tale of Two Cities*, published in 1859, more than a year before George Eliot began to think of writing *Marner*, Dr Manette is 'buried alive' for eighteen years as Marner was for fifteen, also by an injustice. He falls back on shoe-making, and his bench and tools are for him in his isolation and misery in the Bastille what Marner's loom is to him at the Stone-pits. He relapses more thoroughly in personality than Marner, his loss of memory corresponding to Marner's trances, but is 'Returned to life' by the unexpected appearance of his unknown daughter Lucie, whose golden hair recalls his lost wife's, as Eppie's unexpected appearance and golden hair arouse Marner by recalling his lost sister. This experience and the obligation of being a father start a regenerative process in Dr Manette as in Silas which restores his powers of affection and his place in society. The parallel strikes me as too close to be accidental. While Dickens's treatment of the subject is too theatrical to be worth the close attention George Eliot's demands, I am bound to say that the case-history of Dr Manette is much more interesting than what we are shown of Marner in his despair and after. But Silas is meant to be representative, so George Eliot could not afford to do through him the kind of analysis that Dickens did, even if she had been tempted to do a piece of pioneering investigation into the psychological effects of isolation and despair – nor was she, like Dickens, attracted by abnormality. Silas's

state is too predictable. 'Silas was both sane and honest', we are told, and he remains so all through his sufferings. And he is too simple to make new values for himself in contempt of his treatment by his society, as Hester Prynne, the *esprit fort* of *The Scarlet Letter*, had done in her isolation. The robbery occurs such a short time before Eppie reaches Silas that we don't have to ask whether this final loss would have pushed him over the edge, although in fact it is shown to start the process of reintegration for him. Nor is the account of why he became a miser interesting – and it belongs too much to the mere symbolism of the gold.

13 Even the author's generalizations tend to be cast in the same appropriate kind of metaphor, e.g. 'language is a stream that is sure to smack of a mingled soil', and 'that habit of looking towards the money and grasping it made a loam that was deep enough for the seeds of desire' and 'before such calm external beauty the presence of a vague fear is more distinctly felt – like a raven flapping its slow wing across the sunny air'. These and many of the other images in *Marner* are Shakespearian rather than Wordsworthian.

14 Another instance of this is Eppie's insistence when she is planning her garden on taking in the furze-bush, under which her mother was found dead in the snow. '"Ah child!" said Silas, "it wouldn't do to leave out the furze-bush."' The feeling here, left so delicately for us to grasp without help from the author, gets some emphasis by Eppie's adding: '"and just against it I'll put snowdrops and crocuses, 'cause Aaron says they won't die out, but'll always get more and more."' Of course to people like the English poor who religiously planted flowers on family graves and tended them every Sunday, the associations make the feeling clear without any more needing to be said; and Shakespearian as Eppie's poetic statement is, it is still quite plausible in the circumstances as natural speech.

15 George Eliot's understanding of the relation of the peasant to his environment is better, because more intimate, than Wordsworth's, and this she conveys admirably in *Silas Marner* and *Adam Bede*. Cf. Sturt: 'He did not merely "reside" in it; he was part of it, and it was part of him...Out of all these circumstances – the pride of skill in handicrafts, the detailed understanding of the soil and its materials, the general effect of the well-known landscape, and the faint sense of something venerable in its associations – there proceeded an influence which acted upon the village people as an unperceived guide to their conduct, so that they observed the seasons proper for their varied pursuits almost as if they were going through some ritual – and to neglect the well-known signs which hinted at what should be done, was more than bad economy; it was dereliction of peasant duty...and all the customs which their situation required them to follow sustained their belief in the ancestral notions of good and evil. In other words, they had a civilization to support them' (*Change in the Village*: 'The Peasant System').

16 *Change in the Village*, p. 110.

17 *Marner* is the first of her novels to take an anti-Cinderella shape, but

thereafter the pattern becomes compulsive. Eppie who renounces her birth-right as the Squire's heiress to marry a working-man is followed by Esther (in *Felix Holt*) who rejects a rich suitor and forfeits her inheritance to marry a poor, class-conscious Radical artisan, while the same idea dictated Dorothea's sacrifice of fortune and status to marry a Radical politician, who is further to be deplored as an artist. This addition is then developed in the sub-plot of *Deronda*, where the heiress Catherine Arrow-point refuses a future peer and breaks with her county family to marry a foreign composer with subversive political views. The Cinderella story was the basis of much popular fiction but no temptation to George Eliot, who savoured a rarer kind of success. She may have well felt, also, that happiness has to be paid for by some painful sacrifice, as she had found herself when having to choose between 'respectability' and union with Lewes (which cut her off from her family and put her at a disadvantage socially).

18 Cf. Squire Donnithorne and his daughter in *Adam Bede*, and the exploration of the unattractive attitudes both of Arthur Donnithorne himself and of the rector's mother. *Silas Marner* differs only in being more forthright and quite disenchanted in its presentation of the gentry.

19 So striking is this that it leads one to infer that 'Cass' was chosen for its suggestion of 'crass', as Dunstan ('Dunsey') obviously was for its association with 'dunce'.

20 Nevertheless, like the Dodsons in *The Mill on the Floss*, she gets very fair treatment, and the virtues of her kind are scrupulously credited to her. And at the earlier crisis she has given us as well as Godfrey a surprise, in her admirable reaction to the history her husband has so long concealed because he thought it would alienate her: '"Do you think I'd have refused to take her in, if I'd known she was yours?"' – she puts the duties of kinship before all else. Cf. Flora Thompson's record of her knowing a 'rough' countryman 'who, when told for the first time, ten years after marriage, that his wife had an illegitimate daughter of sixteen, and stricken with tuberculosis, said: "You go and fetch her home at once and look after her. Your child's my child and your home's her home"' (*Lark Rise to Candleford*, p. 400).

21 As is his name, not merely biblical but actually that of the High-priest himself.

22 Horse-dealing is said to be the manner in which 'many human transactions are carried on'.

23 It is irrelevant to object that city craftsmen were, at times, better off, or had access to the enlightened culture of the educated class in some northern towns. Carlyle's comment on London in 1831 is significant: 'Miserable is the scandal-mongery and evil-speaking of the country population: more frightful still the total ignorance and mutual heedlessness of these poor souls in populous city pent.'